Clarence M. R_____ Jr.
4 Brompton, Ct.
Elkton md. 21921

Cell = 410-920-6198
Home- 410-398-4124

The Big Book of
Maryland
Ghost Stories

To George

Thanks for your help

The Big Book of
Maryland
Ghost Stories

Ed Okonowicz

STACKPOLE
BOOKS

Published by
STACKPOLE BOOKS
5067 Ritter Road
Mechanicsburg, PA 17055
www.stackpolebooks.com

Printed in the United States of America

10 9 8 7 6 5 4 3 2 1

FIRST EDITION

Library of Congress Cataloging-in-Publication Data

Okonowicz, Ed, 1947–
  The big book of Maryland ghost stories / Ed Okonowicz. — 1st ed.
      p. cm.
  Includes bibliographical references (p.   ).
  ISBN-13: 978-0-8117-0561-5 (hardcover)
  ISBN-10: 0-8117-0561-7 (hardcover)
  1. Ghosts—Maryland. I. Title.
  BF1472.U6O546 2010
  133.109752—dc22
                                             2010017262

Contents

Eastern Shore

Central Maryland

Annapolis and Baltimore

Annapolis

Baltimore

Southern Maryland

Western Maryland

Along the Mason-Dixon Line

Introduction

*T*his is a book of ghost stories. But it is also a book about the land and what happened there. Since the European explorers arrived in Maryland in the early 1600s, portions of what they discovered and what they did have been recorded in court documents and historic newspapers. So much more occurred here though, both before and after the settlers' arrival—so much that we will never know.

The land was here, and while the earth is silent and doesn't keep written records, the land never forgets. Some events—good things and bad things, achievements worth celebrating and tragedies best forgotten—leave an indelible legacy at their locations, a mark or a message that can be retrieved some time in the future. And the essence of those private and public deeds has become the basis for the stories we tell, especially ghost stories.

I live at the northeastern corner of Maryland, within a very short walk of the Mason-Dixon line. I've touched the centuries-old stone markers and traced my fingers in the lines of the letters M (designating Maryland) and P (indicating Pennsylvania) carved on opposite sides of these weathered stones. They were put in place nearly 250 years ago. At night, walking through the thousand-acre forest of the nearby state nature preserve, it's easy to imagine the Indian guides, axmen, cooks, and surveyors who created the internationally recognized geographic boundary. Some of these long-gone people stood on the same spots as modern-day weekend hikers, or camped near the roads and paths so many people routinely travel today.

Certain people believe past events have been recorded and preserved in ways we cannot imagine—much more sophisticated than words on newspaper pages, or information and images on Web sites, or secrets locked in the minds of elders.

Psychics claim they can grab slivers of the past and the future. People calling themselves "sensitives" say they have received "the gift" to hear and see incidents that most mortals overlook or don't know how to access. And ghost hunters—folks I call "ghosters"—roam the night armed with the latest in expensive, high-tech gizmos on a paranormal treasure hunt to catch a spirit on film or capture a ghost in a jar.

This book, containing nearly 150 stories, has taken advantage of all of these sources. The chapters—featuring six sections of the state—are based on personal interviews with paranormal experts, museum guides and administrators, residents of haunted homes, folks who claim direct experiences with entities from the other side, and even a few owners of haunted objects, or "possessed possessions."

There also are a number of stories that were found in old books, historic documents, and both faded and modern newspaper clippings. These were located over the Internet, in historical society file cabinets, and on library special collections shelves. Some were nothing more than scraps of paper, handwritten notes, or faded writing on the backs of old photographs. But the most entertaining tales were given to me by friendly folks during personal interviews. A few of these stories had been written in some of my earlier books, which are now out of print, and others have been updated for this new volume.

The history of the region is the foundation of many of these stories. From the Revolution to the Civil War, from the Underground Railroad to the War of 1812, from Chesapeake Bay culture to Allegheny Mountain settlements, spooky tales have provided both entertainment and information about Maryland's treasure trove of history.

Of course, after writing nearly two dozen books related to the paranormal, it's natural for readers to wonder if I believe in ghosts.

My answer is: I believe there is something that is unseen, unusual, and at times, very evil that does exist. I believe there is a very limited number of people who, for whatever reason, were born with a psychic gift or who have developed the ability to communicate with, or sense, what others cannot. But these gifted individuals are few in number.

I also believe there are many people who see what they want to see, who have very active imaginations and who desperately wish they could encounter a ghost or experience a paranormal event. After talking to hundreds of people that have shared their unusual and sometimes troubling unexplained experiences, my advice to anyone who wants an up-close-and-personal encounter with "the other side" is: Be careful what you wish for.

Thanks very much for selecting this book, and I wish you happy reading.

Eastern Shore

The Pit of Ashley Manor

Most writers believe it's best to begin a collection of stories with a tale that's shorter rather than longer. But circumstances sometimes dictate that certain rules should be broken. This is such a case—because this story is based upon my interview with the owners of a haunted house. It also is one of the first ghost stories I had written.

It was 1992, during the latter part of October. For some this is the most eerie, horrifying, and, for ghost hunters and paranormal fans, favorite period of the year. I was a freelance writer for the *Wilmington* (Delaware) *News-Journal*. But I didn't focus my attention on serious newsworthy happenings. My assignments were features, best described as "fun" or "real" stories about interesting people or unique events. Features are the attention-grabbing pieces most readers turn to when they want to escape from the bad news that covers the front page of the daily paper.

As a story finder, I sought out eccentrics, collectors, tinkerers, award-winners, and hometown heroes—people usually overlooked and whose exploits rarely made the front page. If the topic was a bit offbeat, or a peek behind the curtain, it was my specialty.

One Halloween season I did a story explaining how a local "haunted valley" got its buildings and trails ready for the annual arrival of more than 10,000 visitors. The story's attention-capturing photo showed five recently-hacked-off heads of huge pigs, which the event organizers kept in a freezer and hauled out each night to display and terrify the paying customers. I think that's why the following October I received a call from my editor. "I need an unusual Halloween story, and I figure you're the one who can come up with just the right article," he said, "and I need it yesterday."

"How about another spooky trail or corn maze exposé?" I suggested, figuring that could be done quickly, primarily because the operators of seasonal attractions would do anything necessary to obtain the free publicity such an article would deliver.

"No way!" my boss snapped, as if anticipating my response. "I know what I want, and it's a story about a haunted house." Then he paused a second, and stressed in a commanding tone, "a *real* haunted house."

To some placed in this position such a request may have seemed impossible to fulfill. But I had a contact in place who, I was fairly certain, would be able to give me a worthwhile lead or two.

This friend, George Reynolds, had lived in his own haunted home in Elk Mills, Maryland. I had written about him a few years earlier, and we had stayed in touch. I figured George would once again prove a valuable source to fulfill my editor's last-minute demand.

I was right. Within two days I had the names, address, and phone number of the owners of a first-class, eerie-looking, haunted mansion. A week before Halloween, when the leaves were turning bright colors and falling from the trees, I drove to Ashley Manor, then the home of Clayton and Caroline and their children. The family had moved to Cecil County about ten years earlier and had purchased the three-story, twenty-two-room, Federal-style mansion. A prominent county landowner and Maryland state delegate had erected the structure in the early 1800s.

A plantation of more than 500 acres had originally surrounded the mansion. The home now stands in the middle of a small, three-acre plot at the top of a hill overlooking the banks of a Cecil County creek west of the Elk and north of the Sassafras. The locals call the spit of land a neck, a slender slice of marsh and farmland that seems to reach out toward the wide part of the river like the longest finger of an aging hand.

There is a magnificent view of the upper reaches of the Chesapeake Bay from the mansion's white-fenced widow's walk, perched atop the building's roof. That's where the original owner would go to watch his ships come up the waterway, delivering valuable cargoes of spices, fine cloth, ivory, and slaves.

As a pulled into the gravel driveway, a man and woman were standing on the porch, awaiting my arrival. After I locked my car and began walking their way, the newspaper's photographer was exiting the house. He glanced back at the owners, looked at me and said, "That place is a nightmare."

"What do you mean?" I asked.

Holding his camera toward my face, he said in a frustrated voice, "I had to make three trips out to my van to replace the batteries. The flash worked fine outside, but as soon as I entered into that house, the power died. And the owners, they're a real pair," he said, rolling his eyes.

"Well," I said with a bit of hesitation, "they say in haunted places the spirits will drain the energy out of power sources. Suck them dry. That's why camcorders and tape recorders and cameras seem to go dead at the moment when something exciting happens."

The photographer gave me a look that seemed to indicate he thought I had escaped from a mental institution, and added, "Really?" in a questioning tone. "Well," he continued in his mocking voice, "I'm sure you'll fit right in with the Addams Family up there. But my concern is that something worthwhile comes out from this shoot, because I don't want to have to come back here to frightland and do this over again." As he walked away, obviously glad to be done with the assignment, he shouted back, "Have a nice time chatting it up with your friends in their *haunted* house."

I ignored his sarcasm and turned toward my hosts and their home. I was immediately impressed by the awaiting couple's distinctive attire. It was obvious they had prepared to have their picture taken. Clayton looked like a pirate, in gleaming black boots and dark red trousers. He wore a gray, unbuttoned vest atop his white, fluffy cuffed shirt. A gold and blue scarf accented his open collar.

Caroline, like her husband, was in her early fifties. She was wearing a full-length gold gown. On her fingers were several large stone rings. An ornate, mother-of-pearl comb was affixed to the back of her hair.

My hosts explained they had spent years and a significant amount of money restoring their historic home. Dozens of Caroline's early American plates and teapots sat on shelves arranged along three walls of a medium-sized sewing room. Clayton's collection of muskets and swords hung from the walls of a larger room farther down the hall. Dozens of musket balls found on the property filled a glass bowl.

I complimented them on their historic artifacts, but then tried to steer their attention to the focus of my visit, asking: "What about the ghosts?"

They responded by leading me into the parlor and stopping at one corner, where Clayton carefully picked up a narrow glass cabinet door that had been resting against the side of a large armchair. The surface was covered with dust, but you could see the ripples in the ancient glass, handmade more than a century ago by an unknown craftsman.

The couple had planned to refinish the piece and replace it back onto the bookcase that stood above the antique desk. They said the glass panel had rested for more than five years in the back of an unused closet for safekeeping.

As Clayton turned the panel, he pointed toward the top corner. Boldly written in script lettering, one could read the words that were partially hidden by a fine layer of dust: "Please help me."

"We think it's a message from a spirit trapped in the house," was Clayton's explanation.

"But," Caroline added, "we don't know which one. There are so many."

They had my attention. During the next three hours, as we sat beneath flickering candlelight around a large dining room table, the couple presented a succession of unusual occurrences.

There were the usual: crashing noises in the middle of the night (while everyone was asleep); footsteps walking the halls (when only one person was home); a pungent smell of tobacco (although no one in the house smoked); the distinct smell of roses in the dining room (often in winter when no flowers were in the house); cat footprints traveling up a hanging wall mirror and animal scratching outside the master bedroom door (this began the night after the family pet was killed in the road in front of the house); voices calling out unfamiliar names; conversations originating from the front porch in an unknown language; and chilling, sinister laughs.

I told them I was approaching ghost overload and asked them to start at the beginning. Caroline smiled and said a stranger alerted them that something might be wrong with their new home. Soon after moving in, the couple was buying gas at the general store in the nearby town and the attendant said, "You must be the folks that moved in the old haunted house."

Clayton and Caroline laughed, thinking the man was referring to the home's sad, paint-chipped appearance. Not so.

A few days after they had moved in, Caroline was home alone. Clayton had left for work, and their daughters were at school. While unpacking boxes in the foyer, Caroline heard footsteps that seemed to indicate someone or something was walking along the second-floor hallway. Eventually, she decided the bothersome sounds seemed to be coming down the stairs, toward her.

Startled, she shouted, half in fun, "I don't know who you are, but we're going to be living here together. So we might as well all plan to get along. So leave me alone right now, I'm busy unpacking my things."

She said the footsteps stopped and did not resume that day.

When she shared her ghostly experience at supper with Clayton, the no-nonsense engineer and chemist looked at her and calmly tried to explain, as any twenty-first-century scientist would, that his wife was the victim of an "overactive imagination." Noticing Caroline's reluctance to accept her husband's logical explanations, he looked directly at his wife and said, "Do not tell this nonsense to anyone else. You don't want them to think you're crazy and come and put you away."

Caroline said she controlled her initial impulse to argue with him, and sternly replied, "Fine. You think I'm crazy. Just wait. You'll get yours one day."

When recounting this story, Clayton looked across the room at me and said, "It didn't take long, and I got mine." My host immediately rose from the table and motioned for me to accompany him into the kitchen. Clayton walked directly out the side door, onto the porch, and headed down a set of narrow stone steps. They led to a cellar door located under the outside steps, directly beneath the kitchen entrance. It was quiet and very dark outside. We entered the dirt-floored cellar, which contained several rooms but only one entrance-exit, the doorway through which we had just walked.

Standing beside a modern workbench, Clayton said he spent a lot of time down there, working on projects and items that he needed to repair in the ancient and long-neglected house. He pointed to a locked door. Triple locked, with a small opening—similar to a narrow slit in a jail door. A small metal slot could be slid aside, and the thin opening would allow a narrow object to be passed through it.

"What's in there?" I wondered aloud.

"We don't go in there," he said, pointing to the thick door of the triple-locked room. "I'm careful not to open it very often. They say that was the 'Screaming Room' where they punished the bad slaves."

After a long silence, Clayton took a few steps back from the eerie, thick wooden door and leaned against his workbench. "You want to know why we don't go in there?"

I nodded.

He took a deep breath. "Late one night," he said, rather quietly, "I was working here and felt something, like a sudden chill in the air. I looked up, to my left, toward the door—which is the only way in and out of here—and I saw a black-cloaked figure standing in the door-way. It was blocking my way out. The thing, whatever it was, just looked at me. It was all fuzzy, cloudy, but it had the most piercing red and green eyes. Then the figure seemed to begin moving, floating directly toward me. And those eyes, they actually bored right into my chest. The heat was unbearable. I thought I couldn't breathe. Then, just as I knew I was going to pass out, the cloaked figure began float-ing sideways, eventually going right through the Screaming Room door. And it was gone. That's why I try not to spend too much time down here, especially at night." Then he paused and chuckled, "Unless I have some company, like you."

After that story, I was ready to head back outside and return to the more comfortable and less threatening first floor, but Clayton turned and walked toward the rear of the basement. This caused me a bit more unease, since it was the farthest point from the exit. He stopped and waved me over. When I caught up to him, my host looked down and pointed to a distinct square outline of what seemed to be a well. The opening was about five feet square. He said he guessed it was about twelve feet deep at one time.

"Seems like it should have a fence or railing around it," I said.

"That's one of the things I wondered about, too," Clayton agreed. "Most people assume, like I did, that this was a well. But you know what happens when you assume," he added, smiling. Picking up a small plate, he pointed to a few small relics in the center of a table. He said the family had retrieved the items from the deep hole. There were buttons, shards of broken pottery, a few arrowheads, several musket balls and short slivers of what he guessed was some kind of bone.

He said he found out the story of the hole during a yard sale his family was holding about two years after they had settled in. Clayton stressed that they had not told anyone about the strange experiences they had endured since their arrival. In truth, he said they found most of the unexplained events either annoying or intriguing, but never horrifying or threatening.

A man was standing at a table displaying some of the items on sale. After a while he decided to buy a small trinket. As he passed the money to Clayton, the man referred to the spooky look of the house. "I guess you got a lot of ghosts in there," he said, chuckling.

Taken off guard, Clayton nervously replied, "Oh, we might have one or two."

Suddenly, a well-dressed woman, who was looking over some items at a nearby table, snapped in a sharp voice, "You've got a lot more than one or two in there!"

Surprised, Clayton took care of the man and immediately ran to the woman's side, asking her what she had meant by the remark and demanding more information. As the well-dressed woman ignored his question and began walking to her car, Clayton pursued her, trying to get additional details.

Suddenly, the stranger turned, pointed a finger directly at Clayton's face and asked, "You known that hole in your cellar?"

"Yes. The well?" he responded, nodding that he knew what she was referring to.

"That's not a well," she said in a hoarse whisper. "That's the pit where they used to hang the disobedient slaves." Clayton was too stunned to ask for more details, and the woman got into her car and drove away.

"I don't think more than a few seconds had gone by until I recovered from the news," Clayton said, "but when I looked up, she was gone. It was like she just vanished."

Frantic, Clayton and Caroline closed up the yard sale and called the former owners, two elderly farmers in their eighties who had lived in the house more than four decades. That night the previous residents arrived for a visit and sat around the dining room table with the new and confused owners. The two couples calmly discussed the building's unseen former residents and they shared their common ghostly experiences.

The strong scent of flowers was traced back to days when the dining room had been used as a parlor, where deceased relatives had been laid out for three-day wakes.

The unfamiliar dialect was a language spoken by slaves when they sat near the mansion and discussed topics they didn't want their masters to hear.

The smell of smoke was a remnant of the original builder, who was never seen anywhere without his constantly lit pipe.

After a few hours pondering paranormal pleasantries, the former owners said if they had told anyone about their eerie experiences, no one would have bought their property. Even worse, people would have considered them crazy old coots and tried to "put them away."

After the meeting, Clayton and Caroline admitted they felt better about living in the old building and dealing with the strange and unexplainable experiences in their historic home. "I felt I wasn't crazy, and all the strange events weren't my imagination or just happening to me. Besides," Caroline added with a slight smile, "even when you are home by yourself, you never feel like you're alone."

I asked a few obvious questions: "Why do you stay? Why not move away?"

They offered several reasonable answers. First, it had been their home for more than ten years. They had restored it themselves. They felt it was their way of preserving a small part of American history that had been falling into ruin and neglect. A new owner might not be dedicated to historic preservation.

They also wanted to leave something of value and of themselves to their children—even though their grown daughters, who had lived in the home, refused to return, even for a brief daytime visit. When they came back to the area, they would meet their parents at a nearby restaurant.

Caroline and Clayton added they wouldn't be run off from the home of their dreams. If and when they decided to sell the property, "It would solely be on our terms."

Caroline said she and Clayton had considered inviting a psychic, and maybe even asking a priest, to pay a visit and bless their home. Some suggested both of these approaches might help rid the place of its pesky spirits. After long consideration, they decided not to take any action. Caroline believed the phantoms they had experienced were bearable and described them as "more annoying than evil." Clayton even suggested their unseen inhabitants seemed to be benevolent and protective. If a priest or psychic drove them off, just maybe, something else would come in and take their place.

Caroline wondered: "What if the spirits we knew were actually protecting us from a patiently waiting evil force, resting deeper in the cursed well? That might be more harmful."

"Better live with the devil we know than something that might be worse," Clayton agreed.

As the long night came to a close and the clock approached midnight, I closed my notepad and thanked my hosts for their time and candid comments. Rarely are persons involved in such an unusual dilemma willing to speak so openly about a paranormal problem.

My car was parked on the gravel driveway, not far from the side entrance that led into their kitchen. Beneath the wide set of stairs was the doorway leading into the Screaming Room. I shook Clayton's hand and prepared to leave, but took one last look at Ashley Manor. From the tip of the widow's walk to the uneven windows of its lowest cellar level, the old mansion screamed "HAUNTED HOUSE." Suddenly, we both focused our eyes on what appeared to be a yellow flash of flame, which offered the appearance of a candle passing behind a cellar window. But just as quickly, the uneven light disappeared.

I turned to Clayton, about to ask him if he had seen the same thing. But before I could speak, he looked at me and said, "That's why I don't go down there very often."

Several years later, I was driving along the road in front of Ashley Manor and noticed a "For Sale" sign standing beside the driveway. I turned my car around, drove up the gravel lane, and knocked on the side kitchen entrance door. Caroline answered. I told her we had met a few years earlier, in connection with the newspaper article, and directed our short conversation to the pending sale of their property.

She explained that the home was too large, and demanded too much attention, for her and her husband to handle. She added that there had been a fair number of lookers, but, as of that time, no one had made an offer. Then she paused a moment, offered me a conspiratorial look and said, "At first, potential buyers all seem delighted with the property and home, but after I tell them about our unseen residents they leave without saying a word, and we never hear from them again."

Eventually, the property was sold. The subsequent owner told me the pit-in-the-cellar story was a sensational tale with little substance and he never felt ill at ease in the home. The fellow claimed he felt very comfortable in the historic building, even though he believed there were a few ghosts roaming the rooms and hallways. One pesky child spirit seemed to enjoy stomping up and down the stairs and rattling a door handle, as if demanding to be let out of a certain room. The owner said he solved the problem by leaving that door open so the ghost could move about with ease. But each time he forgets to leave that particular door ajar, the spirit is sure to make its presence known.

Buggy Ghost

The Kent County Courthouse in Chestertown made national headlines in the summer of 2004. One month after installation of a new $75,000 security system, the ever-watchful, high-technology guardian seemed to be well-worth the money. It had captured an unauthorized presence in one of the new building's stairwells.

But after a thorough search, law enforcement personnel did not find anyone matching the description of the intruder on the premises. Computer geeks who were called to the scene also were unable to identify the criminal element involved in the captured-on-film break-in. Eventually, someone spoke up and offered an off-the-wall explanation: Maybe it was a ghostly spirit, moving up and down that particular section of the stairs, that had been captured on film.

One security officer was quoted by the Associated Press as saying of the movement, "It didn't show up to the eye, but it showed up on tape."

Security officers physically walked the stairway in the exact location where the tape indicated the floating spirit had been seen, and where it still remained visible through the camera's lens. But the on-the-scene inspectors found nothing in the area. At one point, a crowd of employees gathered around the camera monitor and actually saw a security staff member "walk through the anomaly." The AP reported that at that same moment, the security officer who had been on the stairwell said he "felt a real chill."

Soon after hearing the news of such a mass paranormal sighting, ghost hunters and psychics converged on the newly identified haunted location. They all wanted to become a part of this significant paranormal breakthrough. Some longtime courthouse employees began talking about unexplained incidents they had been circulating over the years regarding the old building . Some said people saw shadows in the halls. Others claimed they heard doors slam, and some workers swore they had experienced unexplained noises when no one else was in their section of the building.

At the time of the highly publicized camera incident, the Kent County sheriff said he didn't believe in ghosts and stated, "There has to be a logical explanation," but added, "I'm keeping an open mind."

Someone suggested the structure was as good a place as any in this historic Eastern Shore town for a ghost to take up residence. After all, the old Chestertown courthouse is built upon the site of several executions, dating back to 1746. And a 1969 expansion of the building was erected over a forgotten nineteenth-century cemetery, which some said was directly below where the feisty twenty-first-century phantom had appeared posing for the motion-detecting camera.

Orbs, floating dots resembling the water spots on old photographs, was one explanation that seemed to gather the most steam among paranormal experts. But the real answer to the dilemma came after the firm that had installed the high-dollar sentry system examined the equipment and discovered a solitary insect trapped inside the camera's lens.

The resulting appearance to those viewing the monitors was a slow-moving, blurred, out-of-focus specter, which appeared to be invisible to the naked eye. This unforeseen high-tech anomaly initially had caused some of the paranormal experts to claim a specter from a parallel dimension existed in the courthouse stairwell, roaming at will above its old forgotten burial ground.

But in the end, even disappointed ghosters had to give science a nod for solving another supernatural phenomenon.

Holly Hall Hitchhiker

The state historical marker along Maryland Route 213, just north of U.S. Route 40, notes the location of Holly Hall, the manor house built between 1810 and 1820 by local civic leader James Sewall.

Not far from the sign—sandwiched between a busy road and a sprawling shopping mall—stands the three-story brick building that has been the subject of a fair number of ghost stories. Even though dates associated with the building's construction and the owner's lifespan don't coincide with the timing of the local legend, some place more faith in the ghost tales than they do in county historical records. But that's not surprising, because the Revolutionary War-era stories about the spirits of Holly Hall are a lot more interesting than what's etched on the metal highway marker.

It's said that before the Revolutionary War, James Sewall arrived at Head of Elk (the original name for Elkton) and built Holly Hall, a stately brick mansion, not far from the waters of Elk Creek. Sewall's wife had died and he was left to raise a rebellious son, Thad, and a docile daughter, Sarah. Sewall was a wealthy man, with farms and businesses throughout the county. He was a popular personality with a fair amount of influence, and he liked to host parties in the main-floor parlors of his magnificent home. Unfortunately, quite often his guests were distracted from the merriment by the loud sounds of arguments taking place on the second floor between the master of the house and his difficult-to-control teenage son.

Eventually these disturbances became more heated and the subjects of the conflicts became more serious. Rather than fighting over restrictions imposed on a growing boy, James and Thad engaged in shouting matches over unfair taxation, government intrusion, and the impending war between England and the colonies. James Sewall was a staunch supporter of the Crown. His son, and secretly his daughter, had become involved with Maryland patriots actively working to break away from the rule of the King of England.

One day Thad arrived home dressed in the blue uniform of the local militia and informed his father he was leaving to join George Washington's forces at nearby Iron Hill. The British were marching toward Philadelphia, and local soldiers were joining up with the American army to defend the region and stall the enemy's advance toward the nearby Pennsylvania city. Disgusted, James Sewall struck his son across the face and said the young man would never be allowed to enter the property and home as long as Sewall was alive. Thad and his father exchanged further harsh words before the younger man turned, kissed his sister farewell, and left Holly Hall.

Enraged, James ordered his servants to drag all of his son's possessions from his second-floor bedroom and burn them in the back of the property. Then he raced throughout the house, pulling every item that reminded him of his son off the walls, and tossed them into the fire. Sarah, moving quickly into her room, pulled down a drawing of her brother and hid the framed image under her bed. When she was sure her father was out of the building, she pulled up a loose board in the floor of her closet and placed Thad's picture inside her secret hideaway with her treasured possessions.

After that night, Sewall swore he would not tolerate the mention of Thad's name in or out of his home. When neighbors inquired about the younger Sewall, James responded, "I have no son." Sarah, however, kept in touch with her brother by using friends to send and receive correspondence. A year after Thad's abrupt and unpleasant departure from Holly Hall, Sarah was given a message from her brother in which he said he had been wounded in battle. While recovering he had contracted pneumonia, and he needed medical assistance and a safe and warm place to stay. She sent a carriage to pick Thad up from the farmhouse near Germantown, Pennsylvania, that served as a temporary hospital for the wounded. When Thad arrived at Holly Hall, Sarah raced to her now-dying brother, whose body was so thin that his skull seemed to be pressing against a nearly invisible layer of pale skin. Sarah and the coachman stumbled as they dragged Thad's almost lifeless body up the front steps of the brick home. When they reached the main entrance, James Sewall stood in the doorway, his face an evil mask displaying hate and vengeance.

"Who is this?" he screamed, as his eyes traveled quickly from Thad and rested on Sarah.

"My brother, your son," she said. "He is very ill and needs rest and attention." The tone of her voice was a plea, hoping it would generate some degree of sympathy in her father's cold heart.

"I have no son," James hissed. He took a step forward and pushed Thad down the tall flight of brick stairs. As the house door slammed, Sarah screamed and tried to lift her brother to place his body back in the coach. She planned to take him to her friend's home so she could help nurse him through his illness. But Thad did not respond. At the front of Holly Hall, the spirit had left behind the young man's corpse. Sarah's screams filled the frigid winter air. As she cradled her dead brother's body, her father blew out the candles on the first floor of his mansion and retired to his warm bedroom on the second level. When he awoke the next morning Sarah, like her brother, had left home and never again set foot inside the building.

After the Revolution, James Sewall, who had already destroyed his family, also lost everything, including Holly Hall. As new tenants moved in and out of the building over the years, several reports of unusual incidents surfaced and grew over time.

A farmer who worked the property reported hearing screams in the night, and said he was troubled when lightning struck and killed several of his livestock—during a calm, sunny day when there were no storms in the area.

During a Halloween costume party, thrown by a wealthy family who later owned the mansion, the hostess said she heard footsteps on the second floor. Going up to investigate, she entered a bedroom and noticed a young man, dressed as a Revolutionary War soldier. The stranger's back was facing the woman, and she told the guest that he should not be in the room because the party was restricted to the first floor.

When the terrified woman later awoke from her fall down the stairway and into the main hall, she told her husband and concerned guests about the strange man in her daughter's room. In a nervous voice, she said when the intruder turned to face her, he was looking down at a small painting that he had been holding in his lap. As she took two steps to approach him, the thin man lifted his horrifying face in her direction, and it looked exactly like a skull. Terrified, she screamed, ran from the room, tripped, and fell down the stairs.

An immediate search of Holly Hall by all of the costumed guests turned up no person matching the stranger's description. But resting on the bed they found an antique frame holding a small painting of a pleasant-looking young man. Word immediately spread about the "skull-faced" ghost seen on the building's second floor, and within weeks a "For Sale" sign appeared on the front lawn of Holly Hall.

When the again vacant structure was later turned into an office building, employees and visitors claimed they heard footsteps coming from areas where no one worked, and certain spots in the building always seemed unusually cold. When the old estate was turned into a homeless shelter, even the down-and-out vagrants left the building, complaining about loud noises in the attic and a skull-faced boy appearing throughout the building in the middle of the night.

Decades before the area and nearby crossroads were turned into a commercial center, drivers along the hill in front of the property claimed they saw a young man hitchhiking on the shoulder of the roadway, very close to the Holly Hall gate. Depending upon which version was told, the young man disappeared as the car stopped to offer a ride. Other witnesses claimed they saw the apparition walk toward the waiting driver and remove its skull from its shoulders before attempting to enter the vehicle. Each time, the well-intentioned drivers burned rubber as they left the Holly Hall Hitchhiker in the dust.

Deadly Black Cat

Black cats and bad luck go together like mashed potatoes and gravy. The dark-furred creatures have been associated with the dark side since the beginning of time. Some say a black cat was roaming the Garden of Eden along with the snake that tempted Adam and Eve. Witches selected the feline creatures as their favorite pets, taking them along for rides on flying broomsticks. In some cultures, cats—black ones in particular—are believed to suck the breath out of newborn babes and young children. And a strong majority of the population would react negatively if a black cat crossed a person's path. But a Rock Hall man known as Hollis offered a different reason for avoiding black cats. Based on his experiences, each sighting predicted the death of a loved one.

According to Hollis, one night his parents were sitting around the kitchen table when his father looked up and asked, "When did we get a black cat?"

"We ain't got no black cat," his wife replied.

"Well, we sure must do," the father snapped, "'cause I just saw one go across the floor and walk into that pantry over there!"

Immediately, the couple checked the food closet, the kitchen, and the entire house. Finding no evidence of the mysterious creature, they went on and searched the yard, barn, and outhouse. There was no black cat to be found.

Two days later, Hollis's grandfather, who lived in the house next door, died.

Three years passed. The same couple was sitting at the same kitchen table in the same rural home. Just as had occurred a few years previously, a black cat walked across the floor and entered the pantry.

Hollis's father asked, "When did we get a black cat?"

"We ain't got no black cat," his wife replied.

"Well, we sure must do," the father snapped, "'cause I just saw one go across the floor and walk into that pantry over there!"

The couple got up, as they had done three years before. Again they checked the pantry, the kitchen, and every room in the house. Again, as happened before, there was no black cat. The next day, Hollis's aunt, his father's sister, died from an accidental gunshot wound. She lived in the house next door.

After the funeral, Hollis recalled hearing his father say: "I hope I don't never see that black cat again."

Wish Sheppard

There's a ghost in Denton's Caroline County Jail, and we know who it is. Wish (pronounced "Wush") Sheppard is his name, and he's been a resident of the county lockup for nearly one hundred years. The red-brick jail stands in the center of town, along the banks of the Choptank River. That prime location earned it the apt nickname "Waterfront Hotel." The original jail, built in the early 1900s, is in the front of the large building. To its sides and rear are modern additions that have been built since the 1980s in response to the county's increases in both population and crime. Even today, employees and townsfolk still talk about the phantom prisoner that makes occasional appearances in the cells and also messes with the building's high-tech security equipment.

The ghost story begins in 1915, when Wish Sheppard, a black man, was found guilty of raping a white girl and sentenced to death. A wooden gallows was erected at the bottom of the hill, near the jail and along the Choptank River.

Since the public was allowed to witness the execution, which also was a major social event, the townsfolk turned out in force. Some viewed the hanging from boats docked in the river and others climbed nearby trees to get a good look at the proceedings.

Somehow, Wish was able to leave a lasting impression on the cell wall that had been his last earthly home. It's said when they came to escort Wish out to the gallows, he put up a fierce struggle. With one hand, he grabbed onto one of the jail cell's metal bars while he forcefully pressed his other hand against the cell wall, leaving a distinctive handprint in the solid, flat surface.

Sheriff James Temple was in charge of the Sheppard hanging. At the time of the execution, there were four officials up on the gallows, standing beside Wish, and each official put one hand on the lever of the trapdoor. Then Temple came down with his hand and hit the tops of the others. That action pushed against the lever, causing the trapdoor to open and drop Wish through, sending him to his maker. But since there were four executioners, it was not just one man who was responsible for pushing the lever and doing the hanging.

During an interview in his home in 1999, Caroline County Sheriff Louis C. Andrew shared some of the tales he had heard about Wish over the years. The then-retired sheriff had served in office from 1961 until his retirement in 1994, and he had been associated with county law enforcement almost his entire life. In 1938, at the age of ten, he moved with his family into the jail's residential area when his father, William E. Andrew, became sheriff. When the elder Andrew died, Louis took over the job and was elected to eight consecutive terms as county sheriff, serving a total of thirty-three years. He lived in the jail-house building for fifty-five years, a portion of that time with his wife, Joyce, who helped her husband by cooking for the prisoners.

"I did see that handprint," the former sheriff said. "It looked like a man's palm and fingers pressed into the wall. We painted it over, plastered it over, and it always seemed to come back, and not too long a time later."

But, before telling me the stories, he added, "Now, let me say this," he stressed. "I've never seen anything strange in that jail, and I never experienced anything myself: no unusual sounds, no sightings, no stuff like that. All I can do is tell you what I heard from the prisoners and guards. I can tell you their stories, if they're of interest to you."

After I acknowledged his statement, he presented a number of interesting incidents involving the ghost of Wish Sheppard that folks said occurred in the Caroline County Jail.

"Over the years, the prisoners would always say somebody was in there," he said, "and that it was Wish Sheppard. They swore he was in there roaming around. One old fella, he was about seventy-five years old, he's dead now. He was a regular, in for disorderly. He always said there was no ghost in there, didn't believe it. One night, I went down to see how they were doing and there were seven or eight prisoners right up against the door. And the old fella was shouting, 'Sheriff! He's in here! I take it all back. He's in here. I seen him!'

"I went in there and looked around, and they followed me around like a bunch of little kids. They said, 'He went through that wall!' We used to have a real dark area. We used to call it the 'dungeon.' I used to tell them, 'If you act up, I'll put you in the dungeon.' They didn't like that. You used to be able to get away with that in the old days. I threw my light around down there and showed them there was nothing there, but they weren't satisfied. They were scared and said he showed up that night."

Another time, there was a man in the cell where Wish's handprint still decorated the wall. When Sheriff Andrew entered the cell area in the morning, the man claimed that someone had come in during the night, took his watch, and threw it outside through an opening in the window.

"He had scratches all over his arm," the sheriff recalled, "from whatever it was that was pulling on him. He was hollering and hopping around and said none of the other guys in the cell took it. He said it was outside. I went outside the jail and the watch was there, near the window."

The cell where Wish appeared was on the first floor of the jail building. One evening when the jail had a pretty large number of prisoners, the sheriff was concerned that if there were a fire he wouldn't be able to hear the screams of the inmates. To ensure that someone could alert him by banging on a door that led to the offices, the sheriff locked one prisoner in the hallway, outside of the cells.

"It got so loud from him beating on the door," the sheriff said, "I went down and asked what was wrong. He said, 'Ya gotta lock me in the cell! He's here. Wish Sheppard. Ya gotta lock me inside with the others!' I opened the door and he jumped in. He was scared to death. A lot of the prisoners would hear footsteps, and not see him. They'll swing at him, but they can't hit nothing."

Joyce, the sheriff's wife, said, "It was worse on rainy nights. It seemed they used to see him when it was raining. Now, I never saw or heard anything all the years we lived there. But I remember he'd go down to see what was going on and come back and say, 'Old Wish was down there again,' and I'd just laugh. I thought it was all a bunch of malarkey."

But the sheriff said he couldn't resist using the threat of Old Wish to quiet down the unruly prisoners from time to time.

"I'd tell them, 'Boys, it's a rainy night. You know who comes around on cloudy and rainy nights, don't you?' And right away, one or two of them who'd seen Wish would say, 'Sheriff knows what he's talkin' about,' and they'd quiet down."

Sheriff Andrew explained that he usually kept the female prisoners in the second-floor cells. One year, he had a woman in the jail for nine months awaiting trial for murder. When he came in one morning, the woman asked the sheriff, "What are you trying to do, scare me?"

The sheriff replied that he wouldn't do that, and asked the prisoner what she meant.

"Well," she said, "you pulled chains up and down the steel stairway last night."

Denying that he would even think of doing that, the sheriff said he knew the woman was serious. She had been in the jail for a long time, and they had gotten to know each other.

When the sheriff didn't offer her any other explanation, she said, seriously, "I guess it was that Wish Sheppard. He was up and down with them chains all night."

Thinking back to that conversation, the sheriff said, "She swore she heard those chains. She was serious. But I never heard anything. Living in that jail as long as I did, I got up many a night, 'cause I could tell if there was something different or not right. But every noise I heard in that jail, I could explain. I never heard anything that was unreasonable.

"I had one psychic person come in. He came with some radio station, and he said he could tell things by vibrations. So he took hold of the cell door, and he said I can make out something is in there. Then he turned to me and said, 'Sheriff, you don't hear it because you don't believe. But I can tell you there's something here.'"

After the 1980 renovations, the old cell doors were thrown away and the wall with the handprint was covered over. However, that did not seem to get rid of the spirit of Wish Sheppard.

"I had guards tell me that the elevator would go up and down the floors by itself," the sheriff said. "They would tell me at twelve midnight, the elevator would come up, the door would open, they'd go and look inside and there was not a soul inside."

Sometimes, buzzers that would summon the elevators would be sounding during the early morning. But there was no one there to press the button, and it was protected behind an enclosed fence. No one without a key could gain access.

A guard who was out in the recreation yard once told the sheriff that there was a figure pressing the buzzer on the third floor. But when the guard got to the site, there was no one there—and no explanation for who or what it could have been.

"Another guard," Sheriff Andrew said, "he told me, 'I'm not kidding you, sheriff. I was in the control room and it was just a fog that come over me, inside the jail. And it just floated right through here.' He said it hit him right in the face, and he felt it. He believes it was Wish Sheppard."

Shaking his head a moment, Sheriff Andrew looked up and said, "I believe what I was told. I have to believe what they tell me. These are reliable people. People I trust. The other is just prisoners' talk. But you have to understand that this is all of the stories that I was told. They all didn't happen at one time. All this happened over the years I was there. There wasn't something every single day."

According to an interview with Sheriff Andrews, printed in Mary Anne Fleetwood's book *Voices From the Land*, during construction of the new additions to the jail, the sheriff mentioned the ghost to members of the work crew. Soon afterwards the foreman told the sheriff not to say anything about Wish Sheppard's ghost or he wouldn't be able to keep his help.

After almost a century, the story of Wish Sheppard hasn't been forgotten, mainly because of his periodic ghostly visits. On more than one occasion, Sheriff Andrew said he would be walking along through town on Market Street and a friend or shopkeeper would call out a hello and ask, "How's ol' Wish doin'?" to which the sheriff would wave a hand and smile in reply.

"People knew about Wish," he said. "Prisoners talk. Word gets around."

And, apparently, so does the ghost of Wish Sheppard.

Early-Morning Visitor

Not far from the Bay Bridge, the primary connector between Maryland's Eastern Shore and the state's western counties, stands Bloomingdale. The Federal-style mansion was built in 1792 a few miles outside Queenstown, and it is listed in the National Register of

Historic Places. As is the case with many old estates, it's believed there may be a ghost or two roaming about the grounds. More than a dozen slave families worked the property, and their quarters stood close to the main house.

According to John Martin Hammond's *Colonial Mansions of Maryland and Delaware*, a Queen Anne's County newspaper reporter wrote a story in 1879, based on an eyewitness account, of a rather unusual event.

At the time of the incident, the estate was owned by Sally and Mary Harris, two unmarried sisters who were noted for hosting lavish, entertaining parties. One evening, Sally was enjoying a late-night discussion with her friend and overnight guest, Mrs. Nancy De Courcy. After both women became tired from the long but pleasant day, they retired to their bedchambers. A small amount of time passed and they heard a strong rapping sound that seemed to be coming from outside the front door. Although a bit concerned, Mrs. De Courcy volunteered to accompany her host and one of the servants to see who might be calling at such an inappropriate, early-morning hour.

When they opened the door, the women were shocked to recognize the visitor as William Sterrett, a nephew of the Harris sisters. Unfortunately, the sighting caused quite a bit of concern since the young man was no longer alive, having died several months earlier.

Moving silently past the trio of speechless greeters, William's apparition headed down the hall, stopped, and then turned and waved in the ladies' direction, indicating that the two women should follow him. As the stunned hostess and her guest headed cautiously toward the mysterious visitor, the ghost stopped at a closed, locked door. Again he turned, smiled at his followers, and finally faced back toward the closed door. In what seemed like only a few seconds, William's spirit began to disappear as it moved away from where the women stood. Shocked and silent, they watched the phantom pass through the shut door, into what had once been the living man's bedroom.

With hands and key ring shaking, the wide-eyed servant unlocked the dark room, which had been vacant and unused from some time. When the ladies lit the lamp, their eyes were directed toward the usually well-made-up bed. But on this memorable morning, a flowing bedspread littered the floor and the bed sheets were rumpled, as if they had been recently slept upon.

Rushing throughout the house, the two women awoke the other workers, and they all spent the rest of the dark morning searching every room and alcove of the mansion. Nothing unusual was found, and William Sterrett's ghost was never again reported at Bloomingdale.

Lady at the Woodpile

Brumfield and Ned were brothers who lived on a little plot in Queen Anne's County, not too far from Church Hill. They resided in a secluded area, near the woods, in an old farmhouse. Not too big, but the right size for them. One night while they were sleeping, Ned heard something. He didn't know what it was, but it woke him up. He went over to the window. The wind was blowing hard, causing a thin branch to beat against the pane of glass.

There was a full moon, so there was a fair amount of light. Down a bit from the house, but still in the yard, Ned saw a woman in a long, old-fashioned farm dress. On top of it she wore a short, white apron. He noticed the stranger was holding the material of the apron out in front of her with one hand while she gathered up wood chips and small branches with the other.

Ned watched for some time as the lady picked the strips of kindling from the ground around the woodpile and dropped them into her white apron. She kept at it a while, in the moonlight, until she had collected a nice-sized bundle.

By this time, Brumfield was up, too. Both brothers saw the woman coming towards the house, and the men rushed out the bedroom door and stood looking down from the head of the stairs.

Before they could leave the top step of the second-floor landing, Ned and Brumfield watched the lady come into their house, passing right through the locked door. The form was almost like a mist, floating in and forming again after she glided through the solid barrier. Silently, she moved steadily toward the fireplace. Then she stopped and slowly tossed her load of wood chips and twigs into the fire, little by little . . . until they were all gone.

Right after the chips started to burn, she turned, looked up, and saw Ned and Brumfield staring at her. Then she smoothed down her empty apron, smiled, and disappeared. The only thing left behind was the newly formed blazing flames in the fireplace.

"If I told that story once," Brumfield said, "I told it at least a hundred times. I believe it, 'cause I saw it. I was there. Ain't no one gonna ever convince me it didn't happen. And Ned was there right beside me, and he saw it, too."

Hessians' Hole

At the western edge of Cecil County—south of Elkton, where the Elk River meets the Chesapeake Bay—a state historical marker stands near Hart's United Methodist Church. It refers to the largest land invasion in North American military history.

"On Aug. 25, 1777, after a month's voyage from New York, 15,000 British troops led by Sir William Howe disembarked on the shores of the Elk River, approximately two miles east of this site. The fleet of 300 vessels that had transported them was under the command of the general's brother, Admiral Richard Howe. Heavy thunderstorms subsided the night of Aug. 27, when the British began their cautious march toward Philadelphia along both sides of the Elk. On Sept. 11, they engaged and defeated Washington's army in the Battle of the Brandywine."

The people who erect state makers are historians, and they are much more interested in dates and places and major, earth-shaking events rather than ghost stories, folklore, and legends. In the vicinity of the British landing there is a long-told, and still unsolved, local legend about a deadly place called the "Hessians' Hole."

No one knows exactly where it is, and no one is absolutely sure of what happened there. But for storytellers, folklorists, and regular folks that like a first-rate tale to tell, a thorough knowledge of details has never stopped the spreading of a good story.

According to a variety of sources, a massacre occurred in the rural area of the British landing, an area that is still covered by a fair amount of forests, farmland, and fields. George Johnston wrote in his 1881 *History of Cecil County Maryland*: "There is a tradition that 19 of the Hessians deserted, but were captured and shot at Welsh Point (today referred to as Welch Point), and buried there in a common grave. Some indications of a grave of that kind are to be seen at the Point at this time. The depression in the earth that is said to be their grave is called 'The Hessians Hole.'"

Based on these "historical" references and word-of-mouth tales, there are several versions of what may have occurred during the summer 1777 invasion. When asked if he had ever heard of the story of the Hessians' Hole, area personality, archaeologist, and historian George Reynolds of Elk Mills said the Hessians (hired German soldiers fighting for the British) ran off because the King's officers usually placed these mercenaries in the front line of march. This practice caused the foreign troops to be among the first killed or most severely wounded when they encountered the enemy. Apparently, the idea that a small band of Hessians would attempt to desert is certainly possible. In both Reynolds's and Johnston's versions, the deserters were caught and surrounded by British soldiers, who killed the Germans and disposed of them in a mass grave.

But did the British kill these soldiers? Another version suggests Cecil County patriots carried out the executions. There are reports throughout the colonies of citizens in many towns coming upon British soldiers and their allies and disposing of the invaders. Some of the killers were members of the local militia, but others were groups of farmers and townsfolk who took an active role in the defense of their homeland.

Mike Dixon, Cecil County's historian, admitted he receives inquiries from time to time about the mystery, but very little is written or known on the subject.

"People come into the historical society looking for information about 'The Hessians' Hole,'" he said, but added that both the exact spot and the circumstances remain unknown and unsolved. He said that some believe the massacre took place in the vicinity of Welch Point.

Dixon added that one could only imagine the chaos during the landing, with 15,000 troops coming ashore, and the confusion that occurred in the thick forests on both sides of the Elk River. Several months ago, Dixon said, an area resident reported that one evening, around dusk, he had found a depression and thought it might be the Hessians' Hole. However, when the local returned the next day he could not locate the site.

Ever the historian, Dixon questioned whether the massacre actually occurred, or if it was simply a good story to entertain area residents over the years. But if it did happen, the location has remained a puzzle for more than 225 years after the supposed mass murder—and the unmarked grave may host a few dozen restless spirits, eager to be discovered and properly laid to rest.

Pig Woman

One of Maryland's best folktales, and one that seems to have generated considerable interest, involves the Pig Woman. The horrid, witch-like creature has been described as one-third human, one-third animal, and one-third ghost. Although there have been sightings in the mountain counties and along the marshes of the Eastern Shore, a few versions of the story have been passed down for generations by residents in the northeast corner of the state.

In the late 1800s, two young girls were walking down a road a few miles south of the village of North East and noticed a fire blazing in an old farmhouse. As they stood back and watched the flames consume the wood structure, they saw an old woman appear to fall from the second-floor window and crash to the ground.

The girls raced to help the burning woman, who was screaming in pain as she rolled over and across the ground but then stopped moving. As they got within arm's reach of the smoldering flesh, the stench caused each girl to cover her nose and mouth. While they looked down at the back of what they thought was a deep-fried corpse, the old woman jumped suddenly to her feet. With a large halo of gray smoke surrounding her charred body, the hairless hag faced the schoolgirls, who immediately turned and ran when they glimpsed the old lady's disfigured face. Later, they described the victim's head as "a burnt piece of meat that looked like the face of an ugly pig." At that moment, the legend of the Pig Lady was born.

This grotesque-looking monster is said to live in the woods and riverbanks outside the river town of North East. The creature appears late in the evenings, crossing back roads on her way to find food to steal. She is also said to look for an unattended young child to scare to death and take into the woods and eat for dinner.

Others warn nighttime drivers to avoid an old wooden bridge located on a side road in the thick forests south of the town. Some say a solitary car will stop unexpectedly and for no reason. When the confused driver exits the vehicle to check under the hood, he finds nothing wrong. But within a few seconds after he returns to his seat at the wheel, he discovers he is not alone.

Unexplained scratching sounds, originating from the vehicle's fenders, trunk, roof, and hood, break the quiet of the night. When the terrified victim looks into the rearview mirror, he sees the distorted face of the Pig Woman. Simultaneously, the snout of the same wicked face is pressed against the front windshield, and the monster's hoofed hands bang frantically against the vehicle's roof and trunk, demanding entry.

Those who run from the car to seek help on foot are never seen again. Victims who remain in the car are better off, since the vehicle's engine eventually comes back to life, allowing the driver to speed away. But when he or she returns to the safety of the home driveway, the terrified victim notices distinct dents and marks covering the body of the car. Anyone who has survived such an encounter with the Pig Woman refuses to drive that road again, whether alone or accompanied, and during neither the day nor the evening.

This last version of the legend originated in the 1960s, when the Pig Woman was allegedly roaming the area around Rising Sun, in northern Cecil County close to the Mason-Dixon ine.

Teenagers in those days made it a habit to park late at night in an area near the town dump. Somewhat regularly, an old woman with a contorted figure, a round, pig-like head, and a snout of a nose would come out of the woods and beat on the windows of the teenagers' cars. As the scared couples drove off into the darkness, they could see the ominous figure of the Pig Woman, waving her arms and shouting at them in the distance. Each time the story was told, the Pig Woman's story became a bit scarier. As years passed, some parents would show youngsters the old Pig Woman mask they had worn during their high school days, when they terrorized lovers parked near the town dump.

Samson Hat

Furnace Town Living Heritage Museum is located northwest of Snow Hill, in Worcester County, close to a densely wooded portion of the Pocomoke State Forest. Tourists learn about the operation of the Nassawango Iron Furnace, which was established in the area in 1829, and the village of Furnace Town, which housed many of the workers involved in the site's important iron-smelting operation.

A walk through the museum's buildings and shop-lined streets shows life as it was during the iron enterprise's short-lived existence. But there also are some interesting stories about the phantom of one of the nineteenth-century workers, who some say lived in the abandoned ghost town long after it closed up shop. He goes by two names: Samson Harmon and the more popular identity, Samson Hat.

There are several versions of Samson's story, which can best be described as a combination of literary license, oral history, documented facts, and a tall tale or two.

In 1832, the Maryland Iron Company began operating the Nassawango Iron Furnaces, a group of stone structures that eventually was surrounded by a small village. The operation was named after the nearby Nassawango Creek, from which workers would mine bog ore— thick deposits located in the waterbeds of the swamps. They would smelt the raw material from the bogs in furnaces, and the resulting iron bars would be loaded onto barges and shipped through nearby waterways onto the Chesapeake Bay. Eventually, Furnace Town iron was delivered to waiting customers throughout the country.

As more furnaces were erected in distant states, and better-quality iron ore resulted in superior products, Furnace Town closed down its operation in 1847. Eventually, the buildings were abandoned and the once-busy village became a ghost town.

During its peak, a large number of slaves operated the furnaces. Others supplied wood that was essential for the processing, which took place throughout the day and night. Some slaves were charged with growing crops to feed workers and families that lived in the village. One of the slaves was named Samson Harmon, who became better known by his fictional identification, Samson Hat.

In *In Days Gone By and Other Delmarva Tales*, regional author Hal Roth points out that Samson Harmon was the basis for the fictional character, Samson Hat, featured in George Alfred Townsend's nineteenth-century regional novel, *The Entailed Hat*. In that work, the slave's primary duty was to stand at the ready to deliver a perfectly shaped and brushed hat to his master. After the publication of Townsend's work, Samson's actual name faded into oblivion and his created, more colorful identity stuck with the local character.

As the ghost tale goes, Samson Hat refused to leave Furnace Town after the iron operation closed. The old slave, who had earned his freedom following the Civil War, took over one of the buildings and lived on the property with an old black cat, appropriately named Tom.

Samson Hat loved to strike up discussions about the old days with anyone who passed by his squatter's quarters. The legendary and colorful figure offered a fair number of tall tales that seemed to grow larger with each passing season. It's said that in his younger days, Samson could run down a deer in his bare feet and jump in a river and catch his day's supply of fresh fish by hand. The only surviving picture of Samson shows him seated and shoeless—but wearing a hat—in front of a wooden cabin.

In Samson's old age, Roth wrote, forest neighbors brought the hermit food and helped care for him. Eventually, he was placed in an almshouse in nearby Newark, Maryland, where he died somewhere between the ages of 106 and 108.

Area folks seem comfortable preserving and sharing the story of Samson Hat, even talking about possible sightings of his ghost in the nearby forest and old buildings of historic Furnace Town. It's said that on a night lit by the full moon, and only around midnight, if you're patient and quiet, you might seen the shadowy outline of an old man, bent over and wearing a wide-brimmed hat, accompanied by a large black cat, and moving slowly above the ground.

Unquiet Grave

St. Augustine is a sleepy crossroads with a few homes and the remnants of an old historic church. The original Manor Chapel is gone, but visitors can walk the land near a small, white wooden church and read the worn inscriptions of common folks and local heroes who are buried beneath the Eastern Shore soil.

But some visitors come with map, notebook, and camera to find the "Unquiet Grave." The unusually named burial site is said to be that of a young man who lived a few miles from the village and who was stricken by a strange disease. He lived during the early 1800s, and he led a wild, carefree, and wicked life. Some believe the sickness that cut him down in his prime was punishment for a long list of transgressions. Others suggested the scamp conducted so many late-night ramblings that he wore himself out and his body refused to try to keep up with his antics. Whatever the cause, his family knew the boy's condition was deteriorating, and they had prepared him for the Grim Reaper, who was approaching with certainty and speed.

Lying in his deathbed, the frightened young man asked that after his church burial service, when his body was placed in the ground, that no nails or screws be used to seal his coffin lid. He also demanded that no dirt be dropped upon the top of his casket, and that he be buried in a shallow grave with a small, elevated, rectangular brick wall built around his gravesite. Finally, he ordered that the small brick wall extend several layers above the ground.

Of course, a flat slab of granite was to be placed over the young man's elevated crypt, but he requested that one brick be left out, creating an opening in the brick wall surrounding his gravesite. That way, he said, when the devil came into the tomb to take his soul to hell, he would be able to escape the clutches of Satan through the opening created by the missing brick.

Even today, after more than a century and a half, some visitors who come to St. Augustine Churchyard to perform tombstone rubbings, conduct genealogical research, and take photographs of the historic church walk away wondering why there is a brick missing from the elevated crypt that locals call the Unquiet Grave.

Cellar House

Combine a jealous pirate, a lonely wife, a secret lover, an isolated mansion, a hidden tunnel, and a spontaneous moment of rage. To no one's surprise, the tragic result was a gory and certainly memorable murder. The incidents leading up to this crime occurred in the early 1700s, and during the ensuing three centuries the facts have been blended with hearsay to serve up a delicious legend that continues to attract the attention of local historians and ghost groupies alike.

Above the banks of the Pocomoke River in Worcester County, southwest of Snow Hill, stands Cellar House. A French sea captain and shipbuilder constructed the farmhouse in the late 1600s. He and his beautiful English wife lived in the remote area of the county on a large parcel of land. They expected a long, calm, and comfortable country life enjoying the proceeds of the Frenchman's profitable shipping business.

Soon after the young couple's house was completed, the husband's legitimate business began to decline. Experiencing a dramatic drop in his income, the merchant took illegal steps to make up for his lost revenue. Joining up with local robbers, gamblers, sailors, and smugglers, the Frenchman left for long sea voyages, raiding and sinking ships in the nearby Chesapeake Bay and off the Mid-Atlantic coast.

Since the Pocomoke River was among the deepest waterways in the region, the merchant-turned-pirate was able to sail his ships directly up to his property. He stored all of the stolen goods in the area around his home and outbuildings. Eventually, he and his pirate crew dug a brick tunnel that began at the dock and led into the basement of his home. This underground passage is the basis for the home's "Cellar House" name.

Such a secretive and seafaring career demanded long voyages, as the captain and crew kept lookout for merchant ships to attack and plunder. As a result of his new occupation, the Frenchman's lovely wife was left alone for extended periods of time. She spent hours each day lying across her bed, located beside an upper-floor window, looking downriver, hoping to see the sails of her husband's returning ship. Eventually, the lonely wife fell in love with either one of her husband's pirates or a local handyman, who visited Cellar House often to help with repairs and tend to the farm's daily chores. Locals reported seeing the secret lover's small boat docked often, and for extended periods, at the pier below the Englishwoman's home.

When her pirate husband arrived home unexpectedly, he found his wife in the arms of her lover. Although the boyfriend was able to escape from the scene, the young woman was caught and her husband immediately banished her from Cellar House. The woman, now homeless, abandoned by the lover whose child she carried, and rejected by her smuggler spouse, disappeared. Apparently, she took refuge in the home of her brother, William Allen, whose house was located nearby. There the pregnant woman stayed for more than a year.

One winter evening after the birth of her baby, the woman saw a candle burning in a first-floor window of the Cellar House and approached the home. When her estranged husband opened the door, he became enraged upon seeing his wife holding a young baby that was not his beneath a blanket in her arms. Rejecting her plea to reenter her home and return to her previous life, the Frenchman sent her away into the freezing night. A short time later, he heard his wife's screams and ran to the dock. Her boat had capsized and her baby had drowned. Splashing and shouting for help, the crazed woman reached the dock. Holding onto one of the pilings, she begged the captain for forgiveness and help.

Pulling her wet and frozen body onto shore, the Frenchman carried his soaking wife into Cellar House. After entering the warm home, he grabbed her by her long dark hair, dragged her upstairs, and tossed her onto a bed in the second-floor master bedroom. Trembling from fear, but relieved to be rescued from the icy waters, the woman looked up at her savior. But relief turned to shock when the Frenchman took his revenge by stabbing his unfaithful wife in the heart. She died in the upper-floor room, where for years she had waited so many hours for her husband's return from sea and where she thought they might reconcile and embark on a second life together.

After a few days, the pirate realized he would be hanged when his murderous act was discovered. Gathering his most valuable stolen goods from the tunnel, he sailed away with his crew, never returning to the lower Eastern Shore. At first, no one realized the pirate had left the region, and the wife's brother assumed her hoped-for reconciliation had gone well. When a search party entered Cellar House months later, the men discovered a grim scene. Whatever was left of the decomposed remains of the murdered woman rested upon the floor. Since the corpse was found in early summer, the rotted skin and body fluids had seeped from the decayed corpse, creating a near perfect outline of the dead woman's figure in the wooden surface.

In 1966, a *Salisbury Daily Times* article by Orlando Wooten recalled the well-known legend. The piece also mentioned that during restoration work on the property, a skeleton was found in the historic home's cellar, This discovery, along with tales that the house was used by troops during the Revolutionary War and served as a stop on the Underground Railroad, has helped maintain interest in the structure's legends and other regional stories of buried treasure chests and unsolved mysteries.

The Archeolog, published by the Sussex Society of Archeology and History, contained a chapter about Cellar House written by Linda Creasy Krabill. It made reference to the physical impression resulting from the horrible murder by the enraged pirate: "This grisly memento of the lusty days of pirates and smugglers remained visible on this floor until soon after 1916, when the owner had the entire room floor overlaid with wood. The ghost of the slain lady is said to patrol the banks of the Pocomoke wailing for her lost sailor lover and her drowned child."

Road Roamer

The bold headline in the August 4, 1933, *Cecil Whig* asked: "Have You Seen The Honest-To-Goodness Ghost on Phila. Road?" The anonymous newspaper writer reported: "For those who have faith in the theory that spirits of the dead rise again and walk at night, a current story should provide a wealth of material for the imagination. It is reported—and, for that matter, from not . . . unreliable sources—that a 'ghost' has been seen walking along the Philadelphia-Baltimore highway through this section."

The story goes on to describe a "shabby, stooped man of perhaps 40 years, walking at a slow, weary pace, with a look of sadness and resignation upon his countenance. His gaze, it is said, is fixed straight ahead and he is apparently oblivious of passing automobiles."

The story was published first in Baltimore, after reports by "late-traveling motorists." The phantom, it was said, confined his activities to the same area on U.S. Route 40, and always appeared to be walking in a northerly direction. The first reported sighting was given by Louis L. Erhardt, the general manager of a Persian rug-importing house in New York City, who stopped at a local Maryland hotel. "Erhardt claims to have encountered the specter near the top of Bacon Hill, between North East and Elkton," the paper stated.

The salesman reported that his automobile lights "picked up the figure of the pedestrian as he was ascending the long grade. Because of the apparent weariness of the stranger, the driver paid particular attention to his progress, but found that no matter at what speed he drove, the phantom remained just within the rays of the headlights. Nevertheless, Erhardt claims, the figure had the appearance of proceeding at a slow fatigued gait.

"Truck drivers who also allege to have seen the ghost near Elkton say that he carries a pack upon his shoulder, but never asks for a ride, and that he appears and disappears suddenly out of, and again into, the shadows. Sometimes he has been encountered just out of Baltimore, sometimes on the long, isolated stretch beyond Aberdeen, and again on the lonely hills between Perryville and Elkton."

One week later, the ghost story continued to make headlines, with the *Cecil Whig* announcing: "Highway Ghost Leaves Route 40 For Perryville-Port Road." The article stated: "Maryland's highway ghost has forsaken its native Philadelphia Road. First reported near Baltimore, later in the vicinity of Aberdeen, and last week said to have been seen between North East and Elkton—but always proceeding in a northerly direction on U.S. Route 40—the apparition has now digressed from its native haunts and was seen on Tuesday on the highway between Perryville and Port Deposit."

The story referred to Layton Schmidt's sighting, which happened while he was returning to his home in Lancaster, Pennsylvania, from Baltimore through Havre de Grace. He alleged to have seen "the specter in one of the lonely hollows near Cokesbury. Like other accounts of the ghost's escapades, Mr. Schmidt tells that during the early morning hours his car picked up the figure of a shabby, stooped old man walking slowly ahead."

Apparently, Mr. Schmidt was "badly frightened" and reported an "incoherent story" when he arrived in Rising Sun, soon after the sighting of the apparition.

According to the *Whig* article, "Traveling at a rapid rate of speed, Mr. Schmidt avers that he did not doze at the wheel, and like others who have seen the ghost, claims that the figure of the weird pedestrian remained before him in the highway for several hundred yards before it disappeared into space."

Headless Horse

There are a lot of tales about headless horsemen. They are found in every state and in every country around the world. But a longtime Eastern Shore resident alerted me to the story of the Headless Horse of Dorchester County. Thinking I had heard him wrong when he called on the phone, I immediately asked if he meant to say "headless horseman." But in a rather irritated tone, my informant replied, "Horse is what I said, and horse is what I meant." So I quieted up and started scribbling down this rather unusual, but quite fascinating, tale.

Late one fall night, in the area south of Blackwater National Wildlife Refuge, somewhere around Toddville, Crapo, and Bishops Head, three hunters were walking down a dirt farm road after a long day shooting in the fields. Suddenly, they heard a sound to their rear that they all identified as the steady pace of a slow-walking horse. In unison they turned around to make way for the passing creature and discovered they were within ten feet of a large, sweaty black horse—without its head.

Frozen in place, the speechless trio stared as the dark-coated animal passed beside them. One man later said, "It was so close, I could hear the stretching of the leather and the saddle against the horse's hide as it went by."

After the headless beast disappeared around a tall row of dried cornstalks, the men recovered their wits and raced toward the bend, hoping to see where the mysterious animal had gone. But the headless creature had vanished, probably blending into the night's tar-like darkness. Troubled by the sighting, the men decided to make an effort to share their experience with some old-timers in the region, hoping to find an explanation or some history related to the disturbing apparition.

It didn't take long to come up with a fairly plausible answer. According to a local legend, in the early 1800s, Ashley, a heavy-handed overseer, operated a plantation sawmill. The miserable man had a reputation of treating the slaves in his charge very badly. This evil boss man didn't need much of an excuse to lay the lash onto the back of any slave that walked too slow, held his or her head too high, or dared open his or her mouth at an inappropriate time. Ashley believed that making an example of anyone that caused even a slight aggravation to the workflow would insure an uncomfortable, and therefore productive, workforce.

One slave in particular, named Henry, was the object of Ashley the overseer's constant attention and abuse. While working in the sawmill one morning, Henry made an error that ruined a large piece of rather rare and expensive lumber. To teach him a lesson, Ashley—who conducted business from atop his impressive black horse—pulled out his red leather whip and beat the slave mercilessly. The rest of the members of the work crew turned their heads away rather than watch the brutal beating. When the whipping was done, a bruised, bleeding, and beaten Henry crawled through the dirt and disappeared out the wide sawmill door.

Thinking the injured slave was headed back to his hut to nurse his wounds, Ashley started up the large saw and ordered his crew to fetch another piece of lumber and get back to work. With the noise of the steam engine and the resumption of the cutting, no one noticed Henry had returned. The injured slave's beaten figure stumbled across the large room dragging a long, uneven board behind him. Suddenly, the blood-soaked slave pulled back his arms and swung his jagged, makeshift weapon forward. A loud whack sounded as the wood plank connected with the hind end of Ashley's startled horse.

Apparently, Henry had intended that the overseer would be tossed off the animal and land on the whirling saw blade. Instead, the horse's abrupt reaction caused a different result. Ashley was thrown from the horse's back and hit the dirt floor beside the saw. But the startled animal lost its footing and fell across the whirling blade, and its wild-eyed head was severed from its neck.

In a rage, Ashley picked up the board and beat Henry to death. But as he died, the bloodied slave pointed toward the dead horse, saying, "A curse on ya and all yer damned childs. That black horse is gonna folla ya'll to the graves, forever."

Some suggest the three tired hunters were walking on the old sawmill road at the precise time when the restless phantom horse was bound for the home of one of Ashley's unsuspecting descendants—possibly to deliver a final deadly message.

There's a second story in Dorchester County about another four-legged animal. A creature known as the "White Devil Mule" lived on a farm near Tobacco Stick. No one knew where the mule came from. The animal just appeared on the farm one Friday the 13th, and took up residence at the site. It was difficult to handle, and some said it had the temperament of the devil. Others said it was the Devil itself. After the mule died, its spirit never rested. Hunters and farmers claimed they saw the White Devil Mule's ghost wandering along streams and moving on back roads throughout the county. The animal's reputation grew, and the legend spread that if the White Devil Mule looked directly into your eyes, you would be taken immediately to the gates of hell.

One town drunkard was so terrified after a weekend encounter with the beast from hell that he gave up drinking forever and became a preacher. At least a half-dozen times a year, he would deliver a lengthy and spirited sermon about how the White Devil Mule was responsible for leading him away from sin and into the arms of the Lord.

Suicide Bridge

If you were trying to come up with a spooky name that would attract attention, you couldn't do much better than "Suicide Bridge." The span is in Dorchester County, southwest of Hurlock and west of East New Market. It's a part of Suicide Bridge Road, which crosses Cabin Creek, a tributary that empties into the Choptank River. Although the waterway looks narrow and insignificant on a map, it's deep enough to have drowned several victims over the years, and it has earned its place in local history and lore.

They say the first bridge in this isolated part of the Eastern Shore was built of planks in the late 1880s. The next, also made of wood, was erected about 1910. The present-day bridge, a wood structure coated with blacktop, was put up in 1967. And while it has gone by a few different names—including Cabin Creek Bridge and Uncle Joe's Bridge—it's the Suicide name that seems to have stuck.

In a 1985 Associated Press story by Theresa Humphrey, a few long-time residents shared their memories of the span and mentioned the mysterious deaths that contributed to its eerie reputation. The first victim was a postmaster from nearby Hurlock. He shot himself and his body dropped over the side of the bridge and landed in the creek. The next death involved a farmer, who also died of a self-inflicted gunshot, and his body also caused a splash as it fell into Cabin Creek. The third fatal incident occurred when a man named Frog dove off the bridge and hit his head on a piling. At the time of this incident, some locals said it was suicide; others claimed it was the result of foul play. One local recalled that when they pulled Frog's corpse from the creek, they laid the body out on a nearby picnic table. Frog rested there for some time before the local doctor eventually arrived and performed the autopsy right there in the public park.

After the third bridge was built, only about six months passed before tragedy number four occurred. A man was driving back from a vacation. Instead of returning home, he headed to Suicide Bridge Road, parked his car, climbed over the railing, and dove into the water. One old-timer claimed there were bloodstains soaked into a nearby dock where the body was fished out from the water, and the dark marks were visible for years.

Certainly, facts get hazy as decades pass. There are rumors of other deaths and sudden tragic accidents related to the bridge. One modern-day story involves a headless rider—on a motorcycle, not a horse—who has been seen speeding across the bridge on moonlit nights, under a full moon and during dense fog.

A few folks have suggested that Suicide Bridge and the nearby area might be cursed. In *A Visit With the Past, Legend and Lore of Dorchester County*, author Brice Stump mentioned some residents reported seeing balls of light near the bridge. "They were said to be tokens, light which foretold death to come and marked death passing," Stump wrote.

Who's to know whether these lights were warnings of a future deadly event or indications of spirit energy left behind? Some paranormal experts say cursed sites allow those with "the gift" to notice things others cannot perceive. But such locations also may cause other impressionable and troubled souls to be influenced and think they see things that might not be, or do dangerous things they should not do.

Following every unexplained incident or deadly event, a spooky locale's reputation grows, encouraging curious visitors. "Legend tripping" is the term folklore experts use to describe these paranormal pilgrimages.

It's natural to try to find an explanation when a series of tragedies occurs at a specific place. Is the hexed location known as Suicide Bridge a bad-luck spot? Is it the site of a long-forgotten massacre? Does a lost Indian burial ground or unmarked slave cemetery rest beneath the road or along the banks of Cabin Creek?

The answer to the death toll mystery might have nothing to do with ghosts or the unexplained. Suicide Bridge might simply have become a fatality magnet. A random series of coincidences may have attracted people who have had enough and want to move on to the next part of their cosmic journey, and on their own timetable. The structure's unusual name might lend a slight sense of legitimacy to their deadly act. "Why not," one might wonder, "do what others have done, commit suicide at Suicide Bridge?" If so, they won't be the first or, some believe, the last to do so.

Restless Jailbirds

The vacant brick building on North Street in Elkton is haunted. At least that's what one might assume after hearing the story shared by an evening-shift custodian. The older woman had worked in the historic building during the 1990s, and some believe her reports of strange events occurring after dark are certainly possible—especially since for more than a hundred years the nineteenth-century structure served as the Cecil County jail.

The woman's tale about rattling chains and slamming cell doors surfaced when this employee—who cleaned up the former jail building after hours, when it housed the town's senior center—stopped into the nearby Historical Society of Cecil County. While talking to historian Mike Dixon, the visitor, who we'll call Gertie, asked if there ever had been any reports of ghosts making noises in the old brick-and-stone building.

According to Gertie, she usually tried to get her duties done as quickly as possible, especially during winter when the sun descended earlier than the rest of the year. Within about a half hour of sunset, she reported hearing metal doors slamming and male voices calling out for attention. Sometime they demanded food or medical help, she claimed.

"Of course," Gertie explained, "the voices were hard to understand, since the words and sentences were more like whispers that sorta faded in and out."

When asked how often the clanging door noises and unseen voices occurred, she said, "A few times a week. A lot less in the summer. But during winter, it seemed they were a lot more regular. You could almost count on them to get antsy about two or three nights a week. I tell ya, I would work hard at what I had to do, moving real fast, so I could get outta there. I was alone, and I didn't like staying a minute longer than I had to."

Sometimes, the spirits would get so loud that Gertie couldn't stand it. "One night," she said, "they wouldn't let me be. I just got so upset, I shouted out loud, 'Leave me alone. I'm Lester's daughter. So just let me be!' And that quieted them right down. Never heard a peep any more that whole night long."

Gertie explained that her father's name was Lester. Decades earlier, he was a locked up somewhat regularly for minor crimes associated with drinking, bootlegging, and fighting. "I figured some of them jailbirds might know my father, and hoped they would let me alone. After that, whenever I reminded them of Lester, they quieted right down. But the peace and quiet only lasted a day or two, then they'd start up all over again."

But Gertie shared one more unexplained incident from her time working at the old jail-turned-senior center. She said one night she heard the painful cries of a man, who four times in a row called out the name "Alice." The custodian said she heard the voice very clearly, as she passed through the front section of the building on the second floor, overlooking North Street.

"He sounded like he was in terrible pain," Gertie recalled. "I'll never forget the sorrow and hurt in his voice."

After Gertie left the historical society library, Dixon, the town's expert on all things related to the past, said he couldn't get the story out of his mind. Staying later than he had planned that evening, he pulled down a ledger that held bound copies of town newspapers from the last century. One front-page story caught his eye.

In the early 1900s, a prisoner in the front of the North Street jail, where Gertie now worked, shot the county sheriff. At the time of the murder, the sheriff's wife, who lived in the upper floor of the jail with her husband, witnessed the tragic scene from the couple's second-floor parlor window, overlooking North Street. The man's last words, spoken as he lay on his back looking up at the figure standing in the window, was his wife's name—Alice. Witnesses said he called it out several times before he died.

Plain Dealing

Plain Dealing was the name of a mansion in Talbot County on the Eastern Shore. The property was named for a group of early New World settlers, good people who traded honestly with the Indians that lived in the area across the Tred Avon River from the small settlement of Oxford.

Samuel Chamberlain built the estate's home in 1758. One of the heirs, Thomas Chamberlain, moved into the mansion with his young wife, Susan. They planned a wonderful life together in their family's beautiful country estate, but Thomas died suddenly. For seven years, his grieving widow sat in a chair by the window of her room and looked out at the nearby graveyard where her young husband's body had been buried. Susan was so distraught that she instructed her servants to place a lighted lantern by Thomas's grave each night, so when she looked out from her bedroom windows the lonely widow would be able to see her lover's stone marker through the darkness.

Near that same old family graveyard, a large sunken area of the earth was associated with a legend about lost treasure. This tale, related from John Martin Hammond's *Colonial Mansions of Maryland and Delaware*, involves two brothers who at one time lived at Plain Dealing.

After one brother announced he had dreamed that gold was buried beneath the low spot of ground near the graveyard, the two men spent the next day digging at that spot until they found a long-lost treasure. Unfortunately, the gold had been cursed, and one of the brothers lost his mind, wandered off into the forest, and died. The other brother took the gold and purchased an island in the Chesapeake Bay. However, it's said that he too met a tragic death at the hands of pirates. They had tracked him down looking for their treasure, which the young man had taken and which the picaroons had reclaimed.

Hammond's book also claims the Plain Dealing mansion is haunted by the ghost of one of the owners who fell from the home's high balcony above the entry hall and broke his neck. His lifeless body left its mark in the form of a pool of blood, which stained the mansion's polished wooden entrance lobby and remained for years as evidence of the tragic death.

As time passed, the mansion was abandoned, and the family cemetery was reclaimed by nature. Weeds and trees covered the neglected tombstones. What was left of the haunted mansion became the unofficial residence of one of Talbot County's last witches, Katie Coburn. Old, stooped, deformed, and clothed in dirty rags, the ancient sorceress was a memorable and feared sight as she traveled through the area's forests and back roads.

Like all witches, children feared her and adults went out of their way to avoid contact with the spell caster. Villagers said she could make animals talk. With the slightest glance she could dispense the deadly power of the "evil eye" at anyone she chose. Slaves wore mojo charms about their necks, and wealthy merchants carried lucky rabbits feet, to protect themselves from the spells of Katie the Witch. But over time, Katie and tales of her powers disappeared, along with the public's belief in magic potions, mysterious amulets, and the secretive powers of those eccentrics that practiced witchcraft.

Kent Manor Inn

An old historic mansion on Kent Island in Stevensville offers a glimpse of the past. For more than two centuries the Kent Manor Inn has survived invading armies and fierce storms. But its greatest achievement is its ability to withstand the most deadly of all predators: progress. Within sight of the busy Bay Bridge, and not far from the modern shopping outlets, fast-food restaurants, and fast-moving traffic along Route 50, the estate's 200 acres and waterfront views make it an ideal getaway for dining, romance, and solitude. Plus, there's a chance you might bump into one of the original builders, Alexander Thompson—who's been dead for well over a hundred years.

Most will agree that legends associated with old buildings add to their charm, and Alexander is said to sometimes ride up the long driveway and pause in the circle, possibly to survey the present condition of his old mansion before riding off. His stately figure has been seen evaporating, along with his horse, into the distance. One other interesting note: the horse and rider make no sound as they traverse the paved lane. No hoofbeats are heard, and the phantom rider utters no comments.

During an interview in the mid 1990s, then owner Leslie Harper Williams noted that employees often complained that locked doors in the inn had been left open. Also, a figure dressed in farmer-style clothing had been seen in one of the upper-floor guest rooms, quietly sitting on the end of a bed before disappearing.

Room 209, located in the original section of the inn, is believed to have been Alexander Thompson's master bedroom. Some say the spirit of the long-deceased owner and builder occasionally makes his presence known in that chamber and in the hallway nearby.

There have been reports of items being moved around in various guest rooms, of unexplained tapping sounds, and of lights being turned on in locked rooms, but nothing horrifying. Leslie had described the antics as playful and said it's probably just "Alexander being mischievous."

Bigg Lizz

As far as ghosts go, Bigg Lizz is an Eastern Shore icon. Physically, she was, and some believe still is, so big that her name should be spelled with two g's and two z's. She once lived on a sprawling plantation. Today, she roams the swamps and forests of Dorchester County, even though she was murdered during the Civil War.

At that dangerous time, the sympathies of citizens throughout the Delmarva Peninsula were divided. Some were loyal to the North while others had equally strong sentiment for the Southern cause. Neighbors were at odds over the issues of slavery and states' rights, and members of the same family who had opposite views found some sons wearing blue uniforms and others wearing gray.

While Maryland remained in the Union, many of her citizens on both sides of the Chesapeake Bay fought for and supported the Confederacy. Monuments have been erected to honor the legacy of Maryland's sons of the Eastern Shore who fought for the Rebel cause. In Dorchester County, a wealthy plantation owner worked secretly as an agent for Confederate States of America president Jefferson Davis in Richmond.

Sacks of gold and silver coin were delivered to the man's plantation where Bigg Lizz worked, and the "Master" considered her one of his most dependable and hardworking slaves. Eventually, he learned that Bigg Lizz was working as a spy for the Union. Since he had treated her quite well, the Master was immensely disappointed to learn she had been reporting his activities to Federal troops on a regular basis.

One night, when a chest was filled with gold bars and coin, the Master called for Bigg Lizz. She was a large woman with powerful muscles, and he directed her to lift the wooden treasure chest and place it in the back of his wagon. Together they rode in darkness on a moonless summer night into the depths of Green Briar Swamp.

Once there, the Master told her to dig a hole deep enough to hide the large, treasure-filled wooden box. As Bigg Lizz burrowed deeper, less and less of her body could be seen from outside the growing pit. Up and down she went as she dug and tossed aside the dirt. The rhythm of her powerful body took on a steady beat.

In the shovel went, down the body followed, up the head came, into the air the dirt flew. In the shovel went, down the body followed, up the head came, into the air the dirt flew. The pace was so regular that the Master began to tap his foot to the steady repetition of movement.

In the shovel went, down the body followed, up the head came, into the air the dirt flew. One. Two. Three. Four. One. Two. Three. Four. His head nodded. His finger tapped.

When the hole was approaching the desired depth, he ordered Bigg Lizz to dig just a little deeper, to be sure that varmints wouldn't disturb the chest and its important contents. Finally, the freshly carved crypt was done to the Master's satisfaction, and he ordered Lizz out of the hole, directing her to place the box in the bottom of the pit.

That done, Lizz resumed her shovel work. She stood on level land, not far from the Master and his wagon, parked at the edge of the swampy hole.

Again Lizz's actions took on a rhythmic beat. Bending over and twisting, she shoved the tip of the tool into the tall pile of damp earth and released its contents back into the hole.

Turn, bend, dip, pull, toss. Turn, bend, dip, pull, toss. Turn, bend, dip, pull, toss.

Again, the Master began tapping his toe, smiling as he observed her steady pace, the strong muscles of her body at work, the high level of concentration.

He was proud that she was his, that he owned her. A better slave he could not have acquired, but then he shook his head, obviously bothered by what had to be. Busy with her task, Bigg Lizz did not notice the Master, standing on the wagon deck, directly behind her body. A large tobacco knife, about three feet long and razor sharp, was clutched tightly in both his hands.

As her body bent forward, then raised itself into an upright position, Bigg Lizz's massive sweating head was only a few feet from the Master's waist. He tapped his toe, getting into the rhythm of the moment, her rhythm, her steady pace. Then, when her head was highest, closest to the level of his belt line, he timed his motion perfectly. In one flowing, smooth, and rapid swing he pulled back both arms and directed the silver blade of his razor-edge knife forward, catching Bigg Lizz unaware.

A strange look of surprise was frozen on her face as Lizz's round, full head flew into the air and landed with a thunk against a nearby tree. The headless corpse, which didn't yet know it was dead, took three erratic steps forward, tumbling in a heap into the death hole. Within seconds, a headless Bigg Lizz ceased to function, and the lifeless mass rested atop the nearly buried chest of Confederate gold.

With the crypt conveniently prepared and the gold safely hidden, the Master adjusted his riding gloves and began to fill the remainder of the hole. This was one physical task he would trust no one else to do. Slowly, the remains of Bigg Lizz were covered with swamp dirt. On his return to his plantation house, and satisfied that only he knew the site of his treasure chest, the Master thought how clever it was for him to leave the slave's body sprawled atop the chest. With satisfaction, he compared Bigg Lizz's eternal guardian role to the ancient pirate practice where a murdered crewmember was tossed atop a treasure chest to safeguard its contents for eternity.

Then he remembered the woman's head, the shocked black face that had bounced off the moss-covered tree. Stopping his horses, he turned in his seat and thought for a moment about going back and retrieving it. But in the dark it would be impossible to locate. Besides, he convinced himself, there was a good chance the tasty face would be carted off by a wild boar or fox. Laughing, he thought of Bigg Lizz being devoured and all evidence of his treasure and the murder he had committed gone before daylight.

It was nearly three o'clock in the morning when he arrived at the front of his mansion. The Master shouted for Thomas, his favorite servant slave, and directed him to take the horses and wagon into the barn. Even though it was late, Thomas appeared within moments. Everyone knew it was not a good idea to keep the Master waiting.

Quite tired from a full evening of stressful activity, the Master was in bed by 3:15 A.M. and fast asleep moments later. After what only seemed to be a few seconds, he was awakened by a scratching sound that seemed to be coming from a corner of the room. He turned in his bed, pulled the pillow close around his head and ears to block out the sound, and tried to return to his much-needed sleep. But rest would not be his that night.

The annoyance grew louder and sounded closer, much closer. It was as if the scratching was coming from beneath his mattress. Sitting up in his bed, the Master shouted, "What is making such a noise!"

No one answered, but he noticed that the temperature in his room had dropped dramatically. It had been a humid summer night, but his room felt like a winter chill had entered through the open third-floor window. Jumping from his bed, intending to shut the window, his bare feet reacted to the bitter cold of the floor.

"What is this?" he wondered aloud, but he never reached the window. From the corner of his eye, he noticed two small red dots of light. They were about four feet off the floor and heading toward him. As they came closer, a huge figure of a woman dressed in familiar clothing—poor worker's clothing, slave clothing—came into view.

Bigg Lizz had returned and emerged from the shadows. Her headless body glided across the room and toward the Master, who was moving backwards at a very rapid pace. In the dead woman's left hand was her head, which she held by her hair. The red, glowing eyes seemed to direct the rest of Bigg Lizz's immense dead body in the direction it should go. She had no trouble following her prey around the mansion's large master bedroom.

In the ghost's right hand was a rather impressive tobacco knife. The Master knew that its blade was sharp, for he had used it earlier in the evening with good results. However, now the bright silver metal was coated with dried, black-red bloodstains—the blood of Bigg Lizz, whose ghost had returned from the swamp to take her revenge.

The Master was a smart man, and he knew more than most. After all, he owned and operated a successful plantation, and he had convinced his Rebel associates to trust him with their personal wealth.

So he must have realized that his death would occur in a matter of moments, that there would be no reasoning with or mercy from the resurrected ghoul.

But logic does not always prevail in times of strife and danger. The Master pleaded and cried, shouted and cursed, but nothing swayed the phantom from her goal. Terrified at the thought of spending eternity without his head, the Master jumped onto a chair and leapt out the window, crashing to his death on the ground three stories below. His body was found the following morning, and he was buried in the family cemetery on the grounds of his plantation.

The chest of gold and Bigg Lizz's head and body were never located. It's said her banshee remains in the swamp, somewhere in the area of Bucktown, south of Cambridge near DeCoursey's Bridge. She's there to protect the gold, a solitary sentinel standing watch forever.

Treasure hunters with sophisticated metal detectors have visited the area searching for the lost chest of riches. They say they're not interested in Bigg Lizz. Some even laugh when they hear stories about her role as the guardian of the gold. But they are careful to work only during daylight.

Area high school students, who say the slave ghost is the product of active imaginations, have organized outings to locate the swamp monster. But they only make one nighttime excursion into the forests and never go back. When they speak about the experience, they admit the swamp is eerie, very troubling, and not a nice place to play or explore during daylight or after dark. But as years pass others will still go there, to look and maybe even to get lucky and strike it rich.

There are other reports that Bigg Lizz has picked up her noggin and moved. One story tells of a sighting of her head in the Chesapeake Bay, circling small pleasure boats at night and calling out for help, asking to be pulled from the water. Another version says that the old girl has taken the treasure with her, and that she now sits on the chest in the middle of the Pocomoke Forest. But that story seems a bit far-fetched, not as believable as the original tale.

But who's to say what's true and what's not, what's real and what's imagined, what's the way it is and what's the way you want it to be.

The facts are these: Bigg Lizz was real. She was murdered. The Master is dead. The gold remains yet to be found. Even in the twenty-first century, strange and terrifying things still happen deep in the swamps and forests on the Eastern Shore of Maryland.

Aunt Molly

Easton and St. Michaels are the two most popular getaway destinations in Talbot County. Camera-toting tourists flock year-round to chic boutiques, trendy restaurants, and specialty shops. Others are attracted by historic homes, magnificent water views, distinctive folk art, and the Eastern Shore's slowly disappearing maritime lifestyle.

But there are also less visible attractions—secluded old mansions that provide a special, step-back-in-time weekend experience. Most of these former plantations are hidden off narrow, rural lanes, and are not easily visible from passing roads.

Gross Coate is one such mansion. For a time it operated as a popular and highly regarded bed-and-breakfast. Today it's a private residence, but its fascinating history and colorful ghost tales remain part of the Eastern Shore's heritage. Built in 1658, Gross Coate's beginnings predate by more than a century the signing of the Declaration of Independence. Many ancestors of present-day members of the Daughters of the American Revolution hadn't arrived in the New World when Gross Coate was being built.

Like any stately home that's been lived in for more than three centuries, the house holds scores of fascinating stories. But the mansion's two ghost tales—one short and foreboding, and the other more complex and romantic—are the focus of our attention.

Some say when a black phantom coach, driven by an unnamed ghost, drives up to the front of the mansion, it's a signal that Death's arrival is imminent. Early residents would anticipate the demise of someone who lived on the property, since they believed the Death Coach's appearance was a signal that the body of the departed would soon be ready to be carried off and take its final ride toward the other side.

The more complex, romantic, love-lost tale involves well-known portrait artist Charles Willson Peale, who arrived at Gross Coate in 1796 to paint the images of owner Richard Tilghman and other family members, including his wife, children, and his younger sister, Mary (more often referred to as Molly) Tilghman.

During the long periods when the fair subject "sat" for the artist, Peale and Molly became attracted to one another. But their hope to live happily ever after would not become a reality. Molly was a very young, beautiful girl. Peale, on the other hand, was an aging widower, with a busy studio in Philadelphia. He also was the father of several grown children. Eventually, Peale, who was staying at Gross Coate while he performed his artworks, approached Richard Tilghman and asked the family elder for his young sister's hand in marriage. Enraged, the plantation owner refused the artist's request and forbade him from seeing Molly again.

While the wide disparity in the ages of the two lovers was an issue, it was not Tilghman's primary concern. As a well-respected landowner, public figure, and influential community leader, Tilghman considered the artist's low position on the social scale extremely troubling. To have his sister marry far beneath her class would reflect poorly on the Tilghman family's good name.

After hearing about her brother's denial of Peale's marriage request, Molly became rebellious and argued fiercely with her brother. Richard considered his sister to be out of control and locked her in her room. There she was to remain until the young woman got over her lost love and regained her senses (meaning she agreed with her older brother and would eventually marry someone suitable). One can imagine Molly's emotional pain as she was kept in seclusion while her hoped-for, husband-to-be artist remained in the mansion completing the rest of the family portraits.

Upon Peale's departure—a better word might be eviction—from Gross Coate, and Molly's release from her room, she again demonstrated her rebelliousness and lack of good judgment. The young woman married, as they said in those days "the scapegrace of the county," meaning she picked a local as her husband, one who was considered a big-time, well-known town loser.

Years later, when her husband died, Molly Tilghman Roberts, by now a cripple suffering from rheumatism, returned to Gross Coate to live with her two nephews. One of the young men was a proper young man, like his father, Richard. The other was the wild black sheep of the family's subsequent generation. This independent streak allowed him to stake a stronger claim to the elderly aunt's heart. Having an addiction to the bottle, the wayward nephew would roam the local bars, returning to Gross Coate in the early hours of the morning, at which time he required help getting into the house. Aunt Molly, worried about his welfare, would often wait up late for the drunken boy's return. Perhaps she recognized a little of her own stubborn youthful personality in the troubled young man.

Until she died, Aunt Molly attempted to bring about reconciliation between the two young men, but even her deathbed request could not help them resolve their differences. The less reliable nephew agreed to bury the hatchet, but the prim, more formal, and stern brother refused his aunt's request. Shouting at her, he slammed the door behind him as he left her bedchamber. A few days later, Aunt Molly died.

But while the phantom coach may have hauled off the elderly woman's body, a stubborn portion of her spirit may have remained in Gross Coate. As evidence, some point to the muted tapping sounds of a wooden cane, traveling the hallways and along the floors of various bedrooms. Some say it's the ghost of Aunt Molly, continuing her quest of reconciliation by following the paths of her stubborn nephew and attempting to convince him to forgive the transgressions of his rebellious brother.

According to an article on "Ghosts of the Eastern Shore" by well-known Delmarva Peninsula author Helen Chappell, after Aunt Molly's death, some of the Tilghmans who resided in the home claimed if you sat on the bed in the room where the old woman died you would sense her ghost sitting beside you. It was, Chappell wrote, "as if you were the wild nephew, come to tell her about all your adventures before turning in."

Smith Island Specters

Smith Island is Maryland's only inhabited island accessible solely by boat. Each day at 12:30 P.M., a boat carrying the U.S. mail and other supplies needed for daily living leaves the dock at the end of Main Street in Crisfield. It and other craft in the daily caravan are bound for the small patches of land that host Smith Island's three water villages—Ewell, Rhodes Point, and Tylerton.

Located twelve miles offshore and surrounded by the Chesapeake Bay, Smith Island was charted by Capt. John Smith as he sailed up the Chesapeake in 1608. Its earliest European inhabitants arrived from England in 1657. But archaeological finds show that American Indians used the island many centuries earlier for ceremonies, hunting, and fishing.

Today, most of the several hundred residents are descendants of the original European settlers, and some say Smith Islanders have retained a trace of the eighteenth-century British dialect. While farming was initially the island's main source of livelihood, land erosion and other factors caused the islanders to focus on making their living from the sea. Many of Smith Island's residents still work the waters of the bay, and each village has its own working dock and harbor. More recently, the island gained fame as the home of the state of Maryland's official dessert, the multilayered Smith Island Cake.

Jennings Evans, a lifelong island resident and former waterman, calls himself an "unofficial historian." He keeps active by giving tours and speaking to guests at the island visitor's center. In fact, he is the narrator of the informative video that is shown several times daily in the center.

Smith Island is rich in history, and visitors can read and learn much about its association with all aspects of the country's past, such as the Battle of the Barges during the Revolutionary War and British threats and visits during the War of 1812. There are tales of picaroons and pirates hiding out in Rhodes Point—formerly known as Rouges Point—of buried treasure in the graveyards, of secluded mansions, and of the storms that flooded over the entire island.

Stories of the watermen and the hazards and humor of bay life abound, but Jennings also knows a few stories about the island's ghosts. Here are a few spirited tales he was kind enough to share with me during an interview I had with him during a visit to Smith Island in 1998. The stories are transcribed in Jennings's own words.

"Every place has got a lady with her head cut off," he said. "My wife's grandfather, Edgar Brimer, he's the first one that told this story. Back then, before World War II, there was no electricity on the island, except for a few generators that some people had in the backyard. But not all families had them. Electricity didn't get here until 1949. Before there was any lights, there was somethin', I don't know exactly what you'd call it, but there was a mist that came up outta the marshes.

"Now these guys, they wouldn't tell you lies. They've been accused of tellin' yarns around here. But when they telled you somethin' it was true and you believed it. If UFOs had been available then, you woulda believed that they saw one, 'cause they'd tell you, and that's how much dependence you put on a man's word.

"This happened on Ewell. Edgar was comin' from his sister's, from 'over the hill,' that's the west side of the church. He was headin' down the lane, toward his home, when he saw a figure in the moonlight, standin' by this tree. He saw a woman there. In those days, people were polite. So they would tip their hat or even take it off, you know? How sure he was that it was a lady, is that he said, 'Good evening, ma'am.' And when he looked, he said to himself, 'My God! I don't see any head on her! And I know I ain't gonna get an answer.'

"So he kinda walked briskly along. His house was only another two doors down, and he kept lookin' behind, and she was standin' there the whole time. Not gettin' any communication from her, he didn't see no point in elaboratin'. When he went around the corner and into his house she was still standin' there. And when he peeked out the window, she was still there, and he went to tell his wife. His wife thought he was crackin' up, and when she looked, she was gone. And Edgar went outta the house to check, and she was gone. But he told that for truth, and whether it was a mist or some particular gasses that come outta the marsh, we don't know. He believed he saw it, and we believe he saw somethin'."

A different unexplained tale involved one of Jennings' neighbors.

"Now, in late 1945, Stanley Marshall said he was courtin' a girl at the time. She was Mary Ann Evans, and she was stayin' with her grandmother in an old home called Pitchcroft. It was one of the oldest settlements on Smith Island and was used to keep preachers and visitors that came for the camp meetings. It was a place to take in boarders. It had an oyster house and store and an undertaker business there over the years.

"Stanley had to walk to Pitchcroft, a kinda outta the way place, and he said he always heard stories about things. So it was kinda easy to be startled. And he said, 'I think I had been drinkin' a bit, too, before I went over there.' But not after he came out, 'cause he was there two or three hours, just courtin' a girl. And he was from Tylerton, so he left his boat down near the dock.

"After he left Pitchcroft, that's what they called it, he started kinda whistlin' as he walked down a long lane. They had this gate to keep cattle in, and he had to lift this big weight on it. It was creaky like. It was another moonlight night, always seemed to be a moonlight night. I guess you couldn't see anything if there was no light.

"Anyway, he got a walkin' a while. And just before he got to where Cap'n Edgar saw his headless lady, Stanley looked behind him and he saw a woman. Now, this one apparently had a head. He didn't look too closely, but he thought it was a bit strange for her to be out there alone at night. So he started to speed up his walk, thinkin' whoever it was would go into the next house or stop to meet somebody. So anyway, he walked along. He kept lookin' back, and it looked like she was gainin' on him. And he looked at her feet, and it looked like she was floatin' along.

"So he told this for the God's truth, you know? And I believed him. I was a kid when he told it to me. He said he started speedin' up, not quite a run, but he had a long ways to go to his boat. As he speeded up, she tiptoed along behind him. He said, 'The chills are goin' up my back.' And he told me, 'I'da liked to know for sure what it was, but in another way it was so ghastly looking that I was afraid, so I just kept on speedin' up. If I get down to the boat and she's still with me, I don't know what I'll do. Jump overboard, I guess.'

"He said when he got near to the graveyard, there wasn't nothing to do but break into a run as hard as he could go. The last he saw, she was steadily gainin' on him, but then she went behind an old confectionery stand that used to be there, and that's the last he saw of her.

"He said, 'The sweat was pourin' off of me. I'll never forget it as long as I live.' He just left us with that mystery, and he always swore it was true. And I believed him. Stanley Marshall. He died about ten years ago. There also were stories about a headless woman carryin' her head in her hand. I heard different versions. Cap'n Edgar told me himself, and I knew he weren't just tryin' to scare me.

"The way it used to be, all these old men would get up at the store there and they would talk about different things. And somebody would mention a ghost from way back. It would become a subject and they'd start to elaborate.

"You had to sort them out. But when people like Edgar told you something, you more or less believed it. What I hated about it though, I had to go home by myself. But I had a choice of goin' home and not hearin' no more conversation, or stayin' there and gettin' the pants scared off ya. And at night, I had to go over the hill, and there weren't no lights except lightning bugs. Sometimes there were these green lights, the marsh is full of 'em. That's the only light I had. Sometimes I'd break into a run, imagination runnin' away with me."

When Jennings paused at the end of the story, I told him that on the boat ride over to Smith Island, I had met Gene Somers, who said, "Electric lights messed up all the ghosts."

Jennings agreed, saying there seemed to be more sightings and ghost stories before lighting arrived on the island. Then Jennings recalled another story, this one a sighting by Dr. William Stout, a semi-retired doctor that came over to live on Smith.

"Dr. Stout went down the road to Rhodes Point and said he saw this image. It kinda rose outta the marsh. He thought to himself, 'I don't believe in ghosts.' But it just amazed him how that formed right in front of his eyes.

"With it bein' in the marsh, he didn't want to take the chance to go out to it and sink up to his ears in mud. But he stood there and watched it for a while. And, all of the sudden, it started to disappear, kinda break up.

"See, he was tryin' to analyze the ghost that people was seein' around here. From his assessment of it, he thought it was some kinda marsh gas that rose up, and he knew all the people weren't lyin'. But he was brave enough to see what it was, and that was his conclusion—that the marsh sometimes puts out some kinda gas and made a form that resembled a fella with a sheet on, or whatever. It made some sense, too.

"And some people claim they seen flyin' saucers. That's another story . . ."

For another time.

Hexed Coffin Handle

Dexter recalled the brass coffin handle on his mantel that he had displayed in the corner of his living room, above the neat brick fireplace. He said he found it in a cemetery, not too far from the nearby shore. On the Eastern Shore, the water table has a tendency to shove the old wooden boxes holding the long-buried bodies up from the ground. Sometimes the coffin lid breaks the surface. Other times an edge or portion of the coffin is the only part that comes up. When that happens, the local gravedigger either moves the entire crumbling box or tosses on more dirt to keep the casket edges hidden.

In Dexter's case, he said one day he noticed the brown metal handle lying in a small indentation of freshly tossed earth. Dexter figured the artifact had been pulled up toward the surface by a groundhog or squirrel that had been active inside the grave in the corner of the old boneyard.

After polishing up the brass piece in his toolshed, Dexter said he placed his find on display. That night, there was an electrical fire in his kitchen. The next day, the brakes of his wife's car went out and she smashed her car into a telephone pole—on the roadway near the cemetery gate. Two days later, Dexter was cleaning leaves out of a clogged gutter. Suddenly, his ladder slid to the right. He fell two stories to the ground and broke his ankle.

"But, you see, I hadn't made the connection yet. I didn't realize the coffin handle was doing it to us," he said, shaking his head as he recalled the string of bad luck that occurred after his graveyard treasure discovery. After his wife mentioned during a dinner conversation the timing of the bad events, and the possibility of a connection, he figured the old coffin handle might be the cause.

"That night, right after supper," Dexter said, "I went out there with a flashlight and shovel. I dropped that coffin handle right back in the spot I found it. Then I said a prayer of apology and headed home."

Apparently, that did the trick, and the onslaught of bad luck ended for Dexter and his wife. "I figure," he said, knocking on wood, "that we put the hex to rest. But I'll tell ya. That's the last time I'm going to ever take anything outta the graveyard."

I told Dexter that I had interviewed a man who had a drawer filled with coffin handles. He said he collects them and buys them from an old gravedigger on the Eastern Shore. He said they're a very popular item, and you can find them for sale on the Internet.

"Well," Dexter interrupted me and said, "I can tell ya for sure, it ain't me sellin' them things. No way. No how. But based on my recent situation, if you're looking for bad luck, takin' a coffin handle from the graveyard is one sure way to find it."

Chesapeake Island Tales

Life near the Chesapeake Bay marshlands and along the guts and scattered islands required perseverance and ingenuity—particularly for those working on the open water and living alongside the soggy land. Things that city and farm folk took for granted, such as burying the dead, demanded different attention by the water folk. With the high water table exerting significant pressure, coffins of the deceased were buried in high ground. But in island graveyards, which are never far from surrounding water, the boxes of the dead are placed to rest in graves above the surface. While decorative box-like monuments enclose these bodies, there is no guarantee that the dearly departed will remain there forever. Such is the case of the floating coffin.

According to a *Baltimore Sun* article written by Joseph J. Challmes and Tom Horton and published on Halloween Day, 1972, this eerie event occurred on Hooper Island, at the western edge of Dorchester

County. It happened during the Great Storm of 1933. Others suggest it occurred many years earlier, and some even claim the creepy circumstances took place along the southern Atlantic coast or somewhere in New England. But while variations of this water village folktale may differ slightly in certain locales, the gist remains the same.

A sudden fierce storm delivered wave upon rising wave of water onto the saturated island. An aging waterman was trapped on the upper floor of his cabin, waiting for the most certain arrival of his last earthly visitor—a rain-soaked Shadow of Death. With no hope of escape, the old salt had made his peace with the Lord, and the fisherman resigned his inevitable fate to the hands of King Neptune and Davy Jones.

Amid the sounds of the howling wind and splattering rain, which sounded like gunshots hitting his tin roof, the waterman heard a steady tapping against the second-floor window. Over and over the slow rhythmic beating occurred, as if in sync with the crashing waves and surging gusts of the deadly storm. Eventually, the captive sailor crawled to the window, whose base was level with the height of the threatening water. Having trouble seeing through the darkness of the night, he pulled up the window and a wooden coffin floated into the second-floor room. He immediately recognized the long narrow box, for it contained the corpse of his recently deceased wife, who had been planted in the island graveyard.

Some say the waterman opened the lid and the dead wife, stiffened with rigor mortis, sat half upright. Others claim the old man dared not raise the top of the coffin, and was satisfied to read his wife's name that had been burned into the top panel.

In either case, the old salt shoved the well-built walnut box out the second-floor window, climbed aboard, and both rode and rowed his makeshift, life-saving craft throughout the stormy night, arriving safely on an adjacent island.

There's no logical explanation for the series of events that allowed the doomed man to survive being swept out to sea. And locals used to swear that the tale that extended his life for several years beyond the Great Storm was absolutely true. Some even added, with a sly smirk, that upon arriving on to dry land, the relieved waterman proclaimed: "Thanks, old woman! You always did look after me."

Another unusual incident occurred in the Chesapeake Bay a few years later, in 1938, just before the start of World War II. That year the U.S. Navy targeted a deserted island to prepare its future officers for potential naval combat. The strange scenario was reported on May 10 in the *Baltimore Sun*, under the headlines "U.S. Navy Prepares to Bomb Lone Ghost of Sharps Island" and "Spook Warned to Seek Shelter, As Midshipmen Will Use Place for Practice."

Sharps Island, at the mouth of the Eastern Shore's Choptank River, had been deserted for years. In order to provide second-year midshipmen from the U.S. Naval Academy at Annapolis with bombing practice, the island was rented from its owners so that a squadron of twin-motored patrol ships manned by trainees could conduct firing exercises using bombs filled with water rather than explosives.

Apparently, the excitement over the impending practice invasion rekindled tales of the island ghost that was believed to roam the deserted area, which had once been populated by vacationers who stayed in a spacious hotel and numerous summer cottages. Through the late 1890s, Sharps Island was a getaway destination and also a popular site for duck hunters. Only a few folks lived there year round.

Erosion and a rising sea level were the causes of the island's demise, and as the residents departed they left formerly useful buildings behind. The unattended structures slowly were claimed by the rising Chesapeake waters and spreading island vegetation. But before Mother Nature finished her work, scavengers returned to Sharps, carting off anything of value, and useful remnants of the island's buildings began appearing in homes and structures on the mainland.

About this time, reports of the island ghost began to spread. The stories were based on sightings of nighttime shadows and folks declaring they were hearing bumps in the deserted buildings. Eventually, only the stone foundations and the ghost stories remained.

But there was one other myth associated with Sharps Island, based on a story told during the Civil War era in the nearby town of Cambridge. The originator of the tale said he dreamed there was buried treasure on Sharps, and he claimed to know of its exact location. Initially, he was the subject of laughter, but a few days later the scoffers changed their tune. The old fellow, it's said, bought the entire island using several gold coins that were enough to seal the deal—and he never shared the source of his sudden wealth.

Today Sharp's Island, the town, and the old screwpile-style light building are long gone—the latter destroyed by ice floes in 1881. A fifty-two-foot red metal lighthouse stands as a reminder of a thousand-acre island that has disappeared. But the present lighthouse, built in 1882, has more than enough room on which a solitary ghost may roam.

Proof of a Ghost

In a 1959 column in the *Baltimore News-Post*, Tom White wrote about the 1799 appearance and existence of a ghost that was proved in a Queen Anne's County circuit court case. The original story was published in Baltimore, in 1808, in a booklet entitled "Authentic Account of the Appearance of a GHOST in Queen Anne's County, Md."

The tale began late on a March night when William Briggs was riding near a cemetery on his way home. Suddenly, his horse began jumping and stomping. Briggs tried to control the upset animal and, to his left, the rider noticed the ghost of his late friend, Thomas Harris. The phantom was dressed in a blue coat, and the figure stood and stared at Briggs for a few moments before vanishing.

When he arrived home, Briggs kept the incident to himself. He did not want anyone to think he was going crazy, or that he may have had too much to drink, neither of which were the case. He also was certain no one would believe a word of such a farfetched story.

A few months later, on June 1, the ghost of Thomas Harris appeared to Briggs again. First it made its presence known in the middle of the afternoon, when the ghost simply stood and looked at his old friend. Later, in the middle of the night, Briggs was awakened by a loud moaning coming from somewhere in his bedroom. When he arose from his bed to locate the source of the sound, the visiting ghost hit Briggs in the face so hard that it bloodied his nose and blackened his eyes.

Two months later, ghostly Harris made a return visit, and this time spoke to Briggs, explaining what was bothering the troubled spirit. Apparently, while alive, Thomas Harris had said he wanted his real estate sold after his death and the money divided among his four illegitimate children. This had not taken place. Harris's ghost told Briggs to go to the dead man's brother and remind him of the arrangement. The ghost told Briggs the conversation had taken place near the wheat stacks in the family barn and on the day the deceased was stricken with his fatal illness.

Briggs did as his dead friend directed. To his surprise, the brother, James Harris, admitted that the details were absolutely correct, and the brother promised he would follow his dead sibling's wishes. Unfortunately, James Harris died before he could execute the final details. His widow, Mary, claimed she now was the sole beneficiary of her husband's and all of the Harris family property.

To resolve the matter, Thomas's four illegitimate children took Mary Harris to court and sued to receive their rightful inheritance. The testimony of William Briggs, speaking on behalf of the ghost of Thomas Harris, was the main piece of evidence presented by the plaintiffs.

Briggs's comments in the case were critical. His reputation as a Revolutionary War veteran, a reputable citizen, and a person having no direct interest in the outcome of the case also influenced the judges. The defendant's lawyers tried to break down Briggs's story, but in the end the court agreed that the ghostly visits had indeed occurred as Briggs had described. Therefore, the judges admitted in open court to the existence and influence of a ghost.

The illegitimate children received their just payments, and his no-longer troubled dead friend, Thomas Harris, paid no more visits to the living William Briggs.

Headless Farmer

The last two stories in this section take place on the Eastern Shore of Virginia, whose two counties, Accomack and Northampton, are part of the three-state Delmarva Peninsula. The ghostly incidents occurred very close to Maryland's state line.

Assateague is a lengthy barrier island on the Atlantic Coast, extending along the Maryland–Virginia border. Chincoteague is a much smaller landmass, located between the Eastern Shore main-land and Assateague Island. Early settlers of Chincoteague—which in the Indian language means "Beautiful Land Across the Water"—arrived in the 1670s. They were sailors and livestock herders. Their main sources of income were farming, raising livestock, fishing, and salvaging whatever floated onto shore from frequent shipwrecks along the Atlantic Ocean coast.

For a time, a number of families lived and died on Assateague Island. Eventually, the federal government evacuated all residents from that island. Many of these families resettled on adjacent Chin-coteague Island. Some of the Assateague Island homes were trans-ported across the bay, and they became residences on Chincoteague. Today, however, the most famous residents of Assateague Island are a herd of wild ponies.

The island's small horses are said to be descendants of those that swam to shore in the sixteenth century, after a Spanish galleon they were on had wrecked at sea. Since that time, the photogenic ponies have taken over Assateague Island, and they have attracted tourists from around the world. Each July, tens of thousands of visitors arrive in Chincoteague for the annual festival, known as the Wild Pony Round-Up, Swim and Auction.

But there are other fascinating legends about Chincoteague and Assateague. Some involve buried pirate gold. Others are boastful yarns of island market hunters who outfoxed pesky game wardens. Still more recall sad stories of souls lost in turbulent seas, and of the ship-wreck ghosts that roam the scenic shoreline and old historic homes. Then there's the tale of the Headless Farmer of Ragged Point Channel.

More than a hundred years ago, the people on Chincoteague owned or rented land on Assateague Island, where they grazed their livestock. In the late 1800s, a wealthy gentleman decided to head over to Assateague to check on his livestock. A storm was approaching, and he wanted to make sure his animals were secure. At the time, there was little or no distance across the channel to the outer island. In some places, it was so shallow you could practically walk through the water.

The livestock owner's wife begged him to stay home with the fam-ily and to wait until after the storm had passed. But the husband ignored his wife's demands, saddled his black horse, and rode onto

Assateague Island. An hour later, as he was riding home in the dark, trying to outrun the storm, a bolt of lightning struck his neck and severed his head from his body.

The stormy decapitation occurred at the edge of Ragged Point Channel, on Assateague Island, across from the northern end of Chincoteague Island. The horse, having made the ride so often, knew its way home and delivered the headless farmer to his front door. When the relieved wife heard the horse's arrival she raced out onto the porch. After raising her lantern to welcome her husband, the woman's terrified scream spooked the horse away. The husband's headless body was never found.

For years afterward, the dead man's wife said when she went outdoors on a stormy night she would hear the hoofbeats of the phantom horse and hear her husband's sad, frustrated voice screaming as he searched for his missing head.

Some locals say the Headless Farmer of Ragged Point Channel still rides the coastline of Assateague Island, particularly during a lightning storm. He's the fellow dressed in black, sitting—headless, of course—atop a dark horse and frantically searching for that most important part of his body. But he's been riding for a long time, and most folks will agree that he will never, ever find his long-lost head.

Keeper's Death Prayer

Only a few miles south of the Maryland–Virginia border, the water village of Chincoteague is a popular getaway resort, and throughout the centuries the island haven has worked hard to maintain its small-town appeal. It also seems that its old-fashioned charm may have contributed to the presence of a ghost or two, lurking along the sands and above and below the waves.

From 1886 to 1939, Killock Shoal Lighthouse stood above the water, about five miles north of the Chincoteague village, at the southern end of Chincoteague Bay. This small, wooden structure was an indispensable navigational aid, relied upon by both local watermen working the inland bays and captains of large ships sailing the nearby Atlantic Ocean.

According to lighthouse historian Bob Trapani Jr.'s book *Lighthouses of Maryland and Virginia: History, Mystery, Legends and Lore*, a sudden and unusual tragedy occurred in the one-and-a-half-story frame structure. And some believe this deadly incident may be the basis for unusual sightings that have occurred in the area over the years.

In February 1912, lightkeeper William Taylor waved good-bye to his wife as she pulled on the oars of a small boat, heading toward Chincoteague Island to buy supplies. Mrs. Taylor was alone, but she had to make the trip. She and her lightkeeper husband were in desperate need of fresh food, since the couple had been trapped for several weeks by dangerous ice that had built up in the bay. A sudden thaw had offered an opportunity for Mrs. Taylor to make her way through the still-dangerous waters, but her husband had to remain behind and maintain the burning beacon.

A few hours later, while still in town, she and others noticed that for the first time in twenty-six years, Killock Shoal Lighthouse was dark—a very bad sign. Desperate to return as quickly as possible, Mrs. Taylor enlisted the help of several men and they headed immediately toward Killock Shoal Light. Hurrying up the ladder that extended from the waterline to the platform at the base of the lighthouse, every person in the party was anxious. When they reached the door of the building, there was no greeting from the keeper. Sensing the worst, Mrs. Taylor led the men into the building, all fearing their search would not end well. Inside she found her husband—kneeling at his bedside with his hands pressed together, as if in a state of prayer—dead.

His wife rushed to his side, embracing the freezing, lifeless body, as the men searched the building. They found no sign of foul play. The keeper had been in good health. Only a few hours before he had waved his final farewell to his wife as she set off toward town for supplies. The cause of Mr. Taylor's death remains a mystery. But on that winter night of his demise, even as the men left the lighthouse and ferried the cold corpse toward shore for burial, his grieving widow knew Killock Shoal Light had to be relit and maintained.

Before the death boat reached the nearby island, the beacon came back to life, and for a moment those in the makeshift burial party shared approving nods. But their smiles disappeared and an icy chill ran down each man's back when the widow's shrill death moan rushed by them, like a gust of wind, sweeping across the ice-coated bay. And that eerie cry occurs during some winter nights, north of the Chincoteague Island, when the bay is frozen and the moon is full, in the area where Killock Shoal Lighthouse and its keepers used to stand watch.

Central Maryland

Assassin's Birthplace

It's been called a "Birthplace of Infamy" and a "Hero's Homestead"; the "Poisoned Birthplace" and a "Conspirator's Haunted Home." Its real name is Tudor Hall. It's the property where nineteenth-century assassin John Wilkes Booth was born, raised, sowed the seeds of his hatred of the Union and, eventually, formulated his deadly plan to change the course of history.

Today, the Gothic-style home stands at the end of a narrow, tree-shaded lane, not far from a relatively well-traveled main road a few miles east of Bel Air. When well-known Shakespearian actor Junius Brutus Booth Sr. and his wife, Mary Anne, built the home in 1850, the countryside was sparsely populated and, as they desired, far removed from the congestion of the port city of Baltimore. Tudor Hall was going to be a showplace and refuge for the couple and their ten children—among them actors Edwin and John Wilkes. The two famous brothers had been born years earlier in a log cabin that sat on the property.

Since 2006, the historic, and some say cursed, structure has been owned by the government of Harford County, and its bedrooms and parlor have been converted into modern offices. Like any workplace, busy personnel go about their daily tasks rarely thinking about the infamous killer who grew up inside its walls or the invisible inhabitants who might lurk in and about the property. Certainly, it's no surprise that many folks think the old, eerie structure is haunted. This belief is based upon the 160-year-old building's appearance but more so because of its association with the assassin of the sixteenth U.S. president. But there may be some basis to this belief, especially when one considers comments from a succession of Tudor Hall owners, volunteers, and tenants, all of whom have said they experienced strange incidents during their stays.

The Booth connection to the area near Bel Air began when Junius Booth, who had arrived in New York from London, moved to Baltimore. Soon bothered by the town's noise and his cramped surroundings, the actor purchased more than one hundred fifty acres of farmland in Harford County, a fair distance north of the fast-growing seaport. The highly acclaimed stage actor was described as eccentric, brilliant, deranged, and moody. When he got off the vessel that brought him to New York City, he had brought along his pet pony, named Peacock, and had left his wife behind in Europe. After living for a few years in a small log cabin, Junius ordered the construction of the present home, but he died before it was completed. However, his children and wife enjoyed the property he had arranged to be built.

Little John Wilkes was a creative child, and he had decorated his second-floor bedroom with swords, pistols, and hunting trophies. He also left his mark on a window on the first floor, where he carved his initials, "JWB," with, some believe, a diamond ring.

Following his father's lead onto the public stage, John Wilkes was a 1860s celebrity, with the same crowd-pleasing movie star stature as, depending upon your era, Rudolph Valentino, Clark Gable, Marlon Brando, or Brad Pitt. Audiences and critics raved about his talent and performances. But like so many rich and famous personalities, John Wilkes Booth also had a secret side.

John was a fervent Southern sympathizer, hated Abraham Lincoln, and was determined to play a major role in helping the South win the Civil War, even if it meant dying for the Confederate cause. Instead of watching history occur, he apparently decided to make history.

Everyone knows about the events that occurred in Ford's Theater on the evening of April 14, 1865—and in the weeks immediately following, when Booth was cornered and killed in a Virginia barn. Fewer people are aware that upon receiving word of the actor's involvement in Lincoln's shooting, Union troops raced to his boyhood home and surrounded Tudor Hall. Members of the King family, tenants renting the property from the Booth family at the time, were shocked when blue-coated, rifle-bearing soldiers entered the house and searched the premises. The troops then stationed sentries throughout the property, in case the president's murderer returned to hide out in his boyhood home.

The King family had no idea that John Wilkes had killed the president, and at first told the commander of the troops searching the house that all members of the Booth family were always welcome in their family home. The commander replied that the Kings were lucky John Wilkes had not been on the premises, because they would have immediately been heading for a long prison stay in Washington.

Several of John Wilkes' family members were jailed for months during the assassination investigation, and intruders entered the Booth property and grounds in Bel Air, searching for evidence and morbid souvenirs related to the killer and his now-notorious and reviled family. Some time later, a rumor spread that a band of Northern supporters were planning to dig up the bodies of Booth family members from their private graveyard on the Tudor Hall property. To avoid such desecration, a relative had the remains exhumed, moved to Baltimore, and deposited in the Booth family plot in that city's sprawling Green Mount Cemetery.

As decades passed, Tudor Hall's public profile began to fade. Fewer people thought about the assassin's connection, and visits by historians, Southern sympathizers, and Yankee Booth haters became less frequent. Families having no connection to the infamous thespian-assassin eventually owned the building and property. Life in and near Bel Air reflected a peaceful, less agitated atmosphere—until someone reported a sighting of what might have been John Wilkes Booth's ghost. Then Tudor Hall was back on the map—more specifically, the Halloween, haunted mansion, and ghost-hunting map.

There were reports of images and lights passing by the Booth house's windows at night, of strange cries in the nearby woods, and of a foggy figure in a wedding dress floating in the first-floor parlor. Such incidents are commonly seen at many haunted places. But some other strange events at Tudor Hall made folks wonder if an ill force or cursed aura was attracting deadly energy to the old home. A small tornado uprooted a tree on the property where an owner had been standing only minutes earlier. A rumor circulated that a man moving a piano from the porch to his truck was crushed to death in front of the house, but some believe this is a tall tale that grew taller as time passed.

In 1980, *Washington Post* reporter Eugene Meyer visited Tudor Hall and interviewed the late Howard and Dorothy Fox, who at the time had owned the property for a dozen years. The couple discussed a number of unexplained events, including loud footsteps, strange voices in the middle of the night, and the sounds of crashing glass. While these incidents occurred with some frequency over the years while the couple was in the home alone, other unusual actions happened in front of witnesses.

While the Foxes were hosting a meal in Tudor Hall for some friends, the top layer of a cake floated up and flipped over, landing on the center of the dining room table. During one Christmas season, a mirror leapt from its hanging place on a wall and landed face-up in the center of the floor. Howard told the reporter, "It was like someone had lifted it off the wall and put it there."

After doing considerable research on the Booth family, the Foxes agreed that the actors were a "kooky bunch." The Foxes added that based on their experiences as owners of the property, they believed Tudor Hall was haunted.

An incident in 1968 was one of their first strange encounters. As the couple was in their car heading up the lane, a small white pony appeared nearby. Later, the head of the friendly animal peeked in a low rear window of the house, but just as suddenly disappeared. Knowing no one else in the immediate vicinity owned such an animal, the Foxes suggested the uninvited, four-legged visitor might have been Peacock, Junius Booth's favorite pet that he had brought with him to America.

During their years living in the home, Dorothy Fox said she had heard her name called out when she was home alone, was bothered by sounds of crashing glass, heard cabinet doors opening and closing, and smelled scents of strange perfume. But the couple agreed that whatever spirits inhabited the home were friendly and never made the owners feel uncomfortable.

After the couple passed away, the home was auctioned to a young couple and later purchased by the county government. Today Tudor Hall houses the Center for the Arts, and spooky stories about ghost sightings have decreased dramatically in recent years. Whether the constant turnover of owners or reconstruction work on the building settled the spirits is anyone's guess. But some drivers passing the nineteenth-century Booth homestead during dusk steal a quick glance at the remaining "Romeo and Juliet" balcony, projecting from the building's second floor. It was there that Edward, Junius, and John Wilkes practiced scenes from the famous Shakespeare play during more pleasant times, before the Civil War and the Lincoln assassination.

Along Maryland Route 22 east of Bel Air, a roadside historical marker designating Tudor Hall grabs the attention of passersby. But the sign's inscription bears no mention of the home's connection with John Wilkes Booth. The nearest place to find the assassin's name is on a gravestone above the Booth family plot in Baltimore's Green Mount Cemetery, where the killer eventually was buried. Perhaps it is there near his burial site that his restless and troubled spirit roams.

Legends of the Rocks

The area surrounding Rocks State Park in northern Maryland has an interesting history, particularly when the focus involves the unexplained. Legends of witches, restless Indians, hidden treasure, supernatural animals, and a fair number of ghosts all seem to be based within a few miles of the park's distinctive natural stone formations. In several books featuring Harford County folktales, and a ghost story on the Maryland state parks Web site, the area known as "the Rocks" plays an important role.

Since the 1700s, on All Hallow's Eve, now more commonly called Halloween Night, a coven of black-dressed women in pointed hats have descended on the area along Chrome Hill Road to meet at Witch's Rock. These secretive mortals, accompanied by their black cats, have used the secluded site near the 850-acre state park for devilish purposes. An incident involving a young couple appeared in the article, "Spooky Stuff in State Parks."

Late one Halloween night, a young man and woman drove past Witch's Rock and were shocked to see their headlights illuminate their names, which were painted in bright red letters on the hexed stone. The terrified couple drove home and, no doubt, had a sleepless night. Early the next day they returned, hoping what they had seen was the result of overactive imaginations. Relieved but confused, they found, instead of their names, a heavy coat of green moss covering that portion of Witch's Rock.

Another story involving witches is based on information in Rev. Thomas Wysong's book, *Rocks of Deer Creek*. Slightly northeast of the Rocks is an area called Mine Old Fields, which contains a number of mineral deposits, including lead, iron ore, and fool's gold. It was also a meeting place for witches, who would practice their rites and cast spells under the full moon. Some legends said people who visited the area soon after a coven had met would be affected by the remnants of the spells left behind. Doctors were called upon to treat people who seemed bewitched, for they would crawl around on the floor, bark like dogs, meow like cats, and bleat like sheep.

A tale from Mary Wright's *Harford Heritage* features the region's infamous Witch Rabbit. This was the name locals gave to a pesky oversized hare that had apparent supernatural abilities enabling it to jump along the crags of the steepest section of the Rocks. Over the years, even the most skilled hunters were unable to capture or kill the annoying critter, and these proud sharpshooters became perturbed when friends and neighbors ridiculed them for their unsuccessful efforts. After a meeting where they discussed their attempts and shared their techniques, the hunters decided that the only answer was the rabbit was a witch in disguise. Everyone knew it would take a silver bullet to put the evil nuisance to rest.

But silver was a precious commodity at that time and it was difficult to acquire, so the hunters abandoned their quest. For years, the large hare wandered the forests and hills of the county at will. Eventually, sightings of the creature declined and it seemed to have disappeared. Some suggested the animal enjoyed toying with its pursuers, and it moved on because it was bored that the hunters had given up their chase. Others said the Witch Rabbit probably went away to explore the new frontier and torment the settlers that were heading west.

Flora Wiley's *Harford Ghosts*, a group of stories collected by students at North Harford High School prior to 1960, includes the story of the Ghost of Deer Creek. This Indian spirit visits the site of a large boulder located near Chrome Hill, close to Rocks State Park. Longtime residents claimed they had seen a solitary Indian brave, riding a white horse, visit the boulder each year. The ritual occurred during early evening. The phantom visitor stopped at the stone for a few moments, as if paying his respects at the site, and then turned and disappeared into the night.

Some wondered what attracted the unearthly visitor to the hallowed spot. Had he died there in battle? Was the stone a monument marking the grave of an Indian chief, or was it the resting place of a loved one he still adored? Did the stone offer a clue to a massacre site or location of a forgotten hidden treasure?

It's safe to say the reason for this lonely apparition's yearly visit, and the sources of the other legends associated with the Rocks, will remain a mystery. But at least the stories have survived, and they most certainly will be embellished and changed over time.

La Cle D'or Guesthouse

Havre de Grace, originally called Harmer's Town, is one of northern Maryland's more colorful and historically significant water villages. During the early days of the colonies it was a major stopping point for travelers heading up and down the East Coast. George Washington walked the village's streets, as did the Marquis de Lafayette. The town was invaded and nearly destroyed by the British during the War of 1812. In the mid-1800s, it was an important stop on the Underground Railroad.

During Prohibition and the Roaring Twenties there was so much illegal booze available in the small town that it earned the nickname "Little Chicago." Just outside the city limits a long-gone racetrack, nicknamed the "Graw," made the town a getaway location, attracting visits by mobster Al Capone and his cronies. Famous thoroughbreds Seabiscuit, Man O' War, and Triple Crown winner Citation raced at the popular track.

Today, the quiet town is known for its specialty shops, walking tours, popular restaurants, and attractive bed-and-breakfasts. Visitors from across the country enjoy the peace and quiet atmosphere of a less hectic era in the city's restored mansions, which display antique furnishings and interesting artifacts and also provide fascinating stories.

One of the most popular getaway havens is La Cle D'or Guesthouse. Since 1868 this stately former home of members of the Johns Hopkins family has stood on North Union Avenue overlooking the top of the Chesapeake Bay.

Ron Browning and his former partner, Bill, bought the building at auction in 1994. The original foundation was constructed in 1839, and the present house was erected in 1868 following the Civil War. Today, the seventeen-room building includes a few additions and gardens that were not part of the original construction. The name, La Cle D'or, means "Key of Gold," a reference to the gold symbols on the lapels of concierges in fine French hotels. Also, the town had a strong association with the Marquis de Lafayette, who visited the village several times. On one occasion, the French and American general said the area reminded him of the French seaport Le Havre-de-Grace. Based partly on that comment, in 1785 the town formally changed its name.

While preparing to open his inn, Ron decided to use a French name and theme to solidify this historical association. His named guest rooms include the Lafayette Suite and the Rochambeau and De Grace rooms.

The public auction at which Ron bought the building took place on the front lawn of the property in June 1994, and final ownership papers were signed in September. In the interim, Ron said, the bank gave him permission to enter and clean out the property, which needed a lot of work.

"When I was cleaning up things by myself," he recalled, "many times I just didn't feel like I was there by myself. I felt funny, like someone was watching me." Like most people in a similar situation, Ron rationalized his reaction. After all, he was working alone in an old house that had been abandoned for years. It had a lot of unfamiliar areas and dark corners. And all old structures were known to have creaking noises. Ron decided to keep his concerns to himself. If others found out about his overactive imagination and his fear of the dark basement, he would be the subject of endless jokes.

But a number of psychics visited his home over the years, and each offered comments that gave Ron the impression he wasn't imagining things. Eventually, he began to believe a few of the building's former residents might have refused to move away from his popular tourist getaway.

Betsy, the first psychic visitor, arrived at the inn soon after Ron and Bill had moved in. She was a friend of a business associate of Ron and Bill; the friend had suggested the woman visit Bill because his mother had died recently. The neighbor thought the psychic Betsy might be able to offer Bill some helpful comments and counseling, since he was having a rough time dealing with his mother's death. While they were seated in the Hunt Room, Betsy paused and directed her attention toward Ron, who had been silent during the meeting. Betsy told Ron that she felt he wanted to ask her a question. At first hesitant to admit she was correct, Ron eventually inquired if there were any spirits or ghosts in the house.

Betsy casually said there was a woman in a dark Victorian dress in the De Grace Room. She said the spirit was comfortable with how Ron and Bill were restoring the home. When Ron asked Betsy why she hadn't told him, the psychic explained that she wasn't sure how he would react, so she didn't want to bring it up. Also, the purpose of her visit was to help Bill, not investigate the building.

A few years later, Katrina and Fred, two psychics who had moved into the area, were visiting Ron and commented on feelings and impressions they were receiving in the home. After walking through every room in the house, the couple said they saw a woman dressed in black at the top of the stairs entering the attic. Inviting Ron to accompany them to the top level of the home, which is not an area where guests are able to stay, they said the woman stays near the dormer window and looks out onto the street below. The psychics called her a "watcher," and said she is the spirit of a woman who had lived in the home. During her mortal lifetime, the spirit spent considerable time waiting for her husband to arrive back home from his business trips. He was a pharmacist who visited Baltimore and returned by steamboat.

One of the most unusual things these psychics told Ron is that the "watcher" was sitting in the window during the public auction—which was held on the front lawn of the building. The psychic said the spirit had seen Ron and Bill in the crowd of bidders and had picked them out to buy her home.

While that may have been a rather wild assertion, a short time later, Ron discovered that his name had been on the deed to the home long before he purchased the property. During a records search of the list of former owners, he found the listing for "Abraham and Mary Browning of Philadelphia," who sold the property to the Hopkins family in 1868. While Ron said he could not claim any direct connection to the former owners, the Browning name had caught his eye. Could it be a coincidence, or something more, that caused a Browning to come back and claim the abandoned home more than one hundred years later?

Andrea was the next visitor claiming psychic powers. Ron told her nothing about the home's history or any of the comments he had received from previous mediums. When the woman reached the attic door, she turned and asked, "Ron, did you know you have spirits in this house?" Feigning ignorance, he asked her to explain.

Andrea mentioned there was a woman in dark clothing roaming several floors and identified the spirit as Mrs. Hopkins. She said the former owner cleans and dusts rooms in the old sections of the house. "She is the lady of the house," Andrea said, "and she keeps things tidy." The psychic added that Mrs. Hopkins stays in the old section of the home and does not venture into the additions, including the modern kitchen.

Thinking about Andrea's comments, Ron admitted there are certain rooms that seem to be less dusty. But he's hesitant to attribute it to the late Mrs. Hopkins.

The most striking paranormal comments came from Barbara, a voodoo priestess from Philadelphia who visited the house one spring night. A neighbor had arranged for Barbara to offer a number of psychic readings in La Cle D'or's parlor. A full schedule of customers had signed up for half-hour sessions. At the end of the long night, Barbara, in appreciation of her host's hospitality, offered to give Ron a free reading.

As he took his seat, Barbara immediately grabbed his attention. Ron said he would never forget Barbara's first comment. "She told me, 'Your house is so full of spirits that it's very difficult for me to concentrate. You've got four Quakers at the front door—a man, a woman, a grandmother, and a little girl. I saw them as I walked up to the front door. You've got a king who walks around in the breakfast and Russian rooms. There's an Oriental man in the Lafayette Suite. And there's a man entering through the front window of the parlor. He's wearing a bloody shirt and keeps wanting to tell me his story, and I have to keep telling him to go away.'"

Summarizing the backgrounds of the different spirits, Ron said the Quakers are supposed to be the Henry Harrison Hopkins family, who practiced that religion. The Asian man might have been a servant or associated with the accessories in the Lafayette Suite. The king might be associated with an antique seventeenth-century piece of French furniture. He thought the man in the bloody shirt might have been someone injured in an automobile accident, or a victim of a fight or shooting from the days the town had been known as Little Chicago.

The most shocking moment of the reading came when Barbara told Ron, "Your father's in here with us." When she added a comment about the size of Ron's ears, a frigid chill raced down his spine. His father had died only a month earlier, and the man used to tell his son, "After a haircut, your ears look like two doors open on a taxi cab coming down the street."

"There was no way," Ron said, "that she could have known anything about that. It really got to me."

Ron said his session ended abruptly when he asked Barbara about the woman in black who appeared to other psychics in the De Grace Room and in the attic. Obviously upset, Barbara's eyes rolled back into her forehead and she froze, as if in a trance, and said in a different voice, "My name is Miriam, and that's all you need to know. And you better tell your guests to hold the handle down until the music stops."

Suddenly coming out of her daze, the psychic ignored Ron's attempt to get an explanation of the comment. As if he hadn't said a word, she grabbed up her belongings and raced out the door to a waiting car. After she left, Ron said he thought the name Miriam referred to Mrs. Hopkins. A few days later the meaning of the other part of the psychic's comment flashed into his mind when he pressed down on a toilet handle.

"In Victorian times," he suggested, "it might have been more proper to refer to the swirling water of a bathroom toilet fixture in such a strange fashion as 'until the music stops.'"

Ghost investigators have stayed in Ron's inn and reported recording indications on their instruments that might be interpreted as evidence of paranormal activity. A few guests over the years have asked about the presence of spirits. But incidents have been rare. The stream of psychics who seem to have been drawn to La Cle D'or Guesthouse has provided most of the information.

Ron said he can somewhat accept paranormal information about historical connections with former owners of the property, such as the Quakers on the front porch or the lady in black. But the most unusual comment—regarding a "king" in the breakfast room—seemed a bit outlandish, until he had a personal encounter with the phantom royal.

One day, while carrying a soda through the doorway from the kitchen into the dining room—between the new addition and the original home—he felt as if he had bumped into someone. Instinctively, Ron said, "Excuse me!" But thinking back on the moment, he added, "I said it to someone who was not there. But I saw a flash of bright purple and gold and white. I mean, I talked to him, or whatever it was, and I apologized."

Both confused and upset, he walked to the nearby antique shop where Bill was working and sat down. His friend approached and said, "What's the matter with you? You look like you saw a ghost."

To which Ron replied, "I think I just did."

Trying to make sense of the sighting and the "king's" presence, Ron said a walnut vaisselier—a large piece of fruitwood furniture that resembles the base of a hutch—stands in the Russian Room. It's believed to have been made in the 1600s and was imported to America from France. Eventually, it found its way to La Cle D'or Guesthouse. Who knows, wondered Ron, if the historic piece has some connection with royalty, or if the wood that had been used to construct it was cut from a tree associated with an interesting or tragic history. That's the best guess he could make to explain the unusual apparition he sighted inside the Havre de Grace inn.

Before leaving the La Cle D'or Guesthouse, I had to find out what the owner thinks about the magnetic pull his inn has had on psychics and those sensitive to the other side, and also learn his thoughts about the reported spirits that some say inhabit his home.

"I feel very comfortable here. It's a friendly place," Ron said. "Instead of the word haunted, I prefer to think of the residence as 'spirited,' since none of my co-occupants have done me any harm. But I find all of the stories intriguing. It's particularly interesting when visitors who have no idea of the building's past or its former owners tell me something connected to the home's history. And while some may fathom I have entered dementia, I maintain I am quite sane, just more aware of the spirits about me. After all, what homeowner would not like a free housekeeper and four guardsmen at the front entrance?"

Currier House

The beam of Concord Point Lighthouse burns steadily, shooting its powerful signal over Havre de Grace and the northernmost coastline of the Chesapeake Bay. Since 1827, the squat, stone tower's beacon has signaled captains of small craft and oceangoing vessels. In the early 1800s, the light was an illuminated sign of hope for escaped slaves trying to reach freedom beyond the Mason-Dixon line, located only a few miles north of where the light keeper maintained his flame.

On Market Street, about two blocks from the Harford County shoreline, Currier House sits atop a small hill, looking down on Concord Point Light. Built in 1790, the inn survived the British burning of Havre de Grace during the War of 1812 and witnessed Union troops heading south along the town's rail lines during the Civil War.

Jane Currier grew up in the building that has been associated with her family since 1861. The first Currier on the property was Matthew, Jane's great-grandfather. He worked as a ferryboat captain who guided passengers and cargo across the mouth of the Susquehanna River where it empties into the upper Chesapeake Bay. Matthew was the first of five generations of Curriers to live in, and ultimately preserve, the historic inn.

Jane, the current owner, lives on the property and operates Currier House as a bed-and-breakfast in the heart of the town's residential district. She grew up in the home before moving away. In 1994, she moved back to the area and planned to sell the property. But while cleaning out the basement she was overwhelmed by the wealth of family history she found in old trunks, antique furniture, historic paintings, and drawings, as well as numerous artifacts about Havre de Grace's past. Unable to sell off her ancestry, she restored the historic home. Today, most of the items decorating the attractive getaway destination are antiques, and many are associated directly with Jane's family.

It took a few years during the early 1990s for Jane to renovate the property and get it back into presentable and commercial shape. During that time, she said she met a man named Matthew Johnson, who was conducting Underground Railroad tours in the northern Maryland area. Johnson told her there was a very good chance that her home had been used as a station on the railroad's route toward nearby Pennsylvania.

Jane said she was surprised by Johnson's comment, but upon reflection Jane said she began to believe such a thing might be possible. During the mid 1800s, she said, the more established English population in Maryland and throughout America looked down on Irish immigrants, from whom she is descended. "The Irish," Jane said, "were thought of as lesser-class citizens and were treated as the slaves were." She had heard stories that her ancestor, as a ferry captain, most probably worked with the abolitionists to help slaves that passed through the area escape and continue along their trek north. Plus, there were active groups of Quaker abolitionists in the Conowingo–Darlington area, located in the north of the county along the Maryland–Pennsylvania border. Jane's ancestors may have worked with these Quakers.

It was believed that Jane's great-grandfather died in a ferryboat accident in 1865. But the possibility of her family's involvement in the Underground Railroad became more probable when, Jane said, a legend came to light that bounty hunters might have killed Matthew Currier because of his association with abolitionists. Also, there is the "secret passageway," located in the middle of Jane's house, which is just large enough for someone to hide in and crawl through.

Like an old-fashioned chute for a dumbwaiter, a lengthy, hidden chamber extends from a trapdoor in the attic, through false walls hidden behind a partition, and ends several floors below in the home's cellar. It is near this passageway area that strange activity reportedly has occurred. According to Jane, two different psychics, who did not know each other and who had visited the house on separate occasions, indicated sensing a presence in the center of the home, near the passageway. They also said they felt a presence in two of the inn's guest bedrooms. "It may be the spirit of a slave who was hiding in the house and who had been ill and died while en route along the Underground Railroad," Jane said.

While she admitted never having seen the pesky apparition, without hesitation Jane added, "But I have heard her!" The inn's owner also has heard what some claim is evidence of the ghost's presence through electronic voice phenomena (EVP)—phantom recordings captured on a tape recorder.

Jane thinks the spirit is that of an eight-year-old slave girl, who she has named "Gee Zee," after the initials Jane and a friend learned while using a Ouija board late one evening. After asking about her inn's resident ghost's name—from the invisible contact in the other dimension that was directing movement on the board—Jane said the planchette kept repeating the letters G and Z. Hence the nickname that has seemed to comfortably identify the inn's mysterious unseen resident.

While Jane and her daughter, Sarah, who also lives and works in the home business, have accepted the occasional sounds caused by the invisible child, some guests have found the noise and occasional appearances bothersome.

One couple that had arrived at the inn for a getaway from their youngsters became irate, complaining to Jane that she had assured them there were no children staying in the inn that weekend. The guests said they had heard the sound of a child running up and down the stairs, and they had assumed it was an out-of-control youngster, Jane recalled.

Another couple saw a small girl, whose skin appeared to be purple, standing in the bathroom. The figure was lit by the reflection of a nightlight's soft glow. During another occasion, a couple reported seeing a small girl standing at the foot of their bed wearing a head wrap.

A fireman from New Jersey stopped in the inn's kitchen very early one morning, about 4:30 A.M., to talk to Jane while she was preparing breakfast for her guests. He told Jane, very calmly, "I just want to let you know your house is haunted. But don't worry about it, our firehouse is haunted, too, and you get used to it."

Jane smiled as she recalled a couple from the Midwest that had stopped while on a trip to deliver their daughter's belongings to her East Coast college apartment. "They were not the type of people I'd expect to go ghost hunting," Jane said. "They came here to take advantage of an opportunity to see the bay. We all were sitting at the breakfast table, and the husband looked over at his wife and asked, 'Are you going to tell her?'"

Laughing at the memory, Jane said, "Anytime anyone says something like that, I think there's a problem with the plumbing. I put six bathrooms in this house and don't expect them all to work all of the time. But the wife waved me off and said, 'We had a visitor last night.'"

"Now, I'm telling you the honest-to-goodness truth," Jane said, "I am not a ghost person. I thought it might have been Sarah's dog, Sadie, which likes to run. But the wife said she saw a little girl at the foot of the bed. And both of them, the husband and wife, saw her at the same time. Then they said she disappeared into a little Tinker Bell ball of light, which was bouncing around the walls of the room until daylight."

A visit from some female psychics occurred after they had been at the Gettysburg battlefield, where they said they had heard Havre de Grace was "very active," a hotbed of ghostly activity. One of the investigators was sensitive to sounds, and she claimed she could walk the shoreline and hear past conversations of workers along places that had been warehouses, fishing huts, and boat docks.

One of the women had brought her daughter along on the trip. They told Jane they planned to use their visit to Currier Inn as an instructional training session for the young girl. But, Jane said, they were unaware of any specific activity in the home before they had arrived. They had just selected Currier Inn because of the structure's age and excellent views. Before they left the inn, they shared some of the EVP recordings they had captured during their visit and also showed Jane some of the pictures of orbs, supposed evidence of spirit activity, they had caught with their cameras.

A man checked into one of the guest rooms in the afternoon. Before Jane could leave his room and walk away into the hall, he opened the closet, turned toward her, held his hand flat in front of his waist and said, "She's this tall."

"I don't know how he picked up on her," Jane said. Maybe some people are more aware of the other side, she suggested, and they have a gift to be sensitive to these sorts of things.

Taking a break after summarizing the home's fascinating history and the lengthy list of unexplained incidents, Jane stressed that every day doesn't offer a new mysterious adventure or evidence of a ghostly visit. "I'd say things like that seem to only happen a few times a year," Jane said.

"One day during the winter, when things were slow," Jane remembered, "I was hearing a lot of running. And I said aloud, 'Gee Zee, I'd really like to see you. Everybody gets to see you but me.' And there was no sound. Nothing. Suddenly, several of the hangers moved in one of the closets I was near. There's no ductwork, no way a breeze strong enough to move the hangers could have gone through that closet. I just walked away and shut the guest room door."

As Jane stressed several times, there's nothing "scary" or "frightening" about the unidentified spirit's presence. But she admitted one incident was quite bothersome. Years ago, Jane had two dogs, both of which have since died. There was a full house of guests and all the rooms were occupied. "Suddenly, for no understandable reason, the dogs were carrying on something fierce in the back room, in the private area of the inn. They were very agitated.

"I put them out back, in the middle of the night, and returned to the kitchen. In the middle of the floor was a plastic, red water bowl, going round and round in a slow-moving swirl. I stared at the water, and it wouldn't stop. Nervously, I picked it up and poured the water out into the drain. I refilled the bowl and set it on the floor. Immediately, it began to go round and round and round. I shouted, 'Gee Zee! Stop it!' And she did. She had been stirring the water and making the dogs go crazy. I let the dogs back in, and the water had stopped and everything was calm."

People ask Jane if she has ever seen a ghost in her home. Honestly, she says, "I've never seen her." But, she admits some unusual things have happened, and the stories she has heard from her guests are not tales she has prompted or suggested or asked about. For years, she had not told anyone about the unexplained incidents. But the strangers staying in her inn have approached her. "Usually," Jane said, "the people who have seen things are the last people who you would think were going to tell you about seeing a ghost."

Years ago, Jane said, people died from all sorts of diseases, and death was more common for children than it is today. "You had people on the run," she said, "and they weren't healthy in the first place. I'm sure a lot of those traveling on the Underground Railroad died. It was a brutal existence. She could have been a young child who died here. I don't know."

Probably, the identity and circumstances that caused the friendly spirit to take up permanent residence at Currier House will never be discovered. But that doesn't stop the owner from speculating. "It's been taking a lot of effort to try to figure out in my head what all this is about," Jane said. "I know this house is full of history. A lot of the furniture you see, and the antiques, were here when she may have passed through. That may have something to do with her continued presence. All these people during the last few centuries have lived here, and this is all their stuff."

The tangible objects from the past might be what keep the spirit of Gee Zee connected to Currier House. But there could be plenty of other answers. One can imagine an unseen slave spirit, gazing out upon a lighthouse beam that illuminated the adjacent shore. And if you have the gift to see the other side, you might notice a smile on the face of the phantom called Gee Zee—who never reached freedom, but who seems comfortable with her caretakers and the familiar, reassuring beam near her Maryland seaport home.

Spencer-Silver Mansion

If there is one structure that stands out among the many preserved historic homes in Havre de Grace, it is the Spencer-Silver Mansion Bed and Breakfast. The building most certainly lives up to its "mansion" identity, which is reinforced by its corner location, wraparound porch, tall turret, and colorful, eye-catching trim. The solid, gray granite construction and small stone wall bordering the property give the impression visitors are entering an American version of a small castle. But that's only the exterior.

Once inside, the tall ceilings, large entry hall, impressive stairway, and well-appointed guest rooms make the Spencer-Silver Mansion an inviting and enticing getaway destination for weekend tourists. And if the stories passed down over the last few decades can be believed, the impressive home of innkeeper Carol Nemeth might also serve as a pleasant, long-term abode for quite a few friendly ghosts.

A few years ago, the magnificent architectural treasure, which has been owned by only a few families since it was built in 1896, was about to be sold and turned into a clinic. Carol, who had always loved old buildings, bought the property in 1987 to restore it. Upon taking possession of the building and grounds, which include an adjacent cottage called the Carriage House, Carol focused on renovations and restoration. The possibility that there might be ghosts or spirits roaming about was the farthest thing from her mind. But as years passed, some of the guests, who had no knowledge of the home's history, began offering rather unique comments, asking strange questions, and sharing fascinating stories about some unusual experiences during their stays. To her surprise, Carol discovered many of these tales had a strong connection to the heritage of the mansion, some of its owners, and a few of its former residents.

One of these guests was a woman studying to become an Episcopal priest. She had stayed previously in the cottage, which one Dr. Simon, a former owner, had used as his office. The guest described herself as a "sensitive," and said she couldn't sleep in the Carriage House because it was "too busy," explaining that the building was a portal, a pathway for spirits to leave and enter the other side. It was not a terrifying or scary situation, the woman assured the innkeeper, "just active." With her ability to sense paranormal activity, the cottage would not have allowed the visitor to get much rest.

Carol didn't think too much of the comment and gave the guest a different room. Some time later, however, the owner would learn there was an historical connection to the future priest's concerns.

One weekend, a surgeon and a general physician from Johns Hopkins Hospital were staying at the inn. As the surgeon was checking out, she asked if the house had ever been used as a hospital. After Carol asked why the guest was interested, the doctor, who had stayed in the Garden Room of the main house, said she had opened her eyes and saw several men sitting around in a room, holding coffee cups. They were dressed in bathrobes and were mingling and relaxing in a kitchen setting. Their appearance gave the impression they were in an old-fashioned hospital and were possibly recovering from some illness.

Carol later learned that in the 1950s, Dr. Simon, in an effort to earn additional income, turned the building into a place to house recuperating war veterans. Some of the rooms on the second floor served as a ward and kitchen area, where the injured men would gather to pass away the time as they recovered.

To hear something like that, Carol said, was significant. It was impossible that the visiting doctor would have known about such an obscure event in the home's past. "I like when someone provides me with information they couldn't have known otherwise," Carol said.

A visitor from California stayed overnight in the Carriage House. At breakfast, she told Carol, "Don't make up the bed upstairs. I slept downstairs. I fell asleep on the couch downstairs and never went upstairs to bed." The woman said one of the inn's cats came into the building and was resting on her chest. At about 3 A.M., she smelled cigar smoke and heard men talking, dealing cards, and stacking poker chips. The cat noticed the sounds, too, because it jumped off the couch, ran halfway up the stairs to the upper room, and immediately turned and raced back down.

Dr. Simon was a pipe smoker, Carol said. Every Friday night he played poker with his friends. Even after he sold the mansion, he kept the Carriage House so he could continue practicing medicine. He died soon after he gave up his practice.

"The guest didn't know any of this," Carol said, "about Dr. Simon or his habits. That's what makes her experience most interesting."

An attorney from the West Coast arrived in Havre de Grace and made a long-term arrangement to stay at the inn until his business affairs were resolved and his permanent home and office were established in Maryland. Since the man was handy with tools, Carol agreed to put his maintenance and construction knowledge to good use around the property.

Immediately after setting up residence in the Swan Room, the man demanded that he be moved to a different room, complaining that a woman in a black dress, and with her hair up in a bun, had appeared to him. He said the spectral intruder seemed to have been watching him for some time. Carol said the man told her, "If looks could kill, I would be dead," and then demanded, "I need to get out of that room."

As time passed, the boarder became disagreeable, arguing with Carol about changes she wanted done in and around her building. It was as if he began to think of the Spencer-Silver as his own. One time, he told the owner, "This house is mine now."

After Carol concluded their lodging agreement and sent the man on his way, she considered the mysterious appearance of the lady in black, who might have known immediately that the man was going to be trouble. "I always felt that she knew more than I did from the very beginning," Carol said, with a satisfied smile. "A lot of women guests have seen her," Carol added. "Women seem to have compassion for her, they feel sorry for her. They've seen her pacing, as if she is worrying for some reason. She appears a lot in the Swan Room and in Carol's Room. In Carol's Room, a four-year-old girl saw her in broad daylight."

That youngster was in the building while her family was preparing for a wedding. The young girl woke up from a nap and asked her parents: "Where's the nice lady that was talking to me?" Of course, no one understood what she was talking about. Later, the little girl woke up from another nap, but this time she was screaming, "Tell her to leave me alone! She kept looking into my face!"

Apparently, the lady in black was getting a closer look at the young girl, who became startled. The youngster later said she wasn't afraid of the stranger. "She was a nice lady. I like her," the girl added. "I told her not to be so close to my face."

As stories began to circulate about unusual activities in the Spencer-Silver Mansion, Carol said, "People would ask specifically where the lady was seen. Some arrive and ask which rooms are most active." When the producers of the annual town ghost tour found out about the incidents, they added a stop in front of the mansion to their walking tour.

"In fact," Carol said, "only once has anyone canceled a reservation or decided to stay elsewhere because of the legends and stories associated with the Spencer-Silver. I've never had anyone leave here terrified or say they would never come back. I've had people tell me they feel special that they've been selected after their experience here. It's a very positive feeling," she said.

It wasn't until about fifteen years after she had moved into the building that Carol witnessed her own unexplained sighting. It was in broad daylight on a summer weekend. The doorbell seemed to be ringing constantly, from a combination of people checking in and others who wanted to take a look around the building for a possible future stay.

Carol was rushing up and down the stairs, helping guests get settled, showing curious visitors the rooms, and answering questions. As she passed by Carol's Room, she said she noticed a woman sitting on a chair in the corner. At first, Carol didn't give it a second thought. "Often," she explained, "people will come in and sit in a chair, or on a bed, to get a feel for what it would be like to stay, to get a sense of the room. For some visitors, it's a time to enjoy a nostalgic feeling."

But when she got to the landing only a few seconds later, Carol turned and returned to the room to see if the lady sitting in the chair needed anything. But she was gone.

"She had on a long black dress," Carol recalled. "I was so surprised; I looked everywhere, in the closets, in the other rooms. The hair went up on the back of my neck. She could not have gone anywhere in those few seconds. She just disappeared. That was the first time I experienced anything. And it was in broad daylight, in the middle of the afternoon. I had never expected to see a thing in my home," she added. "I go anywhere. In the basement. I don't feel afraid. I don't look for ghosts. But I saw her like I see you in that chair. I thought she had hidden in a closet."

Carol's most unusual and most significant incident occurred in the Carriage House, when a family with small children called her because the furnace wasn't working. After checking through the small building to determine the problem, Carol noticed the door to the utility closet that housed the heater had been opened. After learning the visiting children had been playing in the closets, she reset the heater and warned the children and their parents not to play hide-and-seek in the closets.

Later that night, Carol said she had a dream in which a young man in his twenties asked, "Do you know who I am?" Then he walked up the steps of the house and again asked, "Do you know who I am?" When Carol said "No," the stranger walked to the Swan Room and repeated the question. Again she had no answer. Then the man appeared to be sitting in the front passenger's seat of a car, with the engine running, and said, "If you ever need me, call me!" Then he vanished.

The next day, Carol searched her brain, trying to understand the significance of the unusual dream. Eventually, she thought she might have an answer. A young man who had lived in Spencer-Silver Mansion had died one night when he was out with his friends. Their car had gone off the road and broken down in the middle of a stream during a winter drive. One of the men went to get help while the other three stayed behind. To keep warm, they ran the car's engine and heater, not knowing the tailpipe was blocked by the high level of water in the stream. They all died in their sleep from carbon monoxide poisoning while sitting in the car waiting for help. That young man's handmade pottery hung, in remembrance of him, in the Swan Room.

Thinking the visitor might be trying to give her a warning, she searched the Swan Room, wondering what could be wrong. Discovering nothing that might solve the mystery, Carol attended to her work. During the afternoon, a couple checked into the Carriage House. The wife was connected to a small oxygen tank.

In the middle of the night, Carol's doorbell rang. The husband, who was staying in the Carriage House, said his wife was having trouble breathing. After examining the utility closet in the couple's accommodations, Carol noticed that the exhaust pipe from the hot water heater had been disconnected. Apparently, the children playing in the closets had knocked the connector loose and disconnected the carbon monoxide detector. As soon as Carol reset the sensor, the alarm went off. She reconnected the pipe and prevented a possibly serious incident.

Was the strange dream the night before a warning about a tragedy that might have occurred or merely a coincidence?

"I felt like I had been visited and protected by him," Carol said. "He and his family had lived in this house. People that knew him said he was always helpful and a very kind person." Since that incident, Carol has had those closets locked and inaccessible to guests for their protection.

In these fast-paced times, people tend to move from their residences much more often than in years past. Only six families have called Spencer-Silver Mansion home in its more than 110-year history. After experiencing the comfortable interior of the impressive structure, it's easy to understand why even overnight visitors find it hard to leave.

Carol stressed that she had no particular fascination with ghosts. When she moved into her historic home, preserving its distinguished past for future generations was her main goal. While some people seem to see phantoms in every shadow, she only became aware of her friendly residents through information offered by her guests.

As I was preparing to leave her fascinating home, I asked her: "Is the Spencer-Silver Mansion haunted?"

Offering a slight smile, she thought for a moment, and then replied, "I feel something is going on. But I can't tell you precisely what it is."

Impulsive Lightkeeper and a Strange Sailor

Lighthouses stimulate the imagination, much like ghost stories. But what happens when you put the two fascinating topics together? The result is sure to have captivating and memorable results. Such is the case of the Concord Point Lighthouse, on the shoreline in Havre de Grace, at the upper reaches of the Chesapeake Bay.

The story begins more than a decade before the lighthouse was established, during the War of 1812, when small bands of British rangers and guerilla fighters roamed the Chesapeake Bay aboard His Majesty's ships. Their goal was to terrorize seaside communities and, if the residents did not provide food and allegiance to the Crown, the red-coated invaders would burn the small water villages to the ground.

Admiral George Cockburn had sent word throughout the region, warning any Americans who defied his edicts that their homes and towns would be put to the torch. In 1814, Cockburn's men captured Washington, D.C., and burned the Executive Mansion (White House), so he was serious about carrying out this threat.

On May 3, 1813, Cockburn was aboard the HMS *Maidstone*, near the Havre de Grace shore. He had not made any offensive actions and was simply sailing by the area. American militia had been following the invaders' progress for several days. Perhaps fearing a British attack, or deciding to demonstrate their boldness and courage, the small group of Americans fired a cannon volley at the passing British.

Lt. John O'Neill commanded the American defenders at the town's Concord Point, and he continued to fire upon the advancing British, even though the rest of his small force had run for cover. Cockburn, who was incensed that the people in the town had disregarded his warning, sent a force of about four hundred men to ransack and burn the village. Two hours later, the town was in flames, its charred remnants sending plumes of smoke into the air for several days.

Brave Lieutenant O'Neill was captured and held aboard the admiral's ship. O'Neill's daughter, Matilda, rowed out to Cockburn's ship and begged for her father's release. When the cannon-firing officer returned to what was left of his town, the residents' reaction was surprising. Rather than string up the trigger-happy defender, the now homeless residents proclaimed him a hero. And when Concord Point Lighthouse was erected in 1827, Lt. John O'Neill, local cannon-firing hero of the War of 1812 and defender of his rebuilt town, was named the first keeper of the light.

O'Neill continued in the lightkeeper's role until his death in 1838. His son, John Jr., took over his post, working as keeper of Concord Point Light until his death in 1863. His wife, Esther, served as keeper until her retirement in 1878, and her son, Henry, took over the duties and carried on the O'Neill family lightkeeping tradition until his death in 1919.

For ninety-two years, members of the same family walked the circular stairway of Concord Point Light, polished the brass, refilled the oil lamps, and helped guard the Upper Bay coast. For decades, visitors who toured the restored beacon have reported experiencing a cold chill on the stairway. Some area residents walking their dogs at night have seen a slow-moving shadow in the upper windows of the light tower. And, occasionally, voices have been heard, possibly originating from a dark figure that appears, and quickly disappears, beside the solitary memorial cannon—which stands at the spot where town hero Lt. John O'Neill fired upon the British during the War of 1812.

A few miles to the west, along U.S. Route 40 in the area known as Perryman, there's a tale about a quirky sailor whose body was returned home after decades sailing the high seas. Because of his very unusual funereal request, the dashing adventurer came to be regarded as a local celebrity—but only after his death. This eccentric seafarer's name was John Clark Monk. In his will the seaman demanded that his dead body be buried in Harford County, but his corpse should never touch the earth.

According to the legend, after he died on a ship at sea, per his instructions, Mr. Monk was "pickled" in a barrel of rum or some other alcoholic/preservative substance. Months later, his soaked-through-the-skin corpse eventually found its way to Spesutia Church Cemetery of St. George's Episcopal Parish in Perryman. There his remains were wrapped in a lead shroud, and the tightly encased body was deposited in the grave pit, several feet below the earth's surface. But the gravedigging crew took care to suspend the shrouded body of the sailor from chains or lead straps. This technique insured the deceased's remains would never touch the ground—unless the elements eventually ate through the slowly rusting metal chains.

To casual Sunday cemetery visitors, there is no clue or marker indicating there is anything unusual about John Clark Monk's traditional, aboveground, coffin-like, marble marker. But those who know the full story have searched out the quirky gravesite, bent down and directed flashlight beams between the wide gaps in the dark stones that hold up Monk's large aboveground monument. The reward for their persistence and keen eyesight is a view of the outline of the straps, leading toward the center of the gravesite, where the lead shroud is said to hold the remains of a rather eccentric sailor, who provided us with a marvelous tidbit of unusual boneyard folklore.

While this sailor's creative imagination provided an unusual, eccentric yarn, to date there have been no reports of Monk's apparition or restless spirit roaming the area near his grave. But those sightings probably won't occur until after the aging straps give way and the sailor's encased body falls to the earth. Until then, per his instructions, John Clark Monk still hangs in peace.

Baltimore County Ghosts

From the Chesapeake Bay in the south to the Mason-Dixon line in the north, Baltimore County's history is filled with spirited tales associated with haunted homes, mysterious deaths, and unfinished business. Here are summaries of a few:

Imagine living on Spooks Hill Road. The winding lane north of the Baltimore city limits weaves through the rural countryside near Prettyboy Reservoir and Gunpowder Falls State Park. For hundreds of years, the thickly wooded, off-the-beaten-track roadway has been the subject of a slew of ghost stories. In the old days, several mills lined the flowing, narrow waterways, and strange sounds were heard and flickering lights were seen through the dense woods. Some of these sounds and sights were attributed to a miller who was crushed by a millstone. Another mill worker was believed to have slipped into a spillway and was drowned when his body was caught on the rotating wheel. The corpse was found days after the accident, soaked and shriveled after having been continuously dunked and hauled in a deadly circle by the ever-spinning wheel.

The legend of a large black dog also has been associated with Spooks Hill Road. The creepy canine would appear and disappear suddenly and let out a bone-chilling howl that would cause travelers along the pathway to hurry from the area. One resident said she had heard the sounds of rattling chains, But that may have been caused by the groups of teenagers who visited the area late at night to have parties and keep a look out for spooks.

In 1752, John Berry was punished for planning and directing the ax murder of a neighboring farmer's wife. In the woods near Reisterstown, where the crime had occurred, Berry was hanged for his role in the murder. His body was strung up with chains, as opposed to rope. After the criminal expelled his last breath, the corpse was left to dangle in the wind until it rotted, fell to the ground, and was consumed by varmints. This area became known as Berry's Hill, and a legend grew that on windy nights passersby could hear the rattling of the chains that had held the dead man's swaying corpse.

Jericho Covered Bridge, one of Maryland's seven remaining covered spans, crosses the Little Gunpowder Falls River, connecting Baltimore and Harford counties. The wooden structure is close to Jerusalem Mill, a 235-year-old stone structure listed in the National Register of Historic Places. The covered bridge, about eighty-eight feet long and fifteen feet wide, is located along a narrow rural road. Built in the mid 1800s, this enclosed, wooden truss bridge has witnessed its share of local and national history.

No one knows when the ghost tales began, but along with haunted houses and old inns and cemeteries, covered bridges have long attracted the attention of storytellers, historians and, more recently, ghost hunters. A few legends have seemed to latch onto the aging timbers of Jericho Covered Bridge. One tale mentions sightings of slaves that were hanged from the rafters of the bridge, apparently while trying to escape across the Mason-Dixon Line into nearby Pennsylvania. Because many Marylanders were sympathetic to the Southern cause, there were a large number of slave kidnappers and nightriders, men who would grab up free blacks and sell them back into slavery. These unfortunate escapees were caught within a few miles of freedom. Another story claims a wagon filled with straw caught on fire inside the covered bridge and burned to death the owner as he tried to put out the flames and save his cargo. This angry merchant's ghost is believed to haunt the structure.

Ghost hunters have reported capturing orbs in some bridge photos. Other people claim their cars have stopped inexplicably inside the covered bridge. And one daytime tourist reported seeing women in old-fashioned clothing walking along the roadway and sitting beside the nearby stream. However, when the visitor turned back to view the location of the sighting, the images of the people from another era had seemed to disappear.

In Middle River, at the southern end of the Baltimore County, a plane crash is said to have occurred several decades ago not far from the airport. After the crash site was cleared, reports surfaced of a teddy bear appearing in one of the trees, not far from where the plane wreckage fell. People who began visiting the location late at night said the small, tan, stuffed animal appeared to be looking down on the nighttime visitors—or perhaps hoping to recognize the face of the small child who had been its owner.

Not too far to the east, outside Essex, a pirate named Stammer built a mansion in the late 1700s in the area called Stemmers Run. At that time, the narrow creek was still able to handle a fair-sized craft, and after long voyages Stammer would sail up to the dock near his home with relative ease. Following his death, the pirate's wife refused to leave the home—apparently even after she, too, had died. It's said the buccaneer's spouse did not believe her husband was dead, and she stubbornly refused to leave their home, knowing he would eventually return.

But the persistent ghost did not haunt their house out of love. Instead her motivation was revenge. The loving wife had heard Captain Stammer had been unfaithful and taken another wife while sailing through the Caribbean, where he fathered several children. His Maryland spouse wanted to give him a piece of her mind when he eventually returned, but she died during the long, vengeful wait.

It's not surprising that a quite a few historic mansions claim their resident phantoms put in periodic appearances. In a 1969 article in *The Towson Times*, Bonnie Warr reported on the legends of a few haunts in the northern end of the county. At Stone Hall in Cockeysville a well-dressed aristocrat on a white horse rides up to the front door, waits patiently for the proper amount of respectful attention, and disappears. In the Long Green Valley area, a woman in white flowing robes roams an old house and its nearby grounds.

During restoration at Harmony Hall—built in the early 1800s in My Lady's Manor, near Monkton—a baby's skeleton was found inside a closet. Servants claimed to have heard a mother walking her baby through the house when it was quiet. But after a Catholic chapel was built in the old slave quarters' kitchen on that property, regular visits and services conducted by traveling priests seem to have exorcised all traces of the restless ghost.

Todd's Inheritance

In 1814, while cannons on British ships were bombarding Fort McHenry and parts of Baltimore city, Todd's Inheritance witnessed it all. The four-acre farm site in Baltimore County overlooks the Chesapeake Bay on North Point Peninsula. Today homes and old factories stand a few miles to the north, but in the early days of the country, the Todd family's home stood out among virgin fields and woodlands. For more than three centuries—from 1664 to 1974, through ten generations—the estate that at one time consisted of more than one thousand acres was owned and occupied by a member of the well-known colonial family.

When the Todd family was involved in agriculture, about three dozen slaves worked the property. Later, the Todds shifted their focus to shipbuilding and other businesses. During the War of 1812, the property's strategic view of the nearby Chesapeake Bay made it an important location. American troops were on the lookout for invading British forces and the estate was a critical defensive position during the Battle of Baltimore. After the Battle of North Point, in which the British were defeated and forced back to their ships, the Redcoats burned the original Todd house. It's believed this was in retaliation for the residents' signals days earlier to American troops, alerting patriots that the British invasion fleet had arrived in the area.

In 1954, the nearby Bethlehem Steel operation at Sparrow's Point purchased most of the Todd property, but later sold the grounds and home to the state of Maryland. The Todd residence and about five acres was purchased in 1974 by Elmer Cook, then a teacher at Sparrows Point High School. After Cook died, the home and grounds were acquired by the state and used for farming.

Today the home, family cemetery, and a few acres of ground are a remnant of the area's rural past that is dramatically different than the overdeveloped city and suburbs not too far to the north. Todd's Inheritance Historic Site is operated by a non-profit organization of volunteers, who work to restore the home and preserve and share its valuable role in American history.

But one need look no further than the Internet to see how just such a secluded historic location can attract the interest and imagination of paranormal hunters and those seeking a good ghost story.

According to several Web sites, Todd's Farm (one reference erroneously says it's located in New Jersey) is a haunted home with a fair share of tales to chill the bone. There's a woman with a candle who looks out from an attic window at night, most likely waiting for her soldier boyfriend or husband to come home.

One site says you can see the ghosts of some of the estate's slaves hanging from trees in the Todd family cemetery, directly behind the house. It warns there was no electricity in the old building, but when trespassers entered into the home, lights flashed on. Photographs taken in the building have captured small orbs, which some believe are evidence of spirit energy. There's also the suggestion that the home is haunted because one of the former residents committed suicide in the building, and his spirit cannot rest. But experienced readers of ghost stories realize that many of these are the same incidents attributed to any old, secluded, rural, vacant farmhouse.

A more reliable source, however, has provided a glimpse into some unexplained happenings inside the home at Todd's Inheritance. In two 1976 articles in the *Baltimore News-American*, reporter Edward Colimore interviewed the late Elmer Cook Jr., the high school science and chemistry teacher who had bought the house two years earlier. In Colimore's stories, entitled "Ghostly Visits Enliven North Point House" and "Teacher's Home A Ghost's Castle?" the owner at that time shared some of his experiences and offered his opinions about the presence of mysterious spirits.

Describing the home as peaceful, and anything but sinister and foreboding, Colimore wrote that it is a "serene peaceful place, most of the time. But every now and then the mansion mysteriously comes alive . . . with a cast of ghostly characters." And while Cook said he had "no explanation" for some of the unusual events, the owner could not discount what he had heard and seen. Cook added that he had heard there was a mass grave of cholera epidemic victims near the cemetery, and that the person hanged from the graveyard tree had stolen a horse. There also is a chance the Todds, who had family members living in the Snow Hill area of the Eastern Shore of Maryland, might be some distant relatives to Mary Todd Lincoln. That could explain the report that a former resident of the home had seen the apparition of the assassinated President Lincoln standing on the Baltimore home's front porch.

While working in his study, Cook said he heard a door rattling fiercely, as if someone were trying to get inside his home. Immediately afterward, he heard the clumping sound of heavy leather boots in the area that had been the slaves' kitchen. Looking into the room where the disturbing sounds apparently had originated, Cook said he saw, very clearly, a man dressed in a military uniform. Then the apparition slowly walked toward the room's fireplace and disappeared.

Stating that unexpected events happen with some degree of frequency, Cook related the story of a neighbor who had arrived for a brief visit before all of the doors began slamming. Then a man's voice let out a loud scream. The guest left before taking time to select a place to sit. Knocking on bedroom doors in the middle of the night, rumbling sounds coming from the roof, and voices speaking clearly to residents of the house were common occurrences.

Cook said late one night a guest complained that something had knocked a lit cigarette from her hand. On another evening, a visitor who was washing her face in the powder room said something forced her face into the sink and held it down for several seconds. Another time, Cook and a friend were in the home and heard several loud crashes. When they went to investigate, he said, they "found 'someone' had rolled a barrel down the hall." The owner also admitted he had heard unexplained noises on the roof above the slave quarters.

Perhaps the strangest incident involved Cook's housekeeper. The woman was getting settled in a third-floor bedroom, directly under the cupola. Recalling it was the day she had arrived and was unpacking, she told the reporter, "I heard a woman's voice. She said: 'We know you just moved in here and you better watch your step.'" The next day, the new housekeeper fell through a hole in the porch and hurt her leg. The following day, while walking across the old slave kitchen, a mirror fell off the wall and crashed to the floor, hitting the woman's other leg.

Across the front page of the August 11, 1976, "Women's World" section of the Baltimore newspaper were two very large pictures of strange images that Cook said he had captured on film. One was a shadowy head near a stone wall. The other was a wavy, ghostlike figure behind a window in his house.

It was after Cook saw a black woman standing in one of the bedrooms and a hunchbacked figure moving through the kitchen that he decided to sleep overnight at a friend's home and try to figure out what to do. Eventually, he called upon local psychics, who visited Todd's Inheritance to conduct an investigation. During their visit, the two women pointed out rooms where they "picked up" traces of conversations and the possible presence of spirits. In one bedroom, the investigators said they believed two men were arguing about money and there was some swordplay involved. In another room they said there was a sensation of a fire and a death at some time in the past.

One of the psychics accurately stated that the building had been used as a hospital during the Civil War, and there had been a man hanged from a tree near the house. She also pointed to the location where the slaves lived, and she stated there had been an epidemic that had taken several lives.

The investigators said they had made a number of visits to various locations. In many cases a little common sense had been able to explain what homeowners thought might have been a paranormal event. "But Todd's Inheritance had been most interesting," one of the psychics said.

With a wealth of history that began soon after the settlement of the colony of Maryland, the land surrounding Todd's Inheritance has witnessed some critical historic events. Certainly, because of its prime location near the top of the Chesapeake Bay, American Indians and roving pirates also walked across its ground. If it were possible to discover stories associated with those who were there before the European settlers arrived, the tales would add to the estate's fascinating legacy and colorful folklore.

While talking to the *News-American* reporter, Cook offered an insightful comment that he had heard and which had stayed with him. The statement, by former Todd's Inheritance owner Thomas Todd, may offer a rather eerie explanation for some of the paranormal incidents associated with the mysterious property. According to Cook, "Thomas Todd, in 1916, said the best advice he could give on life is to make a house a home. He said develop it as you would a marriage or a family. But this is the clincher," Cook stressed, "Todd said, 'Then your house will become a home and never, never leave it.' That 'never, never leave it' part got to me."

Old Fort Garrison

In Pikesville, Baltimore County, just north of the Baltimore Beltway, stands Old Fort Garrison. On less than a half acre, in the middle of a development of modern suburban homes on Garrison Farms Court, it is the last remaining original stone blockhouse in Maryland. Built in 1695, the rectangular fieldstone building was constructed with gun windows, which would enable the Maryland Rangers stationed there to defend themselves against attacks by area Indians. The detachment of rangers assigned to Fort Garrison was responsible for patrolling the area between the Patapsco and Susquehanna rivers. Visitors to the site find it hard to imagine that at the time of its construction, the lonely outpost was nearly ten miles from the nearest settlement.

In the late 1600s, Maryland governor Francis Nicholson and his council decided the outpost was needed to protect settlers who were moving into the area north of the port city of Baltimore. The camp also was called Oulton's Garrison, after its commander, Capt. John Oulton, a strict disciplinarian with a horrible temper.

In the History Channel's special program *Haunted Baltimore*, actors recreated an incident where Oulton killed Dennis Garrett, one of his rangers, by hitting the man too hard with the handle of a sword. Oulton was arrested and subsequently convicted of the murder, but he was pardoned by King William III of England.

Because of its unique location in the midst of a modern residential area, the historic site is an attraction for ghost hunters interested in investigating "suburban ghosts." Two paranormal investigators who visited the site shared their experiences on the History Channel special. The man said he had been hit in the face and pushed from behind when no one was anywhere near him. The woman reported seeing an older woman peering down from the window on the upper level of the structure.

Whether the spirit of Oulton or Garrett remains in the preserved historic outpost probably will never be known, but the more than 300-year-old building's survival into the twenty-first century is an achievement in itself.

Hampton Mansion

Hampton National Historic Site, north of Baltimore city, is like many stately mansions found throughout America's earliest settled colonies: erected by the rich, built by proud craftsmen, surrounded by hundreds of acres of rolling lands, worked by slaves, and now operating as a museum that attracts tourists and historians. And like so many other old and famous buildings, Hampton mansion is believed to be occupied by several resident ghosts.

But finding out about the mansion's specters is not as easy as one might hope. Over the years, National Park Service personnel have downplayed the site's paranormal notoriety. But this has not stopped the ghost stories associated with the 62-acre property from being featured in newspaper and magazine articles and books detailing the "most haunted" sites throughout the United States. Many of Hampton's spirited stories seem to have been taken from reports in a booklet, *The Ghosts of Hampton*, by Anne Van Ness Merriam.

The tiny seventeen-page volume was edited and reprinted in 1985 by the Gift Shop Committee of Historic Hampton. But two rather confusing statements serve as a perplexing introduction. The first says descendants of Capt. Charles Ridgely, Hampton's builder, relayed the unexplained historic tales to Mrs. Merriam. But a qualifier, noted with an asterisk, states the stories in the book are "entirely fictional, and have no basis in fact," and that the imagination of the authors is the source of "these interesting fables."

Such an unusual preface doesn't exactly make the reader want to rush into the meat of the hopefully spine-tingling text. One wonders if the hesitancy to perpetuate the mansion's ghost stories was so great that the producers of the book decided to add their confusing qualifier—comparable to advertisements for new drugs that warn buyers to "consult your physician, since using the product might result in serious ill effect, including death."

In his *Baltimore Sun* article, "Shades of History," writer Chris Kalenback spotlighted a number of Baltimore-area legends. In the section about the Hampton mansion, he pointed out that staff members "insist there are no ghosts calling the 200-year-old Georgian mansion home." The curator, in a 1999 Halloween season article, was quoted as saying: "We don't tell ghost stories here, nor do we promote them, because we don't know of any that can be substantiated." But, the reporter added, for 75 cents (the price is higher today) visitors could buy Merriam's ghost tales pamphlet in the gift shop. Certainly, even many historians admit that there is some historic event or basis of truth in many good ghost stories, particularly those associated with famous sites. And historic Hampton probably is no different.

In 1790, Charles Ridgely, a well-known Maryland businessman, politician, and legislator, was pleased to witness the completion of his mansion, named Hampton, in the midst of 2,000 acres of rolling land, just a half-dozen miles north of the center of Baltimore. But the owner was never allowed to enjoy his creation, for within less than a year he was dead.

A nephew who inherited the property enlarged the main building, in which he threw lavish parties. Soon the Baltimore estate earned a reputation as a must-visit entertainment center, offering wine, women, and song. If Hampton had been built and opened in the twenty-first century, it would have been selected for an episode of *Lifestyles of the Rich and Famous*.

Unfortunately, the owner's wife, Priscilla, was never happy. The frail, troubled woman bore her husband eleven children, and died at the young age of thirty-two. (Some think the poor woman might have had about a dozen reasons for being worn out and depressed.) Immediately following her death at a relatively early age, some longtime servants claimed they saw shadows resembling the sad lady floating through the hallways of her former home.

The legend of the crashing chandelier is probably the most often-told ghost story associated with the mansion. Unfortunately, the story goes, whomever becomes startled by the sound of the great chandelier's crash should be worried about more than picking up all of the broken pieces of cut glass. That person, usually the mistress of the house, will probably be the next member of the Ridgely family to leave the premises in a rectangular box carried by six strong friends and relatives. I first heard about this legend about ten years ago from a woman in Wilmington, Delaware. She said she had been a volunteer at the estate several decades before and actually heard the crash. Luckily, her bloodline had no connection to the Ridgleys.

A later Ridgely, Charles IV, was traveling in Europe when a servant at the Baltimore estate claimed she saw the master arrive late one night in a coach drawn by black horses. Convincing herself it was simply a bad dream, the woman relayed the incident to her husband the next morning over breakfast. About that same time, a messenger arrived at the mansion's front door announcing the traveling Ridgely's death while he was enjoying his final vacation on the Continent.

A child's tragic demise is the subject of one of Hampton's most intriguing tales. In the mid 1800s, a young girl was recovering from a severe illness and her family sent her to stay for several weeks at Hampton's healthier, countrified setting. Apparently, the mistress of the house was happy to have the youngster's companionship and made arrangements to hold a special party in her young guest's honor. The night before the grand ball, the sick child had a dream that an old man was chasing her through a cornfield. As the attacker in her dream raced toward the child waving a knife, he shouted that he would catch her "after the ball."

When the nervous child shared the story with her hostess, the older woman told her not to worry. It was nothing more than a silly dream, and the youngster probably was nervous about the upcoming festivities. But the hostess was terribly wrong. While dozens of people waited for the young guest of honor to make her entrance into the Hampton's grand hall, servants discovered the sick girl's cold, lifeless body in her bedroom. The mistress of the house immediately recalled the youngster's threatening dream, which turned out to be a warning that the hostess of Hampton had ignored.

Black Aggie

What the Jersey Devil is to the Garden State and what the Headless Horseman is to Sleepy Hollow, Black Aggie is to Baltimore. For several decades during the twentieth century, this mysterious, dark statue attracted the attention of thousands of Baltimore-area residents. During Sunday afternoon drives, youngsters and their parents made pilgrimages to visit the eerie-looking creature. At night, under cover of darkness, daring teenage couples would arrive and nervously approach the frightful figure that was perched among hundreds of other, less threatening monuments in Druid Ridge Cemetery.

It didn't take long before the gloomy-looking, shrouded sculpture achieved icon status. Its reputation grew with snowball-like momentum, as each horrifying report seemed more terrible and unbelievable than the last.

Mobs of visitors flocked to the hexed gravesite on Halloween night. Each fall, fraternities held midnight initiation rites beside the haunted tombstone beneath a full moon. Evening cemetery visitors reported seeing the statue's glowing red eyes in the graveyard. Pregnant visitors said they were cursed with stillborn babies. The ghostly statue scared a young man to death, and his body was found lying at the monster's feet. And vandals attacked the creature and chopped off one of its metal arms.

For years, parents warned disobedient children that Black Aggie would pay them a visit while they slept. Some of those who had seen the eerie figure in Druid Ridge Cemetery believed that if they dared whisper her name, the monster would emerge from a closet, or from beneath a bed, and strangle the disrespectful child to death.

The story of how an unusual statue became a frightful figure began in 1865, in Washington, D.C. In the nation's capital, noted sculptor Augustus Saint-Gaudens was commissioned by historian Henry Adams to create an original piece of artwork. Henry was the grandson of the sixth U.S. president, John Quincy Adams, and the great-grandson of Declaration of Independence signer and second president John Adams.

Upon completion, Saint-Gaudens' stunning, yet depressing and eerie-looking piece—unofficially named "Grief" by some observers—was erected in Washington's Rock Creek Cemetery as a memorial to Henry Adams's wife Marian, who died while only in her forties.

At the turn of the twentieth century, *Baltimore American* newspaper publisher Felix Agnus, a prominent citizen who had served as a Union general during the Civil War, purchased an unusual sculpture. The businessman decided to use it to mark his family plot in Druid Ridge Cemetery, located just outside the city limits in Pikesville.

The wealthy Baltimore publisher was apparently unaware that the person who sold him the statue had made it from an illegal casting of Saint-Gaudens' original sculpture. With good intentions, Agnus purchased the distinctive artwork to honor his deceased wife, Annie Agnus, and adorn her gravesite. In 1907, this copy of the original creation was placed on its granite base in Druid Ridge Cemetery. Immediately, a storm of controversy erupted over the appropriateness of owning and displaying the unsanctioned copy of the original artwork.

Members of the Adams and Saint-Gaudens families protested the Agnus cemetery sculpture, and lawsuits were filed. Saint-Gaudens' widow wanted the statue removed. Felix Agnus was adamant that his version of the monument would remain atop his Pikesville family plot. Eventually, Agnus's argument against the lawsuit was successful, and the copycat's residence seemed secure. The dark, threatening creature remained perched at the top of a rolling hillside, standing out among granite crosses, carved angels, and thousands of less distinctive markers bearing family names sculpted in stone.

After the court case was settled, the Agnus family memorial did not attract much attention, but in the midst of the wild and carefree era known as the Roaring Twenties, for a reason we will never discover, the sculpture seemed to develop its own personality. Some might even say the silent sculpture took on a diabolical life of its own.

It was shortly after Felix Agnus's death (on, of all days, Halloween, 1925) that the Baltimore monster's legend was born. The contemplative and curious-looking creature seemed to awaken from its slumber and earned its very special name of "Black Aggie."

For more than forty years, from the 1920s through the 1960s, the cemetery area surrounding the eerie metal creation became a must-visit site for curious daytime passersby and brave late-evening adventurers. During weekend afternoons, slow-moving processions of automobiles bearing locals and tourists would drive the narrow lanes of Druid Ridge Cemetery, pausing to take black-and-white photographs of Black Aggie. These pictures later were shown off to friends and neighbors, who made their own weekend trips to the creature's lair. When darkness fell, however, less mannerly explorers arrived on foot, making secretive, unofficial pilgrimages to the sinister shrine.

College fraternities decided Black Aggie would be an excellent assistant to evaluate eager applicants. As part of their initiation rites, club hopefuls were ordered to sit in Black Aggie's lap to prove they were worthy of membership. One folktale claims that a young man died from a heart attack while in the statue's clutches, and the following morning workmen discovered his stiff body sprawled beside Black Aggie's feet.

Naturally, more stories and tales traveled through the friend-of-a-friend message chain, and each bizarre account added to the statue's status as Baltimore's premier urban legend. Some said that even walking beneath the creature's shadow would have dire consequences. Pregnant mothers claimed to experience miscarriages, and others told stories that no vegetation would grow in the shade of Aggie's ominous figure. (Perhaps the latter was due to the constant traffic around the gravesite that destroyed grass and plantings that continually had to be replaced.)

Those unsure of where Black Aggie held court would only have to enter the cemetery and wait until the stroke of midnight. It was at the bewitching hour when two bright-red dots would appear. To no one's surprise, these were the bristling fires of hell, glowing through the evil statue's demonic eyes.

As reports associated with Black Aggie grew more extreme, visits by couples and groups became more numerous. Even midnight escapades swelled in size and multiplied in frequency. Beneath the shrouded figure, young women lost their virginity, drunken parties were held, and wicked, satanic rituals were conducted.

One story claimed that in 1962 a workman found one of Black Aggie's arms, which had been apparently cut off during the night. Another tale reported that the statue was the likeness of an area nurse who was hanged, in error, by an angry mob for an unstated crime. Those responsible for the killing were said to have bought the statue as a penance to atone for their mistake and assuage their accompanying guilt.

By the 1960s, vandalism from unauthorized nighttime visits and the legend's growing notoriety began to cause serious disruptions to the operation, maintenance, and reputation of the peaceful suburban cemetery. It will never be known how many fraternity initiates sat on Black Aggie's lap, felt the heat from her hands, and then jumped away at the last moment to avoid being crushed by the monster's grip. And one can only guess at the number of Baltimoreans who made weekend afternoon and middle-of-the-night trips to catch a glimpse of the eerie edifice in action. But there is no doubt that the numbers are substantial.

Eventually, the cemetery administration and staff decided it could no longer handle the spell that Black Aggie had cast over multiple generations of thrill-seeking Baltimoreans. To help resolve an out-of-control situation, Agnus family descendants decided in the late 1960s to remove the statue that had caused so much strife.

Beau Reid is a lifelong Baltimore resident; during an interview in 2004, he was working as a family services counselor at Druid Ridge Cemetery. One spring morning he escorted me to the site of the Agnus plot, located in the Annandale section, one of the oldest portions of the picturesque graveyard that opened in 1896.

Although Black Aggie is gone, we stood beside the base of the monument where the monster used to hold court. Shaking his head, Reid said, "We get three or four calls a month about her, from people who want to come up and see where she used to be or to find out some information. We're constantly guiding people up here. They want to know the story and also ask how long she's been gone."

Reid said that if twenty or more people visit the cemetery for a service, several who happen to be in the forty-five- to sixty-year-old age range will mention Black Aggie and ask for directions to the Agnus grave. "Some very prominent citizens come up and share some of the high jinks they pulled years ago," Reid said, smiling.

While speaking to Jeff Jerome, curator of the Edgar Allan Poe House and Museum, Black Aggie's name came up in conversation. Immediately, the prominent Baltimore historian smiled and recalled the evening he and a young lady made a pilgrimage along the dark lanes of Druid Ridge Cemetery.

"I'm one of the thousands that went to Druid Ridge," Jeff said. "I was there with a date. It was Halloween night. We decided to go. We were young. It was dark. Eventually, we saw a high beam of light, and a caretaker shouted out, 'Turn around right now!' That's the closest we got to Black Aggie that night."

He added that he has seen pictures of people sitting proudly in Black Aggie's lap. "It's amazing, even though she's been gone a long time, people still make the trip to Druid Ridge, and people still share their stories about Black Aggie."

LuAnn Marshall, tour director at Westminster Hall, site of Edgar Allan Poe's grave and the cemetery's church catacombs, grinned at the mention of Black Aggie. "As a kid," the Baltimore native said, "I remember putting my head under my pillow and saying 'Black Aggie' three times. It was said that if you did that she would appear under your bed, and that if you touched her she would scare you to death. I was terrified. I also remember that they said if you laid in her arms you would die." Then LuAnn added, "She's gone, you know."

When I replied that I was heading off to take Aggie's photograph at her present residence, LuAnn, like others to whom I had talked, became excited and asked for a copy of the legend's picture.

Thanks to very helpful directions provided by Wayne Schaumburg, Baltimore historian and noted tour guide at Green Mount Cemetery, I caught up with Black Aggie in Washington, D.C., only a block from the White House.

In 1967, after she was hauled off her granite podium, Black Aggie was acquired (depending upon which source you use) by the Maryland Institute of Art or the Smithsonian American Art Museum or the National Collection of Fine Arts or the National Museum of American Art. While she may have been displayed in one of these museums temporarily, most sources agree that for several years, Baltimore's version of "Grief" was relegated to a dark corner beneath a stairwell in a museum basement.

In the late 1980s, the mystifying sculpture was transferred to the General Services Administration, which placed her on display in the courtyard of the Federal Judicial Center, located across from Lafayette Square, adjacent to the Dolley Madison House.

Beyond a redbrick, gated archway, with a brass plate proclaiming "Entrance to 717 Madison Place," the Baltimore icon sits alone, beneath a street lamp and surrounded by a sea of shrubbery. Her veiled face gives the impression she is asleep, inactive and benign. Each day she is ignored, or at most glanced at, by federal workers who eat their lunch and chat casually at round picnic tables. Tourists hauling cameras and guide maps pass by, unfazed and unimpressed by the quiet, green-gray creature that seems to be at peace. At most, some consider the statue a rather unusual accent in the lush, manicured garden.

None of the workers or visitors has any idea that in their midst sits a creature that had once achieved a horrifying celebrity status in her hometown. And who would have imagined that more than four decades since her abrupt departure from her Baltimore abode, just a passing mention of the words "Black Aggie" still has the power to delight, entertain, and, in some cases, even terrify?

Belmont Ghost

Belmont Hall, near Elkridge in Howard County, was the early settlement of the Dorsey and Hanson families. Erected on a high hill with an impressive view of twenty miles of rolling countryside, the manor house stands about ten miles west of Baltimore in the high country of the Patapsco River. Today, developments, shopping centers, and highways cover the landscape. But at the time when settlers began to head west and leave the safety of the Atlantic coastline and cities, encounters with hostile Indians were commonplace. When wealthy ironmaker Caleb Dorsey built his mansion in 1738, the house was a full day's horseback ride north from Annapolis. Today, the same distance can be covered over vehicle-filled highway lanes in slightly more than an hour.

Over the centuries, the Belmont mansion has been in the hands of several families, many of them descendants to some degree of the original owners. Today, the historic estate, with more than eighty acres of gardens, woods, and meadows, is a meeting place, available for formal functions, corporate meetings, and wedding celebrations.

Perhaps, however, there may still be remnants of the past repeating their regular visits to Belmont. At least that is what a story written by John Martin Hammond suggests. In his book, *Colonial Mansions of Maryland and Delaware*, the author recounts a spirited tale. To set the stage, Hammond explains that well-known U.S. and Maryland politicians were frequent visitors at Belmont. U.S. senator and congressman Henry Clay of Kentucky was a familiar guest during the 1820s. In fact, when he arrived from Washington, the noted political orator settled into a favorite chair beside the mansion's fireplace. In those days while traveling, gentlemen would wear large footwear, called "great boots." Upon entering a home, they would trade their dirty boots for slippers, furnished by their host.

Hammond wrote that at least once each winter, and sometimes a time or two more on a dark, windy night, visitors and residents at the old house would experience a visit from the Belmont Ghost. "You are sitting, let us say, before the open fire in which Clay delighted," Hammond wrote. "You hear the wind lonesomely without and suddenly there is the sound of horses' hoofs and jangling harness; many horses evidently, and the harness and wheels seem to creak and rumble more heavily than harness and wheels of nowadays."

The startled occupant would begin to head toward the door, to greet the unexpected visitors who apparently were arriving in the coach. But, suddenly, he would hear the sound of other sets of feet, unseen footsteps, in front of where he is walking. Obviously, the host thinks, an invisible spirit is headed in the same direction, attempting to reach the mansion's entrance first. Suddenly, the door opens, and the mortal host stands silent, as he hears the scraping of feet of the invisible people that have entered the building. Alarmed, the confused host wonders: What has happened? Who has generated these unseen sounds?

Over the years, the answer offered most often was: "It is just some of the forefathers of Belmont, coming home from Annapolis in the coach and six." Then the mortal host hears the sound of wheels, driving the carriage away from the mansion's entrance, heading toward the stable. Eventually, the creak of harness, the sound of the whip and the clatter of hooves all disappear. Midnight silence returns. "This," Hammond wrote, "is the Belmont ghost."

Lilburn and Mt. Ida

Ellicott City was established as a mill town in the late 1700s in what was once farmland and forests west of Baltimore. As years passed, the small village became a manufacturing center and, in 1831, it was the site of America's first railroad terminal. With a bustling economy, a rural setting not far from Maryland's largest seaport city, and with ample land upon which to grow crops and establish estates, many impressive homes and manors sprang up in this locale on the eastern edge of Howard County.

Over the years, stories have survived of ghostly activity in several of the area's homes and businesses—enough tales to maintain interest in a wonderful ghost tour conducted in the heart of the town. Thanks to my friend, Troy Taylor, nationally recognized speaker and author of dozens of ghost books, the following stories have been excerpted from his book, *The Haunting of America*.

Since the 1920s, ghost stories have been associated with Lilburn Hall, an impressive gray stone, Gothic-style mansion built in 1857. Some attribute the frequent reports of paranormal activity to several tragedies that occurred to the family of Henry Richard Hazelhurst, the home's prosperous builder who made a fortune trading in iron during the Civil War. The builder lost his wife and several children suddenly, including one daughter believed to have died while giving birth at Lilburn. Outliving most of his family, the elder Hazelhurst died alone at the home at the age of eighty-five.

After another family purchased the home and moved in, tales of unusual events began to circulate. Footsteps were heard in the tower, and other unexplained sounds occurred. After a Christmas fire almost turned deadly and destroyed much of the mansion, the owners rebuilt the home, but they replaced the gothic-style peaks with stone, giving it a fortresslike appearance.

In the 1960s, another family moved in and its members also heard phantom footsteps, and the family dog avoided entering a certain second-floor room. One evening, a chandelier began swaying during a party and frightened the guests. Windows in the tower seemed to open on their own, and servants reported hearing a child's cries and smelling cigar smoke in the empty library. One housekeeper claimed to have seen various apparitions, including a man and a little girl.

In the 1970s, a workman in the home said he was pushed off a ladder, and another worker complained he was locked in a bedroom. During a home-and-garden tour, flowers jumped out of a vase and landed on the floor. Some believe the architectural change made years earlier after the Christmas fire was not appreciated by the original builder, and this may be the source of the ghostly activity. Others say the unseen wanderer might be the daughter who died in the home while giving birth.

Another local mansion, known as Mt. Ida, was designed in the early 1800s, and it is one of the most prominent landmarks of the town. It was built for William Ellicott, grandson of one of the founders of Ellicott Mills. William died at the age of forty-three, unable to enjoy his new home. In the 1850s, a judge and his family moved into the building and descendants of that family lived there until the 1970s. According to author Taylor, it is with this family that the ghosts are associated.

After the judge's death, the house was left to his children. His son died in a boating accident, and his three maiden sisters all lived in the house until they died. The last to pass on was Miss Ida, whom many believe is the mansion's most prominent ghost. Residents and workers claimed to have heard the sounds of rattling keys as Miss Ida roamed her domain. While living, this last family resident would carry a large ring full of dangling keys with her at all times.

Creepy Courthouse

Oak Lawn, also called Hayden House, is a small stone dwelling built in 1842. The original owner, Howard County's first clerk, lived there with his wife and six children until his death in 1850. Over the years the structure has been used by many municipal agencies, including the board of education and the district court. Today it is home to the Howard County Circuit Court. In the 1970s, when the building was occupied by the county office of parole and probation, some staff members reported strange events. Lights would turn on and off by themselves. A coffee pot would heat up, even when unplugged; an unoccupied chair would rock on its own; and the sounds of unexplained footsteps were common. One employee reported seeing the apparition of an unidentified man, but no one was discovered after a search of the building.

There also were smells of soup and bacon and eggs, which could be noticed throughout the building, day and night. When no definite source of the simmering food was discovered, the frustrated searchers dubbed the phantom the "cooking ghost."

One employee claimed to have seen several strange occurrences in the building, including cloth napkins being folded by themselves and a mist-like hazy ball of vapor that appeared and then vanished from view.

Melody Simmons, a Howard County bureau reporter for the *Evening Sun*, wrote about the building's ghosts in an article published on Halloween Day 1980. Under the headline "Alleged Ghost Spooks Workers At Courthouse," her story adds additional details to the legend. Employees reported smells of apple cobbler and bacon, apparently the phantom's favorites. Other staff noted the unseen ghost had called out to various staff members by their proper names.

At times, the invisible resident's antics have frustrated the building's workers, particularly when they had to deal with the lights going off as many as five times a day. The employees first agreed to take turns descending two or three floors into the basement to reset the breakers before they called an electrician. After inspecting the wiring and equipment, the contractor found no logical, earthly cause for the frequent and annoying power outages. One worker suggested the ghost may have been tired of listening to the tedious cases being tried in the traffic and criminal courts, and the phantom simply needed a break.

One day, several workers heard their names being called by a voice coming from a nearby office. When they responded by going into the room, there was no one there. Many workers who have been in the building for some time suggest that the permanent invisible resident is the ghost of Edwin Parsons Hayden, the attorney that built the home and lived there until his tragic death at the age of thirty-eight.

While some may think the idea of a resident ghost would help relieve the dull routines of the average workday, the mysterious presence has some drawbacks. "Many employees refuse to work nights in the courthouse," Simmons wrote in her article, "leaving the building at the 4:30 P.M. closing time. 'I'm just too scared,' one clerk says. 'When I do work at night, I like to have someone sitting in here with me at all times. And I am even afraid to walk upstairs to the bathroom alone.'"

Today the old building is still in use as the Howard County Circuit Court. When I asked a worker there if the old building is still haunted, the staff person on the other end of the telephone paused, and said, "Well. That depends . . ."

"On whom you ask?" I added, trying to break the uncomfortable silence. Then in a relieved voice, the staffer replied, "That's correct."

Annie of PFI

Abandoned schools, hospitals, and military sites are among the locations most favored by ghost hunters, paranormal researchers, and weekend adventurers, sometimes referred to as "legend trippers" (those who dare to check out local haunted locations).

Near Ellicott City are the decaying remains of the Patapsco Female Institute (PFI), a former school for young ladies that opened in 1839. The school, with its Greek Revival architecture featuring tall columns and yellow granite stonework, resembled in its heyday the classic plantation homes of the rich and famous of America's southern society. Many wealthy businessmen and landowners sent their children to the well-respected northern Maryland residence school to receive a fine education.

According to Troy Taylor's book *The Haunting of America*, conditions at the girls' school were much less pleasant than what the young ladies had been accustomed to at home. Unsatisfactory sanitary conditions and poor heating caused outbreaks of influenza and croup, both of which contributed to the deaths of several students.

Taylor related the tale of one victim of pneumonia, named Annie. This daughter of a rich Southern planter had made it known to her family that she was very unhappy staying at the school. Soon after arriving, she wrote home, protesting her "incarceration" and stating she was upset with the institution's isolated rural location near a quiet mill town. Unfortunately, Annie died during her first winter at the school, where it was so cold that the water in the washbowls froze overnight. Her restless ghost, seen wearing a long, bluish-white gown, is believed to roam the abandoned complex, apparently still annoyed with her family, which indirectly caused her early death so far from home.

After the Civil War the school's attendance began to decline, and it closed in 1891. Subsequent owners used it as a private residence and a hotel until 1917, when the former school became a hospital for wounded soldiers returning from World War I. "It is unknown," Taylor wrote, "just how many soldiers may have passed away in the old building, but one has to wonder if any of them chose to stay behind in the massive building as time passed on."

The building's last occupants left sometime after the 1940s. Today, the site is known as the Patapsco Female Institute Historic Park, part of the Mt. Ida Visitor Center in Ellicott City. The ruins of the old school continue to be a magnet for ghost investigators, who search photographs for evidence of spirit energy.

In an October 1997 issue of the *Daily Grind*, a paper published for Howard County employees, Shirley Daniels wrote an article entitled "PFI Spirit Lives On." Her piece included an incident involving a young girl who had become separated from her ghost-hunting friends late one evening while trespassing on the PFI property. As she was trying to locate her friends and wandering alone through the grounds, the lost girl reported seeing a young girl dressed in a flowing white gown exit the front door of the stately mansion. She said the apparition moved across the porch, descended the steps, floated across the lawn, and disappeared. As soon as the mysterious image faded, the nervous witness looked back toward the building. What she saw was a crumbling structure, one that no longer had a porch and looked nothing like the well-kept building from which she had just seen the apparition depart.

Hell House

No place in Maryland, not even the ruins of infamous Glenn Dale Hospital, has grabbed ghost hunters' attention as much as Hell House. This captivating nickname—given to the abandoned Roman Catholic seminary formerly run by members of the Redemptorists, more properly called the Congregation of the Most Holy Redeemer—attracts late-night paranormal adventurers like a empty bar stool during happy hour lures alcoholics. In addition to its image-invoking name and the decaying condition of the isolated structures, contemporary legends shared by word of mouth and over numerous Web sites have added to the lore and attraction of this fascinating, reportedly haunted shrine.

Members of the Ellicotts, the wealthy family after whom Ellicott City is named, established an estate in the country, less than a half-dozen miles southeast of Ellicott City, in the late 1700s. In the 1830s, when a line of the Baltimore & Ohio Railroad passed through the village known as Ilchester, the Ellicotts built a tavern, assuming the site would become an important stop along the growing, money-producing railroad line. But those plans never materialized, and the family sold the tavern and surrounding one hundred-acre estate in the 1860s to the religious order, which in 1882 established Saint Mary's College.

Over the years, the isolated grounds and growing number of large and impressive buildings served as a seminary to train young men for the priesthood. But by the mid twentieth century, enrollment had declined to such a low level that the religious order closed many of its buildings. By the early 1970s Saint Mary's was closed, and in the late 1980s the complex was sold. Some of the acreage became part of Patapsco Valley State Park. Private investors bought the rest of the property, which included most of the old, deteriorating buildings. They immediately put up "No Trespassing" signs. Afterwards, vandals began to deface sites on the property. Fires, particularly a 1997 Halloween-night blaze that devastated the main building, destroyed some of the structures. Soon afterwards the legends were born.

Not surprisingly, trespassers—who have traversed the winding, steep, secluded roads leading to the restricted property—have told tales about moving shadows, strange sounds, loud noises, and whispered conversations. Potential ghostly evidence, in the form of orbs in photographs and garbled sounds on digital tape recorders, has been captured during unauthorized explorations through what is left of the historic, sacred structures. While none of this is irrefutable evidence of ghosts haunting the abandoned seminary, the campus's eerie secluded setting, ruined religious shrines, and decrepit buildings have enhanced the plausibility of the growing number of tall tales.

Some of the stories most repeated include that of an insane priest who had sold his soul to the devil and killed five young girls. After they were dead, he hung their bodies from the ceiling beams in one of the larger buildings and arranged their dangling bodies in a circle so that they faced one another. Beneath the victims' swaying feet, the murderer had drawn a large pentagram and lit black candles at each of the five points of the satanic symbol. The priest's body was found lying in the middle of the red chalk design, with a black dagger sticking out of his heart. Apparently, he had made a human offering to his master before he joined him in hell.

Another legend involves a vengeful caretaker, who along with his family had been abused by some of the religious administrators at the school. He killed several of these superiors and buried their bodies somewhere on the Hell House grounds. Since the killer died without revealing the location of the missing clerics, their ghosts roam the buildings and woods. It's believed these restless spirits are trying to attract the attention of late-night trespassers, who might follow them to the unmarked resting place and, eventually, provide the help the victims need to receive a proper burial.

Despite realizing that the ghost stories are nothing more than tall tales created by imaginative minds and ghost hunters' desires to encounter the unknown, the stories of Hell House continue to be told—and, in some cases, believed.

Montgomery's Mysterious Mansions

Montanverde

Quite a few longtime Montgomery County residents believe Maj. George Peter lives in Montanverde, a Seneca-area home built in 1800. It doesn't matter that the three-term U.S. congressman and three-time husband—who served in the War of 1812 and was a close friend of Abraham Lincoln—died in 1861. There seems to be a fair amount of paranormal evidence that the major is still hanging around.

But rather than dragging chains like Marley's ghost, or wailing in the night wind like an Irish banshee, Montgomery County's mysterious major continues a habit he had conducted before retiring for the evening. Late each night, a servant climbed Montanverde's stairs and delivered a hot toddy to Major Peter's bedchamber. Each night, after draining the spirited contents, the master offered his servant a satisfied smile and immediately smashed the crystal goblet by throwing it violently into the fireplace.

As new owners moved into the historic home, they noticed an unusual and bothersome sound. Initially, they were unable to determine what the noise might be. Some thought a bird might have flown into a window. Others times they suggested a knickknack had fallen and shattered onto the floor. The confused occupants agreed that the sound was more of a fragile tinkle than a heavy crash. But no one ever found any broken item that would explain the strange events.

Eventually, a workman who had been summoned to do some repairs in the home provided the answer. As the worker entered the foyer, he mentioned to the owners that he previously had done some projects at Montanverde. Just before he went about his new task, he turned and asked the new owner if Major Peter was still tossing his wineglass into the fireplace each night. That query ended up solving the mystery of the unusual sounds. Over the years, Major Peter's story has been repeated often. According to Maureen Dowd's article in the *Washington Post* about "The Ghosts of Montgomery," one county historian said, "It's hard not to love a ghost who comes back for the sole purpose of having a drink."

Another owner of the home was warned by a caretaker to beware of "snakes in the cellar and ghosts upstairs." While this family had no encounters with Major Peter, they did see the apparition of an elderly woman, who might have been the ghost of one of the major's wives. The sighting of the strange woman occurred in Montanverde's living room. The ghostly figure was wearing a long white dress with a cord tied around its waist. The witnesses said they could see right through the filmy creature before it waved at the owners and disappeared. On other occasions, early-morning footsteps on the stairs, slamming doors, and stomping boots caused the dogs in the home to howl. Finding items knocked onto the floor, walking through cold spots, and seeing candles sputter and extinguish—and suddenly relight on their own—were examples of other unexplained incidents indicating a paranormal presence in the historic home.

Fair Hill and Nanny

Before it burned to the ground under suspicious circumstances in 1977, the 28-acre Olney estate known as Fair Hill was considered one of the most haunted sites in the county. Three phantoms were said to have inhabited the long-gone mansion. Nearby residents reported hearing high-pitched wails traveling through the sky on windy nights. They allegedly belonged to both an Irish potter who hanged himself in the basement and a slave baby who burned to death in a cellar fireplace located directly beneath the kitchen.

Outside the home, there were sounds of galloping hoofbeats from a phantom horse running hard along the nearby highway. These were attributed to Col. Richard Brooke, a Revolutionary War patriot who often participated in foxhunts in the area and who was buried at Fair Hill. According to one report, the hard-riding colonel is more than a restless sportsman. He's said to have made midnight rides on his black stallion inside the home, racing up one set of the mansion's stairs and descending down the other. County author Roger Brooke Farquhar claimed he had seen the Revolutionary War hero and wrote that the incident "still causes my hair to stand on end and my flesh to break out in goose pimples."

According to "A Haunting Refrain," published in *The Sentinel*, Farquhar was sitting with two friends on the lawn at Sharon, a home near Olney. There was a full moon and the summer weather was beautiful. Only fifteen feet away was a vegetable garden with six-foot-tall cornstalks. Suddenly, everyone heard the rhythmic galloping of a horse, obviously riding hard. The sounds came from different locations, and those emanating from the nearby cornfield were loud and close—but the crops never moved or rustled as the unseen rider passed by.

Before the hoofbeats disappeared, the author recalled that he and his two frightened friends heard "a distinct snort or hiss near at hand, just back of the fence only a few feet from us." Aware of the legend of Colonel Brooke and his nighttime rides, they assumed the phantom had been passing by, just out of their reach.

According to Dorothy Pugh's article "Ghost Stories of Montgomery County," a considerate spirit inhabited a home near an Olney intersection. The owner of this certain house raised five daughters and attributed some of the help she received with her children to a friendly presence she named "Nanny." The resident ghost was both a comfort and a protector. During a thunderstorm and power outage, all of the homes in the area lost electricity, but somehow the power stayed on for the family in Nanny's home. In the middle of a winter night, the owner was awakened by the sound of a bedroom door slamming repeatedly. Thinking it was one of her children, she went into the hall and saw a greenish-colored light. As she focused on the moving sphere, it grew in size until it resembled a sparkling, mirrored dancehall globe. The woman shouted to the invisible force that it must behave if it wanted to remain in the home, and the globe instantly turned bright red and faded away.

On another occasion, when the harried mother could not attend quickly enough to a crying child, the invisible Nanny is believed to have opened the lid of a music box. The pleasing sounds that filled the room turned the baby's cries and tears into laughter and smiles. When that family moved from the home, the mother stopped at the front door, turned back, and invited Nanny to accompany them to their new residence.

Fertile Hill

In the Wildcat Creek area, tragedy occurred at an estate called Fertile Hill. A bridesmaid enjoying herself during a dance at her sister's wedding reception accidentally collided with a lit lantern. Flames jumped onto the girl's veil and the fire spread across her dress. As she frantically slapped at the spreading inferno, her entire body was engulfed in flames and she died two days later. Soon afterwards, servants and residents passing the spot in the home where the tragedy had occurred reported feeling the presence of an eerie, troubled spirit.

Certainly, those who were present at the wedding expected such a reaction, but subsequent owners of the home also have felt uneasy in the dining room, and they have reacted with a shiver when an unseasonal and sudden chill wind traveled through the room. People said they heard a woman's voice in the home singing sad songs, but after searching, the staff said they could find no one else in the building. Owners have been awakened in the morning to the aroma of fresh coffee, but when they have gone into the kitchen to enjoy a cup of morning refreshment they found nothing brewing. Some believe the name of the ghost is Rachel Robertson, who died in 1853 and is buried in the family plot behind the home.

Honeysuckle Hill

In Potomac, an old home hosts a tragic legacy. In 1910, the son of a prominent family accidentally shot and killed his younger sister, Marguerite. Many decades after the deadly incident, an elderly owner, who knew nothing of the shooting, fell asleep in her rocker in an upstairs bedroom. In the midst of her deep nap, the woman said she felt a small creature crawl up into her lap. Assuming it must be one of the home's pets, she never opened her eyes, but softly caressed the friendly visitor and fell back into a sound sleep. When she awoke and instinctively grasped for the pet that had slept in her lap, there was nothing there. When she related her experience, she was told it might have been the spirit of the young girl, who had remained in the room where she had been shot, seeking comfort she had not received during her brief life.

Honeysuckle Hill stands on Brink Road, an old and well-traveled highway, where for generations people spoke of hearing the cries of a young woman moaning in pain. There also were the comforting sounds of a male who seemed to be responding to her concern. Historians reported that there were many mournful goodbyes exchanged in the area of Honeysuckle Hill, particularly during the Civil War. The area was a departure point where hundreds of young soldiers left home and headed for battle, and many never returned.

In the nearby mansion on that hill, built in 1820 by John and Ann Jones, sellers of the home once proclaimed in a real estate advertisement: "Comes With Its Own Ghost!" One legend long associated with the property is based on a rumor that a woman committed suicide by hanging herself to death in the attic. When the house was vacant for a number of years in the 1930s, word spread about sightings of an apparition of the young woman who had been discovered years earlier swinging from a rope in the attic. Apparently, the woman's soul, which was tainted by the suicide, could not leave the property and was condemned to roam the mansion and its grounds.

The Jones family cemetery is on the property, and an unsolved mystery involving a gravestone has become part of Honeysuckle Hill's folklore. Set some fair distance apart from the Jones family's graves is the marker indicating the resting place of Annie P. Linthicum, who died November 24, 1869, at age twenty. The inscription reads: "Though he slay me, yet, will I trust in him." Some suggest Annie was a relative of the family, perhaps a niece, or maybe a servant who lived on the property. Was she the person who committed suicide and whose restless soul wanders Honeysuckle Hill? Was she the lover of a Civil War soldier who never returned? Or was she perhaps the victim of a different, unknown deadly incident? Of course, no one alive knows the answer.

Annington

The Battle of Ball's Bluff, also known as the Battle of Leesburg, took place in Loudon County, Virginia, on October 21, 1861. The evening before the battle, a private dinner was held in Annington, a stately home in Montgomery County. The mansion's owner, Dr. Stephen Newton Chiswell White, sat across the table from Col. Edward Dickinson Baker, a senator from Oregon and commander of the Union troops that would be engaged in the conflict the following day.

During the meal, Colonel Baker mentioned to his host, "Tomorrow night I dine either in Leesburg or in Hell." It's not known whether Saint Peter gave the Union colonel a golden harp or the Devil handed the officer a coal shovel, but it's certain Baker never ate any meal in Leesburg. He died the afternoon of the battle, after being shot through the heart as Confederate troops overran his Union positions. Baker earned the distinction of being the only United States senator to be killed in a Civil War battle, and his close friend President Abraham Lincoln directed that the senator's body be laid out for viewing in the White House.

Not too many years later, strange things began to happen in Annington. Conversations were heard when there was no one in the room. Lights were turned on and off in the empty dining room. There also were tales of the appearance on the property of a man on a black horse, wearing a Union officer's uniform. Those trying to offer a reason for these unusual incidents suggested the source might be Colonel Baker's spirit. In fact, someone said the dining room antics could be the deceased colonel's way of signaling a desire for that after-the-battle dinner he had never been able to enjoy.

According to "Ghost Stories of Montgomery County," by Margaret Pugh, Annington may have several more restless phantoms roaming about. Several tenants and owners reported some unexplained experiences while they lived in the historic home. These include the time a window flew out of the frame but didn't break. There were sounds, but no apparent sources, of galloping horses, a man's heavy footsteps, doors opening and closing, jewelry disappearing but later being found in unusual places, a picture being turned to face the wall, and pets acting agitated.

After a ghostly figure seemed to walk through an outside wall on an upper floor of the mansion, an investigation revealed there had been, at that spot, the entrance to a long-demolished porch. The most frightening incident took place when a resident who was sitting in the kitchen looked up for no apparent reason and fixed her gaze upon the doorknob—which began to turn, and then stopped. Within a few seconds, the door opened very slowly, as if someone were guiding it forward. But no one was there. It was impossible for the door to swing open to its full extension from the hall into the kitchen without some force causing it to occur.

One resident suggested the ghost is named Esther, one of the building's first occupants, who was considered "incompetent," a word used at that time to describe the mentally challenged. Others think the ghost is Esther's daughter, Ann, who married Dr. Smith and who later became mistress of Annington. She died young, leaving behind four children, and she may have remained in the home searching for the family she had lost.

A final theory attributes all of the spirited agitation to the friendly specter of Dr. White, who roams the building late in the evening, probably returning home after making house calls to his patients. The good doctor also may be searching for the spirit of his young wife. Together, they may have decided to remain in Annington and make up for their too-brief marriage that ended with her tragic death.

Beall-Dawson House

According to a story published by the Montgomery County Historical Society, one of the society's buildings in Rockville may host a ghost or two of its own. The organization's November 1988 newsletter featured a comprehensive article on "Ghost Stories of Montgomery County" by Dorothy Pugh that detailed scores of phantoms roaming roads and historic homes throughout the county.

In a section about the Beall-Dawson House, one of the society's historic structures, Pugh wrote that a volunteer, while dipping candles in the old kitchen, turned and "saw a black man on his knees laying bricks in the floor of the carriage entrance." Before the startled woman could speak, the apparition disappeared. Providing a possible historical connection with the sighting, Pugh noted that the original floor in that area of the home had been made in the 1940s of bricks set in sand. "The work," Pugh wrote, "may have been done by a very talented and unusual black man named Nathan Briggs, who did a lot of renovating at the Beall-Dawson House."

Some experts believe ghostly apparitions are sighted because they have a strong association with a certain place. Another theory is that spirits of those who died tragically or unexpectedly seem to stay in the present dimension and are reluctant to move on to the "other side." While Nathan Briggs did not die in the Beall-Dawson House, Pugh stated that the worker's death was a tragic one—the man committed suicide.

Other workers and volunteers at the society's headquarters reported hearing sounds throughout the house, particularly on the stairs and in a second-floor room that once had served as the library. At times the building's burglar alarm would activate, apparently on its own. When police responded and checked the area, they found no one in the home and no evidence of a break-in.

Aunt Betsy

No one knows her real name, but for decades folks have been calling her Aunt Betsy. She's said to be the ghost of an eighteenth-century slave who was lashed while tied to a whipping post erected in the basement of Clinton, an historic mansion believed to be the oldest brick building in Montgomery County. Owners of the home in the mid-twentieth century said a whipping post stood for some time in the structure's cellar.

According to the legend, Aunt Betsy went crazy from the physical and mental abuse she had received, and the old woman would run through the fields screaming as she raced along. Eventually, her masters locked her in the basement, where she died. There have been reports that her ghost still roams through the cornfields at night, and a howling sound accompanies her sightings. The eerie story was passed along by word of mouth and also is preserved in Roger Brooke

Farquhar's book, *Historic Montgomery County Homes and History*. The author wrote, "Aunt Betsy is the authentic ghost of Clinton. She may often be heard moaning in the cellar."

Soon after the old slave's death, doors began slamming and candles were blown out for no apparent reason. That's when residents began blaming Aunt Betsy's spirit for anything unusual that occurred in the home. For six generations, descendants of John Thomas, Aunt Betsy's master, experienced the phantom's annoying antics. One of the last members of the Thomas family to live in Clinton claimed several Aunt Betsy encounters. The owner said she experienced sudden drafts, saw a figure move swiftly by and disappear, found door latches jammed, and saw both doors of a eight-foot-tall wardrobe fly open on their own. Perhaps Aunt Betsy was trying to get even with the descendants of her tormentors, but unusual activity did not end when new, non-family owners moved into the estate in the late 1950s.

According to information in the article, "The Ghosts of Montgomery," by *Washington Post* reporter Maureen Dowd, the Wellens family had experiences with the resident ghost, including candles being blown out, china cabinet doors being opened and closed, switches being flicked on and off, and sighting an unusual form that appeared behind a window and which was captured in a photograph. According to Frances Wellens, who lived with Aunt Betsy in Clinton for eight years, "Aunt Betsy was the greatest. I always enjoyed her pranks. She was noted for being the happy haunt."

Haunted Bridge

There's a spooky railroad bridge in Montgomery County, spanning Seneca Creek between Germantown and Barnesville. The legends have blended over time, but some of the ghost stories are based on events that took place during a small Civil War skirmish that occurred between Clopper Road and Frederick Avenue.

During that engagement, a Rebel solder was decapitated by a Union officer's sword. After the battle was over, the man's head was lost, and the soldier's body was buried without its head. Naturally, and almost immediately, a tale spread about the angry and frustrated headless horseman, who rides throughout the region searching in vain for his long-lost head. Of course, these incidents occur only at midnight, and usually during a full moon. But each time the headless searcher roams, he runs out of time, since his fruitless search must be abandoned before the sun rises, and the hoofbeats of the black ghost stallion fade into the morning mist before daylight arrives. In the years immediately following the skirmish, residents of the farming area stayed inside their homes at night to avoid being frightened by sounds of rattling sabres and groups of galloping horses, perhaps indelible remnants of the deadly incidents that took place during the battle.

Once encounter with the ghost was told in a story by Jo Beck in *The Gazette*, entitled, "Seneca Creek Ghost Yarn Still Captivating." In 1866, a farmer and his family were returning home in their wagon from a barn raising on Clopper Road. It was late October, and a chill was in the air. At a bend in the road, they saw a large horse, which the farmer described as having "glowing eyes, like a blacksmith's fire." In shock, the family stared at the large black animal and the tall, stiff figure sitting atop the saddle. As they watched in silence, the headless being, wearing black clothing and a long dark cape, leaned down. Extending his long, black, gloved hand, the stranger wrote a message in the dirt road. After returning to an erect position, he pulled on his horse's rein, turned, and rode out of sight, vanishing into the fog.

Slowly, the farmer climbed down from his wagon and walked to the spot where the headless horseman had been. The frightened man bent down to read the message. As he used his finger to trace out the initials of some of the words, the farmer pulled his hand back, noticing the tip of his finger was wet and black. Horrified, he realized that the letters of the note had been written in blood. The words read: "I cannot rest until I become a whole being. Stay clear or you and yours may suffer a similar tale." The terrified family raced home, packed up everything they could squeeze into their wagon, and left the region before noon the next day. They left behind a note in their empty home explaining what had occurred and why they had moved on so abruptly.

In another version of the local legend, the headless wanderer is a victim of a train wreck. A third tale involves a conductor, who was looking out a side window of his train and attempting to view the upcoming station, when a tree was struck by lightning. The falling branch separated the man's head from his body.

The last story was found in an 1876 issue of *The Sentinel*, which detailed a mysterious occurrence reported by a number of residents living near Cloppers Mill. For several weeks, at "$9^1/_2$ o'clock," a lantern, erected at the railroad bridge over Big Seneca Creek, "is suddenly darkened, the light being entirely shut off and a flame like a flash of lightening shoots straight up into the air while another of a similar character flashed directly across the bridge."

Groups of up to fifty armed citizens went out and patrolled the area around the bridge to try to come up with an explanation of how the light could be snuffed out without any visible person or object making it happen. Some of the men involved, the paper stated, were veterans of battles in recent wars and "were not afraid of an army of ghosts." One night, the assembled posse did not have to wait long. They saw the lantern light go dark, but could see no apparent cause. They responded by firing several shots into the darkness, aiming for the area where the lantern hung on the post. Immediately, fire was returned, and then everything was quiet.

All the men present agreed that they had seen no one put out the lantern flame, and since the moon was full that evening, no living person could have touched the lantern without having been seen. The reporter could not state whether the cause "be a spirit of hell or goblin damned," and admitted he was not willing to investigate the situation on his own. "We hope," he wrote, "that a solution of this affair will soon be discovered and a cause of terror be removed from the superstitious of that vicinity."

Tommyknocker

One of the minor surprises in Maryland in 1849—rather than in San Francisco, which had received much more publicity—was the discovery of gold on a farm only a few miles from the White House.

Despite the initial excitement, most folks thought it was just a fluke. But in 1861, a Union soldier stationed outside of Washington, D.C., near Great Falls, Montgomery County, discovered a few nuggets while washing dishes in a stream. That was enough for gold fever to strike central Maryland. By 1867, just after the Civil War, some savvy businessmen had established the Maryland Mine. Their initial shaft was located near the intersection of Falls Road and MacArthur Boulevard.

While the amount of ore wasn't overwhelming, the East Coast state's mining and panning operations grew steadily. By 1901, there were a half-dozen companies digging away, hoping to strike it rich. Although no one found a fortune of ore under the ground, exploration and production ambled along until a few years after World War II, when commercial mining ended around 1950. During Maryland's century of golden dreams, most of the companies and workers merely scratched out a living, but some suffered serious injuries and a few unlucky souls died in the mines.

The Maryland Mine, located near the present-day Great Falls entrance of the Chesapeake & Ohio Canal National Historical Park, was the area's largest commercial operation. It sank shafts deep into the ground, hoping to strike a solid vein, but much of what the miners pulled from the earth was pyrite, better known as "fool's gold." While many find Maryland's little-known mining history surprising and interesting, others believe the mines' legends and ghost stories are much more fascinating, particularly the Tommyknocker tales related to the late-night explosion of June 15, 1906.

A crew of miners was ready to set off an explosion in one of the mine's five-hundred-foot-long tunnels. With the dynamite charges prepared, the miners decided to take a short break in the hoist room. This was a small shed-like building that was held by ropes and guided by pulleys. It served as an elevator to deliver the workers in and out of the mine. Planning to relax over a final spirited drink, the miners took off their equipment. Tools and headgear were scattered about. To illuminate the dark caverns, each helmet was equipped with a lit candle.

As the miners passed around the refreshing contents of the Georgetown Bottle—a nickname given to the local spirits they obtained in the area's saloons—no one noticed that one of the helmets had been tossed onto a table next to the explosives. Eventually, one of the miners pointed out the distinct smell of a burning fuse, which had been ignited by the carelessly placed helmet candle. Shouting and screaming, the terrified men charged from the room, trying to get away from the sizzling fuse that would set off the dynamite. In less than a minute, the explosion was heard miles away. While the terrified miners had escaped, the hoist operator, Charles Eglin, was killed when a small building collapsed and crushed his body.

Since miners were a superstitious lot, soon afterwards stories about unusual and unnerving events began to happen in and around the mine. Even the slightest shadow, sound, or misplaced object was blamed on the Tommyknocker of the Maryland Mine.

According to the regional folklore in the mining villages of Wales, England, and Scotland, a Tommyknocker is a deformed elf or gnome-size creature that lives in the ground. It is dressed in miner's work clothes and makes mischief—such as stealing or hiding workers' food and tools, and making sudden scary sounds. Not willing to admit their belief in an imaginary, bedtime-storybook creature, many of the gruff, rugged miners shrugged off the tales. At most, some said they considered the phantom's mischievous antics harmless and annoying. There also was the belief that when sounds of knocking on mine walls occurred just before an explosion or cave-in, it was the Tommyknocker's warning that a tragic event would take place soon and they had only minutes or seconds to escape the tragedy.

While mine owners insisted such noises were natural events caused by the shifting of the earth and straining of the timbers, more superstitious miners continued to believe it was the work of the Tommyknocker. They swore the sounds were not well-intentioned warnings, but instead evidence that the evil creature was hammering on the walls, trying to cause a cave-in and kill the workers. In addition to the Tommyknocker, employees suggested that after a marked increase in eerie events after the 1906 explosion in Maryland Mine, the ghost of the hoist operator had returned to get even with the careless miners who had caused his death.

Horses working near the mine became skittish and unmanageable, particularly as they passed by the entrance to the shaft where the deadly explosion had occurred. The mine's night watchman reported hearing footsteps along the gravel path leading to his office door. But whenever he went to see who was approaching there was no one around.

An article in *The Gazette*, written by Dorothy Pugh and Karen Yaffe Lottes, is entitled "Be Aware of the Tommyknocker, and Beware." In it, the authors share the story of Edgar Ingalls, an underground foreman who received an early-morning phone call from the night watchman. The caller's panicked voice yelled, "Get over here quick!" Ingalls hopped on his horse and galloped to the guard shack, where he found the watchman who had made the call shaking with fright. Years later, Ingalls recalled that the terrified man told him, "A ghostie looking man with eyes of fire and a tail ten feet long crawled out of the shaft and disappeared in the forest. I started to shoot, but remembered the Tommyknocker could throw the shot back in my face. Mr. Ingalls, I ain't doing this job any more!" After that story spread, it was hard to find night watchmen to guard the mine. Those who study folklore know one of the descriptions of the Tommyknocker is that of a creature with glowing eyes and a long tail.

According to the Maryland Geological Survey, nearly two dozen mining operations were active at one time in Montgomery County alone, many along Falls Road between modern-day I-270 and River Road. There were reports of some good-size nuggets being taken from the area of Great Falls. Due to the increase in the price of gold, panning-style prospecting continues, with a small number of hopeful hobbyists and treasure hunters still seeking both fortune and fun through part-time gold mining.

But where history ends, folklore and legend begins. Old mine shafts can be discovered by accident, and some curious explorers have spent their time seeking them out. However, most are on private property and trespassers are forbidden to enter. State and federal law also requires permission to access and explore these sites. Since they have been abandoned for so long, these closed mining operations are dangerous, and personal injury is the more likely outcome than riches. Remnants of the Great Falls operations that have been fenced off to restrict public access include the old Ford Mine, which collapsed in 1890, and several shafts of the old Maryland Mine, one reaching a depth of more than two hundred feet.

Some suggest there is more under the busy urban highways than empty, water-filled caverns. They believe Montgomery County's old gold mines hold the bodies of ghostly miners, those who had been trapped in cave-ins or lost in the tunnels, and that they occasionally return to the surface in the form of Tommyknockers.

Annapolis and Baltimore

Annapolis

Brice House

A mention of the Brice House appears in nearly every book on Annapolis history. In tourist guides and magazine articles the mansion's distinctive architecture places it near the top of the town's most-suggested places to see. More importantly for our purposes, the Georgian-style mansion, located at the intersection of East and Prince George's streets, has been referred to as the city's "most haunted house." According to author and historian Elmer M. Jackson Jr., the building is touted as having "more ghost stories told about it than any other colonial mansion in Annapolis."

If not the most haunted, it certainly is among the largest and most impressive homes in the ancient city. Trying to photograph the massive structure is difficult because its lengthy brick façade extends nearly the length of the block. But in this case, bigger may actually be better, since a larger home may provide a larger number of ghosts with ample room to roam.

Construction on the Brice House property began in 1767. Eventually, the original structures would be torn down or added onto, resulting in the present-day, thirty-plus-room mansion. Also on the property was a carriage house, stable, outbuildings, and gardens. Today the central portion of the building is referred to as the "center block." To either side is a hallway (called a hyphen). Each hyphen-style passage connects to an end building (called a wing) standing at either side of the structure.

The building was built by a successful merchant and remained in the same family for more than a hundred years. At one time it was owned by St. John's College, which used the mansion for faculty apartments. In the attic, exposed beams remain standing, indicating the dimensions of the apartment walls that stood previously on that top level. The last private owners were the Wohl family, whose members restored the home and lived there until the late 1970s. The International Masonry Institute (IMI) purchased the building in the early 1980s. For the last dozen years, the organization's administrative offices have occupied sections of the Brice House, using it for meetings, conferences, a research library, and a central resource center for the organization's U.S. and Canadian members. In addition, the IMI works closely with the Historic Annapolis Foundation, allowing that organization to use the building for special events, lectures, public tours, and educational activities.

If some historic homes in Annapolis seem to take extra care to hide their ghost stories in the closet, such is not the case with the Brice House. In the article "Ghosts Give 'Living History' New Meaning," by Allison Blake in *The Capital*, the writer states, "Anyone who's heard the historic district's haunted tales—and is willing to talk about them—will tell you that spirits dwell in the Brice House." A *Sunday Capital* article by Bradley Peniston quotes Betty Aronson, a town ghost-tour guide at that time, as stating, "The Brice House has the reputation as the most haunted house in Annapolis."

A check of county historical society files and library records served up a slew of newspaper articles about the Brice mansion's phantom residents. "Brice House Ghost Stories" is the headline of one *Evening Capital* story, and another edition of that paper attracted readers' attention with bold print declaring: "Celebrated Brice House Ghosts Now Believed Gone: New Owners Haven't Seen Single One."

The undying fascination with tales of fright and bumps in the night at the massive old residence on East Street seems to prove the old adage, "Where there's smoke there's fire." Following is a summary of some of the eerie events that have helped place the Brice House at the top of many ghost hunters' most-wanted list.

The last member of the Brice family was Colonel (but in some sources referred to as Governor) James Brice, who resided there in the late 1800s. Apparently, the wealthy gentleman was murdered (or died of unnatural causes) in his stately home. By the time his dead body was found in the formal library, the master's faithful butler had disappeared mysteriously. This caused neighbors to suggest that the absent servant should have been considered the prime suspect in the unsolved crime.

However, subsequent sightings of apparitions have been attributed to both the murdered colonel (who returns seeking his killer) and the missing butler (who may be coming back looking for his master's hidden treasure). But some reports suggest the long-lost butler also was murdered in the building, and that his still-undiscovered body may be buried in the cellar, bricked up in a secret passage, or hidden behind an old stairwell. If this is the case, the butler may be roaming about to call attention to his limbo-like situation, seeking someone to place his remains in an appropriate final resting place—preferably a formal cemetery plot.

Legends of hauntings in the house earned some level of respect when a former U.S. Naval Academy faculty member, Allen Blow Cook, reported that he saw four spirits during his stay in the building. The professor lived in the Brice House in the late 1920s, during the period when the building was used as an apartment complex for college professors. In a 1957 interview with the *Evening Capital*, the educator claimed that in the middle of one night he awoke and saw the ghost of the butler standing at the other side of his bedroom. He said he also saw a man, assumed to be the late Colonel Brice, dressed in formal clothing. "He wore a plum colored suit, knee breeches, a lace fichu, and a powdered wig. He was quite diaphanous and walked right through my bed," Cook recalled.

Giving some credence to the belief that ghosts may be attracted to certain people, the professor said he also witnessed a ghostly incident involving a Colonial-era couple arguing in the estate's gardens, outside the rear of the building. Cook said the man disappeared into an area in the gardens between the Brice and Paca houses; the girl returned to the Brice House and paced loudly in the area above Cook's room. In another interview, the professor said he once came face-to-face with a white-haired gentleman in a black suit before the image "gradually melted out of sight like a mist," right before the professor's eyes.

A different story involved a couple that lived in the north hyphen section for eighteen months in the 1950s. They reported their son and his dog were in a downstairs bedroom that led out into the garden. One midnight the boy screamed. At the same time, the child's puppy was shaking in terror, with its eyes bulging out of its head and foam dripping from its mouth. The boy said he awoke and saw someone standing at the foot of his bed. Thinking it was his mother, he lifted his hand to touch the visitor, but no one was there.

There also were reports of tapping and knocking sounds—sometimes in a regular, Morse code fashion—coming from within the building's old walls. Apparitions have been said to disappear in plain sight, and sometimes wispy images drift through doors and walls. But the most fascinating tale is a report of several workmen finding a skeleton in a closet. This occurred during a renovation of the building; the workers were said to have discovered the bones of a woman who apparently had been sealed up inside a wall.

Some people have speculated that the long-hidden corpse was a member of the Brice family, and the woman probably had been mentally ill. Rather then expose the family to humiliation and town gossip, as would have been the case during that era, the troubled woman was kept out of sight and confined inside the home and gardens. When she died, the decision was made to hide any evidence of her existence and wall up the body. No one knew about her life or death—until the skeleton came out of the closet.

Buried treasure was rumored to be hidden somewhere in the Brice House, most probably in the dirt-floored basement. One workman doing chores in the cellar said he removed what appeared to be a loose stone. As he pulled the rock from its place, he was very excited, hoping to discover wealth and riches. Instead, he found he had intruded on the nest of a spider the size of a grapefruit. He claimed the monster bit off the handle of his tool and sent him running for the stairs.

Elmer M. Jackson Jr. writes in *Annapolis: Three Centuries of Glamour* that a servant in the building also tried to locate the hidden trove, but ran off when he was allegedly approached by a "beautiful blonde girl with a halo around her head."

In a 1992 *Evening Capital* article, Hal Burdett wrote, "The most chilling ghost stories told in Annapolis years ago were associated with the Brice House."

During a 2007 tour and interview in the Brice House with Lynn O'Brien, administrative manager of the International Masonry Institute, the woman said she had worked in the building for more than ten years. While aware of the ghost stories, she and most members of her staff had never experienced anything unusual. But, she did admit she had heard two interesting stories.

O'Brien was told the first story in the early 1990s by a woman who had known the last private residents that lived in the house. When one of the female family members was dying in her bed, the old woman told the attending nurse that there was a woman wearing old-fashioned clothing and standing at the foot of her bed. The dying woman demanded that the nurse get the ghost out of there.

O'Brien mentioned another more recent incident that involved the building's caretaker, who usually stayed late after special events to clean up the grounds and home. One evening, after an event was over, the caretaker was in the building alone and heard the sound of footsteps coming from the upper floors. After inspecting the area, he found no one there. "Ever since that night," O'Brien said, "he leaves when the last person is ready to go, and he comes back the next morning to finish up what he hadn't gotten done."

In a 1957 Halloween article in the *Evening Capital*, the writer ended the story with the following statement: "There have been, of course, countless people who have lived at the Brice House and who have never seen a ghost there. History-wise, Mrs. Wohl [the owner at the time] said her research has revealed a number of conflicting tales dealing with ghosts. She says she isn't afraid and from her point of view, there aren't any ghosts. There are just the stories about them." That seems as good an answer as any—but it certainly won't diminish the interest in the unexplained and eerie activities at the "most haunted house" in Annapolis.

Hammond–Harwood House

It's well known that ghost tales and legends are most often handed down through word of mouth. But sometimes a literary work has been the basis of an unusual tale that some believe to be true. In the case of the Hammond-Harwood House, some experts think the home's ghost story may have been inspired from a passage in an early-twentieth century work of fiction.

Stately Hammond-Harwood House stands at the corner of Maryland Avenue and King George Street in Annapolis. The structure is an outstanding example of American colonial architecture. Throughout the year, the building hosts visiting school groups, holds special public events, and offers guided tours.

As visitors pass through the home's formal gardens and magnificent rooms, they marvel at the fine workmanship and attention to detail performed by the original builders. But, according to one legend, focusing too intently in one direction can sometimes have unexpected and unpleasant results. Such, according to one story, was the fate of Mathias Hammond, the original builder of the impressive colonial mansion. In the article "Ghosts Haunt Annapolis," published in the October 1973 issue of *Annapolitan,* writer Dyan Manger described how the builder's care and exacting demands regarding materials and furnishings extended the construction, causing the process to go on for several years.

It's a known fact that most women don't like to play second fiddle to anyone, or anything, including a house. According to the legend, Hammond went about erecting what he was sure would be the most magnificent home in the capital city, but during this time he neglected his fiancée. The aggravated young lady, who had waited patiently for years to witness the completion of the couple's home-to-be, broke off the engagement. When the building was finished, the owner had an outstanding residence, but no one with whom to share it. Some say Hammond decided not to live in the mansion, and instead he resided in his country house, Howard's Adventure in Gambrills, Maryland, where he died and is buried.

Where facts end in such stories, legends and imagination take flight, often in an attempt to make history more interesting. A story, referenced by Manger in his article, began circulating that the neglected woman later changed her mind and returned to the builder, becoming the secret mistress of the house. It's said she would enter and exit the mansion through a secret path, using two keys that were buried beneath loose bricks in the cellar. "One key," Manger wrote, "bore the marking 'secret chamber,' the other 'secret passageway.'"

The mysterious romance continued for some time, and when the woman died her body was buried in a secret crypt under the estate's gardens. There have been reports of occasional appearances of her apparition looking out from windows in the upper floors of the building or strolling through the formal gardens. These sightings might be evidence of the lady's everlasting presence and her satisfaction with the excellent workmanship of her building.

During a 2007 visit with Carter C. Lively, director of the Hammond-Harwood House, I inquired about the legend, asking if he had heard the story and wondering if there was any substance to the tale.

The director acknowledged that various versions of the legend had been circulating about the town for some time. "To our knowledge it's not true," he said. "We have no evidence to either prove or disprove the story." But it is correct, he said, that the builder Mathias Hammond never married. Then, after a few moments, the director suggested that a few elements of the tale—especially references to two hidden keys, a secret passage, and a secret chamber—may have originated from certain details found in a novel published in 1931 by Doubleday, Doran and Company of New York. Entitled *The Brass Keys of Fenwick*, the book was written by Augusta Huiell Seaman of New Jersey, who was associated for a time with St. John's College, located in the center of Annapolis's historic district and a short walk from Hammond-Harwood House.

Lively added that he knows of no secret chamber or burial site in the manicured gardens behind the present-day mansion. But, he noted as we concluded our conversation, "Our gardens are much smaller today than they were when the house was built. Originally, they extended all the way to the Paca House."

If so, one wonders, could the there be a slight chance that the legend might be true? Could the mistress of the house rest in a forgotten, lost grave beyond the present-day boundaries of the estate? As in the case of most ghost stories, we'll probably never know the answers, or discover how much of the story is true and how much is fiction.

Main Street Spirits

If it's ghost tales you seek, the narrow streets of old Annapolis may be among the best places to look. Through the centuries there's been talk of restless specters that periodically have agreed to grant brief, unannounced appearances. To no one's surprise, all of these manifestations have occurred during the peak hours of darkness—between dusk and dawn—when vision is limited and imaginations are enhanced by the shadows of the night and the amount of liquid spirits imbibed beforehand.

There are a variety of unexplained reports, but nothing stirs the imagination and raises the hair on one's neck more than a headless figure, so let's begin there. Of course, the vast percentage of the time you mention a headless horseman, or headless figure of any type, people immediately utter the words "Sleepy Hollow."

The plight of poor Ichabod Crane, being pursued by the pumpkin-wielding Hessian soldier in Tarrytown, New York, was immortalized in Washington Irving's 1820 story and, for later generations, by Walt Disney's 1949 animated version. The story's fame has allowed the small Hudson Valley town to corner the headless sprit market. But there are numerous headless legends told around the world and across the country. In Annapolis, there are at least two reports of such sightings.

The most persistent and repeated incident occurred in the area of Market Space, which began operations as an open-air market very close to the town dock. Farmers and sellers of produce, fish, and meats would arrive by wagon or boat very early in the morning to set up displays of their goods. Merchants were eager to get the best location and be prepared for the first arrival of both wholesale buyers and individual customers.

About that same time of morning, fishermen and crabbers from the town would head to their boats, tied up to the pilings, to set out into the bay for a day working the water. In the late 1800s, a waterman was passing through the market and dock area. Since it was dark and visibility was difficult, he paused when he noticed a man in the area. But as the waterman prepared to pass by the silent figure and offer a quick greeting, the mortal Annapolis resident noticed that the stranger was headless—and holding his face in the crook of one arm.

Without a word, the waterman turned and raced toward home, only to discover the headless man waiting upon the front steps of the frightened fisherman's house. Depending upon the written source or oral version, the tale ends with the startled man:

- Heading in the back door and hiding under his bed.
- Racing into the back of the house and telling what had occurred to his wife, who went outside and checked and found nothing.
- Passed out from shock and was discovered lying in the street by his neighbors; or
- Passed out and was awakened by his wife, who cursed him for drinking so early in the day.

The second tale involves a young man walking on Spa Bridge at midnight, heading home across the creek to nearby Eastport. As he stepped onto the wooden structure, he noticed a man some distance away, heading in his direction from the hill near St. Mary's Church. Thinking he might have some company while crossing the creek, the young man waited for the black-clad stranger to come closer, but he was startled when he saw the advancing figure had no head. The young man immediately beat feet at a rapid pace, moving quickly across the span, his boots slapping loudly on the wooden planks.

As the man looked back, the headless stranger seemed to float over the bridge's surface, making no sound as he glided along. When the young man reached the other side of the water, the headless haunt had disappeared—whether into Spa Creek or into the foggy mist, it did not matter.

Universally, midnight is recognized as the witching hour. On certain foggy midnights, when the St. Anne's Episcopal Church tower clock struck twelve, the sound of hoofbeats would begin to be heard along Main Street. At first, curious residents thought it strange that no horse was in sight, and they initially attributed the sounds to their imaginations or dreams. But as the sequence of events continued to occur, and consistently coincided with the final stroke of midnight, the residents listened more carefully and watched more intently for any sight of the phantom animal.

Accompanying the clop of invisible hooves against the cobblestone surface was the creak of an unseen wagon. Its rolling wheels combined with the sound of rattling chains being dragged along the street. Although human eyes could not penetrate the dimension where these sounds originated, residents agreed that the mysterious wagon seemed to pick up speed. At the same time, the horse reached a gallop as it arrived at the foot of Market Street—at which time all of the sounds seemed to disappear into the river.

Those seeking a source for the mystery speculated that a wagon filled with chains, perhaps carrying slaves, may have sunk at the river's edge, and the phantom team of horses and driver resurfaced periodically to reenact their final, mysterious midnight ride.

At the foot of Main Street, near Market Space and along the edge of the dock, stand sculptures of four figures—a man and three small children. The man represents Alex Haley, author of the book *Roots*, reading to three attentive youngsters. The sculpture group stands near the area where slaves arrived in America, were auctioned along the docks and at nearby taverns, and were shipped to work on plantations throughout the South.

In 1981, a plaque commemorating Kunta Kinte's (the name of Haley's ancestor in his book) arrival in Annapolis was dedicated. Haley's ancestor is believed to have arrived in 1767 at Annapolis City Dock on the slave ship *Lord Ligonier*. But the marker was stolen within two days of its unveiling, allegedly by the Ku Klux Klan. Although the original plaque was never recovered, a replacement was installed within two months. The plaque, which now stands on a pedestal, reads: "To commemorate the arrival, in this harbor of Kunta Kinte, immortalized by Alex Haley in *Roots*, and all others who came to these shores in bondage and who by their toil, character and ceaseless struggle for freedom have helped to make these United States."

On nights of extreme weather at the City Dock, when the wind howls as it blows fiercely into town off the Severn River, some believe one can hear the auctioneers' chants and the slaves' painful wails escaping from sites where bartering of human life took place on a regular basis and left its indelible haunting impression.

Table for Five?

Cheryl and three friends entered a restaurant operating in an historic Colonial-era building near the dock in downtown Annapolis. She did not remember the name of the eatery, but said, "It was an older place, not too far from the water. It was charming, and we went in to get out of the sun and take a break from shopping and sightseeing."

Greeting the group of tired women, the hostess announced: "A table for five?" Turning around after looking among themselves, the quartet turned back and replied in unison, "Four!" But the young girl who greeted them had turned and was walking away, leading them toward an available spot.

While there were several four-seat booths and tables set for a quartet of patrons, the young lady led them to a table for six, smiled and took away one place setting. Exchanging more quizzical looks, the women took their seats and ignored the apparent confusion. They were exhausted, hungry, and looking forward to a cold beverage, midday meal, and an air-conditioned respite. But when the waiter dropped off five menus and glasses of water, they couldn't ignore the situation.

Waving down the hostess, they asked the young woman why she had seated them at a table for five. Without hesitation, the young girl replied: "There were five in your party. All of you, and the older woman who was standing in the doorway with you. I saw her go to the ladies room a few moments after you were seated and you began looking at your menus."

The four confused patrons were speechless and decided not to press the issue any further. Smiling, Cheryl looked up at the hostess and said, "Our friend won't be having anything today. Just tell the server we're ready to order." Throughout the meal, the four ladies glanced frequently toward the head of the table, at the empty chair.

"That was a strange experience," Cheryl said. "I have no idea who or what the hostess might have seen. But I'll never forget that time when I might have been having lunch in the presence of a ghost."

St. John's "Whistler"

It isn't surprising that St. John's College has its fair share of "school spirits." Established in 1784, the Annapolis institution traces its roots to King William's School, the Maryland colony's free school, which was founded in 1696. The St. John's campus is located in the center of the capital city, near the State House. Originally, it was about four acres in size. McDowell Hall, the institution's central building, was opened in 1789. During its early years, the impressive structure housed the school's classrooms, library, and living quarters for both students and instructors.

Early students at the prep school and college included Francis Scott Key, who went on to have a distinguished career as an attorney. But Key's true fame is associated with his poetic talents. During the Battle of Baltimore in the War of 1812, the Annapolis school's most famous alumnus wrote the words to what became our country's national anthem, "The Star-Spangled Banner." George Washington's step-grandson and two of his nephews also attended this recognized center of Colonial-era learning. By 1806, St. John's College had graduated 105 students, including four future state governors, six judges, and twenty-one members of the Maryland state legislature.

Annapolis's location, less than two dozen miles from Washington, and Maryland's role as a border state during the Civil War both played a key role in the college's fate during that bloody domestic conflict. Many students left the college to take up arms and fight. Some students signed on with Union forces, and others fought in the Confederate army. The war caused a dramatic drop in attendance and incoming tuition; as a result, the institution was forced to close its doors for a brief period. Eventually, the Union army assumed control of the campus and used the college's grounds as a temporary housing site for troops. Later the Army Medical Corps took over St. John's buildings, and the wartime infirmaries were referred to as the College Green Hospital.

When the college reopened in 1866, the grounds and buildings were heavily damaged from the school's transient Civil War residents. No one knows the number of wounded troops that passed through the St. John's College structures. But some suggest that the anguished spirits of the wounded who died in the temporary hospitals scattered across the campus might have remained behind.

Today, St. John's College occupies a picturesque thirty-six-acre campus at the northern edge of the town's historic district, extending from College Creek to the area near the State House. Historic McDowell Hall stands at the top of a knoll, overlooking a rolling lawn. Originally called the Great Hall, this eighteenth-century building marks the historic center of the institution. Some say within old Great Hall there might also reside a number of phantoms.

In a 1982 article entitled "The Whistler—and the Wayward Elevator," Becky Wilson, the college's former communications director, stated that some campus security guards have heard "the call of that tantalizing, bodiless 'Whistler' who sends shivers down their spine."

For many years, members of the college security force, as well as some students, have reported hearing distinct whistling sounds originating from an unknown source and indistinct locations. One guard was "teased" by the musical phantom as the security official made his nightly rounds near the school library. In some instances the guard reported that the sound seemed to come from whichever side of the library building he had just left. On other occasions, the sound seemed to be right behind him and also coming from as far away as the school's gymnasium.

Another guard reported hearing the whistling sound coming through an open window in the gymnasium. However, a thorough investigation of that building offered no evidence that would help solve the persistent mystery. Some guards had suggested that the Whistler might be a student, or a group of students, playing a prank. But the sound also occurred while school was not in session. This development caused the security force to discard the prankster theory, and some agreed that the Whistler's presence during school breaks made the invisible tunesmith's melodies seem a bit more eerie.

Apparently, the Whistler can do more than just carry a tune. The mysterious melody-maker also seems to be able to travel at an amazingly speedy pace. In a few instances, his distinctive sounds were heard at distant ends of the campus within seconds—much too far for a mere mortal to travel in that time. In a 1982 article in the *Annapolis Capital*, reporter Jacqueline Duke referred to the Whistler as an invisible, pesky wraith that "for years has teased campus security personnel by luring them from one end of the campus to another with its disconcertingly human call."

Given its long and at times tragic history, one would expect some mysterious entities would inhabit, or be drawn to, McDowell Hall, the college's oldest building. In Wilson's article, one guard summed up the general feeling of many of the security staff that worked the night shift. "You want to get out of McDowell posthaste," the guard said.

The list of unusual incidents reported in McDowell includes:

- Two guards who noticed blinds being raised in an upper-floor window, even when the building was vacant
- Someone, or something, heard walking with a crippled gait on an upstairs floor
- The tower bell ringing off its regular schedule in the dark hours of the morning
- Lights unexpectedly turning themselves on and off
- Voices of children and racing footsteps traveling across the upper floors
- The sounds of doors slamming and furniture being dragged across wooden floors.

According to Duke, "many a guard hesitates before entering the old brick hall and none lingers for long once inside, convinced a phantom resident stalks the place during the lonely hours between dusk and dawn."

In Greenfield Library, formerly the Maryland State Archives Building, one night a security guard was in the empty building, taking a break and warming up from his rounds during a cold winter graveyard shift. While sitting alone about 4 A.M., he heard the sound of machinery moving. He soon identified the source as the building elevator, somehow being operated while the library was vacant and all the doors locked. As he stood in front of the elevator entrance, waiting to see who or what was inside, the doors opened—but the large metal chamber was empty.

Wilson reported the agitated guard said, "I know that elevator has been messed up forever, but on the off chance it wasn't that, I now will go through the library to check it. But I won't sit there."

Sarah Waters, a 1988 graduate, wrote about "The Otherworldly Side of St. John's." In her fascinating paper, she provided details on unusual incidents experienced by fellow students.

During the 1980s, a student residing in a second-floor room in Pinkney Hall reported seeing a cadet in uniform march in through one wall of her room and disappear out the other. In the 1990s, a student studying in McDowell Hall opened the door to a second-floor classroom and saw a man reading by a fireplace in a room decorated with old-fashioned furniture. Startled that she had intruded on someone in what appeared to be a private office, the embarrassed student immediately said, "Excuse me!" and shut the door. Seconds later, she realized what she had seen and knew that it hadn't made any sense. When the young woman reopened the door, the setting was a standard McDowell Hall classroom—and no one was in the room.

The apparitions of ghostly lovers are said to roam the banks of College Creek. According to Waters, the two phantoms are the sorrowful souls of a Native American college student and the daughter of a St. John's College professor. Forbidden to meet and see each other, one winter night the heartbroken lovers joined hands and jumped into the icy waters of the creek and drowned.

In 1974, a student reported encountering two ghosts on the third floor of the Paca-Carroll House, one of the oldest buildings on campus and located west of McDowell Hall. The story was reported in a newspaper article entitled "Ghosts (Civil War Nurses?) Haunt St. J. Dormitory." A student living in an attic room was resting and, while he was in a dreamlike state, said he heard voices of two women in the hallway and a knock on his door. He said he was unable to open his eyes, but he could sense the visitors' presence nearby and recalled hearing them ask a few questions and their departing footsteps. It's been suggested the women might have been ghosts of Civil War nurses who had worked in the historic house and dormitory when it was used as a hospital for Federal troops.

Another student living in the house reported hearing knocking on his door, but when he answered no one was present. The incident had occurred several times. However, within a few moments of each unexplained phantom knocking, a real visitor soon appeared.

In 1781, during the Revolutionary War, thousands of French troops passed through Annapolis on their way to Yorktown, where they helped defeat the British in the final major battle of America's war for independence.

Some believe at least four unknown French soldiers, who probably died of disease, were buried on the grounds of the college campus somewhere along the banks of College Creek. Some think the unmarked graves are located near the French Monument, which was erected to honor these earliest of America's allies. There are reports that wooden crosses had designated the sites of these soldiers' graves, but that the fragile markers had disappeared sometime in the early decades of the twentieth century.

The impressive granite monument honoring the French soldiers was suggested by Henry Marion, a U.S. Naval Academy professor. He had been in France when the body of John Paul Jones was removed from a French cemetery and later returned to America. Marion also was in Cherbourg when the French reverently buried American sailors who had been killed in a Civil War battle in 1864 between the U.S. ship *Kearsarge* and Confederate ship *Alabama*. Marion thought it would be appropriate that the United States honor the more than one thousand French soldiers and sailors who had lost their lives helping Americans win their independence.

The French monument was dedicated April 18, 1911, in the presence of President William Howard Taft and French Ambassador Jean J. Jusserand. Also attending the dedication was Count Rene de Chambrun, a descendant of the Marquis de Lafayette. Baltimore sculptor J. Maxwell Miller designed the monument, which features a female figure and marching soldiers in the background.

The French Monument on the St. John's College campus is believed to be the first monument in the world ever dedicated to unknown soldiers. Somewhere in Annapolis, perhaps in the monument's shadow, rest a handful of foreign soldiers whose names and location remain unknown and who are buried far from their native soil. Maybe their restless spirits roam the historic college campus and the streets of the colonial village.

Joe Morgue

This is a tale of graveyards, dead bodies, an historic church, a colorful character, and names one would expect to find in a Charles Dickens novel—names such as Jeffrey Jig, Jinny Corncracker, and the primary subject of this chapter, Mr. Joe Morgue.

This Annapolis story is about Joseph Simmons, a longtime town gravedigger and well-known eccentric, who died in the summer of 1836 at the age of one hundred. In those days, when wealthy politicians, noted businessmen, and local characters passed away, newspaper obituaries consumed considerable space, chronicling the life's exploits of the deceased. During that era, news stories and reports of death read much like the pages of a nineteenth-century dime novel.

In order to offer a glance at the writing of days long gone, the following exploits of Joseph Simmons are presented as they were shared in the August 1836 issue of the *Maryland Republican*. Read on and take a peek into the life of a remarkable character and his antics that prove the often-stated adage that fact is more fascinating than fiction.

> Mr. Joseph Simmons, the oldest inhabitant of this city, departed this life on Sunday evening last, at the moment the church bell tolled for three o'clock—that bell which from time immemorial he had himself tolled regularly five or six times every day. There lives not this day a native of Annapolis, nay, hardly any one that has ever dwelt amongst, or sojourned without or borders, that will not on meeting his melancholy note, recall the well known sound of our church bell and the striking figure of the old man that has so punctually attended

to the precise moment of ringing the hour ever since the oldest of us can remember.

'Ere the church was a ruin, on the spot where the present edifice now stands, old Joseph was bell ringer. Not one man that ever has been a member of the Legislature, Executive or Superior Judiciary of the State of Maryland, not a student of St. John's College, or a scholar of our humbler schools, but will remember the well known summons which his bell gave them alternately to duties and to relaxation. Alas! Old Joseph rings no more . . .

But it was at grave digging, that the deceased enjoyed the distinction of having held an office longer than perhaps any man ever did, nay, possibly ever will do, in this State . . . In that single field [cemetery] is buried all social distinctions. Long before this field, now studded over with grave stones, on many of which the thick moss of a former century has accumulated, was disturbed to deposit the relics of the dead, was this old man our grave digger. Of all the vast concourse in this graveyard reposing, his hand has prepared and rounded the graves. At length, sinking under the accumulated weight of nearly one hundred years, he is quietly deposited as one amongst the multitude his labors had gathered together . . .

This obituary of Simmons sharply defines the aged sexton's character and includes anecdotes of his oddities and peculiarities.

When he had reached a centenarian's age, he was the object of interest to all. With his white hair flowing over his shoulders, his aged form tottering with the weight of years, his shackling step and the soberness of his occupation, he presented to the mind the apparition of Old Time himself, lacking only the emblematic scythe to make the picture complete.

It was such a character that gave a thrill of terror to the juvenile mind whenever he came in sight, for it was the belief of the children that if Simmons looked at one and said, "I want you," the day of doom for it was fixed. Having occasion then to pass the aged sexton, the children were wont to don their most courteous graces, and with unusual politeness to simper in the softest accents—"How do, Mr. Morgue?" This nickname, and that it was one the children were quite ignorant of, always infuriated Simmons, as the astonished children found by the sexton's vigorous replies that they had missed their mark, and had produced an effect just opposite from what they had intended.

The spirit of Simmons' occupation became more and more a part of him as his years grew apace. He had been known after somebody had offended him to pass an innocent gentleman on the street and to take a ghastly satisfaction in hissing at him, "I'll have you someday," in a tone that indicated that he thought, with him, remained the issues of life and death.

One incident has come down to us that does not reflect his character in an enviable light. There was in Annapolis one familiarity called, "Jeffrey Jig" (from whom Jeffrey's Point took its name), who with "Jinny Corncracker," his wife, lived at the foot of Duke of Gloucester street in a little hut so small they could not stand in it erect. Jeffrey periodically fell into a comatose state and was several times prepared for interment, but always awoke in time to prevent the funeral. On one occasion his resuscitation was deferred until he was placed in the grave. Then as the grim sexton threw in the clods of the valley, a noise was heard in the coffin. The bystanders said Jeffrey was alive. Hardly realizing, let us believe, that the dead was alive, Simmons continued to fill up the grave, tradition says with the remark: "He's got to die sometime: and if he was not dead, he ought to be."

St. Anne's Episcopal Church was Mr. Simmons's charge, where he helped with the upkeep, rang the steeple bell, and buried the parish dead. When the tall building in the center of Church Circle was first erected, the earth surrounding the structure was a much larger burial ground, where the noted gravedigger planted many of the city's most notable citizens. When the church's adjacent boneyard reached capacity, the church and town graveyard was moved to a larger space near Northwest Street along College Creek. Here Mr. Simmons continued to exercise his respected grave-digging talents. Over the course of many decades, the solitary digger deposited thousands of Annapolis residents into their final resting places.

When he died, Joe Simmons was buried in St. Margaret's Cemetery. However, some say his spirit has been seen leaning upon his shovel near his gravesite, perhaps thinking fondly of days gone by. There have been other reports of a longhaired stranger roaming among the gravestones that accent the rolling hills of St. Anne's Cemetery.

The back-row pew in St. Anne's Episcopal Church is another spot that has been suggested to catch a glimpse of Joe Morgue's spirit. There have been occasional sightings of an old man in disheveled clothing, sitting silently in the rear of the church. When people approach the long-bearded stranger, he quietly gets up and walks out (and sometimes through) the entrance doors, disappearing from sight.

Baltimore

Fort McHenry

"We have a number of ghost tales associated with Fort McHenry. And while we don't want to be known as a haunted fort, there's a point where the ghost stories and the folklore become a part of history." So said Vince Vaise, a Baltimore native and park ranger at the country's only National Monument and Historic Shrine, during a conversation in 2004.

Before we begin the ghost tales, it's important to understand Fort McHenry's historical significance. Francis Scott Key, a lawyer, witnessed the twenty-five-hour enemy bombardment of the city during the 1814 Battle of Baltimore. Less than a month earlier, the British had burned the president's home (Executive Mansion/White House) in Washington and planned to capture Baltimore, a major port city. Key was standing on the deck of a British ship on September 12 and 13. During the attack—when the British fleet fired nearly 1,800 shells at the fort—the mammoth 30-by-42-foot flag made by Mary Pickersgill remained flying high for all to see. Key was so inspired by the sight of the U.S. banner that he began writing the stirring poem that would serve as the words to our national anthem.

Like the unsuccessful British navy, the Crown's attacking land forces—after meeting extensive entrenchments and defensive fire on the outskirts of Baltimore City—decided to withdraw. On September

15, the frustrated invaders retreated and sailed south through the Chesapeake Bay. The war would be over a few months later.

While Fort McHenry would never experience another attack, it remained active as a political and military prison during the Civil War. During the latter years of World War I and afterwards, a three-thousand-bed army hospital was located around the fort. If it's true that tragedy, death, and sudden unfortunate events contribute to the presence of ghosts, Fort McHenry has good reason to be haunted.

During the British bombardment in September 1814, an incoming bomb exploded on the gun emplacement at Bastion 3. The direct hit killed members of the Maryland militia, including a lieutenant named Levi Clagett. Some people think his spirit appears occasionally at that site and also walks along the ramparts, sometimes referred to as "Clagett's Bastion." This location is one of five points that jut out from the star-shaped fort. Visitors and employees have reported sightings of a soldier, wearing a uniform appropriate to the 1814 era, walking in that area. A natural reaction to the sighting is to think that the figure in uniform is an actor or reenactor. However, when informed that there were no performers in costume on the grounds on that particular day, the visitors who spoke about the sightings are more than a little surprised.

A former park volunteer said he was leading a tour and mentioned Clagett's death, adding that the solider was considered the fort's most famous ghost. A woman in the group, who said she was a psychic, told the guide that a "messenger" was here as well. Not understanding the comment, the guide asked for an explanation, trying to figure out what kind of "message" the woman was referring to. Shaking her head, the psychic said she had not mentioned anything about a message. She added that a soldier named "Messenger" was killed during the battle. The psychic said that soldier was, at that moment, standing behind the tour guide.

Instinctively, the shocked guide turned to his right, but the psychic said the specter was on his other side. The group of visitors became very quiet and watched the guide look over his other shoulder and react as if shaking off a sudden chill. After the tour, the volunteer looked up the fort's records and said he found that a soldier named Messenger also had died defending the fort.

"From that point on," the guide said, "I made sure to include Messenger's name in every tour I give. But I think he still may be around, hanging out in one of the old barracks buildings." The guide also recalled an evening when he was locking up the fort and heard the sound of heavy footsteps coming down the stairs in an empty building. "I took the steps two at a time and ran out of there as fast as I could," he said, without showing any embarrassment.

Years ago, park staff that worked in a two-story building that for years served as an enlisted men's barracks claimed to have seen a woman dressed in white walking on the building's second floor. They also have reported being disturbed by doors and windows being slammed shut and, at other times, left open. They also have arrived at work and found their office furniture had been moved. There have been sightings of a woman looking out from a second-floor window and reports of footsteps on the porch of the enlisted soldiers' quarters.

A Maryland artist was in this same building reviewing some historical documents. As he walked through a small doorway, he said, "I got hit like I was struck with a frying pan. It was while I was going through the doorframe. I mean, I was out cold. I was gone, out like a light."

The artist said he knew at the time that he had not simply bumped his head against the top of the frame or accidentally ran into a low beam. When the park ranger escort returned, the artist related what had happened. The ranger told the artist he was surprised at the force of the attack, but did not seem surprised that an unusual event had occurred.

"That's our resident ghost," the ranger told the dazed visitor. The park worker then shared his own story about being pushed down the stairs by a woman dressed in early-nineteenth-century clothing. It's been suggested that this ghost had been a sergeant's wife, and that her husband and two children had died from a plague or epidemic that occurred in Baltimore during the 1820s.

Recalling his personal attack experience, the artist said, "I had no cuts, no bruises, no lumps, no nothing. But it was powerful. I hit my knees, and I was face-first down on the floor. I attribute it to the lady ghost."

Perhaps the fort's most often told haunted tale involves the spirit of twenty-eight-year-old Pvt. John Drew, who had been assigned to guard duty along the fort's outer battery on November 14, 1880. Unfortunately for the young soldier, he was discovered in the morning asleep at his post.

Drew was ordered to a cell in the guardhouse, which is located near the fort's entrance building. Upset that his army career was over and his comrades would never give him any respect, Drew smuggled a musket into his cell. Soon after locking the prisoner up, the guards heard a shot from the area of Drew's confinement. When they unlocked the barred metal door, they found that Drew had placed the muzzle of the weapon in his mouth and had used his toe to pull the trigger.

Visitors claim they have felt a distinct chill in the cell where Drew took his own life. Others say they have sighted a figure, dressed in a long watch coat or cape and wearing a military-style cap, walking the same outer battery where the young soldier had been assigned more than 125 years ago. One park ranger slept overnight in the cell on the anniversary of Drew's death, but the employee said nothing unusual occurred.

Another guide, however, did experience an unusual event. While dressed as a reenactor in period clothing and sitting in Drew's cell awaiting visitors, the man heard footsteps in the hallway outside the cramped chamber. After a few moments had passed and no tourists advanced toward the cell where he was waiting, the volunteer shouted, "I'm down here! Come on in!" But no one came his way. Thinking he had not really heard any steps in the area, he sat back against the stone wall to relax and wait for the arrival of the next group of tourists. Again, after a few moments, the sound of footsteps occurred. As before, he shouted out from where he was waiting. As before, no one headed his way.

"After that," he recalled, "I got up and left. Went outside to wait. I didn't feel comfortable in Drew's cell at that time. I can't explain what happened, but I know I wasn't imagining hearing those sounds. Something was out there that day. I've been there since, and each time I listen carefully for those footsteps, but it hasn't happened again."

There's also a report that in the 1970s, while checking out the fort in preparation for a visit by then-President Gerald R. Ford, Secret Service agents spotted a uniformed figure carrying a rifle, which disappeared suddenly. The figure had been sighted on one of the building's porches. The agents were concerned because the unexplained sighing had occurred after the security unit had sealed the fort and made sure it was clear of visitors. When one of the park staff suggested it might be Levi Clagett or John Drew, it's said the worried security staff asked for the addresses of the suspects. When they learned that the park ranger had been referring to the park's resident ghosts who lived in the fort's cell and ramparts, the federal agents rolled their eyes and declined to follow up on the possible paranormal sources of the sighting.

Over the years, documentaries such as The History Channel's *Haunted Baltimore* and numerous newspaper and magazine articles have spread tales of unusual events at the Baltimore fortification that apparently continue to occur.

"A lot of military posts have legends," Vaise said. "Over the years, the stories become part of each site's history. I think that during the Civil War, the troops probably sat here at Fort McHenry and told ghost stories and legends about the Revolutionary War and War of 1812."

Sentry Sighting

During the Victorian era, ghost stories were even more popular than they are today. At that time, supernatural tales were publicized in major daily newspapers and read with keen interest by an audience eager for entertaining reports of life "beyond the pale." In August 1904, the headline "Stories of Ghosts at Fort McHenry," printed in Baltimore's *Sun* newspaper, caught the eye and stimulated the imagination of that periodical's large readership.

Acknowledging that all historic places "lay claim to a ghost or two," the unnamed writer reported soldiers stationed at the famous fort often joked that their ghosts were rather modest, and their spirits were reluctant to show themselves—except to men who had been known to empty the bottles at local saloons while not training or standing guard. But these "temperance ghosts" were not above "giving the men on duty severe frights at times."

In the section of Fort McHenry's "old fort," where the dungeons are located, several British spies had been hanged during previous wars. Their lifeless bodies dangled in the breeze from hooks that were placed at either end of a pathway that passed through the section of the building containing the old dungeons. "And it is here," the reporter noted, "the superstitious solders say, that the ghosts love to prowl and moan. Others say it is only the wind howling through the bars of the dungeon windows, but the others incredulously shake their heads."

Older solders stationed for some time at the fort told the *Sun* writer that during the Spanish-American War, sentries were posted all around the fort. One of the sentry posts included the old fort, where a guard was assigned to pass along the road between the well-known haunted dungeons.

One dark night, a soldier of the Sixth Artillery was walking his post as the eerie atmosphere of "heavy dark clouds shadowing the sky, the low, groaning wind and the gruesome environments seemed to work on the fellow's mind." Trembling with fear, he passed repeatedly below the spots were the British spies had hung. No doubt, in his nervous state, the young man imagined their dangling corpses swaying in the wind with stretched necks and lifeless eyes.

In early morning, an unexpected rifle shot broke through the quiet in and around the fort. Immediately, guards from other posts converged toward the sound of the blast. As they raced to aid their fellow soldier, a loud scream carried through the dark night air. Upon arriving at the site of the trouble, the experienced sergeant of the guard called out for the sentry assigned to that particular post. But he was nowhere in sight. Looking down at the abandoned rifle lying on the path, again the sergeant shouted for the missing sentry, urging him to show himself if he were able.

From the safety of a bombproof bunker, the young man slowly appeared. He was visibly shaken and equally embarrassed to be the focus of attention by his superiors and fellow soldiers. When asked to explain the reason for the shot and his absence from his post, the young recruit replied, with some hesitation, "Ghost. A ghost!"

After his superior demanded a more complete explanation, the frightened soldier said that while he was walking past the dungeon, a faint blue vapor arose from the ground. Thinking he was imagining the vision, the soldier wiped his eyes, opened them and stared intently at the strange, colored mist. Slowly, he said, the cloud took on the shape of a man with a rope around his neck. The astonished and terrified sentry said the apparition's eyes protruded from the face, creating a horrible scene.

"The soldier," the *Sun* reported, "saw the apparition raise one long, shadowy arm and utter a long doleful moan. That brought the sentry to his senses and, firing his rifle at the ghost, he dropped the gun and ran."

The other men of that night's guard waited until their comrade had finished his verbal report "and then each laughed a big horse laugh. Disgusted, the sergeant detailed another man to take the ghost seer's place." The replacement sentry kept a keen eye out for ghosts throughout the balance of the night, but no other unusual sightings of blue vapors or wild-eyed British corpses were reported.

Gallows Ghost

One of the most satisfying experiences is discovering a strong link between an interesting haunting and a historical event. An excellent example of this connection came to light during a conversation at Fort McHenry with Scott Sumpter Sheads, a longtime park ranger and noted author. Sheads's many books, all of which are well-respected historical records of life in Baltimore, include *Fort McHenry: A History; Fort McHenry and Baltimore's Harbor Defenses*; and *Baltimore During the Civil War*.

While Scott has some passing interest in folklore, he's much more concerned with history and with discovering the origins of certain folktales and anecdotes. He admitted that he's not one who shares ghost stories for the sake of entertainment or amusement, and he hasn't spent much time following up on the many paranormal and unexplained reports related to the fort. But as we sat in an office in the historic building that had once housed enlisted soldiers and their families, Scott recalled one particular and rather fascinating incident. He said it had occurred on the fort grounds and been reported directly to him, more than twenty years ago.

Outside the walls of Fort McHenry, in a large open field near the park entrance, stands the twenty-four-foot-tall statue of Orpheus, the Greek mythological figure associated with poetry and music. The statue was erected in 1914 to mark the centennial of the writing of the "Star-Spangled Banner" and the successful defense of Baltimore against the invading British.

This most unusual report of a ghost sighting at Fort McHenry involves an object (the Orpheus statue) and an event (a murder during the Civil War) that at first glance might seem to have little in common. "A lady came up to me in November," Scott said, recalling the decades-old event. "It was a foggy day, and she was visibly shaken."

He said the woman was in her fifties, well-spoken, and told him an unusual story he had never heard before. She said, "I hope you don't think I'm crazy, but I saw what appeared to be a soldier." When Scott asked where her sighting occurred, the woman pointed toward the Orpheus statue. Then she said, "But the man was not on the ground. He appeared to be in uniform, but floating above the ground, in the air."

Scott said he thanked the woman and told her he would make a note of it. However, he did not mention that her sighting had occurred where the fort's gallows had stood during the Civil War. Nor did he explain that her mysterious soldier could have been the spirit of Pvt. Joseph Kuhne, who was executed on March 7, 1862.

According to military records, Kuhne—who was from Company F, Second Maryland Regiment, U.S.A.—had been found guilty of the murder of 2nd Lt. J. Davis Whitson. As reported in Scott's book, *Baltimore During the Civil War*, a wooden scaffold was erected outside the Star Fort on the parade grounds, and a black walnut coffin was placed beneath it. Nearly four thousand federal troops arrived, and residents of Baltimore came to witness the "grim display of a military execution—the first ever at Fort McHenry."

In the *Sun*'s newspaper account, reprinted in Scott's book, the ceremony was described in the very detailed style of the times:

> Shortly after twelve o'clock there emerged a wagon from the gateway of the fort, guarded by a strong military force. The condemned man was in the wagon, and the procession moved with slow and solemn tread towards the dread instrument of death, then while the accompanying band played the "Death March" . . . The rope was adjusted on the neck of Kuhne by the acting provost marshal . . . In another instant the trip fell with a dull, heavy sound, and Joseph Kuhne was suspended in mid-air . . . the drop was only about eighteen inches

but for a few moments no motion was observable. After which his contortions were horrible for a minute, after which he hung still and lifeless.

Park Ranger Vince Vaise said, "On misty days a gallows appears in the area of the Orpheus statue." Was it Joseph Kuhne's spirit that the park visitor reported seeing that foggy day? There is no way to tell, but perhaps the sighting was more than the woman's imagination or mere coincidence.

Sequin

According to storyteller and author Jane Yolen, America has many ghost legends associated with particular locales. However, the ghost tale involving the vanishing hitchhiker "is probably the most popular ghost story still in circulation today."

Urban legend expert Jan Harold Brunvand, author of several books on folklore, including one entitled *The Vanishing Hitchhiker*, said settings for this often-told tale are international. He added that the story's supernatural twist has made it one of the most popular stories told in settings throughout the world.

The mysterious hitchhiker is a man or woman who accepts a ride from a stranger. Over time and various tellings, the vehicle has been a horse, buggy, automobile, delivery truck, motorcycle, van, or tractor-trailer. Other elements of the mysterious tale have involved a young ghost, a nearby cemetery, an article of clothing, and, at times, a special name that over the years remains associated with the story. As a result, the local identity often relates to a particular version in a specific setting.

In the Baltimore account, the mysterious maiden is named "Sequin." Her story takes place along Route 40, and the version contains many of the classic elements of the well-known and often repeated vanishing hitchhiker legend.

Old Route 40, the nation's first intercontinental highway, begins at the Atlantic Ocean and ends in the mountains of Utah. It's a famous road that leaves the New Jersey beach sand, passes through farmland,

and travels through small towns, villages, and major cities, including Baltimore.

In the area where the highway passes the neighborhoods of East Baltimore, reports circulated about a young, blond-haired girl who appears wearing a low-cut, blue-sequined cocktail dress. Some say the story originated when a Sunday school teacher told his students about a young girl with violet eyes and blond hair who would wait outside the church to meet the boys from his class when their lessons were completed. Over time, the attractive young lady dated every one of the boys, and people in the area began describing the girl as immoral.

One Sunday, after the services were over, the fair-haired girl was seated in the back of the church. Some say the girl was there because she heard the preacher was giving away clothes that had been donated by members of the community. When the cleric opened one of the boxes and pulled out a flimsy, blue-sequined party dress, the girl ran down the center aisle, grabbed the fancy garment, and rushed out of the church onto the street. After that incident, the girl was always seen wearing that same blue cocktail-style dress, no matter what the occasion, time of day, or condition of the weather.

That winter the weather was brutal, and the Sunday school teacher and neighbors were shocked to learn that the young girl was discovered dead in the snow. She had been wearing only the blue, lightweight, sequined dress. Everyone agreed she had frozen to death.

A few weeks after her funeral, people in the neighborhood began reporting sightings of the deceased girl, and these glimpses usually occurred late in the evening along Route 40, not far from the church. Initially, no one paid serious attention to the rumors. Anyone with an ounce of sense knew that such an event was impossible.

Several years later, two local college students were driving along the main thoroughfare heading for a dance. They said they saw a pretty girl standing on a corner wearing a blue cocktail dress. They pulled over to the corner, talked to her for a while, and invited her to come with them to the dance. She agreed, and both she and the boys had a wonderful time. She told them that her name was Sequin.

On the ride home through East Baltimore, the girl, who was in the back seat, said she was cold. One of the boys gave her his long tan overcoat. When they arrived at her address, she got out of the car, raced up the steps, waved good-bye, and disappeared into her house.

The next day, when the boy realized he had not gotten back his coat, the two friends returned to the girl's home. An elderly woman answered the door. When the boys said they were looking for Sequin, the woman frowned, shook her head, and replied, "This is rather strange. You two must be old friends of hers. You see, she's been dead for more than ten years."

Shocked, the boys thought they had come to the wrong house, but the woman assured them that they were at the right place. "They found her exactly twelve years ago, last night. I thought someone would be coming here today. I get a visitor each year, usually on a weekend around the anniversary date of her departure."

The woman explained that Sequin was her daughter's nickname. Everyone called her that because she always wore the same blue cocktail dress. The woman said her daughter's real name was Molly, and then told the story of how the girl's body was found near Route 40, frozen to death.

The mother gave the boys directions to the cemetery where they would find the girl's grave. "It's one of the smaller stones, but it has the most beautiful little angel on top of it," the girl's mother said, beginning to cry. "We chose an angel because that's what my Molly, my little girl, was to me. She was a precious little kind and sweet angel. She never hurt anyone. She was just confused. Lived in a world of her own, poor little thing. But it hurts me that she's still not at peace, that she still has that wild and restless side, even after all this time."

The boys thought the old woman was crazy, but they had time to kill and decided to check out her strange story. They drove to the cemetery, followed the directions, and after a bit of searching located Molly's gravesite. The stone was surrounded by taller monuments. But hanging from the girl's marker, and draped over the top of the stone and beneath the angel, was the missing overcoat that the young boy had loaned to Sequin on the ride home from the dance, just the night before.

Haunted Chair

Mark was waiting for me at the diner on Route 40, two miles east of the Baltimore city limits. It was a perfect place to meet a big-city cop: stainless steel siding, neon signs, Formica tables, and a jukebox playing oldies. The coffee cups were plain, with thin gold and brown lines circling the top edge, just like you'd expect in a vintage, 'round-the-clock greasy spoon. Mark wasn't a surprise either. You could easily pick him out from among the small number of patrons who were still there at midnight.

He was a big man, well over six feet tall, with a heavy frame that filled the booth to the right of the cashier. He had been a Baltimore policeman for more than twenty years. Looking at him, it would be hard to imagine a situation where he would be smaller than the person he was pursuing.

We had arranged the meeting for the end of his shift. With court appearances, unexpected overtime, staggered shift work, and limited windows of opportunity for definite time off, it was hard to get a time when we could get together. We grabbed what time we could, and this was it. Besides, the topic of our conversation was one that Mark did not want to talk about in the district headquarters or at his home. Our subject was ghosts, sort of.

Either way, Mark stressed, it was not a subject that he believed in or even cared much about. But, as he had told me over the phone, what happened to him did happen. And after several years, he still didn't have any logical explanation for the strange events.

After brief introductions and greetings, he ordered me a coffee. The waitress came and went, and we got down to the nitty gritty. "Look," he began, "I've been a cop for a good while, and I've had more than my share of unusual incidents that often seemed to start out well but turn out bad. But there was nothing ever like this."

"This" being a bizarre occurrence that happened on a hot August night, when he would rather have been home, watching the Orioles and enjoying a cold one as the AC blasted. "Me and this new kid, Ralph or Rick, I don't remember his name now. But it doesn't matter; he's not on the force anymore. He bailed out a few years ago. We got this call to go to Liberty Heights. I'll never forget that night. It happened in a big old house, three stories high with a wide porch, standing in the middle of a pretty big lot at the end of a block."

As they started to approach the front door, Mark said the two men heard noise, like furniture being thrown around, coming from upstairs. "We figured there was a riot going on in there," Mark said, "and we were ready to fly through the door and charge up the stairs. But this small lady, who opened the front door, led us into the living room, just to the right of the entrance hallway. The whole family— the father, mother, and three kids—are all huddled together, on the couch in the living room, and they look like they're scared to death."

Mark recalled that the father walked over to him and said the noise had started suddenly, about an hour earlier. Everyone in the house ran downstairs, and he called the police. The man and his wife thought some troublemakers had broken a window and had gotten in from the fire escape on the second floor. The family was afraid the intruders were destroying the house. And since they were renting the place, they were worried they would have to pay for the repairs—in addition to being scared out of their minds of being robbed or hurt.

Mark and Rick told the family to shut the living room door and wait for them to return. Slowly, the two officers ascended the stairs toward the second floor.

"Now, before I go on," Mark said, "I want to tell you that I don't believe in this supernatural stuff. Never did, anyway. But as we moved up the steps, we both heard banging. It sounded like a gang was up there smashing up the place."

But as soon as Mark, who was in the lead, reached the second-floor hall landing, the noise stopped suddenly and totally. "It was as if it just disappeared," Mark said, sipping his coffee and shaking his head. He said both he and Rick checked every room together, looked in the closets, and shined their flashlights under the beds. "We even pulled back the shower curtains and then made sure all the windows were locked and secure. I tell you, nobody and nothing was up there. We didn't find a single thing."

As they started to return downstairs, the noise started up again. This time it was coming from the third floor, and it was just as loud as it was before. "We looked at each other, drew our weapons," said Mark, "and I nodded in the direction of the stairs to the third floor.

We went up, slowly, approaching the latest noise that was going full force. I swear, I was sure we were going to find at least three or four guys up there tearing the hell outta the place. And just like before, as soon as I put my foot on the third-floor hallway, the noise stopped, totally."

Mark and Rick checked every room, even though most were empty of furniture. All the windows were locked. Again, nothing was found in any of the closets or rooms. "Thinking back now," Mark said, "I remember thinking to myself there was only this one thing that was really strange. In the largest, practically empty room, there was this huge single chair. It had curved arms, a bright red seat and a lot of carving on the back, like birds' or angels' wings. It was sitting by itself, all alone, way off in a corner like a king's throne. It was really far away from the door. When I looked in that room, it just seemed odd, almost as if the chair was staring at me. I remember thinking that exact thought at the time. Then I laughed to myself and put it out of my mind and shut the door, slamming it tight and hearing the latch catch."

Not finding or hearing anything else, Mark began descending the steps to the second floor and Rick fell in behind. They had holstered their weapons, and neither officer was talking. Mark said they were listening carefully, in case the disturbance started up again. When they got down to the second-floor landing, it was still completely quiet.

"But when we get halfway down the last set of steps, between the second and first floors," Mark said, "and we hear this sound, like something is falling over itself and heading downstairs, in our direction. It was getting louder, sounding sorta like a person was falling down the steps. But it wasn't a person hitting the steps, it was more like wood crashing against wood and scraping and screeching. And it was getting a lot closer."

Abruptly, Mark stopped talking, and I waited for what seemed a long period of silence. With a weak smile, he looked up at me across the booth of the diner and whispered, "I tell ya, I was scared by now. Rather than go back upstairs and look around again, I turned and told Rick we're going down, and fast. So we continued heading quickly toward the first floor. The next thing I knew, Rick was falling on top of my back and knocking me down. And I'm face-down and flat on my chest, and something is flying over my body, heading down, right for the main-floor hallway."

When Mark and Rick pulled themselves up, the chair—the solitary chair that Mark had seen in the large room on the third floor, the one in the room behind the door he had closed tightly—was facing him at the foot of the stairs.

"I know this may sound crazy now," Mark said, "but we both drew our weapons and slowly headed toward the chair. I was going to blast the hell outta it if it moved again. I yelled for the family to stay inside the living room and not come out, and they didn't make a sound." Mark let out a short laugh. "They didn't come out. I guess I didn't have to tell them twice to stay put."

The two officers grabbed the chair, lifted it up, looked underneath and moved it around. There was no explanation for what had occurred.

"We tied the chair with clothesline to the banister in the hall," said Mark, "and we went upstairs and checked the whole building again. There were no drop ceilings where someone could hide, no way anyone could have gotten in and fooled us. It was just us and that damn chair. But I remember shutting the third-floor door tightly," Mark added. "That chair couldn't get out on its own. Someone, something, or some force had to help it get loose."

Mark and Rick agreed not to call for a backup unit. They wrote up the report as a minor domestic disturbance that had been settled; therefore, no arrest or further action would have been necessary. "We told the family that we were getting out of there and that they should, too," Mark said. "In fact, we drove them to a relative's house to spend the night. I went back once to check on them. It was a few months later, but they had moved out and there was another family living there."

Mark paused. "I was tempted to ask the new people about anything strange that they may have seen or experienced," said the officer, "but they didn't volunteer anything when I was there, so I let it go. I did peek inside, just in case I saw the chair sitting there, but didn't see anything familiar. It was gone. I guess it probably walked off on its own one night."

Mark took a final sip of coffee, said nothing else, and went for his wallet to leave a tip. I waited, letting him decide what he wanted to say next. "You can believe it or not," he added. "That's the way it was, and it won't change. I don't know how, or why, it happened, or even why it was me that happened to be there that night. Just luck of the draw, I guess. I gave up figuring out why or what all happened in that place a long time ago."

Then, standing up to leave, Mark looked down and said, "Go ahead and use it, the story in your book. Maybe you or somebody else can come up with some kind of answer that will make some sense. If you ever do, give me a call."

I thought of contacting Mark, telling him he may have encountered a haunted object, a possessed possession. But since he said he didn't believe in that sort of supernatural, paranormal stuff, I haven't bothered to get in touch with him. In his case, I figured it was better to let sleeping chairs alone.

Piano Man

Take an old, nineteenth-century building that originally housed a men's fraternal organization, add a theater group featuring dynamic and experimental productions, and toss in a restless presence that seems drawn to perform on the building's piano—and you've got the makings of unusual story featuring a talented and friendly ghost.

On West Preston Street, several blocks north of the Washington Monument, the Baltimore Theatre Project presents festivals and performances in an ornate building built in 1883 as a men's club for the Improved Order of Heptasoths (IOH). In the late nineteenth century, that area of the city was home to a large number of clubs, fraternal groups, and societies.

The Heptasoths' assembly hall and lecture room now serves as the theater's stage and audience area, but IOH logos and emblems are engraved into the building's interior walls. They also can be seen from the street on the building's stained-glass windows and in the brown capstone over the front entranceway.

The piano player tale has been passed along for decades, and these unexplained incidents—involving the sudden sounds of music or sightings of a stranger playing the piano—occur two or three times a year. The comments are at different times and from different people, who could not have collaborated on their stories.

People would go into a room to rehearse a scene, and immediately come out and report that someone playing the piano was using the practice space. This latter situation sometimes caused people to become upset because they had scheduled the space and were annoyed that a piano player had cut into their time.

The apparition was reported to be male, tall, and wearing a suit and tie. While no one had ever identified the song being played, the music was described as a rag, which would have been popular during the 1920s. During that era, the IOH building was used as a dance hall, so the ghost might be associated with an event that occurred around that time. One person who heard the phantom performer identified the music as a work by Schubert.

This unexplained musical activity would occur anywhere in the building—the main theater, backstage, or out in the lobby—since the piano was on wheels and was moved around quite a bit. It also didn't matter if a piano was replaced; the ghostly musician played on any version of the instrument that was available in the building.

"No one was ever terrified or frightened," a former Theatre Project employee said. "They would just ask, 'Who was that guy?' One person said, 'I was finishing up my rehearsal and a guy came in to play the piano. And he was so good.' They may have thought it was peculiar, but no one was ever scared."

During an interview in 2004, the Theatre Project's director at that time admitted that she had never encountered the pianist and that there had been no unusual reports for the last few years. Despite the phantom pianist's recent reluctance to perform in public, his story seems to have taken on a mysterious life of its own.

Poe Toaster

No visit to Baltimore is complete without pausing beside the grave of Edgar Allan Poe in Westminster Cemetery. The graveyard is at the busy corner of Greene and Fayette streets in the heart of the city— and Poe's distinctive marble monument draws the attention of both tourists and passing locals.

On any day there's a good possibility one will find wreaths, individual flowers, bouquets, and even trinkets and coins resting at the base of the noted writer's tomb. When I stopped at the site, a single penny had been set with care inside the "O" of Poe's last name. A green plastic shamrock, other coins, and small handmade sprays of dried flowers rested against the low ledge at the memorial's base.

Obviously, some of these long-gone visitors had come prepared. Others, seeing the tokens, had dug into their pockets or purses and joined in the custom using whatever they had at hand. Perhaps the visitors wanted to make their presence known, to feel they had made a connection with the famous American writer. Whatever their motivation, they certainly had felt an urge to leave something, no matter how slight or trivial, behind.

One cannot deny that there's a magic associated with Edgar Allan Poe. The interest and fascination with the writer begins in the early years of school, when millions of young learners are introduced to the mysterious man. His captivating poems and eerie stories—of thumping hearts and bodies sealed behind basement walls—and other themes of suspense, romance, and terror have been the basis for oral tales, comic books, plays, and feature films.

But imagine the reaction to Poe's innovative style and controversial works during the days when they were written, at a time when readers and proper ladies and gents in polite society were not accustomed to speaking of grave robbers and murderers. It was a time when reading Poe was a daring act, an invitation to sneak a peek into life on the dark side—and as a result of his taboo subjects, he became a sensation.

Many of America's East Coast cities claim the literary icon as their own. In the Bronx, New York, the Poe Cottage proclaims it is the author's final home, where he lived from 1846 to1849. In Richmond, the Poe Museum boasts the "finest collection of Edgar Allan Poe's manuscripts." Philadelphia hosts the Edgar Allan Poe Historic Site, administered by the National Park Service. The University of Virginia, where the writer attended classes, is proud of its "Raven Society." But Baltimore—site of the scribe's home and, more importantly, city of the author's death, tomb, and corpse—lays rightful claim to the most permanent association with America's first master of horror.

In 1849, when his career was somewhat successful, but nothing like it would become after his death, Poe stopped briefly in Baltimore. It is believed he had been traveling on a train from Richmond to New York City. During his stay, Poe mysteriously disappeared and was later found in a delirious state beside a saloon on Lombard Street, in the city's Cornbeef Row area. He died four days later in a room in Washington Medical College/Church Home and Hospital, which was closed in 2000.

Several theories have been offered as to how and why Poe died—including rabies, depression, alcoholism, drugs, an enzyme deficiency, a beating by angry potential in-laws, and murder because of unpaid debts or at the hands of Freemasons, to name a few.

Poe's remains were interred in the Old Western Burial Ground (now known as Westminster Burying Ground), but his burial plot was located in the rear of the churchyard and, for the most part, unmarked. In November 1875, twenty-six years after his initial burial, his remains were unearthed and moved within the same graveyard to the current location at the corner of Greene and Fayette streets. It is said this transfer was executed to accommodate the steady flow of admirers that wanted to visit the popular author's gravesite.

During an interview for the History Channel documentary *Haunted Baltimore*, Jeff Jerome, curator of Baltimore's Poe House and Museum, explained, "After the Civil War, Poe's fame exploded. Unfortunately, you couldn't see his grave because the gates were locked. In 1875, they moved him to the location near the main entrance. Even if the gates were locked, you could still look through the gates and still see the grave of the famous poet Edgar Allan Poe." A gravestone with the symbol of a raven marks Poe's resting place. The newer, larger, and more ornate monument was financed in part with pennies collected from Baltimore schoolchildren.

Not surprisingly, even in death Poe has the ability to generate additional mysteries. Some conspiracy theorists claim that the author's body was stolen from its grave soon after his original burial in 1849. Others suggest that Poe is not buried at the second gravesite because the gravediggers pulled up the wrong coffin during the exhumation in 1875; others allege portions of his body had been left behind during the transfer.

So, does the author still rest below the tomb bearing a sculpture of a solitary bird, encircled by his famous phrase "Quoth the Raven Nevermore"?

A mysterious gravesite visitor may know the answer, but the anonymous character—known as the "Poe Toaster"—never lingers long enough to engage in conversation. Since 1949 (the one hundredth anniversary of Poe's death), every January 19 (the date of Poe's birth), between the hours of midnight and 6 A.M., an unidentified visitor has entered Westminster Cemetery. Jeff Jerome and a few select "grave watchers" arrive at the adjacent church building several hours before midnight to witness the ceremonial tribute from the windows and warmth of historic Westminster Hall.

Meanwhile, outside, along the streets surrounding the graveyard, groups of people take positions inside vehicles and in lawn chairs, hoping to spot the anonymous visitor when he arrives. From about 10 P.M. on January 18 and into the mid-morning hours of January 19, eager amateur watchers wander back and forth along Baltimore's center-city streets surrounding the cemetery. Many of the sentries are wrapped in blankets, wear cold-weather gear, and carry hot cups of liquid refreshment.

Other than the six-hour window between midnight and sunrise, no one knows the precise time of the Toaster's arrival. Those present watch for a man, who in the past has arrived alone and is often dressed in black except for a white scarf that covers much of his face. With practiced ease, he enters the churchyard and stops beside Poe's original grave bearing the carving of "The Raven," located at the rear of the cemetery.

The anonymous visitor then performs his annual tribute of kneeling to place three red roses and a partially filled bottle of French cognac, from which he pours some of the contents into a glass. As he has done each year for more than six decades, the stranger raises his goblet, toasting the famous American author. There is only speculation about the meaning of the roses and spirits. Some think the flowers are for each of the three bodies resting beneath the family plot—Edgar, his wife and cousin Virginia Clemm Poe, and his mother-in-law and aunt Maria Clemm. No one knows the significance of the French liqueur.

It's believed that several years ago, when the original Toaster became too old to continue the tradition, he passed the torch onto his son. Now a younger man has taken over the responsibility of carrying on the mysterious graveyard ritual. At times, he has left notes along with his floral tribute. One year a message stated, "the torch has been passed." No one, including Baltimore's longtime Poe museum curator, knows the identity of the secretive caller. But as is the case with many of the stories and events related to Poe, the reasons for this unique, six-decade Baltimore custom and the identities of those involved remain a mystery. And that's probably how Poe would have wanted it to remain—forevermore.

Author's Note: On Edgar Allan Poe's 201st birthday, January 19, 2010, the Poe Toaster did not appear at the author's grave, disappointing local fans and others who had come from as far as Texas, Massachusetts, and Georgia. No one, including Jeff Jerome, curator of the Poe House and Museum, had a definitive answer as to why the Toaster had broken the six-decade-long tradition. A sudden illness, a personal emergency, or car trouble were among the excuses offered as possibilities. Jerome suggested the Toaster might have decided the bicentennial anniversary of Poe's birthday held in 2009 may have been an appropriate time to end the custom. In an interview with the *Baltimore Sun*, the curator said he would continue the annual January 19 vigil through 2012. "After two years," he said, "if he doesn't show up, I think we can safely assume the tribute has ended."

Secretive Spirits of Fell's Point

Fell's Point is the one place in Baltimore where ghost hunters and tourists can sample a smorgasbord of ephemeral delights. In a fair number of the restored historic buildings—particularly those housing pubs, restaurants, and saloons—strange events have been reported. Over time, they've developed into stories about friendly spirits that seem very much at home in the neighborhood near the water. But that's not surprising, since many of Fell's Point's buildings have a colonial-era appearance and also operate as taverns and dining sites, just as they did hundreds of years ago. This probably has made their unseen guests comfortable in their restored surroundings.

Many people think the Inner Harbor, a mile to the west of Fell's Point, has always been the center of Baltimore, but that isn't so. The glitzy, modern shopping district, with stadiums, a lighthouse, harbor tours, and the historic USS *Constellation*, is a relatively recent creation meant to lure tourists into downtown. In the early 1700s, Fell's Point was Baltimore's hub. The thriving, working-class waterfront community—established by the Fells, a family of merchants and shipbuilders—was filled with merchant shops, bars, boardinghouses, brothels, and boatyards. The cargo business and nearly twenty shipbuilding yards attracted an odd assortment of characters, ranging from wealthy landowners and businessmen to deckhands and artisans, plus those who made their living serving meals and offering entertainment. To those returning from or heading out to sea, the bustling village named after William Fell was the place to be.

Fell, an English immigrant, founded the site between 1726 and 1730, recognizing its value as a deepwater port. In the 1770s, William's son, Edward, laid out the streets and gave them such English names as Thames and Shakespeare, which exist to this day.

Fell's Point shipbuilding increased dramatically during the American Revolution, and the industry would continue for a number of decades. During the War of 1812, more American ships were needed, and the Fell's Point shipyards were kept busy with orders from Congress. When shipbuilding declined in the 1830s, the area became known as a warehousing center. Later, maritime steam engines overshadowed sail power, and the wooden shipbuilders at Fell's Point were sucked into a long downward spiral that would change their lives and livelihoods. By 1960, more than 225 years since its optimistic beginnings, the area was showing signs of urban neglect. But two decades of community effort and the establishment of preservation societies enabled the neighborhood to survive and restore many of its buildings. Soon Fell's Point became a desirable residential neighborhood, as well as a living history center and popular tourist attraction.

Some believe that along the cobblestone streets, and within the walls of old bars and boardinghouses, those who played a role in the neighborhood's colorful history have remained. Some residents and business owners believe that, at times, these souls from the past make their presence known. If that is correct, there are probably ghost stories on every corner and in every old saloon within Fell's Point. Here are just a few.

Laura Norris, the owner of Bertha's Bar and Restaurant, shared a number of unusual tales associated with the building that was constructed in the late 1700s. Paranormal activity has been noted in the upstairs apartment, where a tenant's cat would freeze to a halt and the animal's fur would stand up across its back. The creature would not move a muscle for an unusually long period of time. Another area on that floor hosts a spacious dance studio, with a large, mirror-covered wall. A worker, walking through the dance hall at 6 A.M., saw a reflection in the mirror of a woman, dressed in black and wearing a big hat. The worker thought "it was an actual visage of person," Laura recalled during a 2004 interview. There also has been a sighting of a male figure in a large hat and dark cloak standing on the nearby stairway.

A waiter reported a sighting involving a little girl, skipping and causing a rhythmic sound in a corner on the second floor. When a local paranormal group conducted an investigation, one of its members noted the spirit of a little girl upstairs in a storeroom near a window. It's believed that the area of the sighting was a closet during the period when the building was a brothel. Possibly, the spirit of the girl still stands where she had been told to hide and remain by her mother, who may have been dealing with an irate customer.

An out-of-town family having lunch asked if the place was haunted. The waiter replied, "This whole neighborhood is haunted. This is the most haunted part of town." The startled customer pointed to a spot nearby, identified as Table 5, and said he had seen an older man, dressed in overalls and with a beard, smoking a pipe. The man looked like a fisherman. But when another customer walked past the area, the old fisherman just disappeared.

Visitors to the Cat's Eye Pub take note of its "Wall of Death," featuring photos of former employees and customers that have passed on. Bar regulars admit that on occasion the place "gets a bit spirited." In particular, there's a history of things falling off the walls, such as model ships and pictures—and some objects even fly across the room. Sometimes it seems they are targeting certain individuals. One occasion involved a bartender who had been talking unflatteringly about a former owner. Within a few moments, a small photograph of an area scene dropped off the wall and landed on her head.

The Whistling Oyster, a saloon featured in the History Channel documentary *Haunted Baltimore*, claims a fair amount of unexplained activity. "There are spirits in this bar that are not contained in bottles," owner Read Hopkins said during a 2004 interview.

The oldest part of the building dates to the 1760s. Some of the early owners had owned slaves, but these workers lived about a block away. Perhaps one of the slaves found his way back and has reappeared in modern times, since a customer reported seeing a black man in colonial-era attire sweeping the floor near the saloon's fireplace.

A small storage closet stands against the wall between the front bar and the back room. Previously, a set of stairs leading to the second floor stood in this area. People have heard phantom footsteps from the site, although the original stairs had been long ago removed.

One night an ash bucket appeared in the aisle near the fireplace. Each time it was moved off to the side, the bucket reappeared in the pathway, blocking the flow of foot traffic. Eventually, the bucket returned there so many times that no one wanted to touch it and return it to its proper place.

In the book *Baltimore Ghosts*, Read offered a possible explanation for the unusual events that have occurred at the Whistling Oyster. His words, however, might apply to the many other spirited inns located throughout Fells Point. "I know a lot of people come here who haven't been in town for a long time, and they had a good time so they come back here," Read said. "It could be that people die and want to come back to a place where they had a good time, and that's right here."

Jazz enthusiasts might want to visit Friends Bar, where it's said famous singer Billie Holiday had performed. It's easy to imagine the singer, nicknamed "Lady Day," singing her soulful laments in the eerie early hours of the morning. Unusual sounds, such as the clicking of women's footsteps and tinkling of glasses, are attributed to the jazz singer still considered one of the greatest vocalists of all time. Since she died at age 44 in 1959, some expected an increase in activity during the half-century anniversary of her demise in 2009. Out of respect, a drink is left on the bar to let the singer's spirit know she always is welcome at the saloon, where the staff keeps her memory alive.

The Horse You Came In On makes two noteworthy claims—that it's the oldest operating bar in the country and it was one of Edgar Allan Poe's favorite watering holes. One rumor is that Poe had been drinking at this particular Fell's Point waterfront saloon very late on October 3, 1849. As the writer headed back to his home, he fell unconscious into the street. After being discovered by a passerby, he was taken to Washington College Hospital, where he died on October 7. The cause of death remains a mystery, but alcoholism often has been suggested as one of the writer's many vices.

Certainly, if The Horse You Came In On was Poe's last stop, he most probably enjoyed himself, since the writer was well-acquainted with liquid spirits. Manifestations of the horror writer's presence include a swinging chandelier, a cash register with a mind of its own that opens and closes intermittently, and moving bar stools.

Along Shakespeare Street, people have reported seeing the figure of a man wearing dated clothing. Some think it may be someone from a period long ago. This finely dressed but rather filmy apparition makes his way along the narrow lane, heading west away from Broadway, before he disappears. Some believe it is the ghost of one of the founders of Fell's Point. To many the explanation seems to have some merit.

In a small plot, marked off by a wrought-iron fence and surrounded by row houses, lie the bodies of four members of the Fell family—Edward and William; William's son, Edward; and grandson, William. The granite marker was placed there in 1927 to denote the founders' family plot. Some believe a mansion stood nearby. But that is long gone; so too are the shipyards and slaves, the clipper ships and wooden-hulled warships. But the stories survive of sailors and sweethearts, craftsmen and harlots, who created the legacy of Fell's Point, and who seem to have decided to remain and reenact pleasant days long gone by.

Baltimore's Ghost Ship

Over the centuries, tens of thousands of wooden and metal ships—powered by sails or steam, and iron men—crossed the seven seas. But a fair number of these craft never reached their destination. Others arrived in port, but badly damaged from the effects of vicious weather, wrecks, pirate attacks, and naval battles. Among those craft most remembered are the vessels known as "ghost ships."

It's said the *Flying Dutchman* has been doomed since the late 1700s to sail the seas forever, directed by a cursed captain who is unable to dock in any port. The *Mary Celeste*, discovered in the 1870s near Portugal without damage but also without any crew, holds fast to a mystery that has never been solved. The *Queen Mary*, one of the world's most famous ocean liners, has been transformed into a hotel in California's Long Beach Harbor. This stately ship is said to host scores of ghosts of former passengers and crew. And like its sister ghost ships, the USS *Constellation*, a popular tourist attraction docked in Baltimore's Inner Harbor, has several unexplained stories of its own.

The frigate was built in Baltimore in 1797. It served in the War of 1812, fought the Barbary Coast pirates, interdicted slave ships, battled Confederate blockade runners during the Civil War, and worked as a training ship for Annapolis midshipmen. Eventually, the *Constellation* returned to the Maryland port city it now calls home. Soon after it was made accessible to Inner Harbor tourists in the 1970s, tales began to circulate about ghosts roaming over, under, around, and through the vessel's decks. Much of this talk is because ghost stories and legends seem to be automatically attached to old ships, and the USS *Constellation* is about as old a ship as you can find.

Reports of paranormal sightings on Baltimore's floating museum have been printed in newspapers and magazines and also featured on the History Channel documentary *Haunted Baltimore*. Three stories seem to be the most popular and most often repeated. They involve seaman Neil Harvey, Commander Thomas Truxtun, and a young boy who died on a lower deck.

During an engagement in 1799, while the ship was in a battle against the French ship *La Vengeance*, sailor Neil Harvey supposedly ran from his post. This demonstration of cowardice was a serious offense, and there are several suggested endings to Harvey's maritime career. The sailor was hanged, or he was run through with a sword, or he was strapped to the front of a cannon and then blown apart. In the twentieth century, the ghostly figure of Neil Harvey—with his limbs all found and replaced in the correct positions—has been reported floating across the decks of the ship.

Commander Thomas Truxtun is said to be the ship's second resident ghost. Congress presented the frigate's late-eighteenth-century captain a medal for his excellent command of *Constellation* during battles against the French in 1799 and 1800. But, in modern times, the old salt seems to enjoy giving guided tours of the ship. In 1964, late one afternoon, a Catholic priest was leaving the ship and passed a few staff members who were closing up the museum. The reverend paused to compliment the staff on the fine presentation he had just received from a costumed guide on one of the lower decks. The staff members, who knew they had no interpreter working on the vessel at that time, went aboard and inspected the entire ship. They found no one else—in or out of historic naval officer's attire—on board.

Young boys known as "powder monkeys" served on sailing ships as messengers, cook's helpers, officer's aides, ammunition carriers, and sick bay attendants. Because of their short size, these youngsters were particularly good at racing through the low-ceilinged bottom decks. It's said one small boy, who served on the ship in the 1820s, was killed—either during a battle, by an accident, because of a prank gone awry, or as a result of a murder or beating. Whatever the reason, there have been reports of a terrified-looking boy phantom appearing to visitors at various times.

In 1955, the *Baltimore Sun* ran a blurred photograph of a naval officer, dressed in a nineteenth-century uniform, marching across the deck of the ship. The photo was reportedly taken by a U.S. Navy officer who had set up his camera on a tripod on the top deck. The story states, "At 11:59 P.M., to be exact, the Navy officer detected a faint scent in the air—a certain something not unlike gunpowder." After his eerie picture appeared in the daily newspaper, the common-held belief that the ship was haunted was reinforced a hundred-fold.

Some say the ship's spirited tales were manufactured to attract tourists when the old wooden ship first opened for business in the Inner Harbor. It's not surprising that these stories have been embellished and exaggerated over the years, primarily for entertainment purposes. But some staff members who give tours of the ship, as well as others who work in the gift shop, claim strange sights and sounds occur occasionally in and around Baltimore's historic ghost ship.

Southern
Maryland

Glen Burnie Tales

The congested Glen Burnie area, south of Baltimore along Route 2 (also known as Governor Ritchie Highway), offers two ghost stories that have survived the test of time. Like many legends, they also provide a glimpse of how the area used to be—before the construction of multi-lane highways, auto dealerships, strip malls, and modern government buildings.

In the eighteenth century, Anne Arundel County was developing into a hub of industry, boasting such successful operations as furnaces, mills, and a brickyard. Several of these mills were operated as commercial businesses, but a number of farmers throughout the region ran private milling operations. The area laborers included freemen, indentured servants, convicts, and a fair number of slaves. A story provided by Mark Schatz of the Ann Arrundell County Historical Society has been passed down orally for generations. It involves a tragic event that some believe occurred at historic Curtis Creek Furnace.

In the mid 1700s, working conditions in all small manufacturing operations were difficult. With no government regulations, all of the laborers were subject to the mercy of the owners and their appointed managers. As expected, conditions were particularly hard on those workers who were slaves. One of the slaves, who had been badly abused by his supervisor at the Curtis Creek Furnace, apparently had reached his breaking point. He decided he could no longer endure any more physical pain and mental pressure. To escape his dead-end existence, which offered not even the slightest hope of freedom or escape, the slave committed suicide by jumping into the deadly furnace. Just before he plunged into the heat of the bubbling fire, the slave is said to have turned to his menacing overseer and shouted "You won't beat me no more!"

A state historical marker located along the northbound lane of Route 2, just north of Sawmill Creek and its intersection with Furnace Creek Road, notes the location and history of the furnace. It states: "The Curtis Creek Furnace, located on the south side of Furnace Creek, one-half mile east of Ritchie Highway, was established in 1759, and with a foundry built in 1829, continued to turn out high grade charcoal pig iron until abandoned in 1851."

Another county tale involves the ever-popular topic of long-lost buried treasure. And what is a safer and more confusing place to hide one's wealth than in a graveyard? To help treasure seekers locate the hoard, a mysterious light is said to appear in and near the rolling landscape of Glen Haven Memorial Park, located on Ritchie Highway in Glen Burnie. According to Schatz, the cemetery and surrounding area was once a farm. The former owner of the land is said to have buried a cache of money on his land, and immediately thereafter murdered the servant or slave who had provided assistance digging the hiding place—proof of the old adage "Dead men tell no tales."

On certain evenings, it's said a floating light appears in the area to help indicate the location where the long-lost treasure might be found. The only catch is that the mysterious glow only is visible at night—a time when few people, even serious treasure seekers, want to roam among the tombstones of the dead and disturb their peaceful eternal rest.

Mount Airy Mansion

One of state's oldest structures, Mount Airy Mansion in Upper Marlboro, claims direct historical connections to the Calvert family, founders of the Maryland colony. Some historians believe one of the first structures built on the property in the 1670s served as a hunting lodge for Lord Baltimore. In 1774, George Washington attended the marriage of his adopted son, John Park Custis, to Eleanor Calvert, at Mount Airy.

Over the years, additions were erected and eventually the building was transformed into an impressive mansion. However, a fire in 1931 destroyed most of the building. Eleanor Medill "Cissy" Patterson, publisher of the *Washington Times-Herald* and a prominent hostess of the era, purchased the ruins and restored Mount Airy to its former glory. It has hosted U.S. presidents, ambassadors, best-selling authors, and other prominent guests. Since 1973, the modern mansion has been part of Rosaryville State Park and is operated as an events and entertainment center.

But there are legends associated with Mount Airy that add color and texture to the bare black-and-white facts of its founding, genealogy, and reconstruction. In his book *Colonial Mansions of Maryland and Delaware*, author John Martin Hammond relates a tale associated with Mrs. Tillie R. Duvall, who bought the property in February 1903. At the time of the purchase, the auctioneer's catalogue described the estate as such: "This beautiful old place now contains about eight hundred and twenty acres of fine grazing, or farming land, well watered by natural springs, having a beautiful lake containing about ten acres, well stocked with fish. About two hundred acres of the land is covered with a natural growth of old oaks and other choice varieties of native trees."

But the advertisement to entice wealthy buyers made no mention of the previous tragic death in the mansion of Miss Eleanor Calvert, the last member of the well-known Maryland family to reside at Mount Airy. Miss Calvert, it is said, had the dangerous habit of using an old-fashioned oil lamp to illuminate her way through the mansion after dark. Despite repeated warnings from her family members and concerned servants that the lit torch was not safe and could cause her and the property serious harm, the matron of Mount Airy persisted in doing things her own way. Late one night, while she was descending the impressive stairway of the home, Miss Eleanor slipped, and the lit lamp fell from her grasp. As had been predicted, the result was deadly. Oil spilled across all of her clothing, and the hungry flames followed the liquid trail. Blazing fire consumed the stubborn woman, and the elderly Calvert family member died from her serious burns.

Hammond reported that a few years after living in Mount Airy, Mrs. Duvall was awakened in the night by a ghostly woman's figure, which one midnight put its cold hands around her throat. Some might suggest that the incident was probably a dream, which the confused victim imagined to be an actual event when she awoke at the bewitching hour. However, additional information offered by the author seems to add some credibility to Mrs. Duvall's paranormal experience.

"There is a room," Hammond wrote, "above the dining room in which no lamp will burn, the strongest, most ingeniously constructed lamp going out meekly the moment you cross the threshold with it. Doors open and shut without cause. Beds sag and creak with no human being on them."

Dale K. DuPont, reporter for *The Sentinel*, wrote about a strange event associated with the funeral for Eleanor Calvert, held in Mount Airy. The matron's corpse was lying in a coffin in the downstairs parlor, awaiting respectful visitors. As the formal ceremony was about to begin, staff discovered the closed parlor door was locked, and the key, which was supposed to be accessible on a table in the main floor's hall, was missing. As an attendant went to find another key to open the door, a series of strange, loud sounds were heard, apparently coming from inside the locked parlor. As the family and staff attempted to enter the room where the corpse was secure in its coffin, the guests and hosts became increasingly alarmed. Eventually, while the noises continued, servants discovered the duplicate key and entered the room. Immediately, the noises stopped, and the original key was discovered lying on a table beside Miss Eleanor's coffin.

Another author provides an additional strange tale. In her book *Homes of the Cavaliers*, Katherine Scarborough reported that during the War of 1812 a band of British troops were approaching the estate. Some of the Calvert ladies hurriedly gathered about thousands of dollars worth of family silver, jewelry, gold coins, and table settings made from silver. Before the enemy arrived, the women carried the household's treasure into the cellar, and ran through a secret tunnel that led to a secluded pond behind the mansion. Near that site, they hid the family heirlooms. According to Scarborough, the treasure was never recovered and "Elizabeth Calvert . . . is said to walk the night in spirit, still seeking the long lost gold at the end of the gruesome corridor."

In his story, DuPont repeated the ghost tale of Mount Airy's "Walking Corpse," originally penned by Clinton H. Johnson in a 1933 edition of the *Baltimore Post*. The subject of the story is Ariana, the very attractive daughter of Benedict Calvert. The young woman was in love with a young man of whom her father did not approve. Succumbing to pressure from her family, Ariana broke off the relationship, sent her lover away, and died of a broken heart. The romantic legend says her troubled ghost roams the garden behind the mansion, waiting in vain for her lost love to return.

DuPont's article, "In Prince George's, a Haunted Hideout," was published on October 20, 1975, long before today's ghost hunters had easy access to high-tech equipment, and decades before the paranormal hunting hobby had reached the crazed level it is at today. But even then, DuPont reported, "The estate [Mount Airy] boasts so many ghosts it has attracted the attention of the London Society of Psychical Research—among the most persistent ghost hunters of all."

Juda of Salubria

The ghosts of dead children were said to haunt Salubria, an 1827 mansion that stood near today's modern Woodrow Wilson Bridge. The frame buildings on the old property were razed in 2003, but the historic site on Oxon Hill Road deserves at least a mention. The early-nineteenth-century frame plantation house was expanded and altered during the five generations it hosted members of the Bayne family. John H. Bayne was an important figure in the fields of medicine, politics, education, and agriculture. But the rich and famous are not immune to unexpected and shocking tragedies.

When it was founded, Salubria's surrounding acres extended for miles from the mansion house, barns, and workers' homes. Today, Apple Grove—the Bayne family cemetery, located two miles from where the plantation house had stood—offers clues to a ghastly series of murders. On the elevated stones are the names of Baynes who had made their mark in their home state. But near the epitaphs of the family's movers and shakers is a pair of small markers, indicating the burial sites of two young Bayne children. In 1834, the boys, ages seven and five, had been poisoned by Juda, their fourteen-year-old family nursemaid.

In her confession, Juda admitted she had killed the young boys. But she also confessed to setting fire to Salubria a year earlier, and poisoning the Baynes's baby daughter, Catherine. At the time of the daughter's sudden death, it was thought the little girl had died from a typhus epidemic that had swept through North America. The execution of the slave girl, who was convicted of the multiple murders, took place in Upper Marlboro. The killer is believed to be the youngest female hanged in America's judicial history. For years, it was believed the ghosts of the three murdered children and their killer haunted the plantation's buildings and grounds. Today, progress in the form of highways and residential developments has overtaken the region, and nothing but the sad story of Salubria's child murders remains.

Haunted Hospital?

More than two hundred acres of open land surround the decaying ruins of Glenn Dale Hospital, located just outside the town of Greenbelt. Because of the aging, crumbling state of the institution's twenty-six vacant buildings, legends have surfaced and stories have spread about ghosts of former patients roaming about the secluded grounds and hiding within the decrepit treatment buildings. Many of these phantoms are described as restless souls, moaning in pain from their horrible experiences in the former tuberculosis sanatorium, which is often erroneously referred to as an "asylum."

Constructed between 1933 and 1939, the large facility, with spacious grounds and numerous medical buildings, was built by the city of Washington as a rural treatment site for citizens suffering from tuberculosis. The construction project was a huge undertaking, and two of the remaining buildings, designed by well-known architect Nathan C. Wyeth, are very large and impressive, featuring brick Colonial Revival architecture. Such hospitals were part of the universally accepted, early- to mid-twentieth century treatment of the infectious lung disease, when cures were thought to include extended bed rest in a quiet, country setting.

But those interested in the supernatural have been known to never let the facts get in the way of a good place to ghost hunt. Paranormal junkies who have secretly visited Glenn Dale—after ignoring "No Trespassing" signs and avoiding security guards—have returned with photographs of decaying buildings, discarded equipment, and shadowy alcoves. Anyone who has surfed the Web and seen pictures that have been posted would certainly believe that evil spirits and agonized specters remain within the neglected walls of the abandoned Maryland hospital.

Since the Prince George's County hospital of horrors was closed in 1981, urban legends have spread, first by friend-of-a-friend word of mouth, and later through Internet lore over scores of Web sites. "Legend trippers," another name for people who visit haunted sites, have described the present state of the buildings as something out of *The Shining*, the Stephen King novel set in a secluded, closed-up-for-the-winter-season hotel. Many trespassers receive directions and suggestions regarding which locations inside Glenn Dale's grounds offer the highest haunted potential. The old hospital morgue is one of the "hot spots," where high-tech ghost hunters attempt to get pictures of apparitions or floating balls of light, called "orbs," which they believe indicate the presence of spirit energy.

Others have reported being chased or followed while prospecting and photographing the ruins. The sounds of footsteps, loud crashes, and whispered voices have been reported, but those incidents are identical to reports associated with any empty old building. The fact that some of Glenn Dale's structures resemble a fortress only adds to the credibility of any unusual experience.

Some of the basements are flooded. Roofs and floors have caved in. Passageways lead to underground tunnels, which were used to move patients and supplies to connected buildings scattered across the massive complex. Rumors include stories of deranged former patients who have returned to Glenn Dale and who still live in the empty buildings. Of course, there are tales about the presence of the ghosts of ill patients that had died in the buildings. Experienced visitors instruct novice nighttime intruders to wear gloves, since touching any of the debris could cause a fatal disease.

A few of the most outlandish rumors claim scores of patients were locked in a burning building where they died during a fire; mentally deranged patients took over the hospital and killed the guards; and scores of patients escaped from the grounds and terrorized citizens in the nearby town of Bowie. One excited ghost hunter, amazed at the size of Glenn Dale, announced, "It's like Disney World. You can't see it all in one day."

In a 2000 article in the *Bowie Blade-News*, Susan Pearl, currently a historian at the Historical Society of Prince George's County, said one reason for the high level of interest in the site is the mistaken belief that Glenn Dale, which opened in the 1930s as a children's tuberculosis sanatorium, had operated as a mental hospital.

She told reporter David Emanuel, "There is no truth to that, either. I think the confusion comes when people think of it as a sanitarium, which is a mental hospital. Glenn Dale was a sanatorium, a TB and health center." If one looks closely at the spelling of the two words, the placement of the letters "A," "I," and "O" makes a huge difference in the meanings.

At the time of the institution's operation, Washington, D.C., had the fourth highest TB rate in the country. There was a steady stream of patients entering and leaving the facility, and the average stay at Glenn Dale was 441 days. By 1960, TB had been controlled and the disease was on the wane. Glenn Dale became a clinic and was used to treat chronically ill and disabled patients. This continued until the facility was closed in 1981.

Perhaps the tales of wandering ghosts roaming through the woods and the presence of forgotten graves in hidden cemeteries sprang up as a result of seriously ill patients dying while being treated during the institution's final years. Certainly, the more authorities claim there is nothing paranormal at Glenn Dale—coupled with the presence of security personnel to keep out the public—the more ghost hunters will try to enter the site and, if locked out, spread exaggerated, unsubstantiated rumors.

But there seems to be one other unusual tidbit to the story, which reporter Emanuel brought up with Pearl in his article, "Glenn Dale Hospital Rich In History, Ripe With Legend." He pointed out that one of the last road signs located in a residential area near the hospital property is named "Legend Manor Road." Coincidence? I think not.

Governor's Bridge

A dead baby. Screeching tires. Car wrecks. Creeping fog. Mysterious screams. Glowing eyes. Hanging bodies. Secret ceremonies. Howling during the full moon. These and other eerie incidents have been reported around Prince George's and Anne Arundel counties' infamous Governor's Bridge. Not surprisingly, over the last several decades the skeletal span's urban legends have been changed and embellished by different tellers, who often raise the level of blood and gore to maintain the interest of their listeners.

Most urban legends are not connected with a specific site. What makes the tales of this southern Maryland ghost-hunting destination special is that Governor's Bridge near Bowie is a real, identifiable place. The metal structure crosses the Patuxent River along a road that links Prince George's and Anne Arundel counties. An added and important feature is that it's rather easy to find, since the bridge is located on Governors Bridge Road.

When approaching the "haunted" bridge from the Prince George's County (western) side, the word "SATAN," painted in red capital letters on a road-caution marker, catches one's eye. Driving across the metal span and parking along the rut-marked shoulder of the road in Anne Arundel County allows visitors to walk back onto the bridge and peer over its side. Standing in the secluded, backcountry setting, it's easy to conjure up images of the various terrifying incidents that have been associated with the structure. Following are summaries of some of the unexplained incidents that have been reported on, near, and below Governor's Bridge.

Travelers have sighted a girl in a white gown, standing in the center of the bridge, who seems to be waiting for a ride. When drivers stop and try to invite her into the car, she disappears as soon as the car door is opened. Other drivers, who are either too afraid to stop or can't do so because the apparition appears without warning, end up driving directly through the misty image. Afterwards, they have reported feeling a frigid "death chill" at the moment of contact when the woman in white passes through the length of the car. When they screech to a halt and lift their eyes to see if anything is there, they observe no figure in the car's rearview mirror. Later, after inspecting their car, they find no damage and no evidence of the vehicle having struck any humanlike figure.

People have heard crying baby sounds, which seem to originate from the water below the bridge. Some witnesses have suggested that a deranged mother might have thrown her young child over the structure's railing. Others say a baby fell into the water and drowned following a car accident. In both versions, the dying baby's cries float over the water's surface at night, repeating the horrifying incident. Some suggest the young child's restless spirit, whose life was snuffed out in its first weeks of existence, is trying in vain to be saved and return to this world.

Late-night travelers who have rounded the bend about a quarter-mile before reaching the bridge on the Anne Arundel County side have seen flashing lights coming from the center of the structure. Thinking the presence of emergency vehicles indicates a serious accident, the drivers have slowed down their cars as they approached the river. Suddenly, the warning lights disappear. As they drive across the bridge there is no indication of any accident, police presence, or roadblock.

Tales persist of ax murderers, kidnappers, and mentally deranged hermits roaming the woods along the river. Some believe the "Satan" graffiti on the nearby sign is a signal to devil worshippers, who meet in the forested area to hold secret rituals that involve human and animal sacrifice. Romantic couples brave enough to park along the secluded road keep a wary eye out for strange movements and lights in the nearby woods. Many times cars have suddenly sped off across the bridge, leaving a trail of burning rubber as evidence of a hasty retreat. These actions are caused by passengers parked in the area who have been frightened by sounds or threats coming from unknown activity in the woods.

Certainly, many of these tales are similar to ones reported for centuries at other locations throughout the country. But the wooded region surrounding Governor's Bridge continues to attract teenage visitors seeking a weekend thrill. This Bowie-area haunted site also is a favorite destination for professional ghost hunters, who search for photographic and audio evidence of phantom visitors.

Vince Wilson, author and paranormal investigator with the Baltimore Society for Paranormal Research, has been to Governor's Bridge dozens of times over several years. While he has never heard any babies crying, the Baltimore resident said he and his associates "have experienced some weird things." He described extreme energy drains, where members of his investigative team felt as if all their energy was being sucked from their bodies.

"On another occasion," Vince said, "we had photographed figures that seem to hang in the mist surrounding the area and seemed, almost, to be magnetically clinging to the metal superstructure of the bridge itself." Centuries ago, the area had been occupied by American Indian tribes. Vince said, "Residents further up the road sometimes reported seeing people walk by in traditional Native American clothing and saw and heard little Indian children playing in the fields."

While exploring the dense woods surrounding the bridge, Vince and his team discovered several old abandoned shacks whose walls, floors, and ceilings were decorated with hand-painted satanic imagery. Vince admitted the drawings caused his group "feelings of dread and discomfort" that shortened their visit. The symbols also made him wonder if rumors of the presence of satanic cults and a Church of Satan in the area were accurate. But shadows and sounds of the night excite the imagination and tend to exaggerate personal tales of terror. People often see what they want to see. Each hoot of the owl becomes a werewolf's cry; each rustling branch announces the impending arrival of black-cloaked strangers or the escaped mental patient with the silver hook hand, sharpened to a deadly point.

But why believe what others say or write? For those interested in paying Governor's Bridge a visit and experiencing their own evening of terror, head west from Annapolis on Route 50. Exit onto Route 301 south. Go approximately one mile south and turn left onto Governor's Bridge Road. Follow the winding, narrow, two-lane road approximately two miles to the bridge—and be sure your car doors are locked.

Faceless Lady

South of Washington, D.C., in Prince George's County, historic Fort Washington overlooks the Potomac River and the Virginia shore. Visitors can still get an idea of the beautiful country view as it was two hundred years ago. Built in 1809 as Fort Warburton, the first defensive structure on the site was destroyed in 1814 by its own troops in order to keep the fortification and its supplies from falling into the hands of British forces, which were heading toward Washington city during the War of 1812.

The present stone fort was constructed ten years after Fort Warburton's destruction. At the time the Civil War began, Fort Washington was the only permanent fortification guarding the nation's capital, although a number of temporary defenses were erected hastily around the important city. After that conflict, Fort Washington continued to serve as an active military installation until 1946. Today, the National Park Service operates the scenic grounds and its museum buildings overlooking the Potomac, and recreational hikers and historical reenactors are a constant presence.

Fort Washington's position on high ground and its thick stone walls made it an ideal defense against attackers in nineteenth-century wars. Its cannons could shoot down at approaching vessels, and the fort's sharpshooters could easily kill any surviving enemy attackers who tried to swim to shore.

Of course, every historic military installation has its share of ghost stories, and Fort Washington is no exception. Its resident phantom is the Faceless Lady. During the British attack in 1814, an American nurse working at the fort was trapped in one of the buildings during the intense enemy assault. Afraid she would be shot if she tried to retreat with the American troops, the young woman hid inside one of the barracks.

When British soldiers entered the remnants of the captured fort, they discovered the woman and decided to make an example of her by carving up her face. Screaming from the painful mutilation, the once beautiful nurse ran from the fort and headed toward the woods, her moans and sobs traveling throughout the forest.

According to the legend, the woman was never seen again, and it was assumed she died somewhere in the woods from her wounds and exposure to the elements. After the war, settlers in the area began reporting sightings of a tall woman who would emerge from the forest looking for food. When the shy stranger dared enter nearby villages, she was careful to keep a veil or scarf over her face. After the local character had not been seen for a fair length of time, stories began to circulate about mournful cries and wails coming from the forest and the area around the fort. Soldiers on guard duty began talking about sightings of the Faceless Lady, who floated above the ramparts of the fort and appeared occasionally in the dark corners of the parade ground and buildings. Some said she had decided to remain at the site where her former life had been destroyed, in hopes of luring British troops over the edge of the cliffs and into the depths of the nearby Potomac River.

America's Lost President

John Hanson must be turning over in his grave. We would try to check—if we knew where the colonial statesman's burial spot was. But the location of Hanson's final resting place is only one of the controversies surrounding this relatively unknown founding father of our country.

Hanson's main claim to fame, of which most Americans are unaware, is his title as first President of the United States of America. On November 5, 1781, the well-known Maryland politician was elected the first president of the young country under the Articles of Confederation. The unanimous vote of approval took place in Independence Hall in Philadelphia by members of the Continental Congress. The election occurred six months before the British defeat at Yorktown that ended the Revolutionary War, and eight years before George Washington was inaugurated as president in 1789. Historians that support Hanson's premier presidential status are eager to point out a number of facts to back up their claim.

In 1781, after all thirteen states ratified the Articles of Confederation, the Continental Congress elected John Hanson as "President of the United States in Congress Assembled," to serve a term from 1781 to 1782. George Washington, the Virginia-born commander-in-chief of the Continental Army, sent letters to Hanson addressing him as "your Excellency." Hanson proclaimed July Fourth and Thanksgiving Day (the last Thursday in November) as national holidays. Under his direction, Congress established the Consular Service, First National Bank, and Post Office Department, and adopted the Great Seal of the United States. He initiated steps for the creation of the presidential cabinet, the census, the decimal coinage system, and the federal mint.

There is an impressive list of other significant actions for which President Hanson is credited. He was a Maryland state delegate from Charles County, raised money and supplies during the Revolution, helped organize the Maryland Line military regiment, and served as a Maryland representative in the Continental Congress.

But under the Articles of Confederation, Hanson was elected the first of seven men who held the young country's highest executive position, each serving a one-year term. Therefore, according to his staunch supporters, called "Hansonians," Washington actually was the ninth U.S. president. "But in 1787," according to *Saturday Evening Post* writer John Kobler's 1957 article, "when Congress ratified a Constitution to replace the articles, John Hanson was already a fading memory."

As years passed, Americans marked former general and war hero George Washington's administration as the country's official first presidency. Hanson, like too many other great men and women, was in the wrong place at the wrong time. As a result, he and his accomplishments have been passed over and minimized by the gatekeepers of American history.

There are a few monuments that honor John Hanson's contributions. The stretch of Route 50 between Washington and Annapolis is named John Hanson Highway. Memorial tablets have been affixed to Maryland homes where the politician lived. One is at Mulberry Grove estate in Port Tobacco, Charles County, about thirty miles south of Washington. The other stands in Frederick, in north central Maryland. Another marker is in Oxon Hill, Prince George's County, where Hanson had been visiting a nephew when the ill politician died. Unfortunately, no one is quite sure what happened to the former president's corpse, and no tombstone marks the burial place, which never has been found. But that hasn't stopped Hansonians and other historians from looking.

In 1971, a newspaper headline asked: "Is Oxon Hill Grave His? New Battle for John Hanson." Amateur historians and archaeologists roamed all over an overgrown area not far from the Woodrow Wilson Bridge, and searched a honeysuckle grove at Oxon Hill Manor. They were hoping that a recently discovered granite crypt might hold the remains of their long-forgotten hero. But a Maryland official stated the burial site was not Hanson's and, instead, was probably that of one of his ancestors whose land had been confiscated during the Revolutionary War because the man's family had sided with the British.

One hopeful Hansonian stressed that a correct and verifiable outcome of the search was serious business, and that locating and properly identifying the remains was critical. It would be highly embarrassing to the group's cause if it were to erect a monument to Hanson the lost Revolutionary hero only to later discover they had placed it atop the grave of a Tory. Many of the searchers said they believed Hanson had died in 1783 while visiting the 230-acre tract of land then known as the Addison estate. It also is said that his body was never transported to his home in Frederick. It was suggested that Hanson's widow, who died in 1812 in Frederick County, was brought to the Oxon Hill gravesite and was interred beside her husband.

Historians said they thought Hanson's original mausoleum had been erected on a hill overlooking the Potomac River, but after the nearby mansion was destroyed by fire the former president's gravesite was overgrown and lost to trees, weeds, and honeysuckle. One newspaper article headline announced, "Oxon Hill Gravesite May Be John Hanson's." That story said a crypt had been discovered on the property in the 1930s. But when the person who had found it returned decades later, he was unable to locate the exact location of the tomb. In the story, the man wondered if highway crews that had been working on the Capital Beltway, which passes only a few hundred yards from the original estate, might have destroyed the mausoleum.

Rev. Alan C. Freed, pastor of Good Shepherd Lutheran Church in Dundalk at the time, also was involved in the 1971 search. He speculated to the reporter that bulldozers, which were in the area to help control a 1960 forest fire, could have destroyed the mausoleum. The paper also added, "He [Freed] said there also was a report that some of the men working on the Beltway 'blew up a stone structure as a lark during their lunch hour one day.'"

As Freed said to a reporter during the 1971 graveyard quest, "It's really not of huge consequence whether we find out or not. If we do, we'll mark the spot with a huge monument. If not, well, we'll still think Hanson was a good man. He's the forgotten American. . . . He was shoved under the rug when in 1789 we made this big, impressive front before all the nations of the world and elected a man who was impressive, a general with gold buttons, braid and all. But it's unjust to those who went before to overlook them. . . . It wasn't a new country when Washington took over. It had been in existence for many years."

Nothing definitive came from that 1971 exploration. The location of Hanson's lost corpse remains a mystery. But if anyone's spirit might have unfinished business on Earth—and have the right to be restless and annoyed because someone else received the fame he deserved—that person is John Hanson.

Silver Buckle

St. John's Episcopal Church at Broadcreek in Oxon Hill traces its origins to 1695. It is the third church building erected on the site. In the early 1900s, late one night, a church elder working in the building noticed he wasn't alone. Somehow a stranger had entered the church without being noticed. The elder, wanting to lock up the building, asked the visitor to come out from the shadows, informing the stranger it was time to leave. Without a sound, a large man, dressed in colonial-era clothing, moved into the light. He was distinctive, in that one of his legs was made of a stick of wood. But when the stranger moved across the building's wooden floor, his peg leg made no sound. The most impressive part of his costume, according to the elder, was a large silver belt buckle that reflected the dancing flames of the church's multicolored candles.

After offering a silent nod, the mysterious figure floated across the room, moved without hesitation through the front door, and headed out into the church graveyard. When the shocked church elder exited the building and looked around the church property, there was no sign of the silent stranger—no vehicles or anything else moving or passing nearby. Whatever the image was, it seemed to have disappeared among the weathered gravestones. As years passed, the stranger was never seen again, but each time a sudden sound in the church could not be explained, parishioners who had heard the story attributed the noise to the man with the silver buckle and peg leg.

In the 1950s, a section of the old church floor was being replaced. Under a rotted section, workmen discovered a large silver buckle. How it got there and the identity of whom it belonged to remain a mystery—just like the late-night visitor who was seen and disappeared suddenly in the church.

Weeping Widow

Residential development has replaced the nineteenth-century historic home known as Pentland Hills. The mansion was built in the 1830s as a residence for the tobacco growers who owned the estate, and was located near Upper Marlboro, not far from present-day Route 301. During the Civil War, the owner joined a Confederate unit and was gone for several years, fighting alongside many of his neighbors for the Southern cause.

Sympathetic to her husband's decision to take part in the "War of Northern Aggression," the mistress of the home ran the family business and waited patiently for her spouse's return. Much like the wives of New England sea captains, the mistress of Pentland Hills stood atop the mansion's widow's walk, looking out for sight of the master, whom she believed would appear marching up the lane in his dashing gray uniform.

Despite the daily ritual, the mistress's husband never returned to Pentland Hills. As years passed, the woman moved her lookout position from the home's roof to a worn, wooden rocker on the front porch. Now much older and lonely, she began hearing voices. Thinking it was her husband, calling out from an area just beyond her sight, she would jump up from the rocker and shout out joyfully to the source of the sound only she could hear. But, of course, it was her imagination, and no one was ever there.

Eventually, she lost her eyesight and hearing, but the mistress still directed her servants to lead her to the chair on the front porch, where she wept for both the loss of her love and the life they would have enjoyed together. One afternoon, the mistress died in her sleep in that worn porch rocker. Soon after her burial, a wailing moan was heard from the nearby family graveyard. Superstitious servants and nervous neighbors attributed the sounds to the Weeping Widow, whose cries continued for some time after her death and floated through the Upper Marlboro countryside on windy moonlit nights.

Devil's Card Game

They say if the devil lives anywhere, he lives in New Orleans. Even if that is true, a well-known legend seems to indicate Satan had made a noteworthy stop in Prince George's County during one of his travels.

In a 1976 article on local ghosts, a longtime resident of Oaklands Manor, near Laurel, said her home is believed to have been the setting for a story about the Devil and a card game. The same story is said to have occurred in a long-ago-torn-down mansion in Croom, as well as a few other sites around Maryland and beyond.

One evening, five men were playing cards in the mansion's library. It was in the late 1700s, during George Washington's lifetime. In the midst of the game, one of the gamblers, a doctor, was called away to respond to a medical emergency. The other men became very upset at losing one of their regular players. One of the frustrated men, who had spent as much of the evening drinking as he had gambling, blurted out, "I'd play cards with the Devil if he were here."

During this period of time, the home where the game was taking place was located on a well-traveled road, and the arrival of unan-nounced travelers was not uncommon. Within minutes of the man's flippant comment there was knocking at the front of the house. When the host opened the door, a mysterious-looking stranger, dressed in dark clothing and with a pair of unusually cold black eyes, entered the foyer.

The owner signed the guest into the registration book and gave him the key to his room. A short time after walking about the downstairs of the building, the late arriver entered the library. For a brief period of time the stranger warmed himself by the fire and seemed to be happy reading a book. However, after an hour had gone by—during which the man had silently observed the ongoing card game—the new guest rose, walked to the gaming table, pointed a long, thin finger toward the doctor's empty seat, and asked if he could join the group.

Initially, the other four men were pleased to have a new player that they might take advantage of, so they happily welcomed the stranger into their game. The five men played cards throughout the night, and the spirited game extended into the early hours of the morning. Just before sunrise, the stranger rose suddenly and said he must leave. A few of the men began to protest, complaining they needed more time to recoup some of their substantial losses. In response, the stranger gave them a sharp, threatening look, and the men's complaints stopped in mid sentence.

As the man gathered up his winnings, the dejected victims dwelled silently on the lifetime of earnings each had lost. Player 1 had signed over control of his bank. Player 2 had lost his shipping business. Player 3 would have to tell his family they were moving out of their plantation home. Player 4 was trying to figure out how to break the news to his daughter that she was to be married in the coming weeks to the unnamed, dark-eyed man dressed in black.

With an evil smile, the winner nodded, announced he would send an associate to handle the legal details and collect his winnings, and then turned away from the table. As the dark stranger walked toward the door, the beaten men noticed a forked tail jutting out from beneath the lower portion of the stranger's greatcoat. They later agreed they also had noticed the distinct, unpleasant smell of sulphur and brimstone permeate the room.

As generations passed, slaves on that plantation told the rest of the tale. They said the sun had begun to rise just as the Devil mounted the steps in front of the mansion. To escape the deadly rays, the stranger ran behind the building and, in the safety of the shade, disappeared through a large hole that had not been there before. Apparently, the indentation remained on the property for centuries, despite attempts to fill it in.

A succession of different owners lived on the estate in the hundreds of years since it was built. In Brian Burns' bicentennial year article, "Spirits That Go Flat In the Night," the home's owners at that time explained that since they raised horses, such a depression—like the one in the story and which they believed was nothing more than a bottomless sinkhole—could cause very serious injury to the animals. They made sure the area around the hole was fenced in so no horse would have an accident and break any of its limbs.

The owner of Oaklands at that time also acknowledged a number of strange incidents over the years. A young girl who lived in the home reported hearing the hoofbeats of running horses, although all such animals were secure in the stables. An overnight guest said he had been awakened during the night and found his bed shaking violently.

The most bothersome event occurred on a Sunday morning and involved a prayer book. An owner could not find her book and began a search. When she glanced toward the floor of her bedroom, she saw several pages from the prayer book scattered across the room. She rushed down the hall to wake her daughter and tell her about the incident, but noticed more pages lying about the younger woman's bedroom. Both women began searching the house for the missing book. When they arrived on the first floor, the prayer book, which had been in good condition with no loose binding, was sitting on the dining room table. It was obvious that the missing pages had been ripped out from the binding; who had attacked the holy book was never determined.

Author Troy Taylor wrote about the history, and several of the ghost stories, associated with Oaklands. Both George Washington and Abraham Lincoln visited the historic home, which had served as a stagecoach stop. One of the early owners was an officer in Robert E. Lee's Army of Northern Virginia during the Civil War. It's believed that this man later suffered from depression and was insane when he died. Later owners attributed sudden sounds and loud footsteps to the ghost of the restless major.

Some residents said they have smelled flowers when none were in the building, and have seen a rocking chair moving on its own. The apparition of a small boy in an upstairs bedroom might be one of the officer's children. Since hundreds of slaves had worked the property, reports of the ghosts of a large, black woman and a black man dressed in work clothes are not surprising. At times, the night silence has been pierced by the sound of a woman weeping from somewhere inside the home, and there have been reports of a shrill scream coming from the nearby woods. Years ago, a woman was murdered in that area, and her killer was never identified.

Cemetery Voices

Did members of St. John's Episcopal Church near Beltsville hear voices, or were the muted sounds nothing more than creaking timbers in the historic house of worship? In a 2007 story in *The Gazette*, reporter Dennis Carter spotlighted a number of unexplained reports recorded in the journal of the wife of a rector of the 150-year-old church.

A report compiled in 1976 detailed a number of strange incidents experienced by the woman at St. John's, which included sightings of fleeting shadows dashing across the church graveyard at dusk and hearing voices. One incident involved the pastor's wife, who claimed she heard a series of sounds that seemed to indicate an unscheduled meeting was taking place inside the church. When she entered the building to investigate, there was no one inside, but she reported she had "the strangest feeling that each and every pew was fully occupied."

One of the woman's daughters told her parents she had seen a man standing alone in a section of the church cemetery, but as she approached the stranger, who was dressed in a gray uniform, he disappeared. When the family members arrived at the exact spot where the young girl said the man had been standing, they discovered a gravestone of a Confederate soldier who had died in the Battle of Chancellorsville.

Surratt House Spirits

After John Wilkes Booth shot President Abraham Lincoln in Ford's Theatre, the assassin rode out of Washington and disappeared into the dark Maryland countryside to the south. His goal was to link up with fellow conspirators, and one of his primary stops was the tavern and home of Mary Surratt, located at Surrattsville, in an area now known as Clinton. Some visitors are amazed that Booth was able to find the out-of-the-way, two-story boardinghouse, which at that time was located along a narrow, unlit road. No doubt the injured Booth was greatly relieved when he arrived at the tavern's doorstep.

After a century and a half, the Surratts' rolling three-hundred-acre farm that had surrounded their family home is long gone. Instead stand congested, fast-moving highways, commercial strip malls, apartment buildings, and modern residential developments. Other than the historic Surratt House itself, little remains of the family farm that once covered much of the surrounding region.

Laurie Verge has been associated with the historic Civil War-era site since 1975, first as a volunteer and, since 1983, as director of the Surratt House Museum. "I've been here longer than Mary Surratt," the director said, cheerfully. "She only lived here twelve years. I've got her beat." Verge agreed that visitors are surprised at the amount of development in the area when they arrive. "I get a lot of calls requesting directions," Verge said. "I warn them, they will be hit by every commercial enterprise known to man. I tell them they are going to be amazed that anything of a historic nature has survived in the area."

Despite the onslaught of progress and the threat of more change, well-trained and knowledgeable guides tell the Surratt story and lead tourists from around the country through the old and, some even say, haunted house. The first-floor post office, meeting room, tavern, and public eating area are laid out as they would have been during 1852, the year Mary's husband, John Surratt, opened the establishment. Unfortunately for the family business, John had a tendency to pop the cork while tending the bar. As a result, much of the saloon's profits disappeared down the owner's gullet.

Speaking of John Surratt, Verge mentioned that as a savvy businessman, "Mr. Surratt saw the commercial potential of this area. He would be absolutely thrilled with the amount of traffic passing near his inn. Also, across the street at the Citgo station is where he had his livery stable. So more than a century ago, horses, as opposed to cars, were fed at that site."

Several rooms in the first-floor private area are decorated as they would have been during Mary's years as owner and proprietor, immediately following the death of her husband. Mary's son, John, lived in the home at times, but he often was away on business. Eventually, he worked as a spy and courier for the Southern cause. The second-floor bedrooms also are furnished with period pieces, and the loft of one of the bedrooms was used to hide weapons, which young Surratt and other members of the conspiracy had hidden for future use.

Over the years, different families and sometimes renters have lived in the Surratt House. In 1965, it was taken over by the state of Maryland. Eventually, volunteers and the Maryland-National Capital Park and Planning Commission dedicated themselves to preserving the historical nature of the site. Today, the property has been restored to what it probably looked like at the end of the Civil War.

The home's survival and claim to fame is because of its owner, Mary Surratt, who was arrested and charged for her reported role in the Lincoln assassination and for her association with John Wilkes Booth. Mary vigorously denied these charges, but after a speedy trial she was hanged in Washington on July 7, 1865, along with three other members of the conspiracy—making Mary the first woman to be executed by the federal government. Over the years, many stories have been told about Mary's ghost haunting different locations where she had lived—including the Surratt Tavern in Clinton—as well as the place where she died, Washington's Fort McNair.

Verge acknowledged that many Surratt House visitors have voiced some level of interest in ghost stories and inquired about paranormal experiences in the building. She said at least one guest has raised the topic, to some degree, on about 70 percent of the tours. When this occurs, individual guides offer general information about reported hauntings and, in some cases, share their own personal experiences.

Noted ghost hunter Hans Holzer, Verge said, put Surratt House on the map several decades ago when he spotlighted the building's haunts in a chapter in his book *Windows to the Past*. In the 1940s and

1950s, a widow rented the home and stories about strange voices on the back stairs began to surface. Some volunteers and guides added their own experiences or impressions to a growing number of spirited stories. One guide said he drove past the front of Surratt House one night after it was closed and saw a tall gentleman in old-fashioned clothing knocking at the front door. A young girl claimed she saw the reflection of a man in one of the second-floor bedroom mirrors. Another guide was leading a group from one room into another on the second floor when she saw a child in period clothing looking under a bed. There was no child on that tour.

A member of a film crew working on a project in the home said he felt someone push him while he was in the family dining room. Someone else claimed he heard a child crying in the main hall, near the closet under the main stairway.

Verge said she and a colleague opened the building one morning, shut off the security alarm, and were standing at the base of the main stairway when they heard heavy footsteps coming from the second floor. The sound of footsteps occurred again, during an evening executive board meeting of the Surratt Society. The gathering was being held on the second floor. Suddenly, everyone stopped and looked up from the table. Every person in the room acknowledged hearing the sound of someone enter the "locked" front door on the first floor and walk across the building toward the back of the house. The group interrupted the meeting, held hands, and slowly descended the stairs and checked the entire building. They found no one else inside.

Today, Verge works in the administration building, adjacent to the historic Surratt House. Years ago, her office was located on the older structure's second floor, at the top of the stairs of the famous home. Because of the small room's central location, anyone, or anything, that used the stairs, hallway, or traveled from room to room had to pass Verge's open doorway.

"There were times," Verge said, "when I was in the building by myself, and I sensed that someone was walking out of one of the bedrooms. It was like whatever it was would stop and look at me, or as if something was watching me. But when I looked, there was nothing there. It gave me an eerie sensation."

When asked to guess at the source of the often-heard, heavy footsteps, Verge said it might be the ghost of John Lloyd. He had been Mary Surratt's tenant and lived in the home in 1865. It was Lloyd who gave the government evidence about the hidden weapons, and this detail eventually was used against the accused conspirators and resulted in Mary Surratt's hanging.

But what if the government was wrong? What if Surratt was aware of the Booth team's earlier kidnapping plot and not the assassination plans? What if her trial and execution were a rush to judgment? In that case, Verge opined, Lloyd's restless, guilty spirit might be roaming the building where he offered damaging evidence that doomed his landlord.

Verge receives requests from ghost-hunting groups to conduct investigations at the historic property. But she declines politely, explaining her desire to focus on the history of the home. "If we decided to allow a group to stay overnight and word got out," Verge said, "we would not be able to handle the number of paranormal investigator visitors. And their interest would overwhelm our focus, which is to preserve and share Surratt House's wonderful history."

Many years ago, while Verge was a volunteer but before she was director, someone had arranged an evening séance in the home without alerting the staff or volunteer board. When a story about the eerie event was printed the next day in a local newspaper, a number of Surratt House volunteers and patrons were very upset that the home was being turned into a "three-ring circus." They believed such activities would detract from the property's historical significance and stature.

On two occasions, Verge said, psychics had gone through the home. One was unannounced and happened to visit on a day when there were a small number of visitors. The other was from Texas and associated with a television crew conducting a documentary about the Booth escape route. Both of the psychic investigators told Verge there were no ghosts in the building. But, they also said the home was filled with emotion and heavy feelings. One said it was a "sick house."

"When I send out letters declining requests by ghost hunting organizations," Verge said, "I share the details uncovered by the two psychics."

Verge said she started out as a firm disbeliever in ghosts and the paranormal. As a result of continuing reports of unusual incidents over the years, Verge said her opinion has changed. She now is open to the possibility that there may be something out there that cannot be seen or logically explained. "But," she added, "if there is such a thing as a ghost, or if any old house deserved to be haunted, it is the Surratt House and the Doctor Mudd House, because of the tragic history and the question marks that still exist regarding the degree of guilt or innocence of those who were involved in the historic events that took place there."

Mysterious (University of) Maryland

Is the College Park main campus of the University of Maryland haunted? A lot of people think so. In fact, each year around Halloween, staff at the University Archives receive a number of requests about ghost stories and legends related to that institution of higher learning. As a result, in 2006, the Office of Visitor Services and Office of Student Affairs asked University Archivist Anne Turkos to produce a ghost tour for parents and students during that year's Family Weekend, which occurred in October.

At the time, Elizabeth McAllister, currently the acting curator of historical manuscripts in the Hornbake Library, was assistant university archivist. She and Turkos created and presented the ghost walking tour on the campus.

"Since this topic seemed to pique the students' interest," McAllister recalled, "and also to be of general interest to the campus community, we thought it would make a good exhibition in our gallery." McAllister collaborated with Jennie Levine, then curator of historical manuscripts, to plan the associated gallery exhibition—"Mysterious Maryland: The Strange and Supernatural on Campus and Beyond."

"That exhibit," McAllister said, "was probably our most heavily visited exhibit that we have hosted in our exhibit gallery since the gallery's opening in 2001. This was mainly because it appealed to a very broad audience, especially our largest campus population: undergraduate students." The exhibition also attracted visits by community groups and was covered in the *Washington Post* and several campus publications.

Thanks to McAllister's generous cooperation, the following chapter—based heavily on campus ghost tour documents and gallery exhibition text—offers an overview of some of the haunted tales and legends associated with the main campus of the University of Maryland.

The Tawes Fine Arts building contains a large theater that has offered a variety of productions over the years. Some say a ghost named Mortimer moved into the building soon after its construction. Footsteps, voices, unexpected sounds, and practical jokes are attributed to the arts building's resident prankster. Some believe Mortimer is the spirit of a former student who was killed while serving in Vietnam, but that is only a guess about the phantom's origin. It's also thought Mortimer might be the ghost of a dog.

H. J. Patterson Hall, nicknamed "Steinberg Castle," has hosted a variety of science-oriented classes from its opening to the present. One evening, a maintenance worker was performing routine duties in the attic. While there he said he saw a strange, oddly shaped shadow move quickly across the wall. There was no one else in the area, and the dark image could not have been caused by any natural or explainable source.

Some believe the ghost of student-athlete Len Bias, who died of a cocaine overdose in his campus residence hall room in June 1986, haunts Washington Hall. The All-American basketball player suffered a fatal cardiac arrhythmia that resulted from the overdose, less than forty-eight hours after being selected second overall by the Boston Celtics in the 1986 NBA Draft. Subsequent residents of that room reported hearing the sounds of a bouncing basketball in the middle of the night. The ghost of a student who died from a fall in the early 1990s from a window in Easton Hall is believed to be the source of unusual events and sightings in that dormitory.

While a ghostly runner has never been seen at Byrd Stadium, evidence suggests a spirited racer may have left his mark on the track's smooth surface. In the 1970s, when the runners raced on a dirt surface, some students said they witnessed puffs of dust. The small clouds of dirt seemed to appear spontaneously, as if an invisible runner, moving at a very fast pace, was circling the interior of the stadium.

The McNamee family cemetery is located near the Stadium Drive Garage, close to the intersection of Valley and Stadium drives. The small plot hosts the remains of the McNamee family, who sold the land to the university in 1938. According to the campus ghost tour, "The University had the cemetery bricked over to prevent anyone from disturbing the graves, although some speculate that it may have been to keep whoever is buried in the graves from disturbing the campus."

One of the most unusual artifacts displayed in the "Mysterious Maryland" exhibition was the coffin of American author Katherine Anne Porter. The Pulitzer Prize-winning writer, and author of the best-selling novel *Ship of Fools*, died in Silver Spring, Maryland, on September 18, 1980. While her ashes were buried next to her mother at Indian Creek Cemetery in central Texas, Miss Porter's coffin was left behind. The writer had purchased the pine box from a mail-order company in Montana in 1974, and she stored it in a closet in her College Park apartment. When she had visitors, she delighted in stepping in and out of it and announcing it was to be her eternal home. The nephew who served as her executor decided that it was unwise to inter her ashes in the pine box. The colorful artifact was passed on to two of Porter's friends, one of whom eventually donated it to the University of Maryland Libraries in 1996. It currently resides—in an unoccupied state—in the Katherine Anne Porter Room in Hornbake Library.

Rossborough Inn

The Rossborough Inn, the oldest building on campus and part of the college since its establishment, is one of the best places to observe paranormal activity. Built before the War of 1812, it was located on the main route between Baltimore and Washington and operated as a tavern, stagecoach stop, and place of lodging. Certainly notable historical figures visited or stayed in the inn, including Revolutionary War hero and French general Marquis de Lafayette. Since the building is located a few miles from the famous Bladensburg dueling grounds, it's believed some of the men who traveled to the area to settle their differences by sword and pistol spent their last nights on earth in the Rossborough Inn.

The ghost of a man who lost a duel near the hitching post in front of the inn is said to haunt the building. It's believed the duelists ran into each other at the inn and decided they didn't have to travel to the bloody dueling ground the next day in order to try to kill each other. The mortally wounded loser of the contest was carried to a room on the third floor of Rossborough Inn and died there. A dark stain, which appears to be blood, can be seen on the floor in that room. Some speculate it marks the place where the defeated duelist died.

Confederate general Bradley T. Johnson used the Rossborough Inn as his headquarters during the Civil War, and his troops erected tents and camped on the present-day university grounds. At different times during the last year of the war, Union troops also patrolled and stayed in the same area and at other locations in Prince George's County. Some troops probably died from injury and illness during their stay, and this might be the cause of reports that a Confederate soldier's ghost walks the grounds near the historic inn.

Another ghost with a Civil War connection is that of Miss Bettie, the woman who managed the Rossborough Inn during the conflict. Her ghost, wearing a yellow gown in a style that was common during that time period, has been reported walking the hallways of the present-day building. In 1981, a dining services employee said he spotted a female ghost in the old inn during renovations. This is consistent with the belief by some paranormal experts that significant reconstruction or renovations of historic structures can stir up the spirits. Several weeks later, a waiter working in the inn said he also saw a woman dressed in an old-fashioned, long yellow dress. Eventually, workers began to attribute any unusual event to Miss Bettie, such as a vase holding a single flower that appeared with no apparent cause in an old bathroom that had been used for storage and securely locked. One night, a caretaker who lived in the building came out of the bathtub, looked in the mirror, and saw a woman's face beside his own reflection. Doors open and close, and lights turn on and off by themselves in the building. There also have been incidents involving sounds of unexplained footsteps coming from the upper floors.

Marie Mount Hall

Constructed in 1940, Marie Mount Hall is named after the dean of the College of Home Economics from 1927 to 1957. Miss Mount loved the college and its students, and at one time lived in the building in a special apartment. According to Turkos's and McAllister's ghost walk script, "She was much loved by her students, and University President Wilson Elkins declared in a 1957 memorial to the dean that 'The character of Marie Mount will live forever.' Dean Marie Mount does just that."

In the 1970s, security personnel, building occupants, and workers told of a number of paranormal incidents involving possible entities from the other side. Doors were heard opening and closing on their own. Toilets flushed when no one was supposed to be in the building. Sudden gusts of wind occurred when all the doors and windows were shut tightly. The exhibition and ghost tour documents suggest the incidents may be indications of the presence of Marie Mount's spirit. Her presence is particularly active during storms with heavy rain and strong winds. During such times, piano music is heard in the building. This might be a sign from Marie Mount, who used to enjoy playing her own keyboard instrument.

Morrill Hall

Morrill Hall is named after Justin Morrill, sponsor of the Morrill Land Grant Act, which established federal land-grant colleges. Among those institutions created was the Maryland Agricultural College, which expanded into the University of Maryland. Built in 1898, Morrill Hall is the oldest campus building with its original facade. One of the requirements of institutions associated with the Morrill Act was offering mandatory military training for male students. At the Maryland Agricultural College, students were organized into companies of cadets. The barracks and administration building—as well as the drill field and parade ground—stood near Morrill Hall. The phantom sounds of marching feet have been reported in the area around Morrill Hall. The drill field also was the site where cadets who misbehaved walked off their demerits by marching back and forth, with a rifle over one's shoulder, for extended periods of time.

A fire broke out in two buildings near Morrill Hall during the night of November 29, 1912, while the cadets were having a Thanksgiving dance. The student soldiers evacuated their dates from the burning building and returned to help put out the fire and save documents, furniture, and personal belongings. By the time firemen arrived, the buildings where the fire originated were nearly destroyed, but the campus volunteers and firefighters were able to save adjacent structures, including Morrill Hall. There were no injuries or fatalities from the blaze, but Morrill Hall is the only structure still standing in the area of the campus that witnessed the Great Fire of 1912.

Modern-day inhabitants of the building, who have no knowledge of the nearly century-ago inferno, have reported smelling smoke in Morrill Hall. Others have told of strange odors, which seem to be particularly strong in the basement of the building.

According to a 2003 article on the University of Maryland Web site, "Recently, workers in Morrill Hall found human remains under a sink while the building was undergoing renovation." Students often wander into the building during the fall to see the "haunted building." During the late nineteenth and early twentieth centuries the building was used as a science and laboratory facility, but it's believed that cadavers were not dissected in the building. Those experiments were conducted at the institution's Medical School, located in downtown Baltimore only a few blocks from the Edgar Allan Poe gravesite.

Greek Ghosts

Greek life and its traditions have been associated with the University of Maryland since Sigma Nu was established as the first fraternity in 1913 and sorority Kappa Kappa Gamma moved on campus in 1920. According to the ghost tour researchers, several sorority and fraternity houses are thought to host one or more resident ghosts.

In Alpha Omicron Pi, some of the sisters have reported music players coming on suddenly and their computers turning on without warning. A fraternity member who had died in a car accident in the 1950s is said to haunt the brothers living in the Delta Tau Delta house. The ghost of Alma Preinkert is rumored to haunt the Kappa Delta house. Miss Preinkert was that sorority's founder and the school's registrar from 1919 until 1954, the year she was murdered in her Washington, D.C. home. The case remains unsolved, and paranormal experts suggest the apparition of the victim's restless soul visits the sorority home that she founded and where she spent enjoyable times during her life. A car accident ended the life of a Theta Chi brother, but some of his housemates believe he came back to say goodbye, since strange incidents occurred in that house.

These are a few of the paranormal incidents reported over the years on the College Park campus, and presented during Turkos's and McAllister's ghost walk. While this is not the only college with resident ghosts, stories of school spirits at the University of Maryland certainly are among the most fascinating, ranging from historical legends to contemporary tales.

Calvert's Mysterious Mansions

Maidstone's Gray Lady

Perhaps the most well-known Calvert County mansion with a roaming spirit is Maidstone. This stately colonial-era home, located near Owings, was built in the late 1600s. Numerous additions and improvements were added to the structure, but some think the most important extra feature is the mansion's resident phantom—the Gray Lady.

Samuel Chew, the original owner of the home and its surrounding two thousand acres, was a prominent landowner. His daughter, Anne Chew, is believed to be the estate's resident spirit. According to a story written in 1960 by Earl Hicks, who owned Maidstone at that time, Anne loved the home and the home loved her. Her grand wedding was held on the property. After the ceremony, she climbed aboard her husband's horse, wrapped her arms around his body, and waved farewell to the home and the large group of family and friends in attendance.

As the happily married bride and groom rode past the front gate of Maidstone, Anne became silent and did not speak during the ride to the just-wed couple's new home. However, the groom became concerned when his bride, whose arms still encircled his waist, would not respond to his instructions to dismount from the horse. Turning and holding onto her slumping, silent body, the young man was shocked to discover that Anne was dead.

In Hicks's story, "A Halloween Tale for Little Girls of Maidstone," the writer suggested that the structure loved the young woman as much as Anne had loved the home, and the possessive building refused to let her spirit leave the property. At Maidstone's gate, the powerful essence of the imposing historic structure claimed Anne's soul, which remains on the estate's grounds and occasionally makes its presence known.

Most witnesses over the centuries have sighted Anne roaming the gardens and standing on the lawn near the main house. On one occasion, a guest in the building claimed the mysterious mistress pushed him off the parlor couch. But that was a rare unexplained incident, and the only one where the invisible phantom came in direct contact with a mortal. The spirit also has been blamed for rearranging pictures and hanging them in different places on the walls. The Gray Lady's nickname is associated with several reports that described the spirit as wearing a long gray gown and matching veil, which establishes a connection with Hicks's story of Anne's sudden death and her attire on her wedding day.

Cedar Hill

In the western area of the county, near Barstow, two ghosts are believed to haunt historic Cedar Hill: a Confederate soldier and a former owner. The Civil War spirit is believed to be benevolent, and he has appeared in the home's study. But a former mistress of the home, said to have been killed in her bedroom by a slave, is considered the more active and disgruntled phantom. She is the cause of a number of bothersome antics, including turning on and off lights, moving a rug after it was put into place, slamming doors, causing footsteps and sounds in the attic, and making it difficult for tenants and owners to open and close the basement door.

John Bigger, a merchant and trader, built Cedar Hill in the early 1700s in the unusual shape of a cross, making it a popular site on the area's periodic home and garden tours. According to one newspaper story about the structure, by Lynda Gallagher in the *Calvert Independent*, "The house's cruciform floor plan also follows an astronomical theme. The sun sets directly down the axis of Cedar Hill on the vernal equinox, the first day of spring."

Hampton's Southern Specters

Several mysterious tales have been associated with the historic property called Hampton (also known as Talbott House), near Chaneyville. A log cabin was built on the property in the 1660s, and original portions of the present structure date to the early 1800s. According to a 1983 interview between a reporter and the resident at that time, late one night in 1946, the owner said she saw a group of about a dozen young men, wearing wide-brimmed gray hats, pass through the front door and silently float up the stairs. The woman added that shortly after that initial sighting another ghostly image appeared from the area of the attic. This friendly phantom told the owner she had a kind and caring ghost living in her house.

Some have speculated that the gray-clad intruders might have been the roaming spirits of long-lost Confederate soldiers. Historical records indicate Southern troops conducted a raid on the farm and stole several oxen from the property. The single ghost might be David Carcaud, the original owner of Hampton, who is buried in a family graveyard located on the property.

Other stories associated with the home include a wailing voice heard near a mature elm tree, but that might be the result of the rubbing of a dead limb that sways during a strong wind. Slaves passed down an eerie tale about blood. The dark liquid would bubble up from the surface of the basement, at the base of a whipping post that was erected there. But the owner said the story was a tall tale, suggesting the old post was probably used to hang smoked hams, and there was no evidence any slaves were mistreated in the basement of the mansion. Subsequent owners have reported on their Web site that they have not experienced any unexplained incidents at the home or on the property.

Taney Place

Roger Brooke Taney, chief justice of the U.S. Supreme Court from 1836 to 1864, was born in 1777 at Taney Place, the family home in Adelina. Roger's most well-known judgment on the court was his 1857 ruling on the Dred Scott Decision. Many believe this controversial decision pushed the divided nation toward an inevitable Civil War, which began in 1861. Because of Roger's significant historical role as the fifth chief justice, a tragedy associated with his father, Michael, that occurred at Taney Place often is overlooked. In a "Know Your County" column in 1975, Betty Briscoe shared a slice of the county's oral history and folklore.

In the late 1700s, Michael Taney and his neighbor John Magruder got into a violent argument during dinner, following a fox hunt held at Taney Place. The subject of their conflict was Barbara Dorsey, an attractive woman who was visiting from the South. In one version, Taney made an insulting remark about the woman, and Magruder slapped the host across the face. Taney pulled a knife from his pocket and stabbed Magruder in the heart. The other story, which the Taney family accepted, claimed it was Magruder that insulted the young woman. Defending the female guest's honor, Taney challenged his neighbor to a duel and they marched to a nearby cedar tree. When the opponents selected their pistols, they found their friends had not loaded the weapons, an obvious attempt to stall the deadly conflict. Still enraged over Magruder's insult to the lady's honor, Taney stabbed Magruder, who fell to the ground holding his hand over his bleeding heart. Taney helped carry the injured neighbor into Taney Place, where Magruder died from the fatal wound. Worried about the legal ramifications of his impulsive act, Taney ran to another end of the house and escaped into the nearby woods through a secret chamber and tunnel.

Briscoe's article did not mention if the master of Taney Place suffered any consequences following the altercation, but that is not surprising. The rich and influential members of society of that period often were not subjected to criminal prosecution. However, the sensational details of the colorful incident have been passed down for generations. Some believe the spirits of Michael Taney and John Magruder appear beneath an ancient cedar tree somewhere on the grounds of Taney Place, which was placed in the National Register of Historic Places in 1972.

Drum Point Lighthouse

Since 1975, visitors to the Calvert Marine Museum at Solomons Island have enjoyed exploring and photographing Drum Point Lighthouse. Built in 1883 and automated in 1960, the distinctive 41-ton screwpile structure helped generations of mariners navigate the Chesapeake Bay. From 1960 to 1975, the automated lighthouse sat abandoned and was experiencing a slow death until it was saved, moved to its current home, and restored.

But a few unusual stories, related in documents provided by staff at the Calvert County Historical Society, suggest there might be an invisible resident or two roaming the historic lighthouse.

Years ago, a few museum interpreters opened the building in the morning and noticed certain items were out of their proper places. The employees insisted they were sure the objects had been left in their correct spots when the workers locked the building at the end of the previous day. Adding to the staff members' confusion, the building's burglar alarm had been turned on, but it had not been activated, which would have occurred during a break-in. Therefore, it was apparent no intruder had been in the building.

Several events have occurred in the lighthouse without any logical explanation: the hat of a former lighthouse keeper was found on the kitchen table instead of on its chair; whenever a certain flower was left in a water vase, the decorative glass was found lying on its side and the flowers were tossed onto the floor (later use of dried and artificial flowers seemed to solve this problem); an icebox door, which has a strong latch that is difficult to manipulate, was found wide open; and footsteps were heard on the upper floors and on a spiral staircase after all of the day's visitors had vacated the old building.

According to a 1980 article by Audrey Osborne in *The Calvert Independent*, the museum director and a friend stayed overnight on Halloween night to investigate the alleged hauntings. While the two men reported seeing no unusual apparitions or hearing any strange sounds, one of the men's watches (which had a working battery) stopped dead at midnight—the bewitching hour.

Some say the lighthouse is home to the spirit of a young, dark-haired woman, who roams the highest level surrounding the light. Standing at the top of the historic building, with her long hair waving in the wind, she appears to be looking toward the Chesapeake Bay, perhaps waiting for someone to return through time from a lengthy, long-ago voyage.

In the nearby museum building, a docent and woodcarver both said they heard footsteps in different locations of the building after it was closed. A search at that time found no one else in the structure and no apparent cause for the noises. Of course, initially, the docent said she was hesitant to mention the incidents and her thoughts about a possible haunting to anyone for fear they would think she was crazy.

Haunted Barn and Church Ghost

During the final years of the eighteenth century, about three miles from Prince Frederick, a settler built a fair-sized farmhouse and a magnificent tobacco barn. The landowner spent most of his working and leisure time inside that sturdy, impressive structure. When a fire destroyed his home, the family was able to move into the working barn, which had ample room to live and work.

Many years passed and the original owner died. The land and barn were sold and the family's descendants moved away from the region. But some believe the spirit of the earlier settler stayed behind. New residents built a home on the foundation of the original farmhouse, but they were never comfortable in the structure. Footsteps, sudden gusts of wind, and even the sounds of gunshots inside the new home caused them to live in a constant uneasy state that was interrupted frequently by moments of sudden and unexplained terror. But things were even worse in the barn. In the middle of the night, the tobacco machinery would start to work, as if a phantom overseer had thrown a switch. The voices of men working in the empty building were loud enough to be heard in the nearby house, but these sounds ceased when the family raced across the yard and opened the barn door to investigate.

People riding along a nearby road raced their horses and carriages past the farm to avoid being assaulted by what folks in the area called the "farm phantom." Word spread that a horseless carriage moved on its own; cattle in the pens awoke at night and raced around in circles, as if being herded, and were terrified by invisible spirits; and unexplained lantern lights appeared in the windows of the barn. No pranksters were ever apprehended, and no logical explanation was ever given for the strange events in the haunted homestead. The best guess is that ghosts of former slaves, buried in unmarked graves somewhere on the grounds, may be the cause of the playful and annoying antics.

At the end of the Halloween season in 2001, Robin Gottlieb wrote a story in *The Calvert Recorder* about the "Lady of All Saints." Apparently, a number of people who attended worship services at All Saints Episcopal Church in Sunderland, as well as a former pastor, had admitted seeing apparitions in and about the historic site, which had been established as a log building in the late 1600s.

Several people said they had caught glimpses of what they believed were specters inside the church. A slave gallery—where African Americans were allowed to sit during services, on an upper level along one side of the building—is one location where a strange figure had been seen. One parishioner said she saw a dark figure in a black cape standing on the stairs in the back of the church building. A former pastor was so convinced there was something to the stories that he asked one of his flock if he had ever seen "people who weren't there." One Sunday, while on the pulpit during a service, the cleric requested that any members of his congregation who had seen unusual ghostly sightings in the church contact him.

Gottlieb reported that a 1975 church newsletter stated the rector at the time was interested in "how many persons in All Saints parish have seen visions, particularly in All Saints Church." The church bulletin further noted that several members of the congregation had already admitted such experiences and the rector was attempting to gain more information.

Stories about the mysterious phantom, nicknamed the "Lady of All Saints," have been told, retold, and embellished over the years. The cause of the sightings remains a mystery, but a clue might be found on the parish's Web site, which describes the church as "older than most countries." Amid the details of the church's origin, history, structures, and pastors is an interesting paragraph. It states that beneath the east end of the building, near the altar, rest the remains of two former pastors: Thomas John Chew and Matthew Johnson. During their days of service, it was a common practice for pastors to be buried beneath the consecrated building where they faithfully had served the Lord and their flock.

Captain Macgregor

In a vertical file in the Maryland History Room at the College of Southern Maryland's library, I came across an old photocopied story. There was no indication of the source of the three pages of faded words, typed under the generic heading "GHOST STORY."

The introductory paragraph claimed the unnamed author discovered the mysterious tale about Patuxent Manor in the Winterthur Files, and the story was attributed to James Hungerford (who visited Calvert County during the summer of 1832 to escape a cholera epidemic that was occurring in Baltimore). The writer stated Col. Albert Musgrove, then owner of the stately manor house, also recommended the interesting tale.

According to the document, Patuxent Manor was one of several houses in Lower Marlboro believed to be inhabited by a spirit. In the 1830s, the Old Brick House (as Patuxent Manor had been called) stood amidst five hundred acres at the northern edge of the village of St. Joseph's. During that time, a Mr. Speers lived on the property, working as caretaker and overseer for the absentee landlord, J. Stafford, Esq.

The origin of the ghost tale, however, occurred when the estate was much larger, extending over nearly three thousand acres. At that time, one Captain Macgregor, who is buried near the Old Brick House and who is now supposed to haunt Patuxent Manor, owned the property. Shortly after Captain Macgregor died, his property was passed down to his two sons, a Dr. Macgregor and his younger brother, Charles Macgregor. Apparently, Charles was angry because the father's property had not been divided equally and his inheritance ended up being less than his older brother's.

Late one night, and after drinking heavily, Charles stumbled to his late father's grave. After cursing the old man, the angry son raised an ax and, in his drunken rage, defaced his father's tombstone. Soon afterwards, slaves on the property reported seeing the wispy figure of Captain Macgregor standing by his grave not far from the big house. Word spread that the spirit of the owner was upset. Members of the superstitious slave community were frightened of the ghost, and they were careful to avoid the area near the Macgregor family plot during both day and night.

When Mr. Speers, the manager of the estate, first heard the story, he laughed at the tale, describing it as the frightened ramblings of illiterate slaves that had too much time on their hands. Everyone knew they spent their evenings creating silly mumbo jumbo bedtime stories to entertain themselves and their children. But the overseer's attitude soon changed. Awakened abruptly in the middle of the night, he glanced out his bedroom window and saw the glowing apparition of the dead captain hovering near his defaced stone in the graveyard. Mr. Speers later told his friends he was so shocked and nervous that he locked his bedroom window and door. He added that he was too afraid to leave his room to make sure the locks on the first floor of the house were secure.

A second, more terrifying incident occurred when Mr. Speers was directed by Mr. Stafford to cut down a weeping willow tree that stood next to Captain Macgregor's grave. Not planning to get his own hands dirty, the overseer ordered several slaves to do the work. Relaxing in a comfortable chair, he watched their progress from his seat on a flat surface at the back of the house. The moment the large tree crashed to the ground, the sky became dark, the temperature dropped, and the mood and atmosphere near the home changed.

A rush of wind, like a small tornado, swirled through the first floor of the house, rattling windows, opening cabinets, and slamming doors. At the same time, a loud, moaning voice cried out from the parlor. Mr. Speers, who had raced inside the building to investigate, later said he saw a large man standing in the center of the room who resembled members of the Macgregor family he had seen in paintings. The figure stared at Mr. Speers and gave off a threatening aura that filled the overseer with a sense of dread and horror. Terrified, Mr. Speers turned and ran from the home and hid inside a stall of the nearest barn. An older slave named Will, who said as a young boy he had belonged to Captain Macgregor, had witnessed the events. Will later identified the mysterious apparition as the Captain, his deceased master. After that sudden and memorable incident, there were no other ghostly disturbances at the home.

In the conclusion of the paper, the anonymous author questions whether the Old Brick House and Patuxent Manor are the same structure, and if the gravesite in the legend and the damaged tombstone exist. Whether the tale of Captain Macgregor ever occurred, or the story is the product of an overactive, creative mind, doesn't matter. Thanks to the unknown writer and careful stewardship at the College of Southern Maryland, this wonderful nugget of county folklore has been saved and is able to be shared and enjoyed.

Devil's Woodyard

Years ago, the Devil had a hangout in Calvert County. It was in a densely forested area overlooking the Chesapeake Bay that few people dared enter. Those who explored the hexed locale were never seen again. The precise location of this secret satanic site, known as the Devil's Woodyard, was unknown, so locals avoided an extensive wooded section of the county. Elders said the Prince of Darkness would meet "somewhere in the wood" with covens of witches on Friday nights, at midnight, under the full moon, as well as on Halloween night. At that time, the band of unearthly revelers would mix potions, cast spells, call out curses, and pay tribute to their fire-breathing, red-eyed master.

One night a local pastor said he was going to accost Satan's servants and clear out the hexed forest. The cleric ignored the warnings of his family and friends and disappeared in the dense woods. After a short time, his faithful followers, who had been waiting at the edge of the forest, heard a piercing cry. Realizing they would soon be announcing a search for a new pastor, they turned and ran back to the safety of their homes.

After that, no churchgoing, God-fearing mortal went anywhere near the Devil's Woodyard, especially after stories circulated that unsuspecting passersby had been pulled from the dark, narrow roads and offered up as human sacrifices to the unholy guest of honor. Eventually, a road was built through the woods, and the stories died, but the legend surfaces every Halloween season.

Also along the Chesapeake Bay, near Plum Point, stands Neeld's Mansion, which was the site of mysterious events. In a 1995 interview in the *Calvert Independent*, the owners told reporter Audrey Osborn of the historic home's tragic legend, which causes an increased amount of interest each year around Halloween.

The folktale's origin is traced to the days when the property was a plantation known as Leitchworth Chance and slaves worked hundreds of acres of peach orchards. One night, a two-year-old child of one of the slaves that worked in the house wandered into the spacious bedchamber of the plantation's mistress. Infuriated that the slave child had intruded on her private domain, the enraged woman grabbed the child, carried it out into the hall and tossed the small body over the stairway railing. The screaming baby fell onto the hardwood surface three floors below, where its seeping blood stained the entry hall. The legend claims the dying child's cries and its mother's screams are heard during stormy nights.

The owners at the time of the interview admitted they had never heard any screams or cries, but the popular legend has survived. The owners also said there was a story that the mistress ordered her slaves whipped and beaten in the nearby barn, for no other reason than to calm her agitated nerves. It seemed that the plantation's mistress said the snapping sound of the lash and the cries of the slaves being whipped helped her relax when she became nervous. Eventually, the slaves realized that the woman of the house never entered the barn during the beatings, so they began whipping a saddle and directed the "victims" to shout out in pain when each lash struck the leather seat.

Nancy

Along Solomons Island Road in Prince Frederick, where Maryland Routes 2 and 4 run together, the Rustic Farm Restaurant operated in the early 1980s. The building resembled an authentic log cabin, and in later years the business was known as the Log Cabin Inn.

On the evening of March 6, 1980, the owner of the business took a revolver from the shelf beside the cash register, told his customers there was some trouble in the back, and walked to his residence, located on the property behind the restaurant building. Minutes later, during a heated argument, he shot his wife in the head. A Maryland state trooper arrested the husband a short time later, and the murder weapon was discovered in the shooter's pants pocket.

As years passed, the business changed hands and operated under several different names. In 1996, it became known as Adam's Ribs. But stories about the restless spirit of the site's 1980 murder victim remained a part of the building's folklore.

Karen Sykes, archivist at the Calvert County Historical Society, said she had a conversation with a former manager of the present-day restaurant. He told her there still were rumors about the ghost of Nancy, the woman killed on the property. According to the manager, Sykes said, "The employees of the restaurant said strange things happened so consistently that the Smithsonian came out to check for paranormal activities. When the manager and bartender were locking up and walking out the door, the TV would come on. They would walk across the room to where the remote controls were and shut off the TV. At this point, another TV set would come on. Patrons reported seeing Nancy at the bar or feel a presence."

It is common for employees to blame any unexplained incidents on Nancy, and female employees have heard their names being called by a woman, but when they turn to respond no one is around.

Scent from the Past

When Geraldine's father died, she inherited the small, twenty-acre farm that the family had owned for two generations. It wasn't a big spread, but it provided enough seasonal crops to supply the vegetable stand they set up each summer along the two-lane rural road that passed by their property.

After Geraldine and her husband cleaned out the farmhouse attic, basement, and bedrooms, they prepared to tackle the outbuildings, which included a pair of barns. The couple took their time going through old tools, unfinished projects, and rusted equipment, some of which had stood untouched for decades. Their four-year-old daughter, Samantha, wasn't much help. She kept busy roaming the buildings, apparently fascinated with the littered junk that covered nearly every inch of the buildings' walls, ceilings, and floors.

After months of cleaning, hauling, and disposing of years of accumulated junk, Geraldine said they were down to two major items: her father's work truck and an ancient Massey-Ferguson tractor. Her husband wanted to toss them both, but Geraldine insisted on keeping the old Ford pickup. It had been her father's work vehicle and also his main means of transportation to town and back. She had fond memories of riding with her cousins in the back bed, waving at passing cars, and playing in the old relic when it was parked behind the house.

"I could still see my father, late at night in the summer," she said, "sitting in the front seat, all alone, smoking a cigarette, and drinking a six-pack of Natty Boh. He would stay out there all night, listening to the Orioles on the radio, whether they were playing at home or away. He'd stay in there until the game was done. But the next morning, when he dropped us off at school or church, the whole truck would smell like stale beer."

About a year after she had gotten the old truck back into operating shape—and two years after her father had died—Geraldine was driving into town to pick up some supplies at the feed store. Her daughter was sitting in the passenger seat. As she pulled into a parking space, very close to where her father had parked the same truck many years earlier, Geraldine said she experienced a flashback. "I saw it happening, just like it was a movie rolling in front of my eyes. There was my father, holding my hand as we walked into the same store I was planning to take Samantha in at that very moment. Then, like a wave falling over me, I smelled the distinct, unmistakable smell of beer. It was so strong, it made me shake my head and pulled me back into the present. The smell lingered in the cab of the truck for at least a full minute." But Geraldine was not the only one who noticed the scent. Samantha turned to her mother and asked, "Mommy! What's that bad smell?"

"That really got to me," Geraldine said. "I could almost discount the incident as my imagination, particularly with the vivid memory I had been experiencing. But my baby had no idea of what I was thinking, and she didn't know anything about her grandfather's habit of drinking beer in his truck. When she noticed the same smell at the same time I did, well, I considered that to be a major unexplained event."

When Geraldine later told her husband, his first reaction was to try to explain away the smell, telling her it probably was her imagination, or just a coincidence. Others have had the same initial response when Geraldine shared the details of that Saturday-morning visit to town. But she remains convinced the incident was much more.

"I really don't care what anybody else thinks," she said. "I know what happened. I know, without a doubt, what I smelled. And I know what my little girl smelled, too, and I saw her reaction at the same time I was experiencing it. I'll always believe it was a visit from my father. I think he was trying, in the best way he could, to let me know he's nearby, looking out over us."

Midnight Emergency

It was during the first hour of the graveyard shift in the emergency room of a small rural hospital. Kathy, one of the nurses on duty, looked at her watch. Ten minutes before midnight. Evelyn, her coworker, was fifty minutes late. But Evelyn was never late, and the one time she had arrived after the shift began, she had called on her drive in and alerted the staff so they wouldn't be concerned. But as the clock approached midnight, Kathy decided it was getting close to worrying time.

The narrow, winding roads that led to the small country hospital had seen their share of accidents, many caused by deer standing on or passing across the ill-lit rural roads. She'd give her friend another fifteen minutes, and then Kathy would have someone call Evelyn's home and try to find out what was going on.

This all happened several years ago, before the arrival of cell phones, which provided ever-present, immediate communication. As Kathy closed the door on the supply closet and began to take some fresh linens to one of the empty rooms, she passed a long, empty hallway. From the corner of her eye, standing about one hundred feet away at the opposite end of a connecting aisle, she saw Evelyn. Her friend and coworker had finally arrived, and she was waving enthusiastically, pointing at Kathy and directing her toward the emergency room entrance.

Thinking her friend had indicated they should meet at the front of the hospital, Kathy dropped off the batch of linens in the empty room, turned, and headed back toward the main admission desk. When she arrived, she asked if anyone had seen Evelyn, but the rest of the staff said they still had not yet heard from the woman. Suddenly, the loud sound of doors flying open and the rolling wheels of a racing gurney interrupted their conversation.

Two stern-faced emergency vehicle drivers had arrived and were pushing a bloodstained stretcher into the lobby. The doctor on duty and Kathy rushed into ER Room 1 to treat the injured patient, but they soon determined it was too late. The accident victim had died just moments earlier, about the time Kathy had seen her friend wave from the far end of the hospital hallway. But that couldn't have happened. Because it was Evelyn's lifeless body, still dressed in her nurse's uniform, lying on the operating table in ER Room 1.

Charles's Haunted Homes

Each Halloween season, newspaper reporters in Charles County offer their readers entertaining and frightening spirited tales. As expected, several reference old historic homes, where some claim a fair number of famous phantoms continue to roam. Here are few of these homes and their well-known, but usually unseen, restless residents.

Prospect Hill

The White Lady haunts Prospect Hill, which stands on a rise two miles east of La Plata. While the house is believed to date back to the early 1700s, little is known about the building's original owner. Edward Hamilton, a wealthy planter, was the owner just before the Revolutionary War. Much more information, however, is available about the mansion's lovely and mysterious ghostly resident.

The incident that started the legend involved a young boy who had been ill for several months and who spent a considerable amount of time in his bedroom. His parents decided to take him to Prospect Hill, owned by his grandfather, where they believed the pleasant rural setting would speed his recovery. Instead, the move led to his death. A few days after arriving, the young boy told his family members that a beautiful lady in a flowing white gown and blue scarf had stopped in his room, leaned over his bed, and smiled down at him. This occurred several times in the middle of the night, and each evening the vision awoke him from a deep sleep. The boy said he was not afraid, but curious about her identity.

The skeptical parents tried to pass off their child's report as an overactive imagination, and they told the youngster he was simply having an unusual dream. They said he shouldn't worry, and they made him drink a glass of warm milk before going to bed. That was a sure cure for his restless nights, they said, and it would ensure a deep sleep. To some extent they were correct: a week later their child went into a sound sleep and never awoke again. He died in his bed during the night.

According to an article by C. Irwin Jones Jr., the ghost of Prospect Hill might be owner Edward Hamilton's second wife, who died in the kitchen while preparing a meal. Sparks from a blaze beneath a kettle of boiling fat leapt from the hearth and landed on the hem of Mrs. Hamilton's dress. As the woman ran away from the fireplace, the resulting rush of air fanned the small flames and quickly turned them into a deadly inferno. Within minutes, the dress and the mistress of the house were consumed by fire. Her beauty was destroyed in the cooking accident, but it's said the lovely lady of the house returns at night and appears to visitors, showing off her former attractive appearance.

Idaho

The ghost of a young mother visited Idaho, a mansion outside La Plata built in 1852 by Judge Frederick Stone. This Maryland home received the name of the western state after the judge had visited Idaho and was impressed with its beauty. He also liked the meaning of the word: "the light on the hill." There is only one ghost, and only one sighting, reported in the old mansion, and it's believed to be a calm and friendly visitor.

Judge Stone's first wife, Maria, died and left behind several children who had to be raised and cared for. Eventually, the widower married his wife's widowed sister, Jennie, who had a child of her own and who also bore the judge additional children.

One night, four children were asleep in a bedroom in Idaho when a soft white light appeared in the dark room. Slowly and steadily the glow grew more intense, until a woman, dressed in a white gown, appeared in a corner and smiled down on the sleeping children. Passing by the beds where the young girls slept, the bright apparition paused and looked down upon each child. At the bed of a young girl who had been an infant when her mother had died, the ghostly visitor bent over and kissed the forehead of her former baby, who was now several years older. As the child stirred from the soft touch, she opened her eyes, looked at the mysterious visitor, and fell back asleep.

The next morning at breakfast, the girl told the family about the pretty lady she had seen in her dream. As the elders seemed to exhibit only slight interest in the story, one of the youngster's cousins, a child of the judge's second wife, said she, too, had seen the lovely lady in the bedroom the previous night. This caught the attention of everyone at the table, particularly when the older child added, "and she looked just like Aunt Maria."

That was the only reported visit of the lovely lady at Idaho.

Dent's Palace

The Washington, D.C., *Sunday Star Magazine* featured an interview with the owner of Dent's Palace, a pre-Revolutionary War home near Bryantown. Considered one of Charles County's oldest all-brick houses, its first section was built in 1720. In the *Star* article, written in 1960 by Jim Birchfield, the owner of the home at the time claimed she and three other residents of the home had seen the same apparition, independently. The ghost, the owner said, had appeared regularly, about once a month, and was pleasant and non-threatening.

Based on the clothing and physical traits of the late-night visitor, it's assumed that the specter is Anne Dent Bean, who died in Dent's Palace about 1839 and who is buried in the family cemetery nearby. Those who have seen the ghost have compared their impressions and all agreed it must be the same person: the spirit was attired in period clothing, wearing a scarf over her head, and her hair seemed in disarray and windblown. Previous residents of the home and a caretaker reported sightings of the spirit of Anne, who died in the home during childbirth when she was twenty-eight years old. Also, at the time of the sightings, the historic home looked much like it had when Anne Dent Bean lived there, making it a familiar place for her spirit to roam and make periodic appearances.

Society Hill

A headless horseman rides in the area of Mount Victoria, at the north end of the peninsula leading to Cobb Island. The ghost is associated with Society Hill, an old mansion built in the early 1700s that was surrounded by hundreds of acres. No one knows the origin of the agitated nightrider, but longtime workers at the estate told tales of the headless phantom's appearance. They said it was not safe to come out of their homes after sundown, and several of those that dared have never returned.

Mount Republic

Built in 1792, Mount Republic was the home of Franklin Weems, considered one of southern Maryland's most well-known and hospitable hosts. The hilltop mansion overlooks the Potomac River, and for several centuries slaves and servants answered to the needs of the estate's rich and famous owners and visitors.

According to an article by Louise Hubbard entitled "The Poker Game Lasted 40 Years," the original owners of Mount Republic entertained their guests with muted elegance and proper British grace and charm. That changed when Franklin Weems took charge. This master of the house hosted twenty-four-hour marathon parties, and he lived by the motto, "Sleep was for weaklings and moderation in food and drink was to be scorned."

More than fifty barrels of brandy and wine were always available in his wine cellar, and he gave his young guests the opportunity to partake of parties in his home three times a week. Often, after staying up all night, Weems would mount his horse early in the morning and dash off on one of the foxhunts he held several times a week.

Guests would arrive at his home and stay for months, and his kitchen staff prepared elaborate dishes, which enhanced the host's reputation as a celebrated gourmet and man about town. Perhaps one of Weems' greatest claims to fame is the story that he had allegedly kept a poker game going continuously on his property for forty years. Details on the how and the why are not recorded, but the unusual nature of the claim has survived long after the bon vivant's trip to that big card game, and twenty-four-hour buffet, in the sky.

Green's Inheritance

Built near Pomfret during the middle of the nineteenth century, Green's Inheritance witnessed the passing of Confederate and Union troops during the Civil War. Tales of blue- and gray-clad phantom soldiers floating across the property and disappearing suddenly have circulated for years. Certainly, with Maryland's sympathy for the Southern cause, Rebel soldiers were hidden in secret passages in the home, and Federal troops encamped in Charles County rode across the estate's lands as they tried to find spies and soldiers working against the Union.

According to Jane Norfolk's *Times Crescent* story about the old mansion, a tale of a tragic love triangle is the basis for a ghost or two. The lover of the woman of the house, who supposedly murdered her husband, was caught and sent to prison. Sounds of a metal object moving across the old home's wooden floors may be the ghost of the jailed killer, slowly dragging his ball and chain. The man's distressed spirit, separated from his lover after being arrested for his crime of passion, still roams the scene of the crime looking for his lost love.

Blue Dog Ghost

For centuries, dogs—particularly black dogs—have been associated with folklore and local superstitions. Their sudden appearances have predicted a wide range of positive and negative events, from impending dangerous weather to the location of undiscovered murder victims to the site of long-lost buried treasure.

The best-known ghost dog in Maryland is not black, but blue. Known as the "Ghostly Blue Dog" or "Blue Dog Ghost," its story has been circulated around the area of Port Tobacco for several hundred years. The small town's history makes it a perfect setting for a ghostly tale. Established in 1634, the community is on the site of an Indian village. The area was sympathetic to the Confederacy during the Civil War, and was part of John Wilkes Booth's escape route after he assassinated President Abraham Lincoln. However, it is the continued interest of ghost hunters in capturing a photo of the Blue Dog Ghost that has made Port Tobacco a paranormal hot spot.

In September 1962, a story in the *Baltimore American* newspaper featured an interview with George W. Hubley Jr., then director of the State Department of Economic Development. Mr. Hubley referred to Port Tobacco as the oldest ghost town in the United States, and he added that the Blue Dog was probably the oldest ghost in America.

The reporter described the Blue Dog Ghost as the source of dozens of stories, rhymes, and ballads. He said the creature "lives on in word-of-mouth tales, affectionately repeated. This makes him a genuine folk personality in an age of skepticism. He was a dog who died defending his master. That is all that is certainly known."

But where certainty ends, the art of creative storytelling takes flight, and various versions of the story have been spun. In the Baltimore reporter's account, the tale goes back to 1658, during Port Tobacco's shipbuilding and seaport days. The tragic incident that triggered the ghost story occurred on the evening of February 8.

It was a cold night when the now-famous dog's master, a traveling peddler carrying his sack, arrived in Port Tobacco. After drinking a bit too much spiked punch and persimmon beer at the St. Charles Inn, his loose lips spilled details about the wealth he was carrying in a money belt tied tightly about his waist.

When the tipsy stranger was pressed by the boisterous bar crowd to prove his claims, the inebriated peddler removed the belt and showed off his large stash of gold to the crowd—certainly making a memorable but short-lived impression. After the pub's closing, the drunken man stumbled up Rose Hill Road, not far from the tavern. That's where the stranger was attacked and murdered, and his faithful dog died fighting by his side, trying to protect his owner.

As proof, however, that folktales change over time, the Web site Our Cities & Towns, featuring Charles County and Port Tobacco, refers to the event happening sometime after the Revolutionary War, more than a hundred years later than the first account. In this version, a soldier was returning home from war with his dog when they were attacked and killed by a Port Tobacco resident who wanted gold and the deed to the soldier's estate. The murderer buried the gold and the stolen deed under a tree along Rose Hill Road. But when he came back to dig up his valuable cache, the Blue Dog Ghost ran the murderer off and the killer soon died of an unexplained illness. To this day, the dog still protects his master and his gold.

Whether you like the first version or second, or one of the others you will certainly hear, most folks agree—or want to believe—that the Blue Dog Ghost returns each year, just before midnight on February 8. And you have the best chance of coming across the phantom protector if you accidentally roam too close to the site of its slain master's unmarked grave and stolen gold—wherever that may be.

Rose Hill

There are several interesting historical incidents, or maybe they're just folklore, associated with Rose Hill. This well-known estate and Georgian home near Port Tobacco has a connection to the Blue Dog Ghost. It's believed the bodies of the faithful beast and its murdered master were buried in an unmarked grave near a large boulder on Rose Hill Road, not far from this eighteenth-century mansion.

In an undated newspaper report in the *Star* by J. L Michael, a story seems to indicate the Blue Dog's spirit continues to guard the treasure that its peddler master hid before he died. One night, an enterprising palm reader and a clairvoyant decided to combine their mystical talents and visit Charles County to prospect for gold near Rose Hill. They claim that when they approached the area of the famous rock the two sensitives heard a growling sound. Whey they turned, they saw the Blue Dog Ghost charging in their direction. The terrified treasure hunters gave up their quest, dropped their shovels, and raced each other to the safety of their automobile.

In addition to its work as a guardian of the gold, a sighting of the Blue Dog Ghost, like the appearance of the Irish banshee, also has been considered a harbinger of death. Olivia Floyd, a Confederate spy and the owner of Rose Hill during the Civil War, told friends she heard a wild howl outside the mansion's entrance late one night. A minute later, she answered a hard knock on the front door. A Southern courier stood on her steps and delivered a note indicating her brother had died in battle.

In his article "Rose Hill and Blue Dog Ghost to Change Hands," Michael wrote, "A few minutes later [after receiving the letter] she told how she looked out the window and saw the unearthly creature [Blue Dog Ghost], tongue out and eyes ablaze, dashing over the hill to a cemetery below."

The old spinster also is said to have confounded Union general Joseph "Fighting Joe" Hooker, whose army was camped a few miles from Rose Hill. One night a secret message was passed to Olivia by a Southern courier. The information was dropped off at Rose Hill, a regular relay station for secret correspondence heading south to Jefferson Davis, president of the Confederacy. Soon after delivering the note, the courier was captured. He admitted to members of Hooker's staff that an important message had been left at Rose Hill. The general rode immediately to the nearby property, entered the home, and directed his men to search the building. While they went from room to room, inspecting the mansion, the Union commander sat in a comfortable chair and warmed himself by the fireplace, resting his damp feet on an ornate, and very large, andiron.

When the search for the document was determined to be unsuccessful—because Olivia had hidden the message inside the hollow section of the andiron the general had been using—Hooker called his men together. At that moment, the mistress of the home, who was indeed a crafty Rebel spy, entered the room waving a pair of mother-of-pearl-handled pistols, which were cocked and aimed at the Union trespassers. Walking up to Hooker, she announced she had caught Yankee thieves out in her chicken house trying to run off with a few of her prize birds.

Hooker is said to have ordered his men to saddle up and leave Rose Hill. "To your tents men," Hooker commanded, placing his hat upon his head. "Better not tamper around a place where the gold is watched by the ghost of a Blue Dog and the house is guarded by a pistol-packin' momma."

Jenifer Portraits

Many years ago, there was an unusual legend associated with Hanson Hill, an old mansion near Port Tobacco. On the parlor walls of the stately home were two portraits. One of the large canvases, both of which were surrounded by ornate, antique, maple frames, bore the image of Daniel Jenifer, who was born in Charles County in 1727 and died in 1793. The other portrait was of Daniel's brother, Daniel of St. Thomas Jenifer, born in 1723 and died in 1790. It's said that Daniel of St. Thomas, an eccentric bachelor, was well known in the region, since he was a member of the Continental Congress, and he also served as a representative at the Constitutional Convention. The noted politician signed the U.S. Constitution in 1787.

Over time, members of several subsequent Jenifer generations have christened their sons with these two names—Daniel and Daniel of St. Thomas. But a strange family legend regarding the paintings had been passed down for years. It's said that the portrait of the married brother, Daniel, has been found on the floor of the parlor prior to the announcement of any marriage in the family. However, when the portrait of Daniel of St. Thomas is discovered below its customary place on the wall, a death in the family is sure to follow.

Centuries ago, a descendant of the brothers was gravely ill and confined to a bed in his second-floor bedchamber. One day, his wife was about to ascend the wide stairway that led toward the sickroom. While carrying medicine and beverages to her husband, the woman passed by the parlor and heard a noise. When she looked inside the large room, she noticed the portrait of Daniel of St. Thomas was resting on the floor. Somehow, the ornately framed painting had fallen from its usual hanging place to the bottom of the wall directly below, but was undamaged.

The confused woman moved slowly toward the painting. After examining the cord behind the frame, she confirmed it was in good condition. She also noticed that the nail protruding from the wall was firm and undisturbed. Suddenly remembering the family curse, she shouted, "Oh dear God in heaven! Uncle Thomas has fallen!" Terrified, she ignored her medicine tray and raced up the stairs. When she opened the door to her husband's sickroom, she found him dead, lying on the floor beside his bed.

Over the years, the portraits were moved to different historic homes in the region, and on several occasions the paintings were reported to have fallen and immediately caused a bit of a scare. One generation of the family believed in the superstition so strongly that the members placed the long-deceased brothers' hexed portraits in a sealed crate—for both safekeeping and to insure the family's personal safety—for more than thirty years.

According to a story by C. Irwin Jones Jr. in *Traditional Tales and Folklore of Charles County*, one descendant wrote a letter to a friend and stated, "I doubt if my mother could be persuaded to enter the parlor alone after dark, so vivid still is her childish fear upon opening the door to find one of the portraits of the brothers standing upright upon the floor!"

The Chamber

Waverly has a great spooky story, but the history of the building's origin is a bit confusing. Some sources claim it was built in the mid-1700s (or early 1800s), and Dr. Morgan A. Harris, after whom Morgantown is named, was Waverly's builder. According to C. Irwin Jones Jr., the good doctor was consumed by the project, and he worked closely with the men who were constructing his country mansion. Unfortunately his wife, a mysterious French Creole woman from the island of Martinique, died in 1825 before the building project was finished. This deadly event is believed to have caused the unexplained occurrences that began soon after the mysterious mistress was placed in her grave—but apparently not laid to eternal rest.

Servants who slept near the room where Mrs. Harris had died began saying they heard moans and screams in the middle of the night. The cries were so loud that they woke up the staff, who could not get back to sleep. While waiting for the safety of dawn, the African-American servants, whose superstitious nature was intensified by the midnight moans, also all claimed they heard the sounds of footsteps—giving the impression a restless spirit was roaming the mansion's halls.

In the days following the nighttime disturbances, word spread among the workers that there were noises coming from the room of death—a place the home's slaves had nicknamed "the chamber." Others called it "the closed room." During the day, groups of uneasy workers clustered in Waverly's workrooms, kitchen, barns, and outbuildings to compare notes and share more stories about the spooky events they thought had taken place during the night.

Dr. Harris became annoyed with the stories, and he also was bothered by their effect upon the estate's work production. He gathered his staff and announced that the sounds were nothing more than the settling of a new building and the overactive imaginations of primitive, uneducated, and superstitious people. Shortly after his speech, the master of the house died in the same room in which his wife had passed away. Word spread that an "evil" presence occupied "the chamber," and whatever it was had been upset with the doctor's comments.

The next apparent victim was John Grant Harris. He had taken up residence in the deadly room after the demise of the non-superstitious doctor. A short period of time passed and John Grant "accidentally" drowned in the Potomac River. When several other members of the family died after sleeping in the hexed room, the entrance was boarded up. Some say it was an effort to seal the evil inside and keep it from infecting the rest of the house.

Many years passed, and future owners decided to disregard the silly rumors. They opened up the spacious bedchamber and turned it into a guest room or "company room," as they called it in those days. These owners believed that the curse pertained only to Harris family descendants, and others would be immune to any reported evil spell. But that didn't turn out to be the case.

One of the first guests to sleep in the chamber's inviting, but still deadly, accommodations was killed the following day when she was tossed off her horse while riding on the estate's grounds. A few serious accidents occurred to other overnight guests who had been given accommodations in the troublesome room. One owner turned the room into a ballroom, where small formal groups would meet. It also was designated as a "supper room," where refreshments were displayed and made available to large numbers of guests during party gatherings. One newspaper article described the results of these efforts by stating, "But even then the curse was not defeated. People who had eaten there contracted singular illnesses, some of them becoming invalids for life." Without fanfare, the chamber was sealed again.

A few overnight occupants of the room had lived to tell their non-deadly tales. One man said he awoke and saw a group of ladies from the weekend house party standing over his bed. When he tried to talk to them, the ghostly intruders disappeared through the walls. A second gentleman, who claimed firmly that he had not had too much to drink, said he awoke in the middle of a deep, early-morning sleep and found several rabbits wearing sunbonnets on their heads, jumping up and down at the foot of his bed.

Eventually, the chamber was converted from a bedroom into a large storeroom. But residents and workers seemed hesitant to enter "the chamber" to retrieve a needed item, and everyone seemed to walk a bit more quickly down the hall as they passed by the closed room's door.

Solemn Promise

In 1966, the "Chronicles of St. Mary's" newsletter, published by the St. Mary's County Historical Society, presented the mysterious tale of George Beckwith. The wealthy gentleman planter lived in Old Beckwith Manor. He was devoted to his loving wife, the former Frances Hervey, a relative of a former governor of Virginia and a member of one of Maryland's oldest and most prominent families.

In 1765, George announced that he needed to attend to important business in Yorkshire, England, the ancestral home of his family. On the day of his departure from Maryland, a large number of Beckwith's friends and family turned out to see him off on his long and dangerous journey. At the dock below Old Beckwith Manor, a crew of slaves from the plantation waited patiently to row their master to the ship in the Patuxent River that would transport him to England. After taking a few steps toward the small boat, George Beckwith turned and walked back to his wife. Holding her in his arms, he said, in a voice loud enough for everyone to hear, "Do not weep, sweetheart, for, living or dead, I shall come back to you." Within the hour, the large ship transporting Frances' loving husband disappeared in the distant Chesapeake Bay horizon.

After a few weeks passed, Frances raced to the dock to greet every ship that arrived from England, hoping for a letter or message from her husband. She asked passengers debarking from both cargo and passenger ships if they had heard any news about George Beckwith. But she learned nothing of her husband's whereabouts or activities. Several months went by and Frances grew more and more depressed. She would spend as much time as possible beneath a large elm tree, where the couple used to talk, laugh, and share their dreams. As months turned to years, the mistress of Old Beckwith Manor became ill. Deciding there was nothing left to live for, the frail woman succumbed to disease, or perhaps a broken heart. On a windy, rainy day, she was laid to rest in a small graveyard near the elm tree that she and George had loved so much.

Eventually, a passerby said he saw a frail, misty apparition, dressed in a black gown, appear near one of the chairs sitting beneath the ancient elm tree. The figure seemed to be very still and gazing out upon the channel, where incoming boats from distant ports still arrived. During each incident, the hazy figure disappeared after a short period of time. As more similar reports surfaced, some said the ghost of Frances Beckwith had returned from the dead. People also decided that the mistress of the house, who now rested beneath the family graveyard, was letting people know she was still disappointed that her husband had never returned, as he had solemnly promised.

Several years later, a large ship with its sails at full mast headed up the Patuxent River. As if on a mission, the impressive vessel floated directly toward the now-sagging dock of Old Beckwith Manor.

As word of the ship's arrival spread from village to plantation to town, a mass of neighbors crowded together on shore near the ancient dock. Most expressed hope that the master of the estate would be seated in the small rowboat now heading toward shore. When the small craft drifted closer, a single figure was seen standing at the bow. It was, without a doubt, George Beckwith. The welcoming crowd cheered as the master of Old Beckwith Manor approached the wharf. But no one wanted to be the first to inform the returning husband that his faithful and loving wife had died while patiently awaiting his return.

Suddenly, a gust of cold wind blew down from the shore, causing everyone to turn around. There, floating down the hill from the area near the elm tree, was Frances, eager to greet her love. As she drifted through the crowd and fell into his open arms, the returning husband said, in a loud voice that everyone heard, "As promised, sweetheart, living or dead, I have returned." And within seconds the smiling couple and the boat in which they stood disappeared.

While members of the speechless crowd tried to understand what had occurred, a new rowboat arrived at the dock. The officer on board, who had not seen what the assembled group had experienced, announced that he had brought back the body of George Beckwith, who had died months earlier in London. The master of Old Beckwith Manor had directed that his body be returned to lie in the family cemetery beside the rest of his family. At the time he gave instructions on his deathbed in England, however, he did not know that his wife had been waiting for his return in that very spot in which he was to be placed.

Today, the original manor house is gone, but the memory and spirits of the faithful couple who had lived there remain. Soon after George Beckwith's solemn funeral and graveside service, people said they spotted the master and mistress of Old Beckwith Manor, standing beneath the elm tree, holding hands and gazing out toward the Chesapeake Bay.

Deadly Civil War Prison

Mass unmarked graves. Polluted water. Sounds of soldiers marching along dirt roads. Shadows racing through the woods. Sudden appearances and unexplained disappearances of hazy-looking men wearing ragged Civil War uniforms. Strange crayon drawings by children of visiting campers. Agitated reactions of normally docile pets. Desperate prisoners hunting rats for food.

These are some of the incidents told in spooky stories, and in comments shared by confused tourists, at Point Lookout State Park. But such tales are no surprise to anyone who has visited or worked at the site. Located at the bottom tip of Maryland's Western Shore, the 1,046-acre isolated area—surrounded by large bodies of water and dense forests, and hosting its very own lighthouse—has been associated with paranormal activity for more than three centuries.

Standing at "The Point," surrounded on three sides by the sea, one can immediately understand why the federal government decided that Point Lookout would be an excellent site for a prison to hold captured Confederate soldiers during the Civil War. It was nearly impossible for the prisoners' weakened bodies—and later a fair number of troubled souls—to escape from this hallowed and haunted ground.

The Point's story began in 1634, when two ships, the *Arc* and the *Dove*, landed north of the sandy beach with about two hundred passengers. They headed north and established Maryland's first settlement at St. Mary's City. Soon more colonists arrived in the region and set down roots at what was called St. Michaels Point (now known as Point Lookout). Since the arrival of the white settlers, there was trouble with the American Indians, and there are reports that natives massacred several colonists. This was the first instance of violent death and the source of some early ghost tales. During the War of 1812, British troops conducted raids in the area, and scores of shipwrecks at the tip of this peninsula have contributed to reports of deaths at sea, floating corpses, and buried pirate treasure.

Over time, the Point's ownership changed hands. By the time the Civil War began in 1861, the Point was known as a resort area, offering tourists accommodations at its hotel and in about a hundred beach cottages. A year after the start of the war, the U.S. government leased the bottom tip of the Maryland peninsula, where it built a military hospital to provide medical care to injured members of the Northern armies. But from 1863 to 1865 this isolated region's purpose changed dramatically. It became the location of the nation's largest Civil War prison, housing more than 52,000 Confederate prisoners during its two-year service. Some sources claim as many as 14,000 prisoners died while in captivity, other estimates refer to about 3,500 prisoner deaths.

It is important to understand that residents of this area of Maryland—like other citizens living throughout the majority of the state—were sympathetic to the Southern cause. St. Mary's County was a hotbed of Rebel activity and had established militia units that were preparing to fight for the Confederacy as soon as the state formally seceded. But if Maryland left the Union, Washington, the U.S. capital, would have been surrounded by hostile territory—namely, Virginia and Maryland. To solve this problem, Maryland governor Thomas Holliday Hicks used political maneuvering to prevent secession from happening. President Abraham Lincoln did the rest when he used Federal force to occupy the state.

Eventually, Maryland's legislators were forced to vote against secession and, on paper, Maryland remained a loyal member of the United States. However, a large number of Free State residents were vehemently opposed to the Union cause. Their sons demonstrated their beliefs by heading into Virginia to fight in that state's military units. Today, graves of Maryland's Confederate soldiers can be found throughout the state. During the war, St. Mary's County residents delivered food, medicine, and clothing to the Confederate prisoners that were under guard at Point Lookout Prison.

In the book *Phantom in the Bedchamber*, Donnie Hammett, former assistant park manager of Point Lookout State Park, stated there are about thirty ghost stories concerning unusual incidents associated with both the lighthouse and events at the former Civil War prison camp. He also mentioned that Point Lookout had been featured on such popular television programs as *In Search Of...*, *Strange Universe* and *Haunted Lighthouses*. Over the years, psychics, authors, historians, and relatives of Confederate and Union soldiers have visited the park and its historic sites—including the re-created area known as Fort Lincoln—seeking their own answers. Some of them have left with more questions and very eerie stories. The park administration usually receives several questions per month related to the "ghosts" at Point Lookout, and probably fields a question a day on that topic during the summer and fall.

There is so much unusual activity to share that the Point Lookout Camp Host Volunteers organization, under the direction of Ralph and Judy Bloor, compiled a pamphlet entitled "True Tales of the Bizarre and Unnatural at Point Lookout." The thirty-two-page booklet features stories that visitors have told to park personnel, as well as strange incidents several members of the Point Lookout State Park staff have experienced.

A park ranger who lived in a home on park property admitted that on certain nights he believes he has heard what seems to be the slow, steady march of prisoners, apparently in a long column, along the old trails nearby that lead in and out of what used to be the prison area. He also has seen his dogs stare suddenly at certain spots in a room in his house, but he and other humans present could not see anything. The dogs, however, continued to look at something that couldn't be seen. "The house where I live lies adjacent to the main road where Confederate prisoners once marched to be placed into the prison pen," the park ranger explained. The walls where the prison once stood are only fifty feet from his home. "Looking out at the beautiful Chesapeake Bay," he said, "it's difficult to believe my backyard was the site of so much misery and suffering for fifty-two thousand men during the Civil War." He also recalled how the atmosphere in a room in his home would sometimes suddenly turn so "stone cold" that he could see his breath, as if he was transported outside in frigid weather. At the same time, his dogs suddenly seem panicked and would bark wildly.

The park also is noted for having two haunted campsites—numbers 136 and 137—considered so because they seem to demand much more attention than all of the other overnight camping locations in the park. For many years, adults and children have reported sightings of men dressed in Civil War clothing when no costumed reenactors were visiting or staying overnight at Point Lookout.

On one occasion, a young boy at one of these haunted campsites said he saw a man who apparently no one else could see. When asked to describe the invisible person, the youngster used crayons to create a rough image of a Civil War soldier in a uniform. What was most intriguing is that the youngster's picture indicated the stranger was dressed in a greenish, butternut-colored coat, as opposed to gray, which is the traditional color most people identify with Rebels. The young boy had no way of knowing the correct historical hue.

Park Ranger Hammett added that the campsite where the incident with the boy occurred is the same place where a woman reported her ankle being grabbed by someone with a very cold hand. But he offered no explanation for why this site seems to host more activity than others. "We have campsites located on old burial sites that we don't get reports from," Hammett said. "We also have campsites in the park that are closer to the site of the Civil War smallpox hospitals, and they don't cause us as much of a problem. But we've had to move a lot of people off those two sites in particular."

There also have been reports of shadowy figures racing across the roads that wind through wooded sections of the state park. Sometimes these images are noticed in a rearview mirror, and other times the figures are seen out of the corner of the eye. In some cases these sightings have occurred near the location of one of two Confederate cemeteries located at Point Lookout, where prisoners who died while being held in the Civil War prison were buried. That same area was also the location of a Civil War smallpox hospital where quarantined Confederate prisoners were held.

Perhaps those searching for a reason for these sightings might find a possible answer in Hammett's comment. "After death," he said, "the bodies were not left to rest in peace. In 1910, the federal government returned to Point Lookout and exhumed the bodies because some body parts were eroding into Tanners Creek. Since a series of woods fires and rot had destroyed the primitive wooden markers which originally marked the soldiers' graves, the workers buried what body parts they could find in a mass grave near the Civil War monument in Scotland."

An impressive eighty-five-foot-tall granite obelisk honoring the war dead is located in the spacious Point Lookout Cemetery, which visitors heading south must pass before reaching the park entrance. Bronze plaques on all sides of the base of the tall monument list the names of the deceased Confederate prisoners, who are believed to have died while captive at the prison. In the same cemetery, a smaller memorial was erected by the state of Maryland "in memory of the Confederate soldiers who died prisoners of war at Point Lookout, from March 1, 1864 to June 30th, 1865."

This hallowed ground was established long after the Civil War, and the remains of about 3,400 war dead were exhumed and brought to this location for a second internment. One rumor even suggests that during the move only the skulls of the deceased were transferred to the crypt beneath the monument, and the rest of the bones were left behind. But that is one story that has never been confirmed.

According to an article entitled "Ghost Busting," in the *State of Maryland Natural Resources Magazine*, a number of ghost hunters have visited Point Lookout State Park because of the hundreds of Union soldiers and thousands of Confederate prisoners buried there. Unfortunately, the bodies of Rebel soldiers were not buried in coffins and some of them washed out of their graves. The article suggested that the "removal of the bodies from the original resting place might be responsible for the many reported sightings of Union and Confederate spirits roaming the park."

If so, the shadowy figures sighted along the park's forest-lined roads could be ghosts of Rebel soldiers that were buried initially in the parkland to the south, but later moved to a different location. These lost souls may be seeking their final resting place, to which they were moved decades after their death.

Anyone who visits Point Lookout has to be impressed by its solitude. Standing on the southern tip of Maryland's Western Shore, one can see only water as far as the horizon to both the south and east. In the distance to the west, about five miles away, are treetops indicating the coastline of the Commonwealth of Virginia. Especially at night, or during early morning at Point Lookout, one can imagine what it must be like to stand on the edge of the Earth.

At that moment, allowing the mind to travel back nearly 150 years, it's possible to imagine how tens of thousands of Confederate prisoners, and hundreds of sick Union troops, prayed to survive. While addressing a meeting in 1890 of the Pickett Camp Confederate Veterans, Charles T. Loehr, a fellow veteran and past commander of the group and a former captive at Point Lookout, shared some of his experiences at the Maryland prison.

On arrival, he described Point Lookout:

A tongue of land where the Potomac joins the Chesapeake Bay, barely over five feet high at its highest point; and herein was the worst feature of the prison. There was no good drinking water to be had; the water was impregnated with copperas, and tasted quite brackish. To this source was a great deal of the fearful mortality that occurred there traceable.

[The rations] were just such as kept us perpetually on the point of starvation, causing a painful feeling of hunger to us helpless, half-starved prisoners. Four small crackers, or a small loaf of bread per day, and a cup full of dishwater, called pea soup, horrible to taste, and a small piece of rancid salt meat, was our daily fare. So hungry were the men that they would eat almost anything they could pick up outside from the sewers; potato peelings, cabbage stalks, or most any kind of refuse that hardly the cattle would eat, was greedily devoured. The scurvy, brought on by this wretched diet, was prevalent in its most awful form. It was not unusual to hear it stated that sixty or sixty-five deaths had occurred in a single day; and it is said that eight thousand, six hundred dead Confederates were buried near that prison pen.

While not sick during his entire service in the war, Loehr contracted such a severe illness that he was noticed by a pair of workers, whose job it was to pack the dead bodies in rough wooden boxes. Referring to his gross appearance, with black and green marks across his swollen neck and face, one of the workers said, "There goes a fellow we will have to box up tomorrow." The next morning, Loehr was sent to a hospital that could only accommodate about twelve hundred. But at least six thousand sick and dying prisoners were moaning and lying in the main building and in tents nearby. Since the conditions and care were so wretched, Loehr attributed his survival to his strong sense of self-determination.

While he was superintendent of the state park, Gerry Sword spoke to a reporter about numerous ghost stories he had heard over the years. In one, a group of fishermen had completed their day on the bay, pulled in their boat, hitched up the trailer, and headed north from the southern terminus of Maryland Route 5, near the Point. Suddenly, the four passengers were jolted as the driver hit his brakes to avoid running over a man who had appeared suddenly in front of the truck's grille. When the shaken quartet raced from the truck to help the most certainly injured victim, there was no one there. They searched around and under the vehicle and trailer. The mysterious pedestrian had disappeared into thin air, or he was never really there.

At other times, someone working at the park will be talking to a group of people, and suddenly, a figure standing off to the side, who the speaker was certain had been there, will be gone. Sword said these apparitions seem to vanish, and there is no apparent explanation.

Sword suggested in his interview with Joseph Norris of the *Enterprise* that most of the unexplained activity "seems to take place just before atmospheric changes, such as a change in the weather. But we have had several people tell us of strange experiences they have had."

Ranger Hammett said there is considerable interest in the unexplained tales at the secluded park. But he stressed that he once told his interpreters there is no need for them to make up ghost stories about the area, since enough real suffering and agony have occurred there.

At Point Lookout, infected limbs were amputated in wretched fashion, worn-out bodies were buried in soggy graves, boisterous prisoners were shot in their tents, and desperate escapees drowned off shore. Many historical sources describe conditions at the prison as "deplorable." Overcrowding, death from exposure, lack of food, and rampant disease were major causes of death. Since no prison barracks were built, much of the time a prisoner's only shelter was a thin blanket and sometimes the luxury of a tent. This was hardly enough to maintain one's health during frigid winters, when moist breezes blew in from the Chesapeake Bay, and during hot, humid summers, when both healthy and sick men succumbed to the deadly combination of oppressive weather and lack of food and medicine.

Many believe that some victims of a painful, lingering death refuse, or are unable, to give up their spirit and pass on to the other side. If so, Point Lookout may be just the place to visit, if one wanted to encounter such unfortunate, troubled souls.

Point Lookout Lighthouse

It was dark one late October night in 1878. The lighthouse keeper knelt in his second-floor bedroom and prayed. His voice mumbled rapidly, creating a string of hoarse whispers as he tried to cover the sounds of the swirling, powerful wind. But there was no way to block out the onslaught of fierce weather. Small clods of wet brown paper, homemade earplugs he had made that afternoon, were pressed into his ears, but they didn't help either.

The small, thin man stopped praying, cocked his head, and imagined a runaway train was headed toward his fragile, two-story frame building. The wind was that loud, its pressure that strong. But there were no railway lines that close to the Point. All there was on three sides of the lighthouse building was water. Lots and lots of water. An endless amount was heading toward him in steady, increasing waves from both the east and south, fed by the bottomless depths of the Chesapeake Bay. From the west and north came the fast-flowing Potomac River. For a man who had lived along and worked on the water for decades, the keeper realized he had never seen so much water in his life.

The man was terrified to leave the house and check on his horse and cow. He would be blown away and disappear in the rising tides before he could reach the door of the small barn, if the door or barn was still there. The intensity of the downpour obscured his view. At least his dog was inside with him and safe, for the time being. But the keeper wasn't a fool. He knew if he stayed in the building he would probably die. There was not the slightest doubt that the water would claim the slim sliver of land on which he was trapped. By morning he and everything around him would be gone. Days later, searchers would discover only the building's foundation. That's all that would be left. The old stones holding up his house would be the only clue, when the bay and river retreated, that something manmade had ever stupidly tried to claim a place on the hexed spot called the Point.

Some would wonder why he hadn't left, run off and saved himself. But he had no choice. He had accepted his duty when he signed on as the keeper at Point Lookout Light, which was, at that moment, still barely standing at the southern tip of Maryland's Western Shore. If by some miracle the house survived, his stern superiors, the inspectors from Washington, would expect to find him there—and with his light burning brightly. Ignoring the devastation of the storm, they would roam about the building, give it a strict inspection, and act as if nothing unusual had happened. Hurricane or not, deluge or not, nothing mattered to them but the continuous functioning of that all-important beam. His life was expendable. He could be replaced. It was just the way it was.

Of course he would stay. But at that moment, early in the morning of October 24, 1878, he wished it would all be over—the waiting, the terror, the noise, every minute feeling like it lasted an hour. He wanted to die.

But he lived. The next day, by mid-afternoon, the winds of what would be called the famous "Gale of '78," had blown out beyond the reach of the light's bright beam. When the keeper opened the door on his front porch, he looked toward the sky and spoke aloud, thanking God that his goodness and grace had helped the man survive. He realized there would be another chance at life, an additional opportunity to plan for a bright and hopeful future. But his improved spirits lasted only until the wreckage and the bloated bodies arrived—the lifeless remains from the 200-foot cargo and passenger steamer, *Express*.

The doomed ship had gone down in the gale, and its cargo and human debris began washing up against the rocks along the Point. That's when the troubled keeper assumed a new role, one not stated in the Lighthouse Keeper's Manual. The Point's newest gravedigger began dragging the nameless corpses ashore and buried them in shallow, unmarked graves.

While a few of the *Express* passengers survived the wreck and moved on with their lives, the others never left the Point. Some people who have worked at the lighthouse and Point Lookout State Park wonder if a few of the victims of the Gale of '78 might occasionally have made an appearance or two. If so, they are not alone. Apparently, a number of other poor mortals, who were unfortunate to take their last earthly breath in the water near, or on the sands of, Point Lookout return fairly often and make their presence known.

In the introduction to a story about the historic area at the southern end of St. Mary's County, a writer in the October 2000 issue of *Bay*

Weekly Online summarized the reputation of the eerie location when he wrote: "Among all of Maryland's legendary haunted spots, none has the fright capacity of Point Lookout. Here, for over 350 years, humans have massacred, imprisoned, tortured, and starved one another. Add shipwreck, fire, famine, disease, and war, and the stage is set for ghostly encounters unequaled in our state."

But it seems the lighthouse, perhaps because of its location and the aura of mystery and seclusion associated with these structures, has been singled out for special attention by a wide range of experts. These include historians, architects, documentary producers, artists, folklorists, photographers, maritime experts, environmentalists, and paranormal investigators.

Point Lookout Light was built in 1830. Because it is on land, the structure is one of the few Chesapeake Bay lighthouses still easily accessible to visitors. When people consider its long history, isolated location, and association with the Civil War prison camp that stood nearby, it's no surprise the beacon has frequently been called "America's Most Haunted Lighthouse."

Bob Trapani Jr. is executive director of the American Lighthouse Foundation in Wells, Maine. Charged with preserving and presenting the history of more than two dozen lighthouses, Trapani has studied, visited, and lectured on the history, architecture, and folklore of scores of U.S. lights on the mainland and on remote islands. In his book, *Lighthouses of Maryland and Virginia: History, Mystery, Legends and Lore*, the author wrote: "There is no other Chesapeake Bay lighthouse, and arguably none other in America, which possesses such a connection to grisly suffering and death—all of which occurred directly below its lifesaving beam—than Point Lookout Lighthouse. In fact, the light station's history is littered with unfavorable circumstances, seemingly bad luck, and unexplained mystery."

The first keeper died suddenly only two months after taking over his post. A subsequent keeper's cat contaminated the oil and broke more than two dozen lamps, causing the keeper to be denied his pay for a full year. But the biggest impact to the light and its keepers occurred immediately after the Battle of Gettysburg, when ten thousand Rebel prisoners were deposited at the Maryland peninsula—suddenly transformed into a prison—surrounding the light. In the coming months and years, misery, disease, and death would increase to epidemic levels, as more than 55,000 prisoners would be sent to Point Lookout. Eventually, anywhere between 3,500 and 14,000 of these wounded and ill Rebel soldiers would die during their stay.

Many years later, the U.S. Navy, and subsequently the state of Maryland, took possession of the lighthouse and rehabilitated the structure. Former tenants of the lighthouse began reporting their experiences, and stories surfaced involving unexplained voices, sightings, and other phenomena. These tales, of course, generated interest in Point Lookout Light among groups far removed from Civil War reenactors, historical societies, and lighthouse preservation chapters. Paranormal investigation teams, armed with high-tech equipment, voiced their interest in learning more about the building, and they wanted to visit the lighthouse in hopes of recording evidence of a ghost.

Gerald (Gerry) J. Sword, a state park official who had lived in the lighthouse, made a list of unexplained experiences. Many of his stories are included in considerable detail in the county historical society's book, *Legends of St. Mary's*, and in area newspaper and magazine articles. His personal stories are associated with crashing objects, a glowing wall, snoring sounds, voices and footsteps in the hallway and on the stairs, strong odors, lights turning on and off, doors banging shut, and his dog reacting to apparently unseen activity.

Noted paranormal investigator Dr. Hans Holzer visited the light with several associates, including Nancy Stallings, a medium with the Maryland Committee for Psychical Research. Photographer Ron Stallings captured a photo in 1980 of what appears to be an apparition of a Confederate soldier leaning against a wall in a second-floor bedroom, on the Potomac side of the lighthouse building.

Laura Berg was the last tenant to live in the lighthouse building, from 1979 to 1981, and she visits periodically to conduct tours and paranormal investigations along with Robert Hall of the Paranormal Research Society of North America. Berg has reported a number of strange experiences. These include hearing someone walking in the hallway outside her bedroom door and noticing strong smells. Visitors to the lighthouse during Laura's residency reported hearing whispered voices and seeing apparitions. Laura has been featured in numerous articles and television programs. A detailed account of her experiences, the history of the light, modern and historic photographs, restoration efforts, and séances and psychic investigations held at the lighthouse can be found at http://www.ptlookoutlight house.com

To Laura, unusual activity at Point Lookout is nothing new. She said investigators have found reports of people speaking about unusual experiences that date back more than half a century. Despite the unsettling events that sometimes occurred at Point Lookout, when asked what it was like to live in the lighthouse, with its truly magnificent view of the lower Chesapeake Bay, Laura said, without hesitation, "Every day was a blessing."

In *Phantom in the Bedchamber*, a park ranger reported a strange incident that occurred along Maryland Route 5, which travels through Point Lookout State Park and ends at the main entrance to the lighthouse. This tip of land has an eight-foot-high chain-link fence that encloses the lighthouse and its surrounding grounds. The entire restricted area is off-limits to the public because the U.S. Navy operates a radar tracking facility just a few yards away from the lighthouse.

One evening a young couple in a Jeep Wrangler stopped a park ranger as they were heading north, away from the Point. They were only about a hundred feet from the lighthouse. After flagging down the ranger's vehicle, the Jeep's driver reported that his girlfriend had seen someone patrolling the lighthouse area, inside the fence line. She said, "I swear, I saw someone inside the fence, close to the lighthouse, just a few minutes ago. He was wearing a dark uniform and had on a small, flat hat, and he was pacing back and forth. He was carrying a long rifle on his shoulder with a long knife sticking off the top of the gun."

The ranger said no one was permitted inside the fenced area, but he also realized the young woman had accurately described a Civil War soldier on guard duty. He told the young woman, "You are not the first person to report seeing a possible ghost, and I'll add this to my list of stories."

Based on two-and-a-half years of living in the lighthouse and conducting investigations since, Laura, who now resides in Baltimore, was asked if Point Lookout Lighthouse is haunted. Her answer: "Yes. I have no doubt that there are multiple spirits haunting this lighthouse."

After the Civil War, in October 1878, the steamer *Express* sank in the bay off of Point Lookout. A ship's officer named Joseph Haney is said to have attempted to row to shore to gain assistance from the lighthouse keeper, but because of the raging storm he never made it to Point Lookout's shore. Haney's corpse washed up along the beach a few days later, and he was buried in the immediate area.

Nearly a century later, a former resident of the lighthouse reported seeing a man at the back porch of the building who looked as if he was distressed and who was wearing clothes from a historic period. When the resident of the lighthouse opened the door, the figure floated across the lawn and disappeared toward the bay. Perhaps it was the confused spirit of Mr. Haney, trapped in another dimension because of his sudden and violent death.

Some people believe progress, in the form of rampant development and neglect of old buildings, is a serious threat to both historic and haunted stories and sites. In order to protect the spirits and stories of the lighthouse, as well as the nearby buildings and land, interested citizens formed the non-profit Point Lookout Lighthouse Preservation Society Inc. (PLLPS). The group hosts monthly open houses and paranormal investigation events in the mild-weather months.

In 1998, The Learning Channel included a segment filmed at Point Lookout on its program *Haunted Lighthouses*. George Steitz, writer and producer of several other television documentaries, including *Ghost Waters*, made several visits to Point Lookout during the filming. "Lighthouses," he said, "are romantic and spiritual places. They evoke a sense of history, especially in America, where they seem to be our answer to Europe's castles."

But are any of them haunted?

"I did not see or hear any ghosts myself," Steitz said. "The closest I came to a supernatural experience was a strange and unsettling feeling I had at Point Lookout Lighthouse. I can't explain it because I don't think we have words to accurately describe this type of experience. At another location someone once commented that in certain places there may be rips or holes in time through which we can sense activity in another dimension, one inhabited by what we call ghosts. I thought about this at Point Lookout. It may in fact be a genuinely haunted lighthouse."

Bothersome Brick

For thirteen years I worked as a history/ghost tour guide at Fort Delaware, a Civil War prison on Pea Patch Island in the Delaware River. The site held 33,000 Confederate prisoners in the 1860s, and nearly 3,000 soldiers died on the overcrowded and diseased island.

The evening candlelight tours I conducted featured a mix of history and folklore, focusing on stories found in old documents, plus spooky tales passed down from local folks on the nearby mainland and from workers on the island. Now owned and operated by the Delaware State Parks system, the fort's ghost tours and daytime living history programs attract tens of thousands of visitors each year. Quite a few of these tourists have shared their own unusual stories, which they claim they had experienced while roaming the granite-walled fortress. But sometimes these folks want to talk about unexplained incidents they were involved in at other Civil War prisons, particularly at Point Lookout in St. Mary's County.

At the end of one evening ghost tour, a couple approached me after we had departed from the ferry at the Delaware City dock. The husband and wife said they had been at the Point Lookout Lighthouse. While touring the inside of the building, the man said he gave into an impulsive urge and stole a brick from the basement of the haunted structure.

"I'm telling you," the husband said, "that night I had nightmares about a man in a dark cloak coming after me. It was so real that I woke up screaming. Then the next two nights he was back. It was so threatening; I thought it was really happening. I told my wife that I was afraid to go to sleep the next night."

Not surprisingly, the man's spouse had advised him against removing the brick from the haunted lighthouse, but he had ignored her. Following the dreams, however, he didn't hesitate to follow her suggestion to return the ill-gotten artifact back to its proper place. "I took off from work the next day," he said. "We drove back to the state park. There was no way I was going to keep that brick after what happened to me during those three nights in a row. And just to give you an idea of how serious I was about all this, I made sure I was wearing gloves whenever I touched that brick."

Unfortunately, the gate leading to the area surrounding the lighthouse building was locked when the couple arrived. The structure had been open for tours the previous weekend, but it was closed during weekdays. The locked gate didn't stop the terrified brick thief from accomplishing his mission.

"I wasn't going to take that thing back home with me and wait for the next weekend tour to get rid of it," he said. "So I looked around, to make sure there was nobody nearby watching me. Then I pulled back my arm and heaved that brick as hard as I could. It went sailing over the chain-link fence and landed outside the lighthouse, but real close to it. Then I got in my car and we drove off."

I wondered if there were any similar dreams during the following nights.

"Nope. I guess I broke the curse. Thank God," the man said, as he turned and offered a weak smile to his wife.

After I thanked them for their story and they began to walk toward their car, I shouted out a question: "Did you take anything from Fort Delaware?"

The couple stopped, turned slowly toward me, and the wife said, "You've got to be kidding."

While on Guard Duty

Ron and Jerry were reenactors, so they were familiar with the history of the Civil War and they also knew how their fellow reenactors operated while at historic sites. The two men were part of a Virginia unit that was camping out one weekend near Fort Lincoln, located in the woods on the grounds of Point Lookout State Park.

All of the twenty-two men in the company were accounted for, Ron explained, adding that he and Jerry were performing guard duty, roaming the perimeter of their campsite during early morning. It was dark and eerie, they admitted. When Ron heard something moving in the nearby woods, he called Jerry over and the two men tried to peer into the overgrown brush and trees.

"We were expecting to see a deer, or some small animal roaming nearby," Jerry said. "But we froze when we saw the figures of three men in Confederate uniforms, carrying lanterns, pass near us."

"They were about forty or fifty feet away," Ron said, "but you could make out their images from the glow of the lights. They looked bad, sick-looking, like they had been out there for a while. At first we thought they were reenactors from another unit."

Jerry interrupted, "But that wasn't the case. They just didn't seem quite right. They were too dirty. They looked sick, and their clothes were ragged and looked like they didn't fit."

After the strangers passed out of sight, Ron and Jerry raced back to the camp and woke the other men. Their comrades had been sound asleep and were annoyed at being awakened. The consensus was that the two men on guard duty had experienced a bad dream, or they had been drinking while on watch. Everyone had a good laugh, except for Ron and Jerry.

"That really got us miffed," Ron said. "So on the way out of the park, after the weekend was over, we stopped at the main office." The two men told the ranger on duty what they had seen, and they asked if there had been another group of reenactors at the park that weekend. When they found out their unit was the only one camping there at the time, the two men decided to press the issue and asked if there ever had been other strange reports of unusual sightings in that area of the park.

"The guy behind the desk looked at us with a sort of smile," Jerry said, "and he told us, 'Guys, are you kidding? This is Point Lookout. We get all sorts of reports like yours. I'll add it into the records, along with the hundreds of others we've collected over the years.'"

Bloody Bladensburg

If the theory is true that ghosts are the remnants of wandering souls of those who had died tragically, then the area of Bladensburg in Prince George's County, originally a colonial village, should host a concentration of spirited activity. After the small town was settled in the early eighteenth century, it boasted a busy wharf. During the Battle of Bladensburg in the War of 1812, some of the town's oldest homes were used as temporary hospitals to treat American and British wounded soldiers. Like any colonial town, Bladensburg had both poor and wealthy neighborhoods, and its business district offered everything the city and nearby country dwellers needed, including several of the period's primary recreational outlets—taverns.

Today major highways crisscross what once had been known as a rural, getaway destination for Washington, D.C. politicians, military officers, and powerful and wealthy gentlemen and their ladies. But the upper class's escape to the Maryland border town wasn't always about pleasure. Often it was about business, and a very deadly and personal business it was.

A Maryland state historical maker stands along Route 450. Even with its unusual title, "DUELING GROUNDS," the plaque is hardly noticed by harried commuters and fast-moving tourists, many of them heading to the nation's capital. But the gray metal sign marks the site of one of the country's most infamous killing zones: "On this site, now part of Anacostia River Park, more than 50 duels were fought during the first half of the nineteenth century. Here, on what became known as 'The dark and bloody grounds,' gentlemen of Washington settled their political and personal differences."

Duels were often held in early morning. To arrive promptly for the deadly appointment, and also to be well-rested on the day one was to kill or be killed, some duelists and their parties stayed overnight at Bladensburg's public house and stagecoach stop, built in 1732. It stood on old Route 1, the main north-south highway at the time. George Washington was a regular visitor. In later years, the tavern's name was changed to the George Washington House, and its clients included such nationally known politicians as John C. Calhoun, Henry Clay, and Daniel Webster.

Dueling was an accepted practice in colonial America. The tradition was brought over from Europe, and one-on-one, deadly contests were considered an honorable way to resolve all sorts of disputes. In keeping up with advances in technology, swords and staffs were replaced eventually by guns and pistols. However, not everyone was enthralled with the idea of two men trying formally to kill each other. Benjamin Franklin described dueling as a "murderous practice" that decided nothing. During the Revolutionary War, General Washington frowned on the practice. Since he needed his limited number of trained officers to fight the British, the American commander-in-chief did not want to lose any of his experienced field leaders in this manner.

Informal challenges had settled arguments throughout America's earliest days. Many were spur-of-the-moment fights held behind wilderness taverns and in the alleyways of larger cities. Defending one's honor, and more particularly the good name and reputation of a gentleman's loved one, were accepted reasons for calling out an opponent for a fistfight or a shootout. But Bladensburg's location near the nation's capital attracted a number of famous opponents. Since the participants' names were easily recognizable, the circumstances leading up to their formal duels, and grisly outcomes, gained quite a bit of attention and publicity.

It was big news when Daniel Key, the son of Francis Scott Key, author of the "Star-Spangled Banner," was killed at Bladensburg's dueling grounds. Apparently Daniel took his argument with his friend, John Sherburne, very seriously. The disagreement occurred while the two Annapolis Naval Academy students were on an extended voyage at sea. At some point, the young men argued over the speed of two steamboats. The conflict stewed and was never resolved. When their ship docked in Maryland, the friends and classmates agreed to decide the argument with loaded pistols, and the twenty-two-year-old Key died from a single shot on the field of honor in June 1836.

There were formal procedures to follow if one intended to issue a challenge, and also correct ways to respond to a dueling invitation. While Bladensburg had gained a reputation as the country's premier dueling ground, similar contests took place at locations throughout the country. Some notable citizens were involved to some degree in duels, such as Button Gwinnett, a signer of the Declaration of Independence and governor of Georgia, who was shot outside Savannah by Gen. Lachlan McIntosh. Gwinnett died from the wound in 1777.

In the blog, "The Ten Miles Square," which features historic events associated with Washington, D.C., its Duel of the Month Club column featured the story of a duel held at Pimmit Run in Arlington, Virginia, between U.S. representative John "Crackshot" Randolph and South Carolina senator Henry Clay. It occurred after Randolph had called

Clay a "blackleg," meaning a cheater. Randolph demanded that the duel be held in his home state of Virginia, as it was "the only place worthy of his blood." Both men survived the contest.

Before he was elected president, Andrew Jackson was involved in at least two gunfights, and he was considered a calm and effective duelist. In 1806, outside Nashville, Charles Dickinson and Jackson became involved in an argument over horse racing and an insult directed at Jackson's wife. After the two men paced off, Dickinson, an accomplished duelist, fired first at Jackson, wounding the future president in the chest. As Dickinson watched Jackson carefully take aim and awaited the blast of the pistol, Jackson's gun misfired. Calmly, Jackson reloaded, which was in accordance with the dueling rules, again took deliberate aim, and hit his mark. Dickinson died a few hours later. The earlier wound to Jackson was severe, entering his chest and shattering two ribs. While some called Jackson's actions murderous, it was agreed he had followed the accepted and proper rules of dueling etiquette.

Alexander Keith McClung, a lawyer, editor, and army officer, earned a reputation as a feared duelist. With the nickname "the Black Knight," McClung's duels attracted audiences that would bet on the outcome. Despite his fearsome reputation, McClung may have been troubled or haunted by the unsettled ghosts of some of his victims. The last shot the Black Knight fired had no trouble hitting its mark, but it was an easy shot. The feared duelist turned his gun on himself and ended his killing career in a solitary room in Jackson, Mississippi, in 1855.

The most famous duel in America took place on July 12, 1804, on the banks of the Hudson River in Weehawken, New Jersey. That morning, Secretary of the Treasury Alexander Hamilton fired first, but purposely wasted his shot by firing his pistol into the air. Vice President Aaron Burr fired second, but he took deliberate aim, and his bullet struck Hamilton in the abdomen. Suffering considerable internal damage, a paralyzed Hamilton was transported to his home in New York, where his family and friends visited him during his final day on earth. The nation's first secretary of the treasury, whose portrait today graces the ten-dollar bill, died that night from wounds received in the early-morning duel. Burr, the third vice president of the United States, was not charged with any crime associated with the duel. However, he would later be accused of conspiracy and treason against the United States; he was eventually acquitted but was disgraced.

Despite the fact that bloody dueling fields were scattered around the country, Bladensburg, because of its proximity to the District of Columbia's rich and famous, was the preferred place to settle differences in the gentleman's way, and make the front page of the country's major newspapers.

James Barron, a U.S. naval commander, was criticized vehemently for what some considered his cowardly actions at sea against the British in the Napoleonic Wars. Barron's most vocal critic was one of his former subordinates, Commodore Stephen Decatur, known throughout the country as the "Conqueror of the Barbary Pirates." Decatur, a native of Berlin, on Maryland's Eastern Shore, was considered a national hero and his critical statements about Barron were well-publicized. Insulted by Decatur's charges, Barron issued a challenge for satisfaction on the field of honor. On March 22, 1820, the former friends greeted one another, stepped off eight paces, turned, and fired. Both duelists were struck and injured, but Decatur's wound was deadly. He bled to death that evening in his Washington, D.C., home, one block from the White House overlooking Lafayette Park. In honor of the war hero's tragic death, the U.S. Senate adjourned to allow its members to attend Decatur's funeral ceremony and procession.

In February 1819, a political misunderstanding over a lost election caused former Virginia senator and War of 1812 veteran Gen. Armistead T. Mason to challenge his cousin, Col. John M. McCarty, to meet at Bladensburg. At sunrise, the men loaded their one-shot muskets, stepped off ten paces, and fired. Mason, who was only thirty-three years old, was killed. McCarty did not walk away unscathed. Physically, he was wounded in the hand and never regained the use of his right arm. Mentally, his responsibility for the death of his kinsman haunted him for the rest of his life, and some say he eventually lost his mind.

In 1838, a duel at Bladensburg had far-reaching effects. Jonathan Cilley of Maine and William Graves of Kentucky fired shots that resulted in Cilley's death. But the duel became famous because both opponents were members of the U.S. House of Representatives. Cilley's death was an important factor in the passage the following year of Washington, D.C.'s anti-dueling law. But the legislation was ineffective, since dueling continued in nearby Bladensburg, and the adjoining state of Maryland had no such law. To settle a score, gentlemen continued to make the short carriage ride across the boundary, where they could settle disagreements with pistols, muskets, and sometimes swords. Eventually, public acceptance of dueling waned, and the practice died out after the Civil War.

Because of the dueling ground's deadly reputation, the stream nearby, a tributary of the Anacostia River, earned the gruesome name Blood Run. The name was changed, and now it is identified as Eastern Branch. The location of the famous duels had been considered part of the Bladensburg area when they were fought, but because of realignments, today the dueling grounds lie within the boundaries of the area called Colmar Manor.

According to Troy Taylor, author of dozens of books on the paranormal, "The events that took place here many years ago have left an indelible impression on the area. Ghosts still walk here today, victims of the fifty duels that were fought on these grounds, and men like Stephen Decatur have left phantoms behind in their place, doomed to walk these grounds in an endless replay of events now forgotten."

Western Maryland

Creepy Carroll County

Ghost stories are a big deal in western Maryland. In Westminster, the Carroll County Public Library has been holding ghost tours since the early 1980s, long before paranormal and Halloween-season ghost tour events had reached the popularity they experience today. With a wealth of material that blends local horror and regional history, the library has put together a self-guided walking tour of Westminster that spotlights several of the area's best haunted locations. Much of the tour's content was based on the book *Ghosts and Legends of Carroll County, Maryland*, compiled by Jesse Glass Jr. and published by the library in 1982. The library also offers guided ghost walks each fall season. The October/November 2005 issue of *Carroll Magazine* also presented a summary of the county's most spirited sites in an article by Shelley Sykes, entitled "Things That Go Bump in Carroll County." Following are brief summaries of a few of these tales.

Cockey's Tavern on Westminster's Main Street claims the ghost of a Confederate cavalryman who rode through the town during a Rebel advance into Union territory. He seems to have enjoyed his visit so much that he's decided to remain in town and take up permanent residence in that historic building. The popular gin mill's Civil War ghost is believed to be the cause of loud bootsteps, of candles blowing out and relighting, of rattling glasses, and of the unexplained rearrangement of pictures.

In the Old Courthouse on Court Street, the smell of freshly cooked food was said to fill the building's first-floor courtroom. Some speculated that the ghosts of the structure's previous residents caused the appealing aroma. In earlier times, the courthouse basement was a temporary residence for the homeless and poor who lived there and cooked food over open fires set in the building's dirt floors.

A lost silver mine—protected by a pack of snarling, red-eyed demons, growling black dogs, and a swarm of hissing snakes—exists in the forested and secluded area of Rattlesnake Hill. The belief is based on a tale involving an immigrant German silversmith who befriended the chief of a local Indian tribe. The Indian chief allowed the old man to take valuable ore from the mine, as long as the crafts-man gave the tribe a steady supply of ornate jewelry in return. They also made the man promise he would not tell anyone about the mine's existence or location.

After much badgering, the man's daughter convinced him to take her to the secret place, and she was astounded by the size of the silver vein and the great number of treasures that filled the large cave. But she was unable to keep the information to herself. She returned late one night to the site with a group of friends and stole a large amount of silver. Furious at being betrayed, the Indians massacred the silver-smith's daughter and beheaded the traitorous craftsman. The legend says the headless silversmith, riding on a black horse and holding a lantern shaped like a skull, roams the area near the cursed mine. Fol-lowing the silent nightrider to his mountain hideaway is the key to locating the vein of long-lost silver and the Indians' treasure-filled cave.

Headless Tom

According to a story in Paula Strains' *Tales of Mountain Maryland*, Westminster's Old Town Jail, located on North Court Street, was the site of a tragic mid-nineteenth-century incident that caused the death of a man named Big Tom and also created the unlucky man's ghost. The well-known local character was resting comfortably in a cell he had visited so often it had become his second home whenever he had too much to drink at the local saloons. A familiar occupant at the town lockup, Big Tom knew all of the constables on a first-name basis, and usually was a polite and quiet customer. But because of his large size and tremendous strength, on those very few occasions when his arrest developed into a problem it took the efforts of several deputies to sub-due Big Tom and force him into his favorite lockup.

On one particular winter night, the sheriff and his men had a very rough time of it, as Big Tom was on a wild tear and appeared to be dangerously close to inflicting injury on himself and others. To play it safe, the sheriff decided to send Big Tom to the much larger Baltimore Penitentiary, thinking that the big-city jail would be able to handle him better and send him back home after he had calmed down.

Big Tom overheard what was in store for him and then waited until the sheriff had locked up the building and left for the night. When the deputies entered the jail the next morning, they found Big Tom lying in a pool of blood on the floor of his cell. The prisoner had taken his own life by cutting his throat. In another version of the story, Big Tom had hung himself and the weight of his heavy body separated his torso from his neck. When the sheriff opened the jail cell, he found Big Tom's head dangling from a rope tied to an iron bar in the ceiling. The rest of the large corpse was surrounded by a pool of blood on the jailhouse floor.

Word spread quickly about the unusually gory death of the town's minor celebrity. And the tale reached the ears of a well-known phrenologist—a scientist who studied an individual's actions based on the shape and number of bumps on one's head—who happened to be passing through the area. The doctor raced to the jail and somehow obtained permission to take possession of the recently deceased's large-sized head, probably by explaining that such a rare specimen could be very useful and aid him greatly in his research. Unfortunately for Big Tom, the sticky-fingered doctor departed town soon thereafter and never returned the noggin. Apparently, he was so impressed during the cranium's examination that he added Big Tom's skull to his phrenological specimen collection.

As a result of the sheriff's generous, but involuntary, donation to medical science—and the authorities' inability to recoup the most important part of Big Tom's identity—the unlucky prisoner was laid to rest in a local cemetery, minus his severed head. Some claim a headless spirit wanders the streets near the old jail seeking its missing noggin. Another story says a very large headless spirit floats among the tombstones of a local graveyard, bending over periodically, apparently searching in vain for its missing body part.

Opera House Ghost

In 1850, an announcement was made about the planned construction of a new building in downtown Westminster. The structure was completed in 1854 by the International Order of the Odd Fellows, which used the upper floors as its lodge, complete with offices and meeting rooms for the men's fraternal organization. The lower level was designated as a town meeting site and entertainment center. Its large stage hosted local productions and traveling acts that passed through the area on their way to larger East Coast cities.

Eventually, the brick building became known as the "Opera House." It attracted large weekend audiences of local residents who were eager to enjoy the wide range of acts that provided temporary relief from the backbreaking workday routines on their farms, in their shops, and at outposts at the edge of the frontier. Whether the marquee advertised jugglers, actors, comedians, musicians, classical plays, or trained animal acts, excited patrons arrived early and formed long lines, eager to get a good seat in their Opera House.

In the years immediately after the Civil War, when wounds had not yet healed between Northern and Southern sympathizers, one particular actor's routines seemed to light a spark that could not be doused, and his questionable program resulted in a tragic offstage ending. The performer's name was Marshall Buell, and he was believed to hail from the Deep South, possibly from the state of Alabama. Dressed as a Northern carpetbagger, the short fellow with a very noticeable Southern drawl took the stage in a sleazy costume and began his well-rehearsed act. While his string of clever dialogue and political humor may have gone over well in places located far below the Mason-Dixon Line, northern Maryland's pro-Yankee audience didn't respond well at all. To say the least, the traveling comic's verbal routine—consisting of jokes and satire directed at former Union general (and then U.S. president) Ulysses S. Grant—bombed big time.

Certainly, a fair number of patrons responded favorably to Buell's well-presented routine and professional dramatic skills. But a much larger number of ticket-buying customers did not like what they heard and what they had paid good money for. During intermission, a few of the disgruntled customers had apparently gone out into the street to get appropriate supplies for the rest of the show. A noticeably nervous Buell returned to the stage to begin his second act. The weak scattering of applause was drowned out by a louder chorus of catcalls, along with a fair number of assorted flying vegetables.

The experienced actor, who by now could tell his audience contained an increasing number of unappreciative members, decided to speed up the pace of his final act. He was halfway through a rather intense story when a large rock landed with a deafening thud beside his feet. When he looked down, a second black stone sailed through the air. But this one did not miss its target, and the missile hit Buell in the chest. The sudden, brief silence that filled the hall was broken by a hailstorm of stones, ears of corn, and heads of lettuce that rained upon the Opera House stage. As some of the ammunition hit the actor and other projectiles caused loud crashing sounds, Buell tried to protect his bruised body and ran hastily from the stage.

The theater manager suggested that the actor leave town immediately, but Buell declined and instead decided to hide out in the basement of the Opera House. He thought it would be safer to allow time for the hall to clear. Hopefully, the troublemakers would reach their homes, forget about him, and retire for the evening. Then, when the town was quiet and the streets were deserted, Buell would slip out of town unseen.

Unfortunately, a few of the annoyed ticket holders had anticipated the actor's plans. When the comedian entered the alley behind the hall to approach his waiting horse, several men attacked the actor and beat him to death. The next morning, Buell's bruised and bloodied body was discovered. His throat had been cut from ear to ear. (Some reports claim his head was missing, and days later it was placed atop a tall post outside the theater entrance.)

In the weeks following the murder, some Westminster citizens began spreading stories about a ghostly figure that had been seen roaming the streets around the Opera House. The spirit was waving his hands, and assuming it was Buell, it looked as if he was performing the stage act that had gotten him killed. One person suggested the actor's ghost had come back to complete the second act of the program he had been unable to finish. Others had a different story, claiming they saw a headless body standing on the back stairs of the Odd Fellows Building. A town drunk confirmed these reports to police, but no one seemed to take him seriously until he offered a description of the phantom, which matched the attire that Marshall Buell had worn on the night he gave his final live performance.

For decades, the building where Buell was killed continued to offer entertainment. In the 1940s, it was used as a movie theater, but that eventually closed and the structure was vacant for several years. Today the historic building, which has been restored and placed in the National Register of Historic Places, houses the Opera House Printing Company—and maybe the ghost of Marshall Buell.

Black Mattie

In the remote countryside of northern Carroll County, a fifteen-room brick farmhouse, built in the late 1700s, seemed to promise its new owners a secluded, peaceful existence. Instead, a series of unexplained events, believed to be caused by phantoms of former residents that apparently had decided never to leave, delivered worrisome, sleepless nights.

The story appeared in 1976 in the pages of the now-closed *Baltimore News-American* newspaper. During that bicentennial year, history was a very big deal. But when reporters had exhausted an area's often repeated, fact-based tales about local battles, famous heroes, and historic sites and monuments, these writers became desperate. This caused them to shift their attention to ghost stories and legends related to local colonial-era history. Proving this point, a 1780s-era homestead provided writer Dean Minnich with a great article that ran beneath the eye-catching headline: "Carroll County Farmhouse Is 'Spirited': Ghostly Happenings Are Recounted."

The hair on the family cat's back stood up stiffly as the hexed spirits walked down the old building's hallways. A three-year-old boy's screams were his reaction to a pair of glowing red eyes. A six-year-old relative who was visiting the home one weekend was too frightened to speak about what he saw, but the lad later told his parents he would never return to that cursed home. And following a psychic investigation, the paranormal expert told the residents she was afraid for their safety, and vowed she would never again visit the heavily haunted home.

The owner, who stated she had "never had a supernatural experience," showed the reporter six typed pages she had assembled, documenting more than five dozen strange incidents that had taken place in her house.

Within days after moving in, the woman and her son heard mumbling and footsteps just before sunrise. That was the first hint they were not alone. Soon afterwards a "man in gray" passed by in the hall, a fast-moving shadow crossed a work area, and noises were heard coming from a nearby cottage on their newly bought property. Doors opened and closed with no assistance, footsteps clacked across wooden floors, and voices seemed to be coming from behind sealed-up fireplaces.

When the owner told her daughter about the strange experiences, the younger woman was skeptical, and even suggested her mother was losing her mind. But her attitude changed after she moved into her parents' mansion and felt someone, or something, try to push her down the stairs. That same, newly arrived mortal resident woke up in the middle of the night and saw a gray figure standing over her sleeping children, then saw the threatening phantom disappear in a flash.

The psychic who had visited the home told reporter Minnich that she had identified several "energy forces." She identified them as a Confederate soldier who had died in the home; a gentle old lady, dressed in blue, who likes to visit her former residence; a harmless, pleasant young girl; and the source of most of the problems, "Black Mattie."

The last phantom was a large, threatening woman dressed in black clothing with "piercing eyes" and who appeared holding a meat cleaver. She might be the ghost of a servant who had poisoned a family member who had lived in the home, the psychic guessed.

"I wouldn't go back," the psychic told the reporter. "Not without a crucifix. You couldn't pay me enough to spend a night in the house. I told them to put crucifixes in each room, and to put this thing aside—let it alone."

The owner said she eventually became accustomed to the occasional visits by unseen and unknown entities, and she stated she had no intention of moving from the historic structure. The source of her calmness occurred, she said, when she took a rare visit to the building's cellar, a place she always avoided unless a trip into the underground chamber was absolutely necessary. Exhausted from frequent incidents that caused her worry and tension, the owner said she sat down and cried like a baby, flushing out her emotions. During that emotional purging, she felt a hand patting her on the shoulder, as if assuring her that everything would be all right. After that incident, everything calmed down and she wasn't afraid any longer.

Starners Dam Bridge

Every region has its own Crybaby Bridge. In northern Carroll County, a single-lane bridge on Starners Dam Road—not far from Haney, between Taneytown and Gettysburg—is believed to be the setting for this region's version of the often-told, tragic legend.

One version claims a teenage girl was desperate to hide her newborn baby, and while crossing the bridge she slipped and the infant fell from her arms into the creek below. Another story says a pregnant mother-to-be was struck by a car while crossing the road late one night. The woman's body fell over the side of the bridge and was never recovered. A third tale suggests the unwed parents of the expected child were involved in a violent argument at the bridge, and the boy strangled the girl and tossed her body into the creek to hide evidence of his crime.

Stories of a crying baby and a screaming mother have been reported at the bridge, as well as stories of cars stopping for no apparent reason while crossing the span. Some drivers and passengers have sworn they have seen an apparition standing in front of their car and disappearing as suddenly as it had materialized.

One driver claimed he felt a chill in his car immediately after passing over the bridge on a summer night. When he looked into his rearview mirror, he saw a woman inside his car, wearing a filmy white gown and cradling a baby in her arms. When the frightened driver screeched to a stop and turned his body around to look into his back seat, nothing was there, But he noticed the car was still extremely cold, and when he let out his breath he saw a cloud of frost form in the air inside the car. Ghost hunters have taken pictures at the bridge and some claim they have captured electronic voice phenomena (EVP) of what they believe is a young woman's voice.

Peddler Jack's Dog

There are a few tales of ghost dogs in the wooded high country near Taneytown. Whether the elusive canine is the famous Snarly Yow (see page 300) or another phantom hound, there are several stories that feature spirited versions of Man's Best Friend.

One of the most told legends is the tale of Peddler Jack's Dog. As the tale goes, Peddler Jack was a friendly sort who drove his sagging wagon from village to town. Always present alongside the wagon, or seated at Jack's side, was his pure white dog. During the decades he responded to the needs of housewives and shopkeepers, Peddler Jack earned the reputation of a friendly character that was constantly in good spirits and never hesitated to offer credit to a patron in temporary financial difficulty.

During those days, traveling peddlers earned their reputations based on their wares, and many different hucksters offered their own special signature concoctions and products. In Peddler Jack's case, his trademark was a cure-all, wonder-drug tonic, said to address every ill from head and backaches to fever, arthritis, and the gout. While the precise quantities of the various ingredients in his tonic were a secret, folks could guess from the taste that Jack included a fair amount of whiskey, prunes, sugar, cloves, and unknown Far East narcotics in his mix. Having the likeable peddler stay overnight in one's home or barn was considered a treat, for he would share tales of his travels, adventures, and exploits—as well as a few free samples from his wagon—with his hosts. One night, after a full day of commerce in the nearby hamlets and a full and satisfying meal, Peddler Jack fell fast asleep in a soft mound of hay in a hospitable farmer's barn. Unfortunately, that would be Peddler Jack's last night on earth. When his host entered the barn to invite Jack into the house for breakfast, he discovered the friendly traveler had died of natural causes during the previous night. After selling off the peddler's wagon and wares, the farmer arranged for Peddler Jack's burial, adding some money of his own and a few donations from local customers, who all agreed the friendly merchant should have a proper sendoff.

It's said Peddler Jack was buried in an unmarked grave, not far from an old apple tree in Baust Church cemetery, close to Taneytown. Present at the burial were the farmer, some local merchants and customers, and members of the church's congregation, plus the recently deceased's snow-white dog. As the mourners turned to depart from the graveyard grounds, they noticed Peddler Jack's dog refused to leave his master's place of eternal rest. One farmer agreed to adopt the animal and take it to his home, but he had to tie a rope around the dog's neck to drag it away from the freshly covered grave. In the coming weeks, no matter how many times that farmer tied the canine to a post outside his farmhouse, he would soon find that Peddler Jack's dog had escaped and made its way to the Baust Church cemetery, where it was sprawled out atop Peddler Jack's grave.

Eventually, the white dog disappeared. It was assumed it had wandered off and died, probably of a broken heart. But on certain foggy nights under a full moon, folks driving past the ancient cemetery say they have seen the filmy image of a white ghost dog, lying in a corner of the cemetery. Folks assume it's resting atop the unmarked grave of its master that the faithful dog returns periodically to visit.

In *Carroll Magazine*'s 2005 October/November issue, the article "Things That Go Bump in Carroll County," by Shelley Sykes, featured a photograph of the graveyard near Emanuel (Baust) United Church of Christ, outside Taneytown. The caption states, "Walter Calahan, who shot this picture, swears that when he was setting up for the photograph, he heard a dog panting behind him. When he turned around, he says, there was nothing there."

Sykes's article also included reports of a large black ghost dog, similar to the Snarly Yow, which appeared at various locations in the county. At times, that canine apparition had been spotted growling, exposing its sharp fangs, and disappearing suddenly. Drivers on secluded roads said they swerved off the road to avoid a large dog that seemed to materialize out of nowhere and then vanish. One county resident even reported sighting a dog-human beast, with a canine body and the head of a man. But none of these incidents compares to the tale of Peddler Jack's ever-faithful four-legged companion.

Spirited Frederick

A *Baltimore News-American* story entitled "Favorite Haunts in Frederick County,"published during the Halloween season in 1975, featured several popular regional legends.

There was a house outside of Frederick where no one could sleep or work, because of the constant playing of an unseen piano that disturbed the residents during the day and the night. The source of this tale told the reporter that he had lived in the house when he was a youngster, back in 1915. The man swore he heard the eerie, nonstop music himself. As years passed, more and more tenants kept moving in and out of the hexed place. When it was apparent no one could stay in the home for long, and the landlord was losing money, he entered the home and searched the building from attic to cellar. At the end of the exploration, he discovered an old, cobweb-covered, broken-down piano resting under a ragged cloth in a corner of the attic. How the heavy piece of furniture had gotten there, no one knew. But the owner of the home decided to hire several strong men to remove the instrument from the premises, and that was the end of the music.

When word spread that the pesky piano's removal had cleansed the haunted house of its spirited songs, a longtime neighborhood resident recalled that many years earlier a young teenage musician had lived in the old house. The old fellow said the young man was a musical talent, and he loved to play the piano, but one day he disappeared. A large search party looked for the boy for several days, but found no trace of the missing lad. About two weeks later, the family sensed an unusual odor coming from the third-floor attic. When they entered the infrequently used area of their rented home, they found the missing boy's body swaying from a rope he had tossed over one of the thick beams.

Another tale involved a child and father who rode in the family buggy along Opossumtown Pike near Rose Hill. Suddenly, the normally docile horse "reared up and shrieked with fright." The driver jumped from the carriage seat to settle the agitated animal. At that moment, both the man and his son saw "ghostly forms circling overhead." After the driver arrived in town and told his story, word of the incident spread like wildfire across a tinder-dry field. The following night, superstitious residents and bored townsfolk headed to the spooky spot in droves to try to catch a glimpse of the Opossumtown Phantoms. While there, some also kept a lookout for the old blue dog that roamed the region (see page 239). They used to say if you were able to follow that mysterious, dark-coated animal, the spot where it stops and barks is the location of a chest of hidden gold.

Auburn Mansion, an old home built in 1805 in Catoctin Furnace, is said to be the home of the ghost of Maj. Edward McPherson. The noted Frederick County resident served with Gen. Winfield Scott in the Mexican War. After the major's death, he returned to the old home where he felt most comfortable. A lady who lived in the building as a young child in the early 1900s said she and her girlfriends would stay in the back bedroom and pretend to be asleep. They would whisper and wait for the sounds of the "dragging footsteps" of Edward, as the mansion's resident ghost slowly climbed a secret stairway that no one ever found.

Over near Walkersville, a farmer would meet with his friends each night to kill time and toss around tall tales. During late October, the man's horse would become skittish and difficult to control as it passed a fair-sized graveyard that extended from a copse of trees right up to the edge of the narrow road. When he told his cohorts in the small-town general store about the horse's negative reaction to the graveyard, the men laughed at the farmer and called him a number of unflattering names.

The next night, as he approached the bothersome boneyard, the rider decided to force his steed to the edge of the path, making both horse and rider pass as close as possible to the troubled burying ground. As the horse had gotten about halfway past the area of the graveyard, the animal rose on its hind legs and let out a harrowing bellow. At the same time, the frightened farmer felt something fall from the tree and land on his head. Wasting no time, he turned the horse around and raced at full speed back toward his house. When he arrived at his property, the terrified rider jumped off the sweating animal and led it into the barn. He didn't care about missing the evening gathering with his chums, and he didn't care if anyone questioned his courage. The farmer was thankful to be home safely, and he prayed aloud, directing his sincere appreciation to the Lord.

The man walked into his kitchen, and everyone in the room immediately became quiet and stared directly at his head. When he asked what in blazes they all were looking at, his wife picked up a hand mirror and passed it to her husband. Looking into the reflecting glass, he saw the clear impression of a solid white handprint in his full, jet-black crop of hair. His grandmother said it was the "mark of the devil," and the distinctive design stayed with the farmer for the rest of his life.

For many years after photographs came into common use, a number of older people believed that having one's picture taken was bad luck. They claimed that the process allowed the picture taker to steal a portion of the subject's soul. It wasn't until the end of the nineteenth century that the majority of people became comfortable with the picture-taking process.

In the mountains of Frederick County, an old woman swore she would never allow anyone to take her picture. She was dead serious, and she warned every person in her family, "If you do, I swear to the Lord, I'll come back to haunt you." When the old woman died, someone brought a camera to the wake. Several of the younger members of the family were seated in the deceased woman's parlor where the ceremony was being held. Since the proceedings were moving along slowly, the teenagers began to talk about their great-grandmother's crazy, old-fashioned ways and her quirky sayings. Someone mentioned there was no photograph of the old lady, and another person recalled the deceased's well-known threat that she would haunt whoever took her picture.

Saying that was "all a bunch of nonsense," a young man grabbed his camera, walked toward the open coffin, stopped, and snapped a picture. A few weeks later, he picked up the developed roll from the pharmacy and gave the image of the dead lady, laid out in the funeral parlor, to his aunt. On the drive back to his home, the young man was killed in a freak automobile accident.

Several years later, an elementary school-age child was glancing through a family photograph album to get ideas for a school project. Suddenly, the little girl let out a blood-curdling scream and sat frozen on her living room sofa. Across her lap were the open pages of the photo album. When the child's mother looked at what the girl had seen, she gasped and brought her hand across her mouth. The only picture ever taken of the elderly matron of the family showed the woman lying flat in the coffin—but instead of an undertaker-embalmed-and-painted corpse, there was a skeletal figure of a bare skull and frail bones.

The owner of a plantation outside Frederick discovered his eldest son, and the heir to the family fortune, had become involved with his housekeeper's attractive daughter. Despite the fact that the young couple was very much in love, the elderly master of the house decided he could not allow his family's fortune to eventually fall into the hands of commoners. The son was immediately shipped off to study at a private school in England. The girl was not as lucky. One stormy night, she simply disappeared.

Despite a search of the countryside, the young woman was never found. Many decades later, it was learned she had been murdered and walled up behind a rarely used kitchen closet on the first floor of the large home. Some claim the girl's apparition has been seen on stormy nights, roaming the hallways of the old estate, sobbing and crying as she tries to find either her lost love or someone willing to place her remains in a proper final resting place.

From 1808 to 1942 there stood along Route 40 a large demijohn, or wine bottle-shaped stone, marked the site of a bridge crossing along the Monocacy River. For nearly a century and a half, the stone arch structure nicknamed Jug Bridge carried traffic across the scenic river. Among those using the span were westbound pioneers, the Marquis de Lafayette, Civil War soldiers, and drivers of modern automobiles. It's said Civil War soldiers hid bottles of whiskey near the unusual marker. Residents of the area said they often heard mysterious voices and laughter at night in the area around the Old Jug Stone.

Veiled Lady

If you lived in the Maryland mountains, you knew it was going to be a bad day if you experienced a sighting of the White Woman, Woman in White, or Veiled Lady. The apparition might be one of three different supernatural entities or she might be a single roaming creature that appeared in different locales and was given different names. But the western Maryland mountain folk believed the specter's appearance meant a tragedy would occur or someone close to the startled witness would die soon after the sighting.

In the valleys and small towns scattered throughout Frederick County's South Mountain area, the Woman in White appeared sporadically and suddenly. Each appearance would set off a string of rumors that traveled like wildfire from farms to isolated villages to larger towns. Timothy L. Cannon and Nancy F. Whitmore wrote in *Ghosts and Legends of Frederick County* that an old man saw the Woman in White rise right out of the surface of a dirt road in front of his home. As the terrified witness froze in his tracks, the apparition floated slowly through his small hut and disappeared. He told everyone he knew about the incident. He died suddenly only two days later. Shortly after his funeral an unexplained fire destroyed the old man's hut.

A grandmother who was raising her orphaned two-week-old granddaughter reported another sighting of the South Mountain banshee. The shaken relative said she saw the Woman in White, who resembled the child's recently deceased mother, standing in a corner of the infant's room. The ghostly figure appeared to be playing with the child, who was sleeping comfortably in its cradle, and the intruder vanished as soon as the grandmother opened the door. Within a few days, the baby died in its sleep, apparently called to its eternal home by its lonesome ghostly mother.

Stories in the *Hagerstown Cracker Barrel*, printed in the 1970s by Patricia Cushwa and G. M. Farley, refer to the Veiled Lady, a legend associated with the Halloween season in the Williamsport area of Washington County.

In Farley's story, the creature was described as a "mysterious lady who wore a shadowy veil and crept stealthily through Williamsport's dark alleys." Some said she was the troubled spirit of a dead woman who was buried alive, or who was so evil the ground refused to accept her black soul. Maybe, some suggested, the ghost had unfinished business and had returned to complete her work on earth. Others said the woman returned to terrify her still-living husband, who had been involved in an illicit affair that had caused the Veiled Lady's death.

Cushwa's story suggested the Veiled Lady was nothing more than a man, dressed as a mysterious woman in black, who roamed the town and spoke to no one as he searched out the whereabouts of his unfaithful wife.

As years passed, more versions of Williamsport's floating phantom surfaced, but no one could ever pinpoint the origin or provide proof of the real story. As in all folklore, the tales frightened local youngsters, were embellished over time, and eventually died out. Nowadays, the legend of the Veiled Lady surfaces infrequently, and only when old-timers relate the tale as a fond, fiendish memory associated with their wild and carefree youth.

School Spirits

Hood College traces its history to the Women's College of Frederick, founded in 1893. Four years after the school's founding, it moved to a rural area outside the city, and today it is considered a leading center of learning in western Maryland. According to a 2005 Halloween day article in *Hood Today* by Jennifer Hill, there have been numerous reports of ghosts in Brodbeck Music Hall. In fact, the chairperson of the Department of History and Political Science stated, "There's more lore and ghost stories about Brodbeck Hall than any other building on campus. It has this distinctive aura, this atmosphere to it."

Apparently the legend has attracted the interest of student ghost hunters, some of whom have visited the building and captured alleged spirit energy through orbs in photographs. Some have attempted to document evidence of electronic voice phenomena (EVP) through digital recordings. Reports of unexpected footsteps and cold spots have caused some to believe unseen spirits inhabit the building.

Built in 1868, Brodbeck Hall is the oldest building on campus. Prior to becoming part of the Women's College of Frederick it had been used as a tavern, social hall, flower shop, farmer's home, and warehouse. However, contrary to rumors, there is no evidence it had been a German-immigrant brothel. After being acquired by the college, it first became a residence for faculty and students. Eventually, renovations and additions turned it into its present-day cultural center and administrative site.

A faculty member who was alone in the hall one night reported hearing music coming from one of the upper floors as he was leaving the building. A student reported hearing wailing and also the sounds of slamming doors late one evening. While the article stated many people believed the ghost stories were intriguing and added to the structure's colorful history, some students nonetheless preferred to use the music practice rooms during the daytime.

Mount Saint Mary's University and Seminary rests on 1,400 acres in the Catoctin Mountains of northern Maryland. Founded in 1808, it is believed to be the second-oldest Catholic institution of higher learning in the country. It also is the home of more than a few pesky ghosts. But this shouldn't prove surprising. After all, nearly every college campus boasts its share of school spirits. But the Mount's rural location—and its proximity to the famous Mason-Dixon Line and the historic battle of Gettysburg—makes it an ideal site for a substantial share of local lore.

The school's most famous phantom appears to be that of Rev. Simon Brute, a former president of the college who died in 1839. The cassock-wearing apparition has been reported to glide at a smooth and steady pace across the attractive campus, and the specter often offers a nod to passing students and faculty. Naturally, it's not surprising that he's believed to hang about in Brute Hall, a dormitory named in his honor. Some say this particular specter's favorite haunt is Room 252.

One year, a visiting priest was assigned to live in the room. The cleric checked in, took a walk around the campus, and returned to find all of his belongings spread about, as if someone had tossed them in a fit of anger. Another priest, who owned a pet cat, was given the room, but he moved out after his pet began hissing at an unseen being and spent its time cowering beneath the bed.

In a 2002 Halloween article in the *Washington Post,* reporter Linton Weeks noted that students who had stayed in Room 252 told of unexplained flushing toilets, flicking light switches, and changing stations on the television.

Weeks also reported a tale associated with McCaffrey Hall involving a servant named Leander, who had worked at the college in the 1880s. When Leander was accused of stealing, his left hand was severed, and according to legend the limb was buried in the college quadrangle. Certainly, this tale is a gift for those interested in perpetuating creepy fright-night tales, and Weeks's article adds, "To this day, residents of McCaffrey report seeing a severed hand here and there, or hearing fingers scratching on dorm windows." No doubt, the troubled hand is seeking the rest of its body, and it's said Leander's limb will roam the campus until its long search is over.

Mother Elizabeth Ann Seton established St. Joseph's College for Women in Emmitsburg in the early 1800s. The school closed in 1972, and many of its students transferred to Mount St. Mary's. But ghost stories about the now closed campus seem to have survived. The girls at Mount Saint Joseph's used to report hearing unearthly moaning and groaning in the middle of the night. They also said they saw the image of Mother Seton, whose grave is located there. The saintly founder's ghost was seen roaming the campus being followed by a man, who floated silently behind the mistress and carried a black doctor's bag. Perhaps, some suggested, it was the spirit of a medical doctor who worked on wounded soldiers during the Civil War. At that time, the campus was used as a hospital for both Union and Confederate troops, who were nursed back to health by the Sisters of Charity.

Washington College is a small school in Chestertown, on Maryland's Eastern Shore. It was the first institution of higher learning named in honor of the nation's first president, and it's said the American hero gave his personal approval for his name to be used. Founded in 1782, it is among the first dozen colleges chartered in the United States. Because of its age and location—in a historic village where one of the revolutionary tea parties was held in 1774 to protest British taxation—it isn't surprising that it's believed to host a resident ghost.

The often-told legend involves a spirit named Ariel who is said to haunt Reid Hall, originally a dormitory only for female students.

According to an alumna who lived in the building for three years, resident assistants in charge of the dormitory make it a point to tell each new student assigned to live there about the residence hall's phantom, "so they wouldn't freak out when Ariel made her visits."

The ghost is believed to be a former student that died while attending a secret gathering on the third floor, which at the time of the incident served as an attic and storage area. "It was a place where the girls would sneak up to party," the former resident said. One night, one of the girls fell out a window and died. Soon afterwards, stories began to circulate about appearances of Ariel's ghost. "The ghost doesn't do anything," the former resident said. "She just makes her presence known. It seems like she enjoys being around the new students, but you get the impression she also likes scaring the girls."

Another version says the Reid Hall phantom committed suicide and is cursed to roam the building forever. This theory is supported by a tale that the apparition, with an aimless gaze, has been seen roaming the hallways and standing in doorways of the building. While there is no official record of anyone dying or killing herself in the residence hall, that doesn't stop the retelling and elaboration of the popular tale.

Wise's Well

Disposing of bodies left on a Civil War battlefield was a difficult and disturbing task that had to be dealt with rapidly. Sometimes fellow soldiers placed their fallen comrades in hastily dug, shallow graves near the killing fields. When opposing troops left battle areas quickly, local farmers and townsfolk were forced to bury the dead left behind, often performing brief and informal ceremonies over the bodies of both Union and Confederate soldiers. On some occasions, the government hired area residents to bury corpses. Many of the young soldiers, who died far from their homes, ended up in unmarked graves.

There's a legend associated with an engagement that was part of the much larger Battle of South Mountain. It occurred in 1862, in the western part of Maryland between Frederick and Hagerstown, near the site of the Reno Monument. The marker indicates the spot where

Maj. Gen. Jesse Lee Reno, commander of a corps of Union volunteers, was killed at Fox's Gap. Near the site, in an old cabin, Daniel Wise lived peacefully with his family. But when the war reached the farmer's doorstep, the Wises fled into the woods and hid there during the battle. Afterwards, they returned to find their property littered with the bodies of dead soldiers from both sides.

At this point, the legend takes a fork in the road. In one version, a Union burial detail was at the Wise homestead and had planted their comrades in graves around the family cabin. However, the Yanks had dumped nearly five dozen dead Rebels down the Wise family well. Afterwards, the ghosts of the restless spirits haunted Wise and others who came near their inappropriate burial site.

Another explanation has a Union Army officer paying Old Man Wise five dollars for every soldier he buried. To make the most of the government's generous offer, it's said that the farmer, without proper ceremony, tossed dozens of dead soldiers into a nearby dry well that was no longer used by the family.

Soon afterwards, the disrespected spirits began to haunt anyone passing near the well. But of more concern to Wise, some of the soldiers' ghosts visited the greedy old man in his sleep, threatening to haunt him forever. To break the hex, the troubled farmer had two options: move away or provide the bodies with their expected—and paid for—decent burial. Wise wisely selected the latter choice, and somehow he retrieved the bodies of the troubled ghost soldiers from his dry well and gave them a more respectful sendoff.

According to one version, a dead soldier returned to Wise in a dream on several successive nights, complaining that his body was buried in an "uncomfortable position," and he demanded that Wise turn him over so he could rest in peace. The next day, Wise dropped into the well, grabbed the topmost body and flipped it onto its back. The decaying face matched that of the agitated spirit who had been haunting the farmer nightly in his dreams.

Whether Wise reburied all of the corpses or simply addressed the concern of his nightly visitor is unknown. But one can only imagine the horrifying task that awaited Old Man Wise as he descended the deep pit filled with rotting bodies. To accomplish this job he had to lower himself into a dark cavern, gather up decaying body parts, and fight off the stench and horrifying sights that attacked all his senses. After he was far into this effort, there were times when he probably wished he had selected the first option and moved away from the area, leaving the restless spirits to roam at will. Of course, he could have avoided most of his troubles by fulfilling the original terms of the deal, but he succumbed to human nature's tendency to make a quick buck—and eventually paid the price in full, and then some.

Spook Hill

Spook Hill, or Gravity Hill as it is sometimes called, is said to exist in the area of Burkittsville. Some say the legendary location is closer to Frederick. Others will direct ghost hunters and interested parties to locations between Sharpsburg and Antietam. There even are listings of Gravity Hills near Baltimore and in southern Pennsylvania—plus a dozen other sites around the country.

In each case, the essence of this well-known tale is the same: Stop your car and shut off the engine at a specific spot in the road. Place the gearshift in neutral, exit the vehicle and watch in amazement as your person-empty car moves mysteriously UP the hill, apparently on its own power, or with a little bit of unseen ghostly help.

The logical explanation, that you are experiencing an optical illusion and the auto is actually heading downhill, is often the same. But the more interesting, paranormal reasons for this supernatural occurrence depend upon several factors, including the teller, the time of the occurrence, and any tragic or historical events that took place at the particular haunted "Spook Hill" site.

At the hill between Frederick, Maryland, and Harpers Ferry, West Virginia, the cause is placed on the apparently bored and restless shoulders of invisible and ever-present ghosts of Civil War soldiers. During the night prior to a battle, Rebel soldiers moved through the darkness pushing and pulling artillery pieces across the mountainside forests, trying to get them into position on high ground before the next day's fight began. Before all the Confederate cannons were placed in position, Union soldiers charged out of woods and killed many of the Rebels, who were unable to return fire and defend themselves because they were concentrating on hauling the heavy artillery. Some believe the ghosts of desperate Civil War soldiers—in most reports they are Rebels but in a few tales they are said to be Yankees— have been seen, repeating their futile efforts to direct their phantom cannons into position. The ghosts of these men killed at the Battle of South Mountain in 1862 seem to have remained on the hillside, still pushing and pulling as they try to resolve their unfinished mission.

Some ghost hunters have seen strange lights, which they believe might be ghostly campfires on the dense hillsides. There also have been reports of sightings of soldiers in gray or blue uniforms and the sounds of horse hooves and cannon fire in the area. Paranormal investigators have used digital recording devices and cameras to try to prove that the spectral artillerists are pushing stopped automobiles, thinking they are the Civil War cannons they had hauled during that bloody night. One recommended evidence-securing technique is to place a layer of white powder on the car's rear bumper and inspect the area for indications of finger or hand marks after the car stops moving. For those interested in visiting Spook Hill near Burkittsville, ask the locals for the mysterious site, which is said to be on Gapland Road.

Phantom Flutist

There's a floating melody that travels through the wooded hillsides near the town of Emmitsburg. Most pass off the snatches of a high-pitched melody as the swirling wind. Others claim it's the screeching of night owls or some disturbed forest creatures. But longtime locals know the real source: it's the musical ghost.

Larry Dielman is his name, and playing the flute is his game. That's the answer that has been given since the tale began in 1884, soon after the first tune took wind. But that's the middle of our story. It's best that we start at the beginning.

According to word of mouth tales—and articles in the *Emmitsburg Chronicle* (as early at 1884) and *Baltimore Sun* (as recently at 2001)— the kindly tale begins with Professor Casper Dielman, a German musician of some note who came to America in the early 1800s. In 1834, after composing inaugural marches for four U.S. presidents and directing orchestras in New York City, Philadelphia, and Baltimore, the accomplished musician arrived at Mount Saint Mary's College. There he planned to enjoy nature and mold young musical minds.

In 1838, a son, Larry, was born. The younger Dielman eventually received some musical training, and soon enjoyed playing a number of instruments at the side of his father. But the son was somewhat of a musical disappointment. Apparently, he never took his lyrical talent to new heights, instead being content to use it in a playful way to attract the attention of the ladies and entertain his friends. Larry became a grocer, married the love of his life and, for a time, seemed to have a perfect existence—until his bride ran off and left him to endure a solitary life. Neighbors recall a picture of Larry as an older, lonely man, sitting alone on his store's front porch singing aloud of his lost love.

In the early 1880s, the old professor died. That following Christmas, Larry walked to his father's gave, stood above the stone and lifted a flute to his lips. People in the nearby town recalled hearing the shrill strains of a lamented melody. The song was "When Glory Lit the Midnight Air," a song composed by Larry's recently deceased father. In response, the locals wrapped themselves in winter garb and walked to the gravesite, located near the Grotto of Our Lady of Lourdes. In silence, they witnessed the musical expression of a lonely son's special love.

As years passed, the event became an annual tradition, with Larry leading a small procession up the steep hill to stand beside his father's gravesite. Over the years, the tradition changed slightly, with the musical tribute occurring on Christmas Eve. But as Larry grew older he was unable to make the climb, and friends placed his frail body onto a sled and pulled him up the hill so he could continue to perform.

One version of the story states that in 1923 Larry Dielman died, along with the tradition. A more eerie rendition of the tale, written by Frederick N. Rasmussen for the *Baltimore Sun*, suggests that despite the most bone-chilling temperatures and falling snow or sleet, Larry never missed a Christmas performance. But his last, in 1922, will be remembered most. "Townspeople heard the notes from his flute," Rasmussen wrote, "which then abruptly stopped. He was found unconscious in the snow and died the following spring. He was buried in a plot next to his father."

So ended a musical family's custom that had developed into an anticipated local event, but others claimed this was not the case. In an *Emmitsburg Chronicle* article, the unknown author wrote, "Old-timers say that if you listen very carefully on Christmas Eve or Christmas morning you can still hear the ethereal strains of beautiful flute music floating down from the cemetery. A short time later, it is gone, not to be heard again for another year."

Flag Folklore

While Philadelphia's Betsy Ross receives a lot of attention for her design of one of the earliest American flags, the Keystone State to the north has to take a back seat to Maryland when it comes to history, stories, legends, and even a ghost story associated with our nation's most cherished symbol.

During the War of 1812, in September 1814 during the Battle of Baltimore, lawyer Francis Scott Key wrote the words to the "Star-Spangled Banner." His inspiration was the courageous American defense of the Maryland harbor town and the immense flag that Key watched flying over Fort McHenry throughout the battle.

The banner's creator, young Mary Pickersgill, sewed the 30-by-42-foot American flag in a Baltimore brewery with the help of her daughter, several nieces, and some African-American servants. After more than six weeks of intense work and using more than four hundred yards of material, the flag was finished. Each of the fifteen stripes was two feet wide, and each of the fifteen white stars measured two feet in length from point to point. The decision to fly such a huge flag was made by Fort McHenry's commander, Maj. George Armistead. Expecting a British attack, he reinforced the fort's defenses and engaged Pickersgill to create the banner. At the time, he told her to make it "so large that the British will have no difficulty seeing it from a distance."

The young Baltimore flagmaker could never have imagined her creation would inspire an amateur poet and a young nation, and eventually be the basis for our country's national song. Pickersgill's restored flag is among the most cherished national treasures in the Smithsonian Institution.

Several decades later, during the start of the Civil War, Southern sympathizers in Maryland played a role in a story associated with the first Confederate flags. During the first Battle of Bull Run in Manassas, Virginia, in July 1861, Confederate general Pierre G. T. Beauregard surveyed the fighting and noticed a large body of troops moving through the valley towards his left. Because of the dust and smoke, he was unable to determine if the advancing force was Union or Confederate, and thus unable to determine whether to attack or retreat. The commander and his staff attempted to identify the still-advancing troops by trying to locate their colors (flag), which they hoped would provide the answer to their critical question.

Unfortunately, this was the first major land battle of a very young war, and there had not been any uniformity in the size, shape, and colors of the Confederate flag. To Beauregard, all of the flags looked similar, and his anxiety increased as the critical time neared. Even the keener eyes of his younger staff officers were unable to determine the precise colors and design being carried by the still-moving mass of troops. Finally, a gust of wind blew the thick smoke from a section of the battlefield, and they recognized the banner flown by fellow Southern commander Jubal A. Early. The Confederates won the battle, shocking not only the Union army but also hundreds of well-dressed picnickers and sightseers who had traveled from Washington to enjoy an afternoon of entertainment observing the fight from the hillsides.

Mass confusion reigned as hundreds of carriages of shocked Yankee fans clogged roads leading back to the capital. This congestion impeded the embarrassing retreat of the Union forces. Newspapers wrote how gentlemen and ladies, dressed in their Sunday best, competed for space on dirt roads with cowardly blue-coated soldiers, who pushed through the civilian crowds desperate to escape from the victorious Rebels.

Confederate military staff members were delighted with the outcome of the battle, but they agreed with Beauregard that it was critical to develop a uniform flag design. It also was critical that they begin immediate production of a standard battle flag for the new nation and its victorious army. The eventual result was the Stars and Bars, a blue cross with white stars on a red field. Beauregard personally presented his troops with the first three flags sent to the army. Maryland Confederate sympathizers Hetty and Jennie Cary of Baltimore, and their cousin, Constance, of Alexandria, Virginia, made these flags from material taken from Southern ladies' dresses.

But Hetty Cary's association with the Southern banner was noted again when a group of Yankee troops were riding through Baltimore, which was filled with Southern patriots. From an open window on the upper floor of her home, Hetty Cary leaned out and waved a Confederate flag. It's said one of the Union officers raced his horse forward to ask his commanding officers if he should arrest the young woman. According to an eyewitness, Mrs. Louise Wigfall Wright, the Union colonel looked up at the defiant, but also lovely, flag waver and told his underling, "No! She is beautiful enough to do as she damn pleases!"

In Frederick, a legendary and inspirational flag incident reportedly occurred on September 10, 1862. Confederate forces under the command of Gen. Stonewall Jackson were passing through the small town as they marched north toward Sharpsburg, where they would be involved in a battle remembered as the bloodiest one-day engagement of the Civil War.

From a window of her home, ninety-six-year-old Barbara Fritchie (also spelled Frietchie) watched the Rebels advance. In an impulsive act of patriotic defiance, she waved her Union flag—which she had retrieved from within the pages of her family Bible—in the faces of the advancing enemy soldiers. General Jackson, it's said, told one of his men to shoot at the flag, or tear it down. But the elderly, patriotic flag waver defiantly shouted, "Shoot if you must, this old gray head. But spare your country's flag."

The actions and words of the feisty Marylander were reported in newspapers around the country. Eventually, poet John Greenleaf Whittier popularized her statement and story in his lengthy 1863 poem, "Barbara Fritchie."

Over the years, historians have questioned the accuracy of the legendary incident. Some scholars have referred to newspaper accounts of similar actions by people in other states. Other researchers have produced letters from Frederick residents who witnessed the invasions of Rebel armies in their town and who had disputed the accuracy of the Fritchie incident in September 1862. Despite these assaults on the legend, the patriotic actions of the elderly hero, who died two months after her defiant flag-waving display, served as an inspiration during the second year of the Civil War. The story and poem continue to stir the imagination of schoolchildren and adults today, particularly those who visit Frederick's Barbara Fritchie House and Museum.

This final flag tale involves an unusual incident at an old home in northern Maryland that, at first, seemed perplexing. Later the owners learned they might be sharing their residence with a defiant, unpatriotic Civil War spirit.

One source said the haunted home stands near Dickeysville, while a second person insisted the story took place outside Frederick. A third version claimed the event occurred in nearby southern Pennsylvania, outside Hanover. Despite this location dilemma, which is common when similar ghost stories are passed around, the main facts are about the same.

A young couple bought an old "fixer-upper" home and energetically spent more than a year and a half restoring the building to a very presentable condition. The husband and wife, with the help of family and friends, took special care to maintain the building's historic charm, while including many up-to-date conveniences—such as central air conditioning and modern plumbing, lighting, and furnishings. During their second year in the home, they threw a gala July Fourth picnic, and they appropriately decorated their restored home in red, white, and blue.

When they had finished attaching the patriotic bunting and banners along the second-floor open porch that spread across the front of their home, the couple walked down the stairs and headed out onto the spacious entry lawn. Looking back up at the house, they noticed that a section of the red, white, and blue material had come undone from one corner of the second-floor porch. Together, they went upstairs, made the repair, and returned to their viewing spot on the lawn.

This time when they looked at their decorated home, the bunting was falling from the opposite side of the front porch. Again, they went out onto the wide, balcony-like porch and reaffixed the dangling decorative material. Now a bit confused and frustrated, they went downstairs and outside to look at their fine work. This time, all of their decorations appeared to be fine.

Early the next morning, they headed directly into the backyard, where they spent much of the day setting up chairs, tables, and dining plates and plasticware for their soon-to-be-arriving guests. Since they had not bothered to check the front of the house, they were unaware of the scene that greeted the guests that parked in the front of the home.

About a half-hour into the party, when everything seemed to be going well, a relative said, "It's a shame what happened to your decorations. You must have had a bad windstorm last night." Confused, the hosts had no idea what their guest was talking about, until she said, "We picked up the American flag and placed it back in the holder on the front porch. It just wasn't right to leave it lying the ground, especially on the Fourth of July."

After racing to the front lawn, the couple looked up to see most of their multicolored bunting dangling from the upper porch. Only two sections were still affixed, and the flag that the guest had replaced in its stand was lying on the ground.

The wife took the flag inside the home, and the husband removed the disrupted decorations. They did not replace them that year, or the following. Over the years, they discovered that whenever they put out an American flag, a short time later they would find it lying on the ground. It was as if someone pulled it from its metal stand and tossed it aside.

Eventually, an older person in a nearby town heard of their dilemma and said his grandfather had told him a story that might be the answer to their unusual experiences. According to an old legend, the owner of their home during the Civil War had a son who fought for the South and was killed in battle. Defiantly, a Confederate flag flew from the front porch each day until the old, bitter man died. That man refused to ever fly the Stars and Stripes, because he said he hated the country that had killed his son. However, the Stars and Bars always had a place of honor, waving proudly in the breeze from the front porch.

South Mountain Spirits

There are a number of ghost stories based in the South Mountain region, including tales of wild dogs, Civil War soldiers, Indian lovers, treasure hunters, and a pesky poltergeist (German for "noisy spirit"). In 1982, when Stephen Spielberg's movie *Poltergeist* was released, Ora Ann Ernst, a *Daily Mail* reporter, reminded western Maryland residents that such activity was old news in their part of the woods.

Ernst's article, "'Poltergeist' Nothing New for Washington County," shared a tale found in an old book, *South Mountain Magic: Tales of Old Maryland*, written a century before by Madeleine Vinton Dahlgren. The collection of folklore features a poltergeist story set in a log house near South Mountain.

The home's evil spirit was attracted by the actions of a wicked old man, who was well known to have a surly and violent nature. Following a heated argument with his sister, the fellow, whom we'll call Hans, remained bitter and refused to talk to her for many years. But when the woman learned that her brother was dying, she rushed to his home, entered his bedroom, and knelt by his bedside. In a kind voice, the sister told Hans he had been in her prayers, and she pleaded with him to forget their differences and said she hoped to effect reconciliation before he passed on.

According to Dahlgren's book, "At this point, he fell into a furious rage, and glowered upon her in a savage way, pointing with feeble motion to a glass tumbler nearby. As she handed it to him, with the sudden force that filled his soul, he hurled it at her face." That evil act would be his last, for Hans died as he attempted to inflict harm upon his well-intentioned sibling. When the tumbler missed its mark, the old, broken man fell back onto his bed, glared at the ceiling, let out a groan, and expelled his last earthly breath.

Months later, when Hans's vacant house was finally rented, the new tenants complained of hearing strange noises, feeling cold winds blowing through the rooms, and living in a constant state of unease. After a short time they moved on. Subsequent renters followed the same pattern—a brief stay and out the door they went. Neighbors who could see the home in the distance reported lights appearing in the empty home. Others said pale blue lights would flicker and move from window to window on both levels. The sounds of barrel making, which was Hans's trade, traveled through the hills, along with the clear sounds of rolling barrels and rattling chains. According to Dahlgren's book, there's a belief held by some mountainfolk: "Where sin and death shook hands, still rage torment and loud lament."

The author also included a chapter about a tribe of Skiliton Indians that roamed the narrow paths of the mountain. In later years, soldiers from many different armies moved along the same trails, originally used by wild animals and later by local tribes. One young passing soldier stopped at a local tavern and fell in love with Sadie, the owner's daughter. When the tavernkeeper forbid his daughter to continue seeing the soldier, Sadie hid her lover in an old Indian cave on the nearby mountain. At night, she carried food to him in secret, and announced her arrival by imitating the cry of a wildcat.

One night, a passing hunter heard what he thought was the call of a wild animal. Carefully, he aimed his rifle at the area where he thought the sound originated. His shot hit its mark, killing Sadie. Worried about being caught and hanged for murder, the shooter buried the young woman in an unmarked grave. Hikers have reported seeing phantom campfires and hearing the sad moan of an injured animal, but they have never been able to locate the source. Some say it is Sadie, crying out for her lover and, perhaps, hoping to be discovered and given a proper burial.

Snarly Yow

There's a fierce and elusive ghost dog living in the mountains of western Maryland. This centuries-old nocturnal beast goes by several names, including Dog Fiend, Devil Dog, Vanishing Dog, and Black Dog. But the name that seems to have become part of the region's folklore is the unusual and memorable handle of "Snarly Yow." (Snarly because it reveals its trademark snarl, and Yow probably because it has been known to let out a loud, blood-curdling yowl.)

Where the Snarly Yow hangs out is as much a mystery as its origin. It has been claimed by folks living in the South Mountain area between Frederick and Hagerstown. But it's also been known to roam as far south as the wildlands surrounding Harpers Ferry, West Virginia. Stories about the Snarly Yow written during the last half century all seem to have been based, to some degree, on a lengthy account penned by Boonsboro resident Madeleine Vinton Dahlgren in her 1882 book *South Mountain Magic: Tales of Old Maryland.* But the exploits of the Yow also have been featured in *Ghosts of Antietam* by Wilmer McKendree Mumma, *Haunted Houses of Harpers Ferry* by Stephen D. Brown, and *Ghosts and Legends of Frederick County* by Timothy L. Cannon and Nancy F. Whitmore.

A combination of these texts, plus articles in regional Maryland newspapers, offer a fairly good and generally accepted description of the elusive creature, as well as examples of some its more memorable appearances and antics.

Although a Snarly Yow has never been killed, trapped, captured, or photographed, there is little doubt that one or more Yows exist. Generally, it has coal-black fur, a very ugly-looking red cavernous mouth that is surrounded by sharp fangs, eyes that flash bright red when the beast is aroused, and an extremely large body. It also is able to change shape and size in an instant, and it can vanish as suddenly as it appears. One report said that although it generally looks like a dog, the Yow can have the face of a cat and has a bristly, as opposed to smooth, coat.

Somewhere near the Old National Road, now known as Route 40 between Boonsboro and Hagerstown, Yow hunters have the best chance of catching a glimpse of the nighttime prowler. Many tales note that the dog seems to "appear" on the side of South Mountain, heads down into a stream valley, and laps up a considerable amount of water. Then it turns and climbs back up the mountain and disappears, apparently heading to its never-yet-located lair.

Travelers along the old highway have reported sightings while riding horses, seated in carriages or automobiles, or walking and hiking. Most times the Snarly Yow materializes in an empty roadway, at times blocking the pathway. Those drivers who have been unfortunate to notice the beast before they could stop their vehicle have said they thought they ran over and through the creature. After skidding to a halt, they have rushed onto the road to see how badly they had injured the creature—only to find no carcass beneath or behind their car. Instead, standing unscathed on the highway behind their stopped vehicle, is a healthy and threatening black dog.

There are several stories of men who came upon the infamous creature while they were walking home from a big night on the town in Boonsboro. One man told Ms. Dahlgren about his encounter. She wrote that he described the creature as "black and bigger than any dog he had ever seen, and it stood guarding the road in such a way as to forbid his crossing."

To get past the fierce obstacle, the man fought the animal, which grew larger and stronger as the battle continued. But every time the man punched his hand against the animal's body, he said his arm connected with nothing but air and his clenched fist flew through the solid-looking apparition. Another man experienced a similar late-night encounter and decided to walk around the animal that seemed to be blocking the narrow roadway. But the man claimed that the Snarly Yow grew larger in both width and height, making it impossible for the man to pass the snarling, frothing canine. Terrified, the man ran back the way he had come, and he waited until daylight to head toward his home.

A skilled hunter attempted to shoot the Yow, but his bullets—which never before had missed their mark at such a close distance—went through the legendary ghost dog, leaving it unharmed. A similar experience was had by a man who threw two rocks directly at the snarling dog's face. Like others before him, he turned and ran back in the direction from which he had come when he saw the rocks pass through the Snarly Yow's black body.

In earlier days, the Snarly Yow appeared in a mist and raced alongside horses that galloped at full speed, trying to separate themselves and their masters from the threatening monster. In more modern stories, the beast of South Mountain effortlessly keeps pace with fast-traveling trucks and cars. Astounded drivers have reported seeing a black beast, which they watched rushing beside them on the highway, suddenly disappear from the roadway before their wide-open eyes.

There had been a few reports of possible Snarly Yow sightings up until the 1970s. But no significant stories have surfaced in recent decades. Like all fascinating folklore, the legends of the Snarly Yow have survived much longer than many might have expected, probably because of repeated recitations of the beast's stories around camp bonfires and during Halloween hayrides. No doubt, many want to believe that in the forests of South Mountain there is a coal-black, red-eyed, frothing dog with fangs that glisten in the light of a full moon. And if there isn't, there ought to be a Snarly Yow out there, if for no other reason than to keep its colorful name alive.

Haunted Farmhouse

The new family was excited when it moved into the old, pre-Civil War farmhouse north of Hagerstown just prior to the school year. The thirty acres of rolling fields and forests were going to be the perfect refuge from advancing development and monotonous weekday work life. A few weeks after they moved in, the wife heard the clear sounds of a grandfather clock, chiming seven o'clock. Knowing they did not own such a distinctive piece of furniture, she assumed her husband had purchased one as a present. He probably had hidden it away in one of the many empty rooms and hallways in the large homestead.

That Christmas morning came and went. No grandfather clock was waiting beneath, beside, or behind the gaily decorated live Christmas tree they had cut from their own fields. But, occasionally, the wife still heard in the ensuing months the unmistakable sounds of seven loud chimes. No large timepiece, however, was ever found or brought into the home.

The following summer, the family's two young boys were playing under the front porch and pulled out two round-topped tombstones. The markings were illegible, worn away by the elements. The parents recalled hearing there might be an old family graveyard somewhere on the property, but they had never come across it. Could the house be built over a boneyard? Impossible, they thought. Someone must have left the old gravestones hidden under the front porch for safe-keeping. If so, where did they belong? Whose graves were they supposed to mark?

When the parents began tearing off old wallpaper and knocking down a few walls to enlarge one of the rooms, the pace of unexplained and unexpected incidents increased. Tools disappeared.

Shadows moved across walls. Dark images appeared in corners. Hazy apparitions materialized and just as suddenly disappeared.

The wife began to wonder if the resident ghosts were upset about the way the new owners were redecorating. The husband ignored the comment, deciding if he didn't acknowledge their existence the spirits would move on. No such luck. Annoying incidents escalated to a more substantive level. One night the wife entered the master bedroom and said she saw nearly a dozen slaves standing in a circle in the room. One of the apparitions turned to the others and discussed how they were to get to their next stop, in adjacent Pennsylvania, on the Underground Railroad route. When the wife later described the scene to her husband, she said it felt like she was watching a live, dramatic presentation. She also knew she was still inside her own bedroom, but had the sense that the people in the room had been there many years before, and had done exactly what she saw.

Later the couple kept their infant daughter in a crib in that room. At times, it appeared that the child was laughing and was responding to an unseen presence above her in the crib. The wife named the unseen spirit "Nanny."

Several guests in the home inquired if there was anything "unusual" about the place. A few said they had been pushed, heard strange voices, and even had seen a young girl pass along a hallway. Eventually, a person who had lived in the area for many years told the owners there had been quite a few deaths of young children inside their home. The person suggested that the spirits of those individuals might be hanging around to play with the new children who had moved in, and to see what the latest owners planned to do with the historic property.

As the couple's children grew older, the parents said, their farmhouse ghosts seemed to lose interest or disappear and move on. Maybe they took up residence in another home in the area, one that needed someone to tend to a young family with a few youngsters and a new infant or two.

Antietam Battlefield

In late summer of 1862, Confederate general Robert E. Lee believed he could end the one-and-a-half year-old Civil War by marching his army into the north and attacking the Union on its home ground. Up to that time, all of the battles, most of which had been Rebel victories, had been fought in the South. A major Southern victory in a state north of the Mason-Dixon Line, Lee thought, would demoralize his enemy and cause President Abraham Lincoln to accept a negotiated settlement. Everyone knew Lincoln, whose bumbling and ineffective generals had lost a long series of battles, was under extreme pressure in Washington to put an end to the unpopular war.

By early September 1862, Lee's army was exhausted, low on ammunition, and nearly out of supplies. But as would occur many times during the war, luck was again on the Confederate general's side. Union general George B. McClellan was in command of the Army of the Potomac. His forces outnumbered Lee's by more than 30,000 men, but McClellan believed that he was greatly outnumbered by the Confederates. Therefore, the Yankee commander was hesitant to engage the Rebels in battle. McClellan's approach was to stay out of sight and have his scouts keep an eye on Lee's northward-advancing troops.

But Lady Luck delivered an unusual offering regarding the opponent's strategy to the cautious McClellan. Lee had sent a copy of his northern invasion plans to all of his generals. When Lee's most trusted commander, Maj. Gen. Thomas "Stonewall" Jackson, received his orders, he directed an aide to make an additional copy of the document, which Jackson immediately sent by courier to his brother-in-law, Maj. Gen. Daniel Harvey Hill. However, Hill had already received his own copy, and the duplicate that had been sent to him by Jackson was lost—but not for long.

On September 13, a detachment of Union troops settled in an area that had been used previously by Rebels commanded by Hill. One of the Yankees found a copy of Lee's orders, apparently the duplicate sent by Jackson, wrapped around several cigars. The discovered orders were rushed to McClellan, who was delighted to be in possession of his adversary's secret plans. Excited and confident, McClellan proclaimed, "If I cannot whip Bobby Lee, then I will be willing to go home."

But Lady Luck had only so much mojo to give, and the ever cautious McClellan, who had been criticized by Lincoln and Washington politicians so often in the past for refusing to act boldly, again waited too long to take advantage of the strategic gift. Instead of ordering an immediate pursuit of the Confederate forces, McClellan waited overnight, and then timidly headed west to South Mountain, still believing that Lee's dirty, hungry, and tired army heavily outnumbered his Union force. After a few days of strategic moves by both sides, the opposing armies met along battle lines drawn near Antietam Creek.

On September 17, at about five o'clock in the morning, Generals Lee and McClellan directed a bloodbath of a battle that ultimately would end in a tie. Antietam National Battlefield, adjacent to the small village of Sharpsburg in northern Maryland, would become famous in history as the site of the bloodiest single-day battle of the Civil War. The number of casualties (soldiers killed, wounded, or captured) totaled 22,720, including more than 3,600 killed in action.

One of the most famous open-air killing fields was the result of Union general Joseph Hooker's accurate artillery fire, which efficiently mowed down Stonewall Jackson's attacking troops as they charged in waves across an open field. Eyewitnesses said the cornstalks in the field were "cut as closely as could have been done with a knife." This deadly harvest of human limbs that began at sunrise lasted throughout the day, with opposing soldiers moving back and forth and falling on grassy knolls, as each side alternately took and then lost precious, blood-soaked ground.

The center of the Confederate line was at a site called "Bloody Lane," a sunken road that served as an excellent natural defensive position. Multiple times, Union forces attempted to overtake the gully, but they were easily beaten back by Confederate riflemen, who themselves sustained extremely high casualties. Eventually, Union forces established an offensive position on higher ground and fired shells down into the Rebels' defensive depression. This area ultimately became a killing zone where dead Rebel bodies were stacked several soldiers high.

As a result of the high concentration of deaths that occurred along Bloody Lane, this area in the battlefield has been reputed to host the restless spirits of some of the heroes who died during the deadly engagement. Ghost hunters claim to have captured evidence on tape recorders of electronic voice phenomena (EVP), which sound like rifle shots, cannon blasts, clashing sabers, and horses' hooves. They also point to photographs, taken at many locations throughout the battlefield, showing spheres called orbs, as well as pictures indicating ghostly images or apparitions of Civil War-era soldiers.

Antietam, one of the country's most visited battlefields, has become well-known as a site of potential hauntings. Some visitors have reported hearing shouts, similar to military commands, as well as orders being given near some of the monuments. There have been claims by tourists that they have heard the famous battle cry of the colorful Irish Brigade near the area of Bloody Lane.

The men of Francis Meagher's Irish Brigade, mainly from New York and Massachusetts, had arrived in the U.S. in the 1840s to escape their homeland's Great Hunger. When the Civil War began, these immigrants signed up to fight for the Union by the thousands, and Meagher's unit became well known for its fierce bravery in battle. At Antietam, the Irish Brigade attacked the Confederates at Bloody Lane and lost nearly six hundred of its one thousand men. Sounds of the unit's battle cry—"Faugh-a-Balaugh," Gaelic for "Clear the Way"— have been heard on the historic battlefield.

Troy Taylor, author of scores of books on haunted sites and unexplained incidents throughout the country, writes of the Bloody Lane haunts:

> Reports over the years tell of the sounds of phantom gunfire echoing along the sunken road and the smell of smoke and gunpowder, which seems to come from nowhere. I spoke to a man who visited the battlefield a few years ago and he told me of seeing several men in Confederate uniforms walking down the old road. He assumed they were reenactors, present at the park for some upcoming event, until they abruptly vanished. And ghostly apparitions are not the only things experienced here.

According to one report, there were more than five thousand Confederate casualties in Bloody Lane. Perhaps the most famous ghost story associated with the sunken road, said Taylor, involves a group of boys from a Baltimore school. The students' daylong tour of the battlefield ended at Bloody Lane. Before they left, the boys were allowed to wander the historic site and were told to think about what they had learned during their visit. They were asked to record their impressions for a history assignment, and several of the students wrote brief remarks and poems related to their field trip.

"But the comments that got the most attention from the teacher," Taylor said, "were written by several boys who walked down the road to the observation tower, which is located where the Irish Brigade charged the Confederate line. The boys described hearing strange noises that became shouts, coming from the field near the tower. Some of the students said that it sounded like a chant, and others described the voices as though a group was singing a Christmas song in a foreign language, a song like 'Deck the Halls.'"

When asked to elaborate, the boys described the words as sounding like the lyrical part of the Christmas song that goes "Fa-la-la-la-la." They said the singing began strongly and then faded away. "But," Taylor wondered, "what if the singing had not been a Christmas song at all, but the sounds of the Irish Brigade 'clearing the way' with the fateful cry of 'Faugh-a-Balaugh'?"

Another popular paranormal site at Antietam Battlefield is Rohrbach, or Burnside, Bridge. The stone structure with attractive arches was involved in violent fighting toward the end of the daylong battle. Union general Ambrose E. Burnside, with a force of about twelve thousand soldiers, attempted repeatedly to cross the structure. However, a much smaller force of Confederate sharpshooters, numbering only about three hundred and under the command of Brig. Gen. Robert Toombs, held the high ground. From their elevated positions, the Rebels were able to shoot down on their enemy and hold off the Union attackers for hours.

Hundreds of men were killed on and near the bridge, and it's said their bodies were buried close to where they fell in battle, in unmarked graves in the hallowed ground around the bridge. Some visitors claim they have seen colored orbs floating around the bridge at night. The sound of an eerie drumbeat has been reported, along with sightings of misty apparitions of both Union and Confederate dead.

While every student of the Civil War is aware that the Battle of Antietam was the bloodiest single-day battle of the entire conflict, nothing puts the number of dead, wounded, and captured into more perspective than the annual custom that occurs on the first Saturday in December. Each year, volunteers at Antietam Battlefield set out more than 23,000 luminaries—lit candles in paper bags. Each glowing memorial represents a casualty of that bloody day in 1862. The battlefield is open for visitors to drive through the national park in darkness, except for the hallowed glow of the memorial candles.

Visitors who have witnessed this respectful tribute are moved by the significance of the loss of human life, and the valiant sacrifice of America's Civil War heroes, when they see row upon row upon row of flickering lights as far as the eye can see.

Pry House

Battlefields where soldiers suffered and died are not the only locations believed to be haunted. Some structures used as meeting places, hideaways, and hospitals during and after a bloody battle also are sources of unexplained events and interesting legends.

The Pry House, located north of Sharpsburg, served as Gen. George McClellan's headquarters during the Battle of Antietam. Today it is a part of the national battlefield park and open daily, serving as the Pry House Field Hospital Museum, which is associated with the National Museum of Civil War Medicine. This use is historically appropriate, since the farmhouse and grounds, once owned by Philip Pry, also served as a field hospital where wounded officers were treated. A nearby barn on the property was used as a medical site for enlisted men, where it's estimated that at least five hundred wounded troops were cared for during the battle.

Two ghosts that might haunt the property are Mr. and Mrs. Philip Pry, who were not happy their home was invaded and confiscated by the Yankees. These military invaders disrupted the owners' lives and showed little care and respect for the family's possessions. Other phantoms might be troops that died in the nearby barn and officers who breathed their last inside the Pry home.

Among those who were carried into the Pry House breathing, but who left without a beating pulse, was Union general Israel Bush Richardson. The West Point graduate and native of Vermont had served valiantly in battles throughout the war, and he had been promoted to major general in July 1862. During the fierce fighting at Bloody Lane, he was mortally wounded by Confederate artillery fire and was carried to the Pry House for treatment. Unable to be moved, he died in the building on November 3, 1862, less than two months after being wounded.

A related ghost story involves a deathbed visit after the bloody battle and a contemporary fire. In the mid 1970s, an unexplained blaze destroyed a significant portion of the Pry House. While fighting the inferno, some firefighters claimed to have seen a woman looking out from one of the second-floor windows. However, after investigating, they found no one inside. Also, the second-story floor had caved in prior to the sighting, making it impossible for anyone to have been standing in a room on that level. Some believe the mystery woman may have been the spirit of Mrs. Richardson. The wife of the dying general had visited her husband shortly before he passed away in the room where the apparition was sighted.

According to Troy Taylor, during a meeting in the Pry House of park personnel, a person who was not part of the gathering said she saw a woman dressed in old-fashioned clothing coming down the staircase. When she asked the others present that day about her possible sighting, no one else had seen the stranger and no one could offer a reasonable explanation about the lady in the long dress.

A short time later, some workers arrived at the house and said they saw a woman standing in the window of an upper-floor room, and it happened to be the bedroom where General Richardson is believed to have died. The workers searched the house and found no one who shouldn't have been at the meeting. But after going upstairs, they realized the room where the woman had been standing had no floor.

Perhaps the persistent apparition was that of Richardson's wife, who cared for him on his deathbed.

According to Taylor, subsequent sightings of the ghost caused workmen hired to repair the historic home to abandon their projects and not return. Others suggest reports of phantom footsteps, often heard in the building, might be those of Mrs. Richardson, who climbed the stairs several times each night to check on her dying husband—or the boots of nervous generals, pacing back and forth as they worried about the outcome of the bloody battle.

Devil's Banquet

It was Halloween night. In a isolated house on South Mountain in Washington County, the table was set with fine china, the tall, tapered candles flickered and danced, the colorful bowls were filled with ripe fruit, and thirteen chairs were set, awaiting the evening's invited guests. Earlier that afternoon, a young stranger traveling along the Old National Road (also called Cumberland Road and Route 40), had stepped from his coach and entered a popular tavern. He located the owner and showed the hefty, bearded man behind the bar an impressive engraved invitation. Its words were written in black script, and the envelope still bore the exterior seal, featuring a large letter "M," engraved in a thick blotch of black wax.

The nervous bartender looked at the letter, but was careful not to let his fingers touch the correspondence. He nervously glanced from side to side, checking out the darkest corners of his busy inn. Leaning forward, he whispered to the young man, "There's still time to leave. A coach will be heading east within the hour. Before dark. You'd best be on it, and save your skin."

"Nonsense," the traveler replied, his tone indignant, as if he had been insulted by the barkeep's recommendation. "I've an appointment, and I intend to keep it. I was told I could obtain a driver, who would drop me off this evening and who will come back and be waiting early tomorrow for my return."

Shaking his head, the larger man smirked. "I can get you delivered there, stranger. But they'll be no need to bother with setting a time for your return."

"Why so?" the unruffled visitor inquired.

"Because you won't be able to come back. Like all the others, you'll be dead."

Tossing a handful of bills across the drink-stained bar, the young man ordered, "Get me my coach. I've a bet to win, and tomorrow morning I will return without fail. Then I will show you the color of my gold." Turning abruptly, the traveler headed out the door.

On the ride into the forest, along the narrowest trail he had ever traversed, the young man reflected on the bet he had made with the mysterious stranger when they had met two months earlier at a corner saloon in Fell's Point, Baltimore's shipbuilding district. The young man—who was now heading through a tree-blanketed canopy toward a so-called "haunted mansion"—had bet he could stay overnight in the house, where he was told a band of evil spirits had claimed every other person who had been foolish enough to try. If he lasted the night, his prize was to be five hundred dollars in gold coin. If he lost, the evil spirits of the home would own his body and soul, and he would be unable to escape, bodily or spiritually, from the hexed house.

But the stranger had never been one to believe in hocus-pocus. He told that to the well-dressed, sophisticated gentleman who had shaken the man's hand and struck the deal. He had been instructed to arrive at 6 P.M. on Halloween night. He would dine, retire to his room, and fall asleep. Whether he left the next morning or not would be determined. Such were the agreed terms.

As he exited the mud-splattered coach, the up-to-this-point confident visitor felt a slight twinge of concern as he stared up at a dilapidated, crumbling structure that looked as if it might be blown over by the slightest wind. By the time he turned to glance back down the narrow lane through which he had just passed, his rented coach was out of sight. No doubt the local driver had no interest in being lost in the woods, or anywhere near the reputed haunted home, when darkness fell.

After stepping up onto the porch, the man knocked on the only door that led into the building. Slowly, it creaked open and a gaunt-looking housekeeper of indeterminate ancient age nodded. Tossing her thin head and pointed chin toward the dark interior, she did a quick about-face and led the way into the dining room.

Startled at the ornate and sparkling interior of the structure, the young man's eyes scanned the well-maintained mansion. If the outside looked like it had never seen a coat of paint, the inside appeared to match any painting he had seen of Europe's most splendid castles and estates. But his sense of awe ended at the threshold to the candlelit dining room. As he passed into the eating chamber, he stopped abruptly as his twelve dinner companions rose from their seats. The word "strange" would not adequately describe the scene. "Bizarre" would be a better word to illustrate the unique cast of memorable characters.

Certainly, it was Halloween, and he had come attired in proper staid, formal clothing. But the sight of five witches, three pale-faced military officers, a couple of formally dressed vampires and a short, ragged hunchback presented a surprising scene for which he had not been prepared. As he tried to stifle a loud gasp, his host—a tall, refined gentlemen bedecked with a considerable array of jewelry adorning his black-and-red caped ensemble—approached and shook the newcomer's hand.

The visitor felt his host's sharp nails scratch against his skin and winced slightly. Still holding tightly to the guest's wrist, the leader of the event, who said his name was Mephisto, directed the young man to take the last chair at the far end of the table.

When all were seated, and the fast-moving, formally attired servants had deposited platters in front of each diner, a unison series of polite nods and smiles passed among the witches, soldiers, vampires, hunchback, and guest of honor. Finally adding his approval, Mephisto ordered them to begin. Having regained his composure, the young man raised a hand and called out, "As a moral and church-going man, and one who certainly appreciates such a bountiful feast, I believe it proper that we first pause and say grace, to thank the Lord on high for his generosity in granting this abundant feast."

Mephisto's hand gripped his silverware so tightly that the fork and knife began to melt. The rest of the assembled diners glanced toward their host, whose eyes had turned the color of bright red embers. Steam escaped from his nostrils, and the white tablecloth beneath his plate began to smolder, as if at any second it would erupt into flames.

"I think not!" the host roared. But by then the young man had already pulled his Bible from the inside pocket of his frock coat. Opening the Good Book to its middle, he produced a small notecard and announced he would pray the words that had been handed down to him by his deceased mother, "as saintly a woman as ever lived and died."

Speechless, the worried faces of the invited wiccans darted from host to guest, scanning the length of the table with each glance. The hunchback began bouncing frantically, like a small monkey, upon the seat cushion of his chair. Attempting to relax their nerves, the two vampires gulped the contents of their goblets of dark red wine, as did the ghost soldiers.

As Mephisto began to rise from his throne, the stranger prayed aloud, "Dear Lord in Heaven, grantor of all that is good in this world and powerful conqueror of all that represents itself as evil . . ."

A moan spread about the dining room and the fruit in the baskets turned from fresh to sour, deteriorating into a moldy state of greenish-black decay. Spiders scampered across the clean linens, and a foul stench, like that of a stable full of dead animals, filled the air of the room.

"Let us give thanks to your greatness and charity, as we strive to share your example of love with all creatures, good and evil . . ."

As this supplication continued, a strong wind traveled through the room and snuffed out the tall red candles.

"And enable all of us present to kneel at your feet, dear Lord, and pay homage to your grace, goodness, and your unlimited power over everything, in word and deed, that still exists in this world. And from your celestial home, bless all assembled here in your name with a strong shower of your grace, which will cleanse them from all sin, evil intent, and wickedness."

This last supplication cleared the room of all the guests, leaving only the host and his nemesis. Enraged at the young man's actions, Mephisto again tried to rise, but found he was still stuck in his chair. Smiling, the young man stood. Slowly walking the length of the table, he retrieved a silver cross and consecrated hosts, blessed by the high archbishop in the cathedral in Baltimore. Standing over the festering demon, the stranger dropped one of the blessed wafers onto the beast's hand and watched the demon's skin sizzle and steam.

"I will give you one chance," the guest said. "Give me the bag of gold and promise me no harm, and I will allow you to leave. Decline my offer, and I will press this cross into your forehead, and you will roam the halls of Hades with the sign of the most blessed symbol of heaven's king. To wear the sign of the blessed one, I believe you realize, would not be in your best interest nor impress your vile associates."

Realizing he had been bested, the Devil nodded and told the young man where to find the hidden treasure. Satisfied that he was safe from the demon of the house, the young man cleared off the dining room table and settled into a deep sleep. Just before sunrise, the young man released his evil host, who raced toward the bottom of the fireplace and disappeared with a soulful howl into a pile of ashes resting at the hearth's base.

Securing a black stallion from the house's stable, the stranger rode back to the inn, tossed a large gold piece with the letter "M" at the tavernkeeper, and said, "Here's your proof that I got the best of your neighbor. I doubt you'll have another guest arrive next Hallows' Eve."

During the hour the young man waited for the coach to take him back east, he sat alone on a bench outside the inn. Of course, word of his story had spread, and there was much speculation about what specific events may have occurred in the haunted house during the previous evening. But no one would ever know the real story, for no one dared approach the man who had bested the fiend. All they knew is that somehow the young stranger had survived the Devil's Banquet, and he was leaving the area with a fortune in demon gold.

Dan's Rock

There are a few stories associated with Dan's Rock, Allegany County's spectacular scenic overlook in Dan's Mountain State Park. This nearly 500-acre recreational area preserves the rustic beauty of western Maryland, and visitors to Dan's Rock are offered a spectacular, twenty-mile view of the Potomac River, West Virginia, and the nearby mountains.

Dan's Rock, near the top of 2,900-foot-high Dan's Mountain, is named after Daniel Cresap, a mountain man and pioneer. He was the son of Col. Thomas Cresap, who fought in the French and Indian War and who eventually moved his family into the western part of the state. Later, the colonel became one of the first and best-known settlers in Allegany County.

His son, Daniel, became a local explorer, hunter, and trapper, and he was well-known to members of local Indian tribes, with whom he traded. According to a story in J. Thomas Scharf's *History of Western Maryland*, the mountain got its name after Daniel was killed at the site. He had been tracking down a group of Indians who had attacked several area villages. When he came upon the band at the top of the mountain, both Daniel and the Indian leader fired at each other at the same time and both men were killed.

A different tale tells of a bear hunt involving Daniel and his Indian friend, Nemacolin. The two men separated and agreed to meet later at the top of the mountain. While alone, Daniel tracked some bear cubs that had climbed up a tree. The hunter decided to hoist himself up into the tree to get them, but a rotted branch broke and Daniel's body crashed to the ground. In one account, he hit his skull on a rock and died at that spot. In another version, he was dragged home by his Indian companion and eventually recovered. In either case, some say his spirit has remained at Dan's Rock, the site of the fall, and since the incident the peak has been referred to as Dan's Mountain.

But a longer story can be found in the *Frostburg Mining Journal*, written in 1906 by J. B. Odor and reprinted in *Legends of Allegany County*, a book of local stories compiled by Harold L. Scott Sr. in 1994.

In Odor's account, Dan was a mountain man in the area of Cumberland, shortly after Gen. Edward Braddock built the fort there in 1754. Only a few hundred white settlers were in the region at the time, and they were concerned about a fierce tribe of Indians led by Chief Wampagoc. Of course, the two groups—longtime Indian residents and late-arriving English immigrants—did not like, trust, or associate with each other. While hunting and exploring in the mountains, Dan accidentally met and became attracted to the chief's daughter, an Indian princess.

As time passed, the pair met in secret and fell in love, but they knew neither the girl's tribe nor Dan's friends and relatives would approve of their relationship. Eventually, they agreed they would have to leave each other or move from the area and start a new life where no one knew them. Also, one of the strongest Indian braves in the tribe loved the princess and wanted to marry her. She was concerned that the jealous brave would speak to her father about her relationship with Dan and urge her father, the chief, to attack the settlers. A few days later, while sitting on the high rock waiting for Dan to arrive, the princess looked at the countryside below and saw the jealous Indian approach her lover on a narrow trail. As the two men faced each other, neither allowing the other to pass, they reached for their weapons. The Indian grabbed his tomahawk, and Dan pulled out his knife.

As if watching a horrifying vision of the future, the princess saw bloody scenes in her village and at Fort Cumberland. The bodies of members of her tribe and families of settlers were covered in blood, and Dan and the Indian brave were the leaders of the opposing war parties. Knowing she was the source of the impending and unstoppable bloodshed, the princess called out from her rock high above the two strong young men. When they turned to locate the source of the familiar voice, the princess jumped from the edge of the rocky ledge. Her thin body fell silently, slowly at first and then quickly gaining speed. Within a few seconds, it crashed against the earth close to the spot on the trail where the two men stood. When the warrior and the hunter reached her battered and bloody body, the princess took each man's hand in hers and whispered her request that they promise her they would not start a war. Just before she closed her eyes for the last time, she saw them both nod silently and agree to her dying wish.

The men carried her body to the top of the mountain and buried her near the rock, where she loved to sit and view the beautiful country that was the home of her tribe, and which would become the land of the new settlers. As years passed, individually, and sometimes together, the two men would visit the young woman's grave, recalling days past and silently experiencing the presence of her spirit. When Dan died years later, his friends followed his instructions and placed his body in the ground beside the princess, who he had told everyone was awaiting his arrival. Many believe that's how the top of the mountain got the name Dan's Rock.

Braddock's Lost Gold

There's a fortune in lost military gold waiting to be found somewhere in the thick forests of western Maryland. Some believe it has remained unfound for hundreds of years because it is guarded (depending upon whom you believe) by angry Indian spirits, wandering soldier ghosts, or strange as it may sound, a band of pesky Irish-American leprechauns.

In Allegany County, near Frostburg, a Maryland historical marker states: "General Braddock's 2nd camp on the march to Fort Duquesne June 14th, 15th, 1755. The old Braddock Road passed to the southeast of the National Road from Clarysville to the 'Shades of Death' near 'Two Mile Run.' The National Road was begun by the Government in 1811."

The sketchy reference makes note of the passing of troops led by British major general Edward Braddock during the French and Indian War. Unfortunately, Braddock's expedition had little success; he was the victim of his own poor planning and the inaccurate information he received regarding the rugged geographical hurdles he would encounter on his journey. The naïve and well-intentioned officer set out from central Maryland with several thousand men—plus supplies, food, and several pieces of heavy, hard-to-maneuver artillery. He was heading to Fort Duquesne, located near what is today Pittsburgh. Braddock's mission was to engage the French in battle and occupy the critical Forks of the Ohio.

The British general's map indicated the location of several rivers he was prepared to cross, but the charts left out the more difficult terrain involving mountains, cliffs, and swamps. The commander also had not planned on numerous surprise attacks by hostile Indians, plus thick brush, dense forests, lack of roads, dangerous wild animals, swarms of insects, and intense, nonstop summer humidity. In order to move his large guns, Braddock's Irish and Scottish troops spent considerable time and energy chopping away brambles and cutting trees to widen the Indian trails he was following. This effort to accommodate his weary column of slow-moving troops and supplies took a heavy toll on his frustrated and constantly sick and exhausted men.

In the minds of many, Braddock's March was considered a military failure and a financial disaster. In the latter case, the general had brought along a significant amount of gold, which he had planned to use to purchase supplies from farmers and villagers along the route. Those who survived his march claim that Braddock ordered the heavy bags of gold coin buried when he was involved in a battle, or when he was concerned about an impending attack. Thinking he might not make it out of the wilderness, the general was determined to keep the valuable government treasure from falling into enemy hands.

No one knows the location of his buried treasure, since Braddock never shared the secret before he was mortally wounded in battle on July 9, 1755. The general's nearly 1,500 British regulars were attacked as they crossed the Monongahela River by an enemy force consisting of a few Frenchmen, a larger group of American Indians, and a smaller number of Canadians. These attackers numbered only about nine hundred, but they effectively employed backwoods, guerilla-style fighting. Braddock had been warned to be ready for such an attack by the colonists he had met before he began his march, but he did not heed their advice. The Battle of Monongahela turned into a horrendous defeat because of the deadly rifle fire the French and Indians directed at the British from their hiding places on the dense mountainsides.

When the British witnessed the Indians taking scalps from the dead soldiers, the demoralized and terrified redcoats began a hasty retreat toward Fort Cumberland. Nearly 1,000 of the force of 1,460 British regulars were killed or wounded, including 63 of the force's 89 officers. Braddock had four horses shot from under him. He died within a week, on July 13, at Great Meadows near Uniontown, Pennsylvania, and is buried there. For years ghost hunters have circulated reports of sightings of the general's phantom near his grave. But his apparition also has been reported in the mountains of Allegany County, where some suggest his restless spirit is still guarding the gold he had left behind.

Treasure hunters say the best places to start hunting for the riches are near historical markers that mention Braddock or his march near Cumberland. That's probably one good way to find whatever valuables the general left behind. Since Braddock's name also is featured on a fair number of historic plaques in Garrett and Montgomery counties in Maryland, as well as on others in Pennsylvania and Virginia, there are plenty of places to search. But other clues and legends related to the gold have surfaced through a wide range of stories over the centuries.

According to a March 1957 article in the *Cumberland Sunday Times*, a Confederate army veteran who settled near Bloomington, near the Savage River and the West Virginia border, passed a story down to his grandson. The older man talked about an abandoned coal mine formerly operated by E. J. Ross Coal and Company that supplied fuel to the West Virginia Pulp and Paper Company. The veteran said as a youngster he and his friends would roam the woods on summer nights. During a fair number of evenings, they would see a moving lantern, heading west, carried by a dark-clothed being. The older man said the group would call the light "Braddock's ghost," and they believed he was searching for the lost treasure that should have been returned to Fort Cumberland after the general's defeat and death.

Believers in this legend claim the lost gold was buried in the Westernport-Bloomington area. The story is backed up by the belief that retreating Virginia militia, who had been under Braddock's command at the Battle of Monongahela, had taken a shortcut toward Winchester, as opposed to following the Braddock Road (now known as Route 40) toward safety in Cumberland. The newspaper article stated that many old-timers were convinced a heavy chest of gold and silver was hidden at the base of the cliffs, in a hollow somewhere near the spot where Cold Spring enters the Savage River.

Another article by J. William Hunt in a February 1968 issue of the *Cumberland Sunday Times* offers a fantasy-based explanation—involving leprechauns, the Irish little people—as to why Braddock's long-lost treasure has never been found.

When Braddock's expedition sailed for North America, it departed from Cork, Ireland, and several leprechauns, who had heard much about the fascinating new country on the other side of the Atlantic, stowed away on one of the troop ships. When the army arrived at Fort Cumberland, which became Braddock's headquarters, the little people decided to settle in the area, establishing villages in the dense and undisturbed woods. Eventually, they multiplied in number and claimed a fair amount of the forested region as their own. Because of the long-held association between pots of gold and leprechauns, and the little creatures' ability to make treasure disappear whenever a seeker gets close to discovering its location, they must be the logical reason for the continuing difficulty in locating Braddock's pots of hidden gold.

A different unfound treasure, involving precious jewels, is associated with an inn that stood near Old Braddock in the 1830s. The drinking house was located west of Frederick, approximately where the National Road splits, dividing Route 40 from Alternate Route 40. This main highway was an extension of Old Cumberland Road, which led to Baltimore, and it was well-traveled by both area residents and commercial haulers. Locals and fellow haulers would stop at the popular watering hole to share tales and catch up on news while downing glasses of brew. Quite often these raucous sessions extended into the wee hours of the morning. Whether the principal in our story was a guest at the inn or a teamster driving his rig, no one is sure. But the tale that's been handed down said an unnamed traveler or driver buried a chest of gold and jewels near the Old Braddock-area tavern, or along a nearby mountainside, and left the area.

Two years later, when the driver returned to dig up his hidden wealth, he was fatally injured during a sudden mountain storm. The tavernkeeper came to the traveler's aid, but the stranger's injuries were fatal. While dying, the visitor told the innkeeper about the buried jewels, which he had hidden for safekeeping somewhere nearby. He said they had been stolen from European royalty. Unfortunately for the good-intentioned innkeeper, the stranger died before sharing the treasure's exact location.

Without success, the innkeeper spent the next several years digging up the area near his tavern. Some believe the lost chest of jewels remains, waiting to be found by a persistent and lucky treasure hunter. The only clues are that it rests on a hillside, or near the site of a long-gone tavern, somewhere within eyesight of the split in the Old National Road west of Frederick.

Deadly Apple

The mountain village of Mount Savage sits in northwestern Maryland, at the base of Big Savage Mountain in Allegany County. Founded as a farming settlement in the early nineteenth century, the hamlet gained national attention in 1844 when it pressed the first iron rail in the United States. In no time, it became the fifth-largest city in Maryland and was headquarters for a short-line railroad and the Cumberland and Pennsylvania Railroad. Today it's hard to imagine the secluded mountain community was a thriving industrial center with factories that attracted large numbers of employment-seeking immigrants.

The original Indian tribes and the arriving foreigners created a blend of languages, cultures, religion, and, during the mid- to late-1800s, a fair number of seriously-held beliefs of a superstitious nature. In their efforts to ward off sickness, cure a sudden illness, and protect themselves from bad luck, folks in those days did a lot of strange things. Here are only a few examples:

- Tossing an egg over their house
- Burying offerings under a full moon
- Having blessed smoke and incense waved over one's body
- Spinning a silver needle, suspended by cat's gut, over one's head

- Shooting a silver bullet into a tree bearing the chalk-drawn image of a witch
- Drinking magic potions made from reptile blood
- Wearing a talisman to ward off effects of the evil eye
- Reciting poems and chants from a magic book
- Carving the holy cross on one's barn, home walls, and skin
- Visiting the local wizard or witch for advice

Being the victim of bad luck, or even of an isolated or infrequent misfortune, would cause superstitious victims to rush to the local healer for help. But if one was the victim of a curse, the need for supernatural aide to negate the evil hex was critical. A story about the Curse of Old Coombs Farm, near Mt. Savage, was part of a presentation in 1953 by Mary Miller Bowen to the Homemakers Club of Mt. Savage. According to the ancestry.com Web site, Joyce Reiss discovered and transcribed the material, which also is printed on the Maryland Ghost and Spirits Association Web site.

Before the Civil War, a butcher named Mr. Ceese lived on Old Coombs Farm, and it was common for area residents to walk up the long lane to purchase portions of meat—much like today's Sunday drivers pull off the highway and follow the lure of rustic, hand-written advertisements common in farming areas. However, in the days before refrigeration and ice deliveries enabled long-term storage of perishables, folks would buy meat products several times a week, so visitors to the Old Coombs Farm butcher outlet were commonplace.

One morning, a little girl arrived at the farm to buy meat. As the youngster walked along the long lane of the plantation heading to the meat barn, she paused to look at the grove of apple trees that lined her path. It was early fall, and the bright red, juicy fruits were hanging low on the bough. Hungry and thirsty from her long walk, the girl climbed through the fence, stopped under a tree, and picked up a fresh red apple from the ground. As she bit her teeth into the soft skin, she heard a threatening sound and turned around to face the source of the growl. Terrified, the girl dropped the apple, screamed, and ran back toward the fence. But a wild dog, along with several others from the pack, caught the escaping child and mauled her to death.

Later, the girl's parents learned that the plantation's slaves had been ordered to keep strangers from picking the farm's apples. When a group of the slaves, who were afraid of being whipped for not following orders, saw the girl taking an apple without permission, they sent the dogs to scare her off. Unfortunately, the animals went a bit too far and the child was killed.

Naturally, the dead child's family was shocked and angry. But the plantation owner claimed he could do whatever he wanted on his property; while regrettable, the girl had brought the calamity on herself. This unrepentant attitude enflamed the anger of the girl's family. Her mother, who practiced the black arts, placed a curse of the plantation owner and his entire family, as well as on the overseer, farm manager, butcher, and the slaves who had been in charge of the dogs.

Specifically, the witch predicted that the plantation owner would die, along with anyone else responsible for her daughter's fate. She said the curse would last one hundred years, and it would be passed on to the head of each subsequent generation of that family, who would also die violently. According to Mrs. Bowen's remarks to the Homemakers Club, seven members of the family died very suddenly, with five of them experiencing a violent demise. But those in the area can now relax, since well more than a hundred years have passed since the little girl ate the deadly fruit.

Lovers' Leap

Find a high mountain, and you'll find a spot named Lovers' Leap—a place where a romantic couple allegedly decided to take the plunge. But in this case the term doesn't refer to the big-step decision to marry; it's the big step off the edge of a very high cliff.

At Hawk's Nest State Park in West Virginia, two young Indians took a dive off of Lovers' Leap, a high point over the New River George. They did so because the lovers were from battling tribes. In one version of the legend, the romantic victims were not Indians, but instead white settlers from two feuding mountain clans.

At Lovers' Leap on the coast of Jamaica, a young slave couple jumped to their death from a 1,700-foot cliff rather than be forced to live apart.

In Great Britain during the nineteenth century, a young woman jumped off a cliff after learning her lover had been killed in a war. But her skirt caught onto a strong branch and she was not killed. When she was returned to her home, she found her lover there, having just returned home from battle.

In North Carolina, a young man jumped to his death, upset at being rejected by his love. But a strong wind blew his falling body back onto a mountain ledge. Later, he learned his girlfriend had not abandoned him and was grateful he was still alive.

In Allegany County, the area known as "the Narrows," near Cumberland, is associated with a similar story, involving a rock atop Wills Mountain, which stands 1,652 feet above sea level. The original story was published in J. Thomas Scharf's 1882 book *History of Western Maryland.*

Jack Chadwick was a mountain man, Indian fighter, and well-known hunter and trapper. His exploits had made him a local legend, and he had established a good relationship with the local Indian tribes. One chief in particular had been a friend to Jack, and this older man and his wife had welcomed the hunter into their lodge on several occasions. Eventually, the chief's daughter, who Jack had hardly noticed when she was younger, grew into a beautiful and intelligent young woman.

As time passed, Jack and the princess began to spend considerable time together. They fell in love and announced to the chief they wanted to be married. While the princess's father liked Jack, the older man believed the man of the mountains was too poor and would not be able to offer his daughter a secure and comfortable life. He told Jack and his daughter that he had already promised the princess's hand to an officer at Fort Cumberland. The young girl would be married to the man her father had selected.

Dejected, Jack left the village and headed back to his hut. Along the way, he stopped and sat beside a stream, placed his cupped hands into the water, and took a drink. His eyes caught sight of a glittering flash that was reflected in the sunlight. As he placed his hands in the stream, Jack grabbed at the object and pulled out a silver nugget. He had discovered a valuable vein of silver. Jack excitedly ran back to the village, brought the chief to the stream, and offered him the claim as a dowry for his daughter's hand.

Immediately, the chief agreed, and they set a wedding date. Two days later, Jack returned with his best man. But the chief had changed his mind, kept the silver, and told Jack the princess would marry the army officer, as had always been the plan. Without hesitation, Jack and the young Indian maiden ran into the forest and decided they could not live without each other, but they also couldn't escape the power and reach of the chief. As they slipped farther into the woods, Indians from the tribe appeared and blocked their way.

Jack and the princess ran to the top of the mountain. Without a word, they grasped each other's hands, viewed the beautiful countryside extending from their position at the edge of the outcropping of rock, and together stepped over the side.

Jack's best man and several Indian braves found the couple's lifeless bodies at the base of the mountain. They buried the lovers together in a grave near the entrance to a cave where they used to meet. The legend said their spirits remain, joined in peaceful eternal sleep. Some hikers who have passed by the unmarked burial site, under the reflection of a full moon, have seen the transparent shapes of a young couple, in old-fashioned clothing, dancing and smiling at the base of the Narrows, a site known as Maryland's "Lover's Leap."

Big Bill

A coal miner named Big Bill worked in a number of mines in western Allegany County. Every mine owner knew Big Bill was an expert miner, but he also was considered the meanest and strongest man in northwest Maryland. Big Bill was well known for his evil ways that included hard drinking, hard cussing, hard gambling, and hard fighting. Worst of all, he showed absolutely no interest in and respect for the Good Book or the Lord God.

Whenever Big Bill entered a building, heads would turn, noise would stop, and men would move to the far end of the room. His clothes were stained with tobacco drippings, his body stank from lack of washing, and his mouth spewed out the vilest and most threatening phrases and insults ever heard. It wasn't a surprise that Big Bill traveled alone, ate alone, and lived alone. But inside a mine, every worker knew that Big Bill was the one man to turn to first in times of trouble or danger.

In the late 1800s, Bill got into a Friday-night bar fight at the Black Nugget Saloon. Three strangers passing through the area made fun of Big Bill's rustic clothing and foul-smelling body. After Big Bill had ignored a fair number of insults, the traveling trio tossed a glass of beer in Bill's direction. This got his attention, and he decided to teach the group some manners.

Two of the mean-looking strangers happened to be prizefighters who made their living putting on shows in towns throughout the region. The third man was their manager. At first, the confident strangers seemed eager to take Big Bill on and demonstrate their pugilistic skills to the country bumpkins. The pair surrounded Bill, and charged at him from both sides of the room. The fight lasted only about ten brief minutes. When the dust had settled and the noise had stopped, the customers cautiously reentered the Black Nugget. Big Bill was standing alone at the bar, pouring himself a drink of whiskey. All three of the men were knocked out and lying face-down on the floor.

Unfortunately for Big Bill, and even more so for one of the professional fighters, the saloonkeeper turned to the crowd and announced that the largest of Big Bill's opponents could not be revived because he was dead. News spread quickly, but not as quickly as Big Bill's disappearance out the back door of the Black Nugget. The miner beat feet up the hill outside town, arriving at the Town Mine just in time for the start of his shift.

Not saying a word about the deadly fight, Big Bill joined the rest of his work crew. Silently, the men put on their gear, entered the cave, walked to the lift, and descended into the earth.

That winter, Big Bill's crew had been working the graveyard shift. They had been putting in a fair amount of overtime in an effort to break the shift record for the largest amount of ore hauled to the surface in the shortest amount of time. A number of folks later said Big Bill's crew had been pushing too hard, moving too fast, and ignoring basic safety practices. But not one of the crew cared, especially when they heard a rumor that a nice bonus would be coming their way if they finished up work in their section of the mine ahead of schedule.

But dreams of extra money evaporated when a sudden blast from somewhere inside the mountain caused heads to turn and blood to run cold. From what had been a solid wall directly behind the miners, a flood of ink-black, freezing water burst through a seven-foot-wide hole that had formed in the middle of the rocky surface.

As most of the men stood frozen in shock, Big Bill directed the crew to an adjacent tunnel that led up a slight incline toward the surface. Men who were unable to grasp onto something solid screamed as their bodies were swept away in the fast-moving black current. Eventually, Big Bill directed a group of survivors to a small patch of high ground, but they could hear the advancing water nearby as it filled up more and more of the hollow mine shafts.

When the terrified men began to pray, Big Bill refused to join in, saying, "I've never knelt down and begged for anything in my life. And I don't intend to start now!" Growling, he turned to his terrified crew. "Ain't nobody at home upstairs to hear your prayin'. So get up right now, ya pack of pansies! Ya can either stand up and follow me to the top, or stay down here and die in this stinkin' hole on yer wet knees."

While the black water rose, a few men continued to pray. More than half of the crew got up and fell in behind an apparently calm and whistling Big Bill, who led the survivors toward a narrow seam that would serve as their escape route. Using his broad, strong shoulders, he lifted a crumbled beam and directed the frightened men to crawl to safety through the passage he had created.

According to J. B. Odor's version of the story in the *Frostburg Mining Journal* of 1892, if things didn't work out, Big Bill screamed, "We'll go to hell howling and defying the devil." Then Big Bill spewed out a stream of vulgarities that would have made a boatload of ancient sailors uncomfortable. He followed that verbal volley with a spirited, steady, and familiar whistle. Straining as the weaker men scrambled for their lives, Big Bill continued to whistle, perhaps to calm the nervous miners or maybe to sustain his own weakening body and spirits.

By the time the powerful miner reached the end of his tune, there was no one left in the trapped room and he had no energy left to save himself. Suddenly, an unstoppable avalanche of heavy earth fell upon Big Bill. His spent, strained, and broken body was buried beneath the beams, coal, boulders, and earth of Town Mine.

Big Bill's corpse was never found, but the half-dozen survivors spread the tale of his bravery to everyone they met. Outside the doomed shaft, the survivors all knelt down to offer prayers for Big Bill's brave body and wretched soul. Among the gathered crowd, waiting for word of any survivors, was the local sheriff. He had planned to arrest Big Bill for the murder of the traveling boxer. However, folks later said, "The Devil had rights to Big Bill for a long time, and the Hounds of Hell claimed him first"—proving Satan's reach extended beyond the shorter arm of man's earthly law.

After the mine reopened, workers reported hearing the sound of whistling and heavy, pounding footsteps in various sections of the underground complex, not only in the section near the cave-in where Big Bill had died. Soon after the tragedy, a lot of people heard the whistle, particularly family members of those who were saved and those who were lost that night.

Dog's Best Friend

In the summer of 1964, when Janet was fourteen years old, her family took an extended weekend vacation to the mountains of western Maryland, not far from Grantsville. Since they lived in the city of Baltimore, a weekend in the country was going to be a wonderful adventure. They made arrangements to stay at a four-room cabin owned by a friend of Janet's father.

"When we pulled into the parking area near the front door," Janet recalled, "we were really excited. My sister, Jane, and I started running around the outside of the cabin. But our father's friend, who had met us there, told us to be careful of the tombstones scattered all around the place. He said he didn't want us to trip and fall and get hurt. The mention of the word 'tombstones' got our attention, and we settled down immediately."

Janet said the man told them the grave markers indicated the names of dogs that had died and were buried at the site by a previous owner of the cabin. "At first, the fact that the markers didn't belong to dead people made them seem a little less threatening," Janet said, thinking back several decades. "The man explained that the former owner had loved his dogs, and he wanted to make sure that each of them had a special place to rest when it died."

Janet said that even though there was an innocent explanation for the graves, later in the day she and her sister decided that they still didn't like the idea that they would be sleeping in the middle of a pet cemetery. "I remember that from the moment we stepped into the cabin," Janet said, "we had a feeling that something was out of sorts. There was a definite chill in the air. And Sammy, our small white dog who came along on the trip, was upset and was not acting like his usual happy old self."

Janet said that during the whole weekend little Sammy seemed to be looking off in the corner of the main room, as if he could see something that no human being would ever be able to visualize. The dog also acted like it could hear things beyond the range of human senses.

"At times," Janet said, "Sammy began to bark continuously, and he acted as if he wanted to go outside to get out of the building. Of course, neither Jane nor I wanted to take him for a walk through the cabin's pet graveyard. And Sammy was normally a quiet dog, so all this agitated barking was very unusual behavior."

The family had planned to stay overnight Friday, Saturday, and Sunday and return to Baltimore on Monday morning. On Sunday night, after Janet, Jane, and their parents arrived back at the cabin from an early-evening dinner at a local restaurant, it was dark and spooky. Sammy had been left in the cabin alone. When the family returned and their car pulled up in front of the building, there were no sounds at all. It was as if Sammy, who normally became extremely excited and barked loudly when any car came near their home, was not even there. Worried, the two girls ran up onto the porch and looked in the window.

"We saw Sammy," Janet said, "sitting calmly near the bottom of an overstuffed chair at the feet of an elderly man who was slowly stroking the head of our dog. We turned, shouted to our parents to look inside at the strange man. But by the time they got to the window, the stranger was gone."

Racing into the cabin, the family saw Sammy still resting peacefully near the chair. He didn't even get up to acknowledge that the family had come back into the building. "Sammy had the same contented look on his face that we saw through the window," Janet said. "But there was no stranger anywhere. We looked through all four rooms, but found no one inside. All the doors and windows were locked, just like we had left them. There was no intruder anywhere. It was just crazy."

The family's last evening in the cabin was a restless one, Janet said. Her father slept in a chair in the living room with Sammy by his side, in case the reported intruder returned. When they awoke the next morning, no one had any logical explanation for the strange man that the two sisters claimed they had seen.

"As we left that vacation spot," Janet said, "my sister and I were sure of what we had seen the night before. To this very day, I swear that there was a kind, gentle, older man stroking Sammy's back in that cabin. I remember that the man had a smile on his face. Maybe our dog reminded him of one of his dogs. Maybe Sammy was upset that we were gone, having dinner, and that we had left him behind. The poor animal was all alone in a strange place.

"Perhaps the soul or spirit of the old man who had owned the cabin—and who had loved his own dogs so much—came back, even if just for a short time, from beyond the grave to care for Sammy on that one particular night."

No one will ever know for sure. But no one will ever convince Janet that she didn't see the ghost of the best friend of the dogs, whose names are carved in handmade tombstones scattered beside a lonely cabin in the woods north of Grantsville.

Deep Creek Tragedy

A story entitled, "Who's Afraid of Ghosts? Spooky Stuff in State Parks," on the Maryland State Parks' Web site recalls a Christmas-season tragedy in the area of Deep Creek Lake.

The scenic region in Garrett County is a popular getaway destination featuring Maryland's largest manmade lake. With more than 110 campsites, a boat launch, fishing areas, forested hiking trails, and interpretive recreational programs, the state park attracts visitors from Washington, D.C., and even the Midwest. While it is a popular summer attraction, the winter months offer seasonal opportunities at Memory Cove at Deep Creek Lake. Cross-country and downhill skiing, half-pipe snowboarding, ice fishing, and snowmobiling are available in a setting that receives an average of 110 inches of snow a year.

One Christmas season, a family's holiday vacation at Deep Creek Lake ended tragically. Since they were going to be staying at a rented cabin on Christmas morning, the family members brought along some presents to exchange. The biggest surprise gift was a brand new, very large snowmobile for Dad. Thrilled and shocked out of his mind, the patriarch of the family insisted that all of the men in the room saddle up their own snowmobiles and head out onto the ice. He was eager to try out his new toy.

After bundling up for his virgin ride across the frozen lake, the father hopped aboard and began what would be the first of many fun-filled trips. Unfortunately, the Christmas-morning layer of ice was deceptive and not thick enough to support the weight of the snowmobiles and riders. Far from shore, the ice gave way and the vehicles descended into the frigid water. Three of the six ice riders died that not-so-cold Christmas morning.

As hours passed, the wife of the new snowmobile owner began to wonder just how long her childish husband was going to be out there playing with his new toy. As dinnertime approached, her wonder turned to concern and finally to fear. In a state of panic and ready to call the police, the woman heard a weak knock at the cabin's front door. Rushing to the sound, she pulled back on the handle and saw her husband standing on the front porch. A chill ran through her body as her eyes saw the look of terror on his face and at the ice that was attached to his frozen body and wet clothing. Slowly, she walked toward him to take his arm and lead him into the warmth of the room. She planned to help him change and place him in front of the blazing fire.

But when her hand reached out to touch her husband's arm, the shivering apparition disappeared, seemingly melting away. As her mind tried to grasp what had just occurred, a police officer ascended the cabin steps. He stood in the same spot where the vision of her husband had been only seconds before. The officer said he was there to report that her husband had died in a snowmobile accident that morning in Deep Creek Lake.

Along the Mason-Dixon Line

Haunted Neighborhood

Haunted houses are the meat and potatoes of ghost hunters and ghost writers. Give either group a lead or a story associated with an active eerie site and they will flock there like pilgrims to a holy shrine. But can several homes and parking areas in a neighborhood be haunted? I mean *really* haunted? I think so. I lived in one.

For centuries along the Delaware–Maryland portion of the Mason-Dixon Line, forests and farmland set the scene. With modern development rampant, it's now hard to find much open space. Little nature pockets exist here and there, but for the most part they have been overrun by rapidly erected strip malls, developments, and apartment complexes.

As new residents see bright sun shining through clear windows, smell freshly painted walls, and walk on soft, clean carpets, it's easy to understand why everything in their new home seems perfect. But soon after moving into certain new homes, some unlucky home-owners notice troubling and unexplainable events start to occur. That's when the occupants start to think that they might not be alone—but, initially, they hesitate to share their "crazy" concerns with anyone else.

Some people believe there's a troubled neighborhood within the town limits of Elkton, Maryland's northeastern-most city. For years, calls from residents continued to draw me back to its neat homes standing alongside tree-lined streets. Actually, there are several communities on either side of Delancy Road, the first north-south, two-lane roadway west of the Delaware–Maryland border, just off of U.S. Route 40. But some people report that certain homes in one particular development, named Turnquist, seem to be associated with paranormal activity. While there's no way to prove if this claim is true, the steady number of leads from this locale makes one wonder if there might be something to the rumor.

It's generally believed that the source of this area's haunted reputation is an event that occurred more than fifty years ago, when the region was mostly farmland and open fields. That was especially fortunate in December 1963, when an airplane passing overhead with eighty-one passengers and crew was struck by lightning. Experts say the Boeing 707 was circling over the area while waiting for landing clearance at Philadelphia International Airport, about forty miles to the north. That's when a freak late-autumn thunderstorm occurred. A lightning bolt hit the left wing, causing a deadly spark in a reserve fuel tank. The explosion was immediate, and much of the human remains and plane wreckage fell upon farm fields surrounding Delancy Road. One area resident said there were so many holes in the area after the crash that for a time folks called the rural lane "Crater Road." Mention "the crash" in the Newark, Delaware–Elkton, Maryland, area and some people are eager to talk about where they were the moment the explosion occurred. Others claim to have seen the flash of light or heard the loud, unusual sound when the tragic incident happened.

There were no survivors. Authorities closed off the roads, and the rescue workers respectfully gathered every physical remnant of the crash they could find. But it was impossible to discover and secure everything. Years went by. Land was sold. Developers erected townhouses, multi-story apartments and, more recently, larger single-family homes. During the construction of each new residential neighborhood, locals who were aware of the airplane disaster would say, "That ground is haunted," or "I wouldn't live there, on top of those poor lost souls." But to others, such talk was silly folklore, old-fashioned superstition, mumbo jumbo nonsense, and old wives' tales. Besides, most of the new residents were out-of-towners, unfamiliar with the area's history. What they didn't know couldn't hurt them. Ignorance is bliss—usually.

Sandy's story is typical of several I have heard over the years from residents of homes located on both sides of Delancy Road. A young mother in her early thirties, Sandy resides in Turnquist with her two children. She said she's lived in two houses in that same development. Her current residence is fine, quiet, with no unusual activity. But, she said, shaking her head, "I couldn't wait to get out of that other one."

During our conversation she said her previous residence, only about two blocks away, caused her a lot of sleepless nights. "I was having a nightmare. I had a lot of nightmares, there," Sandy said. "It felt like there was a presence. I couldn't wake up out of my sleep. When I did get up, I was shaking. On other nights, I felt something pressing down on me in my bed. I couldn't get up, couldn't move. I was scared. I thought there was something wrong with me."

These nightmare incidents—combined with strange sounds throughout the house, feelings as if she was being followed, footsteps running along the upstairs hallway, and reports by her son and daughter that someone was lurking in their doorway at night—caused Sandy to approach her pastor.

"At the time, I was trying to get my life in order, and wanted to get closer to God," Sandy said. She waited after church on Sunday morning and, even though embarrassed, explained her unusual and troubling home life situation. "He agreed to come to my home and perform an exorcism. He and another couple he brought with him, we all joined hands, formed a circle, and prayed together. Then we went from room to room and prayed out loud. I remember him announcing he was in my home to 'cast out the evil spirits.'"

Sandy said her pastor mentioned that he thought Sandy might be the focus of "spiritual warfare," with dark and light forces fighting for her attention and control. She also added that living on top of the plane crash site, "with who knows what was under the houses," might have been a contributing factor to her problems.

"I knew about the crash," she said. "Everybody around here has heard about it." She added, offering a weak smile, "There are lots of stories about things moving around in the houses in this neighborhood, and people who live here seeing things. But you don't think about all of that, don't really believe them, unless things start happening to you."

I wondered if the disturbances had calmed down after the spiritual cleansing.

"It lightened up a bit," she said, "but only for a short time, then they started up again. We were renting, so we moved out as soon as we could get out of the lease. But a number of people have come and gone very quickly after we left. There's something wrong with that place."

Sandy stressed that she thought she was going crazy, and the only other person she dared share her problems with was her mother. She is the one who suggested Sandy talk to her pastor. "Sometimes, when I think back on that time I lived there, I thought maybe someone was murdered in the house and that an evil spirit had stayed behind. Or that there were bad things under the spot it was built on. Since I now only live a few blocks away, I pass by it a lot. And I wonder if whatever it is might still be hanging around, bothering somebody else who is living there now."

Author's Note: I lived in a home in Turnquist for five years. I had no knowledge of the tragedy before I moved in. And, yes, there was unusual, unexplained activity of the cold spot, door-closing, phantom footsteps, and cabinet-slamming variety in my house. My son still believes that house was haunted. Periodically, the *Cecil Whig* newspaper runs a column about the plane crash, and the reporter often interviews various area residents, focusing on their opinions of the ever-growing list of local ghost stories. The writers never seem to lack sources. In a May 22, 2002, article, the headline above staff writer Michael White's *Whig* article asked the question: "Haunted Neighborhood?"

Of the thirteen people polled for the piece, ten residents acknowledged hearing ghost stories about their community. White presented reports of sightings involving small children appearing to youngsters and their parents, of images of "children screaming" in a fireplace, and of spirits simply "milling around." Most of those quoted stressed that the spirited visitors are "friendly or sad, not hateful or vengeful."

One resident, who did not want her name revealed, offered the reporter a classic ghostly tale. She awoke in the middle of the night and saw "a little blonde boy" standing at the foot of her bed. Initially, she thought it was a dream, or her young son roaming the house in the middle of the night, until it occurred a few more times. Not wanting to bother her child or husband, she kept the incidents to herself. Eventually, her husband told her he was bothered about seeing a "little blonde-haired boy" in the middle of the night. At first, he said, he thought it was his son, but then realized it wasn't. When the man reached out to touch the youngster and asked, "What's wrong, buddy?" the little boy vanished.

During some family gatherings at the woman's troubled home, she said she had noticed young children standing at the foot of the stairs, looking up at the second-floor landing. Whenever such an incident occurred, the homeowner said she would grab the youngster up and lead him or her away from the area before the child had an opportunity to talk about what he or she might have been watching. Sometimes the woman would say, "I don't even want to know what you have to say."

As expected, however, over time the original facts and effects of the airplane disaster have taken on legendary status. White reported that one rumor, eventually proved to be untrue, told of a local resident who "went insane from the gruesome scene of blood and body parts that rained from the sky." Today, discovering reports of more believable supernatural incidents has become elusive. Most tales about paranormal activity around the area seem to be based on friend-of-a-friend sources, overactive imaginations of teenage minds, and blatant creative elaborations.

Is the area near Delancy Road haunted? Some residents think so. Others say the reports are nothing but silly stories, tall tales serving no purpose other than a source for spooky campfire conversation. But if the best folktales and legends are based on some element of truth, then the ghostly reports along this section of the Mason-Dixon Line trace their origins to a specific incident—the plane crash on December 8, 1963, which the Guinness Book of World Records lists as the largest number of people killed from one lightning strike.

JFK Conspiracy Theory: Following the September 11, 2001, terrorist attacks there was considerable speculation about the cause of the airplane crashes into the Pentagon, World Trade Center, and a Pennsylvania farm field. Suggestions ranged from reasonable to outlandish. One in the latter category suggested that the horrifying events were the result of U.S. government involvement, caused by members of secret intelligence or military organizations.

On the afternoon of the 2001 attacks, several days before these conspiracy theories surfaced, one Elkton resident brought up the December 1963 Maryland plane crash, saying of the 2001 crashes, "I hope it's not another Delancy Road deal." When asked to elaborate on his remark, he explained there was a rumor related to the crash of

Pan Am Flight 214, which occurred only two weeks after President John F. Kennedy's assassination. It was said a witness to, or someone involved in, the president's killing was on that plane, heading toward Philly, to give a sworn statement about a conspiracy to Department of Justice officials in the Philadelphia Federal Building. But the mystery witness had been silenced when he was blown out of the sky. Who's to know?

Tombstone Tale: There is one more interesting anecdote worth noting. In 1993, to commemorate the thirtieth anniversary of the deadly crash, Elkton town officials placed a granite memorial marker at the landscaped area at the entrance road of the development. It states: "In memory of the 81 men, women and children who lost their lives when Pan Am Flight 214 crashed on this site December 8, 1963."

To residents, visitors, and prospective buyers it might seem strange to announce the location of a plane crash, and a troubled site that more than a few residents believe might be haunted.

Fire Phantom

Meryl called me a few weeks after a fire did serious damage to her 1830s stone farmhouse, located a half-mile from Maryland's northern border. After describing the condition of her charred home, she explained that she and her husband were living in a trailer on the property. The attic and roof of their home were damaged in the blaze, and water and smoke damage had affected sections of the first and second floors.

"There's going to be a lot of reconstruction, so we'll be living in temporary housing for quite a while," Meryl said. "But at least no one was injured, and all of our pets are okay." They had lived in the stone-and-wood home for more than thirty years, and a lot of the family's history was destroyed in the blaze. Meryl's mother had resided in a room on the third floor, but the elderly woman had passed away a few months before the blaze.

A few days after the fire, when the state inspectors and insurance agents had completed their investigations, a cleaning crew arrived. Their job was to sort out destroyed and salvageable items and clean out the structure before construction workers would arrive to start rebuilding. "I went up to what was left of the third floor," Meryl said, "and as soon as I entered the area where the three cleaners were working they stopped talking and all of them turned away, avoiding eye contact with me. It was strange so I asked them if something was wrong."

At first no one responded, Meryl said, but then one of the workers asked, in a hesitant tone, if there was "anything strange" in the house. "I had no idea what he was talking about," Meryl recalled. "When I pressed him to explain what he meant, the man said all three of the cleaners agreed they felt a 'presence' with them on that floor. They said it was as if someone or something was watching them, or hovering over their shoulders."

Meryl assured them that in all her decades in the building, she had never had any such experience, even though her home was quite old and had a number of owners and tenants over the previous centuries. "There were rumors of the cellar being a stop on the Underground Railroad," Meryl said, "but we're less than a mile from Pennsylvania, and every old house near the Mason-Dixon Line claims it had that connection. Who's to really know the truth? But, I told the workers, we never saw or heard anything, and we've been here for more than thirty years."

Apparently calmed by Meryl's comments, the cleaners got back to work. But three days later, less than an hour after they had started working on the second floor, all the cleaners were outside, huddled together around their truck.

To Meryl it was apparent there was something wrong. Concerned, she walked over to the group and asked why they weren't cleaning up her home. Clearly embarrassed, one of the women said they were afraid to go back inside, and they needed a few minutes to pull themselves together.

Frustrated and curious, Meryl asked them to be more specific. After a few silent seconds, they all responded and told the same story. They were on the second floor, where a guest bedroom was filled with dolls and stuffed animals. As they were bagging up the objects, they all heard a soft, melodic sound. It was coming from behind them, like someone was singing a lullaby, but they couldn't make out the words. The three cleaners all froze, made eye contact, and slowly turned to look for the source. But nothing and no one was there, and the singing stopped.

For about twenty seconds, Meryl said she and the workers were quiet. No one in the front yard had anything to add. "That's when," Meryl said, "they told me a small baby stroller, the one my grand-daughter used to push her dolls in, rolled toward them from down the hall. They said it wasn't just a few inches. It moved at a steady pace, a good ten or twelve feet, on its own. It was as if some invisible person was pushing it. That's why they left the house and needed a break to regroup and gather their thoughts."

The workers went back inside, but only after Meryl agreed to sit with them while they worked. "I stayed up there for about an hour," Meryl said, "talking to them about all kinds of stuff. But no one mentioned the singing or the stroller again. After a while they were okay and I left. After that, during the next week they were there, nothing else strange happened. Or, if it did, they never told me about it. But I could tell when they left they all were glad to be out of our place."

Thinking about those unusual events, Meryl stressed that she had never believed in paranormal events. She never watched any ghost hunting or haunted house programs. The subject had never interested her. But after the experiences of the cleaning company workers she went online to learn about what might have caused the unusual incidents.

She said her mother loved the third-floor room, which was previously the elderly woman's bedroom. Meryl's grandmother also loved playing with her great-grandchildren. "She felt very much at home here," Meryl said. "When the house was on fire, and I was standing outside watching the firemen fighting the blaze, I remember thinking, 'I really want my mommy.' I really missed her at that time. I wanted her there with me. Maybe, I thought later, she had come back to give me some comfort and make sure I was okay. I don't know. It's just a thought, and not something I could ever prove. But I never felt or heard or saw anything that the cleaners said they did. Maybe they were supposed to alert me that she was here. I know it sounds crazy, but the thoughts went through my mind."

The inspectors told Meryl the fire had started in the walls between the second and third floors. It was lucky she was home to call it in when she smelled the first traces of smoke; otherwise the home would have been a total loss. But Meryl and her husband weren't supposed to be home that night. They were on the road, heading to a party. At the last minute, they decided to stop at home to check on the pets and pick up an item they had left behind. Had they not returned to their house, their pets, which had been caged for the night, would have been killed in the fire and the entire house would have been destroyed.

"I think my mother called us back here," Meryl said. "I know I can't prove it, but I like to think that's what happened. She loved the pets, this house, and us. I don't think it was just luck that we were here when the fire started and were able to call 9-1-1 so the firemen could get here in time."

Ticking Tomb

At the northeast corner of the Mason-Dixon Line, Maryland meets the adjoining states of Pennsylvania and Delaware at a unique geographical region known as "the Wedge." For centuries, this forested no-man's-land was both claimed and ignored by the three states. An assortment of robbers, murderers, and moonshiners lived in the Wedge, since law enforcement personnel from the three states tended not to bother with crimes perpetrated by criminals hiding in this area of questionable jurisdiction.

The lengthy tri-state boundary dispute was settled, and permanent borders were drawn, in the early 1900s. But area residents still refer to the old no-man's-land region as the Wedge, and still pass down tales of disappearances, murders, and ghosts. In London Tract "Hardshell" Baptist Graveyard, only a mile north of the Maryland-Pennsylvania border, is the "Ticking Tomb," sometimes called "Ticky Tomb" or "Ticking Stone." This grave is the basis for one of the most well-known legends of the Mid-Atlantic region, and many visitors swear they have heard its mysterious message, particularly during late-evening graveyard visits.

Some say the sound is the steady plea of the broken heart of a lover who had lost a mate. Others believe it is the rhythmic pulse of a watch, an ancient timepiece, beating within the chest of the entombed. Those who are more logical argue the sound must be an underground stream, or a nest of some family of varmints. To find the real answer, we must travel into the past. Our destination is 1764, almost 250 years ago, when two well-respected surveyors—Charles Mason and Jeremiah Dixon—were in the area to mark their famous boundary.

The Mason-Dixon Line was created because the Calverts of Maryland and the Penns of Pennsylvania and Delaware didn't know exactly what they owned. And the people who lived in the border areas of these colonies didn't know where, or to whom, they belonged. For many years, residents of towns like Rising Sun, Maryland, and Oxford, Pennsylvania, were paying taxes to both the Catholic Calverts and the Quaker Penns. To be honest, the Calverts and the Penns didn't care as long as they got their taxes; and the people couldn't do anything about it, so they paid and kept quiet. But the dilemma really caught the attention of the Penn family when sea captains who came up the Delaware River to pick up and deliver supplies told the Philadelphians that, according to their navigational instruments, the prosperous City of Brotherly Love was located in the province of Maryland.

This got the attention of the authorities, and soon representatives of the two bickering colonies went to London to resolve the border dispute. In 1760, an agreement was signed, and Mason and Dixon were contracted to draw an accurate boundary. The two men arrived on Philadelphia's cobblestoned streets in 1763. By 1764, the solitude of the region around Newark, Delaware, and the Head of Elk (Elkton), Maryland, was broken as the two surveyors arrived. A large party consisting of chain bearers, rod men, ax men, cooks, baggage handlers, Indian scouts, and camp followers accompanied them. For a short time, the two surveyors bedded down at the old St. Patrick's Inn, located just east of the present-day Deer Park Tavern on Main Street in Newark. It's said, for entertainment, Mason and Dixon had brought along a pet bear, which caused quite a stir in the remote village.

Soon, a rural tent city had formed, consisting of a ragtag assembly of pack mules and their handlers, gypsies, fiddlers, plus an assortment of peddlers, pickpockets, and preachers. Many would eventually travel the length of the Maryland–Pennsylvania boundary and watch the workers leave a nearly three-hundred-mile trail of stone border markers. But before the historic journey would begin, an unusual event occurred.

Charles Mason was an Anglican and a member of the Royal Observatory of Greenwich, England. It's said he was of refined upbringing and that he possessed a serious scientific spirit. His colleagues described him as a "serious, methodical man, lacking in humor but competent and devoted to his assigned tasks." On the opposite end of the personality spectrum was Jeremiah Dixon. A bachelor Quaker and the son of an English coal miner, Dixon was noted for his impulsive spirit, steady courage, speed with details, and worldly, street-wise savvy. The two men created an unusual pair, but they got along well and accomplished their work with painstaking attention to detail.

Several decades earlier, the famous scientist Sir Isaac Newton had convinced the British government that there was a need for an accurate, portable, chronometer—a timepiece—that could be used at sea to determine both time and longitude. In 1714, the British Parliament announced a reward of twenty thousand pounds sterling for a chronometer-like invention. For half a century, the greatest minds on the Continent and in the British Isles were at work on the much-needed instrument that would insure one international fame and a very rich reward. Among the notables in the running was Charles Mason.

At the moment that particularly interests us, the surveyors were working in tents, not far from the present-day town of Landenberg, Pennsylvania. Scouts had returned with supplies from nearby Maryland, and Mason was at work on a final version of his chronometer. He already had devoted many years of effort to the project, and he continued to fine-tune his invention during his survey work in the New World.

On this particular day, a fishwoman from the nearby Maryland town of Head of Elk, a small village a few hours hike from the site of the camp, had arrived. She planned to sell her freshly caught wares to the hungry members of the survey party. Following along at her side was the filthiest, fattest toddler one had ever seen. The grotesque child, named Fithian Minuit, was known in the counties of Chester, Cecil, and New Castle for his huge, insatiable appetite and unpleasant, dirty appearance. The young scamp would devour anything—

be it animal, vegetable, or even mineral—that he could shove between his bright-red, chubby cheeks.

Mason's attention was pulled from his invention toward the sound of Fithian's mother, shouting outside the tent: "Fresh fish for sale! Fresh food for the surveyors! Fat and full cut shad! Crabs for the steaming!" Responding to the woman's pleas, Mason left his tent to look at the quality of the catch. While Mason was negotiating price, the monster child crawled into the surveyor's tent. Mason's assistant noticed the child and picked it up off the ground. Suddenly, for no reason, fat Fithian began to cry, then scream, then shout, and finally, beat the assistant across the chest.

Becoming nervous, the assistant surveyor picked up the small metallic object that Mason had been working on. Hoping the sight of a bright, sparkling object might amuse and quiet the small child-devil, the assistant waved Mason's invention, a bright ticking sphere, in front of the unruly beast's face. At that moment, the fat child, thinking it was something new to eat, reached out his hands. In a flash, he opened his mouth, shoved in Mason's timepiece, and swallowed the metal object.

Frantic with fear, the assistant tried to retrieve the precious invention from Fithian's clenched mouth. But luck had deserted the poor assistant, and it did not intend to return that day. Within seconds, Fithian was held upside down by his foot while being pounded on the back by the terrified assistant demanding the return of his master's ticking globe and most precious invention.

Responding to the confusion, the surveyor and fishwife entered the tent. "My baby!" cried the mother, who saw the swollen cheeks and blue color of Fithian's chubby face. "My chronometer!" shouted Mason, who accurately read the look of helpless terror on his assistant's face.

Taking control of her smiling child, the mother swung Fithian back and forth, like an oversized pendulum, while Mason's worried assistant continued to beat on the baby's back. Dixon, who had entered the tent in the midst of the bedlam, was anything but calm. When he discovered that the bothersome invention had been consumed, his reaction was a combination of laughter and relief.

"Finally," he said, "we can be done with this nonsense of the invention and direct all of our attention to the survey!"

Sadly, Mason looked at those in his tent—the mother, the baby, his assistant, and his partner Dixon. The depressed surveyor picked up a half-filled bottle of dark red wine, poured himself a full glass of the liquid, and raised a toast to the small, filthy, monstrous child. With goblet held high, Mason said, "May this fishwoman's child have a long life, and keep my invention safe within him for the rest of his days and beyond."

That is the end of our association with the two famous British surveyors. Soon after their meeting with the troublesome Minuets, the survey party set the great stone in the northeast corner of the colony of Maryland and moved their camp westward. Eventually, their boundary would claim an important place in the nation's history. But, for the rest of his natural life, until his death in Philadelphia, Charles Mason told those he met of how a strange, fat child of a Maryland fishwoman had eaten his greatest invention. He also explained how in less than a minute's time, the hungry little demon had consumed thousands of pounds sterling in one single bite.

Eventually, little Fithian Minuit grew and developed a rotund figure and an interest in carpentry. This led to a respected career in clockmaking and repair, and he opened a shop in the small village of Christiana, Delaware, in a modest stone-and-frame home beside a narrow bridge that spanned a small creek.

In his shop was a vast array of clocks, sundials, watches, and hour-burning candles. He would travel the Delaware Valley and Chesapeake Bay region, buying from individuals with homes along the Smyrna, Bohemia, Sassafras, and Chester rivers. He was well known, and his shop offered excellent grandfather clocks and smaller pieces that he would repair, trade, and sell. It was said he had "a delicate way" with timepieces. On the wall of Fithian's shop, which was full of the sound of steady ticking, was a plaque inscribed with the words "Time never stops, even though the timepiece does."

Eventually, Fithian met a woman named Martha, who he married within a year. On their wedding night, the wife was startled at the steady rhythmic sound coming from her husband's side of the bed.

Fearing first an illness, then some sort of superstition or witchcraft, she eased out of the bed. Carefully, Martha searched the entire bedroom for the source of the steady rhythmic beat. After looking on the bureau, on the nightstands, under the bed, and in the closet, she found no reasonable source of the strange, rhythmic, ticking sound.

Fithian, observing her concern, pulled her to his side. The sound intensified as she rested her head upon his chest. He explained the story of his unusual meeting, at a very young age, with Charles Mason. Then he retold the tale, exactly as his mother had first told it to him. Together they laughed and decided that the sound of Mason's invention would represent their mutual love, and it would beat until the end of all time, even past their death here on Earth. For more than forty years the couple lived together, until Martha died. She was buried in the New London Baptist graveyard, off South Bank Road, just north of the starting point of the Mason-Dixon Line.

Fithian devoted himself to his work even more after her departure, and he took comfort in playing his favorite fiddle. After a long day's work, he would sit in his rocker on the front porch of his shop, swaying back and forth as if keeping time to a secret rhythm. Some neighbors passing by said he often seemed to be talking to someone, although his small store was vacant of anyone else. Fithian, who became somewhat of a philospher in his latter years, warned visitors to his shop to use their time wisely, explaining that the precious commodity passes quietly, unnoticed, and much too quickly.

One weekend, a passing wagon with a group of hunters out seeking game discovered Fithian in the quiet graveyard. His body was flat on the ground, by the side of the spot where his wife, Martha, was buried. At the age of close to eighty, he had fallen into a state of deep eternal sleep. Those who found him said his face seemed fixed in a smile, for he was finally reunited with his beloved Martha.

Out of respect, drivers of passing coaches and families in farm wagons stopped. As word of the friendly clockmaker's death spread, both city dwellers and country people came to pay their respects to the pleasant, well-known man who had given the best of times to them all.

They laid him to rest beside his bride, and there he remains, for all eternity. And even today, hundreds of years after his death, the story of Fithian Minuet and his colorful meeting with Charles Mason still lives on.

Minuet's ancient gravestone is cracked and worn, the hand-carved writing is faded and gone, and the ground within the cemetery walls is sloped and sagging. But if the wind isn't blowing too hard, and if the rushing waters of the nearby White Clay Creek aren't too loud, and if there are no sounds from passing cars racing along the nearby road, and—most importantly—if you know which stone to approach, take a moment and kneel on the damp grass, as so many have done before. Then gently place your ear against the cold, stone marker and be patient and listen. If it's meant to be, and if you truly believe in the legend, you might hear the steady tick, tick, tick of the Ticking Tomb.

And those who have heard it smile with satisfaction, for they believe Fithian Minuit is there, telling us that Charles Mason's chronometer is still held safely within the pleasant colonial clockmaker. And the old timepiece remains in good operating order for all eternity—along with the deep love shared between Fithian and Martha.

Author's Note and Directions: The Hardshell Baptist Church and Graveyard still exist. But the house of worship has been turned into a visitor's center for the Pennsylvania portion of the White Clay Creek Preserve. A sign on the side of the stone building identifies the site as the "London Tract Meeting House." The site is not far off Route 896, a two-lane country road that winds through Delaware and Maryland and north into Pennsylvania. Follow these directions and you will find the gravesite you seek.

Go north past the Delaware–Maryland border. After you enter Pennsylvania (crossing the Mason-Dixon Line), designated by the large "welcome" sign, travel three-fourths of a mile. Turn right onto South Bank Road. Follow this winding route for about a mile and a half, as it leads down to the bottom of a steep hill. You will see the stone church/visitor's center and graveyard.

The easiest way to locate the Ticking Tomb is to ask a park guide in the visitor's center. However, if no one is on duty, enter the graveyard through the white, wooden gate and head toward the doors of the church/meeting house/park center. Walk to the end of the sidewalk and then continue in the direction of eleven o'clock on Charles Mason's timepiece. Approximately twenty feet past the end of the building, next to the small, elevated, heart-shaped gravestone marked "John Devonold," you will find the Ticking Tomb. The rather small, gray stone maker is flush with the ground, and it bears the initials "R. S." or "R. C." (Why R. S. or R. C. if the grave is that of Fithian Minuit? I do not know and cannot guess.)

A note of caution: do not think that the Ticking Tomb is "outside" the gates of the cemetery, in the midst of a small, grassy, triangle-shaped island, at the intersection of adjoining roads. This stone structure that looks like a set of steps that have lost its house is exactly that—steps used as a carriage mount for ladies, so they would not have difficulty entering high carriages or stagecoaches. In error, some people have knelt and placed their ears to the top platform of the carriage mount, thinking the set of steps is the Ticking Tomb. Save yourself unnecessary embarrassment and spend your time more fruitfully by conducting your search in the interior of the graveyard.

Late-Night Initiation

A fraternity from the nearby University of Delaware decided to use the Ticking Tomb as the final step of its long initiation process. Nervous pledges were ordered to visit the gravestone known as the Ticking Tomb at midnight—under a full moon, of course—place the fraternity's pin on the weathered marker, and return to their clubhouse. The next morning, the society's officers said they would visit the cemetery and check to see if the aspiring club member had braved the eerie setting and completed his assigned task. While that's what the hopeful club member was told, the reality of the plot was quite different.

When the nervous student walked past the stone wall, through the wooden gate, and over the ancient bodies long ago buried in the historic boneyard, several longtime members of the fraternity were hiding behind the centuries-old, scalloped-topped tombstones. Dressed in Halloween-style costumes—including skull and werewolf masks, black cloaks, and wielding devil pitchforks—they waited silently for the edgy aspirant to kneel down and set the club pin in its proper place. As the victim completed the assignment and rose from his kneeling position, a dozen demons and monsters leapt up and screamed, causing the terrified pledge to think he was the victim of an attack by the undead.

Rushing toward their prey, the laughing, shouting comrades ended the evening by patting him on the back and welcoming him as a member of their select society. Then they drove off on the dark, narrow roads and headed to the fraternity house, where they partied until dawn.

This scenario worked well for about seven years. The episode that ended the initiation rite occurred when the pledge in the graveyard happened to be at the college on a track and field scholarship. Reacting to the sudden screams of the Halloween-attired phantoms like they were the signal to begin a race, the experienced runner blasted off and escaped their grasp. As he raced toward his car, which was parked in pitch darkness on the other side of the old stone wall, unexpected tragedy struck.

Charging through the ill-lit graveyard, the frightened pledge crashed into an unmoving, 250-year-old granite tombstone. After his body flipped over the undamaged grave marker, his comrades discovered the unconscious applicant. Unfortunately, one of the boy's legs was facing an unnatural direction. Pulling out a cell phone, a fraternity member who had been giving chase dialed 9-1-1. When asked the address of the location of the "accident," the nervous boy shouted, "The ticking tomb! The ticking tomb!"

Since no one knew the proper address of the legendary site, it took a bit more time than usual for emergency medical personnel to arrive on the scene. So ended a rather unique initiation process. But the memorable incident has achieved legendary status, and, not surprisingly, the story lives on in the memories of those who were involved and has been embellished with each passing year.

Blacksmith's Revenge

The Fair Hill Natural Resource Management Area preserves a 5,600-acre historic wilderness in northeast Cecil County. In addition, 3,400 adjacent acres in Delaware's White Clay Creek State Park and Pennsylvania's 1,300-acre White Clay Creek Preserve combine with Fair Hill to offer more than 10,000 acres of trails, wildlife, and history.

In recent years, numerous cougar sightings have occurred in the three-state wilderness. But strange and eerie things also occur at night. That's when the tri-state's restless ghost rider appears. During colonial times, a rich man lived in Fair Hill. He owned several plantations and was an official of the Maryland government. He was rich, older, prominent, and rarely in good spirits. At the age of sixty-five, he married a young, beautiful woman who was only in her twenties. She was confined to her master's home, and was told her main job was to wait for her master to return from his business trips, which were lengthy and numerous.

The young bride, who we'll call Mary, begged the master to take her along on his travels. She longed to see Annapolis, where she wanted to visit the shops in the busy city while the master met with merchants, politicians, and other plantation owners, but he adamantly refused her repeated requests. Home alone, she took care of the grounds and became friendly with the plantation blacksmith. The strong young man was closer to her age, and he worked in the shop not far from the main house. Eventually, the blacksmith accompanied Mary on walks. They also went on picnics, and he talked to her when she sat on the mansion's front porch. It was no surprise that the two friends soon fell in love.

One day, the blacksmith announced that he was planning to head west, to start a new life on the American frontier. He asked Mary to go with him. At first she refused, but two weeks later, following several heated arguments with her husband, she decided to leave with her lover.

Knowing the master would never allow her to go, Mary began to make plans to run away with her new love while the master was away on business. The two lovers packed a small wagon with supplies and, early one morning, were walking out the manor house door. The blacksmith was carrying Mary's belongings when her husband unexpectedly rode into the courtyard. The master was enraged. At first he thought that the blacksmith was stealing valuables from the mansion. When he realized that his wife was the prize and she was trying to escape, the master jumped down from his horse, grabbed the young woman and threw her to the ground. Then he pulled a whip off the wagon and hit his wife across the back. As the blacksmith ran forward to defend his lover, the master pulled out a pistol and shot the young man in the chest.

The shocked wife crawled toward her lover and held his dying body in her arms. Crying, she announced that she would not leave the dying blacksmith. The master, still in a rage, whipped her across the back and neck until her skin was raw and her blood ran together with her dead lover's. The young woman died on the spot as a result of the beating.

Several slaves approached, and the master chased them away, except for his most trusted servant, Lucas. As Lucas picked up the woman, the master told everyone he was taking her into the house to nurse her back to health. Working together that night, the master and Lucas dug a deep hole, near the side of the blacksmith shop, and dropped the two bodies inside, standing upright and facing each other. "That way they can stare at each other until the end of the world," snarled the master.

After they covered over the bodies with dirt, the master directed Lucas to place a large tree stump and huge iron anvil directly on top of the hole. This, he decided, would conceal the evidence related to the two murdered lovers. The owner swore Lucas to secrecy and promised the slave his freedom, as long as he and no one else on the property said a word about the horrible incident.

No one outside the plantation learned what had happened that day. There were rumors, of course, but no slave dared speak of what really took place. Word spread throughout the county that the mistress of the house and the blacksmith had left together one evening. People expressed pity and sadness for the master. How horrible it was for the ungrateful young wife to betray her loving and generous husband. Eventually, the rich man found another young woman, and she agreed to be his new bride. On the evening of their wedding day, a huge party was held in the plantation house. Every notable citizen from the region was invited to attend, as were wealthy landowners and politicians from Annapolis and nearby Delaware and Pennsylvania.

As the best man raised his glass to make the wedding toast, the smiling guests were distracted by a clanging sound coming from outside the home. Initially, most of the guests tried to ignore the distraction, but the sound grew louder and was soon accompanied by the loud whinnying of a horse. When members of the wedding party ran to the windows, they focused their eyes on a large white stallion that was tied beside the blacksmith shop. The animal was rearing up on its hind legs. Furiously, it was slamming its front hooves against the top of the anvil. The clanging grew louder, and several guests that had ran onto the front porch were amazed at what they saw.

The horse, which was out of control, was trying to break away from the anvil to which it had been tied. As the animal yanked back on its reins, the anvil overturned. Fearful of being injured if they tried to calm the animal, a few men who had been standing nearby backed away. But instead of running off, the horse began to pound at the earth where the tree stump and anvil had rested. The animal was not stamping, but seemed to pawing, actually digging, at the soft ground. The frantic horse appeared to be looking for something hidden below the surface. On the porch, holding on tightly to his new bride, the master stood frozen, his eyes fixed on the scene. The wedding party and guests also watched in silence.

One of the three men who had tried earlier to subdue the horse was close to the action and shouted that he saw the top of a human skull in the fresh hole that the horse had dug. When the animal slowly backed away, a few men grabbed tools from the shed and began to toss aside the dirt. Soon they pulled out bones that appeared to be human skeletons.

When the witnesses recognized the clothing as that of the master's former wife and her blacksmith, women screamed and men began to race toward their carriages. The new bride was horrified and moved away from her groom, hiding behind members of her family. The master, babbling incoherently, said he knew nothing. He claimed to be as surprised as anyone. A few close friends believed him, but most did not. The riddle was solved when Lucas, the old slave, walked out from his shed and described the murders. He added that he, his family, and all the other slaves had been threatened with death if they ever spoke the truth.

"Lies! Lies!" shouted the master. "Besides," he said, almost snarling, "the testimony of a slave is not admissible in a court of law." But as soon as the words passed his lips, the master groaned, realizing that just that very morning, during the excitement of his wedding day, he had signed the old servant's freedom papers—the ones Lucas was now waving in the air. His former slave had spoken as a free man.

Before the county sheriff could be called, or anyone could detain him for the crimes, the master ran into his house. A group of men raced up the stairs, charging after him. When he was cornered in a top-floor bedroom, the master refused to surrender. Rather than face the disgrace of a trial and eventual hanging, the murderer raced across the room, broke through the window, and fell to his death in the courtyard thirty feet below.

Eventually, the manor house was destroyed, the land was sold off in parcels, and a large area of the property was reclaimed by nature. Today, forests and fields have covered over all traces of the home, slave huts, and the wooden blacksmith shed where the skeletons had been discovered. But for many years, walkers in the woodland preserves during dusk, and others who camped in the forests overnight, claimed to have seen strange things. The most memorable was the sight of a large white horse, standing on its hind legs, carrying a ghostly rider wearing a tall black hat and cracking a whip. Others reported hearing the steady clanging of a metal hammer, as if sounding a signal against the top of an unseen blacksmith's anvil.

Dancing Ghosts

You know you're traveling back roads when the towns bear countrified names like Golts, Millington, Sudlersville, Vandyke, Blackiston, and Massey. Of course, to call some of these places towns might be a bit of an exaggeration. Crossroads might be more correct. You get to these secluded places by traveling along winding, narrow lanes that began as animal paths, became Indian trails, grew into wagon lanes, and today carry fast-moving automobiles. But behind thick rows of pine trees, on hidden panhandle lots far out of sight of the roadway, there are good stories, and very good ghost stories.

Golts is in Kent County, Maryland, only a half-mile from the Mason-Dixon line. It's not stretching the imagination to say the Mason-Dixon surveyor's crew probably worked and rested on land that the village now occupies. Herman was a retiree and lived with his wife in a frame ranch house in Golts for more than three decades. After she died, he said, "the visitors came." But, he explained, they might have been coming to his home long before that. He only noticed them then. The first time was very early one morning, when he couldn't sleep and decided to get out of bed and watch some television.

He said he went into his recreation room, which was next to the kitchen, and sat in his recliner and turned on the TV. The set stood on a table beside the entrance to the kitchen. It was about three o'clock in the morning. As Herman was focused on the screen, he said he noticed something move across the doorway in the kitchen. "It was quick," Herman remembered, "like a fast-moving shadow. I took off my glasses and cleaned them with my shirt, thinking they might be dirty. Then before I put them back on I rubbed my eyes. It was early in the morning, and I wasn't used to being up at that hour. Less than a half-hour later, I saw it again. Like a blur, moving fast across the doorway."

Herman got up, turned on the kitchen light, and found nothing unusual. Thinking it was his imagination, he shut the lights, turned off the TV, and returned to bed. Nothing else occurred for about two weeks. Then, one weekday night, he said he had been watching TV when he fell asleep in his recliner and awoke a little bit after midnight.

"That was the first time I saw them clearly," he said. "It was a man and a woman. They came to the kitchen doorway and looked at me. I didn't move. I didn't want to scare them off. I wanted to see what was going on. I could see their lips moving, but there was no sound whatsoever. They just looked at me for about a minute, and then they just faded away."

Looking at a nearby clock, Herman said he checked the time and went to bed. But the next night he stayed awake and shortly before midnight the ghostly couple returned. As the months passed, their visits were frequent, sometimes every night of the week. "Usually," Herman said, "they stay in the kitchen. They don't pass the threshold of the doorway to my TV room. But two times they came close and looked at me. Then went right back. You can't move, or they'll disappear. You have to sit perfectly still."

Eventually, Herman said, he would prepare himself for the visits. Since they were occurring nightly, he organized his day and got a lot of rest in the afternoon. At night, when the late news came on, he settled in his chair, which he had moved slightly so that it offered the best possible view of the kitchen.

"You can't hear them," he said. "They don't make any noise. It looks like they are having a party and slow-dancing and laughing. Usually, they stay for a few hours, but the last few times they kept going until about daylight. None of it makes any sense to me. A few times there were more than just the first two, and the others were pointing in my direction. It was as if they were all in there having a discussion about me. But, like I said, I'm never able to hear anything. I admit I look forward to their coming every night, to see what is going to happen next."

As the months passed, Herman said the ghostly guests grew in number and ventured more frequently into his recreation room. As long as he remained perfectly still, some sat on his sofa. One time, one of them brought a pretty little baby and rested with the infant in a rocking chair. "A few times they really got to me," Herman admitted. "Most of the time they keep to themselves, but now and then they'll move things around—car keys, my wallet. Things like that. I think it's just their way of trying to play games with me. When that happens, I shout out, 'Put my stuff back, right now!' And I'll leave the room for a few minutes, and when I come back in whatever it is I couldn't find is back where it was."

Before I could suggest that the incidents might simply be the result of old age or forgetfulness, Herman said, "I know what you're thinking, and I did, too. That it's just a sign of that old-timers' mind-loss thing. But I don't think that's it. After all, it seemed to start happening after that night I got up suddenly, and I discovered the visitors were here. I haven't had any forgetful spells about anything else, or any accidents. I think we're talking about ghosts or spirits, or whatever they are, so who's going to come up with any logical reasons for any of this?"

Ultimately, the main question in Herman's mind is: Are the visits really happening?

"I began to wonder if all this is actually taking place. And if it is or isn't, is there something wrong with me? I'd really like to see if somebody else is seeing what I'm seeing."

However, being up there in years—Herman was seventy-nine at the time of our conversation—he admitted being quite hesitant to share his strange experiences with anyone else, particularly members of his family. "You know what they'd say," he volunteered, "'The old guy's lost his marbles' or 'He's a few bricks shy a load.' No sense calling that kind of attention to myself over this. I like it here, living by myself and in control. I don't want somebody sending me off to a doctor's for tests and observations, and then maybe to an old folks' home for permanent safekeeping, if you understand what I'm saying. So I decided to just use my best friend, Max, as my partner in solving this mystery."

A sleepy-eyed, twelve-year-old golden retriever, Max was Herman's constant companion and ever-agreeable confidante. Unfortunately, it appeared that it would take quite a bit to get Max to stir from his soft-cushioned corner of Herman's recreation room.

"I've seen the visitors walk right through Max, and to him it's like nothing's happening," Herman said. "So far, he can't see them and doesn't even notice they're there. I started to do some research about ghosts. Got some books out of the library and all. A few times, I came across the theory that pets and young children are supposed to be ghost sensitive, but not Max here. Unless," Herman added, "he's been aware of them for years before I noticed what was going on. If that's the case, they're like part of the family to him, and they don't bother him since Max figures they belong here. If that's so, I'm just a Johnny-come-lately to the party."

Patty Cannon

It's a quiet, three-way crossing where Reliance, Maryland, meets the state of Delaware. The intersection is on the north-south segment of the Mason-Dixon Line, on Route 20, only a few miles west of Seaford, Delaware.

Go there at night, if you dare. It's spooky and quiet, real quiet.

"Deadly quiet," folks say.

Passing cars rarely stop, especially at night. During the day, drivers speed by on their way to someplace else, someplace important. Reliance is just a pass-through spot.

"Hardly nobody heads there no more," say the locals.

But years ago they did, quite a few as a matter of fact. Many of those who thought they were just passing through Johnson's Crossroads, the original name of Reliance, stayed forever, but were never seen again.

When the moon is hidden behind thick clouds, especially in the fall, and the wind blows across the open fields, you can almost hear the screams. Some come from slaves being separated from their children, who were sold at the highest market-value price. Some moans are from the throats of traders and travelers who were murdered in their sleep. And a few pleas are from members of a gang who were butchered to keep them from sharing secrets they had pledged to keep.

Talk to certain people, and, in a whisper, they'll admit to having seen spirits hovering over the fields and floating along with the thick gusts of autumn wind. Watermen will talk about really bad things their elders said happened on small, unnamed islands in the nearby Nanticoke River. Some people believe there are bodies yet to be uncovered in the fields near Reliance, under rocks on the islands, and in thick woods outside hamlets. They claim to know about secret tunnels the killers used that exist under stately mansions in Georgetown, Snow Hill, Cambridge, and Princess Anne.

But sophisticated newcomers—retirees and executives from far-away states—scoff at the silly tales of the natives, wondering what kind of uneducated fools believe in ghosts. "Undiscovered remains? Total, absolute nonsense!" "Secret passageways? What delightful imaginations these quaint, country folk seem to have!" And why, in heaven's name, would these phantoms choose to hover near Reliance, one of the most out-of-the-way, hard-to-find places on earth? The answer is whispered in two words: "Patty Cannon."

During the nineteenth century, the people on Maryland's lower Eastern Shore and in Delaware's lower counties associated Patty Cannon's name with fear, hate, and dread. Her story has been told many times, often with different details, some reaching intense heights of horror and gore. Scholars believe Patty's saga will never be told accurately. No one, including her family and gang, knew the real background of where she came from and who she really was. But a mixture of folklore, newspaper articles, eyewitness accounts, and hand-me-down tales has given us a dark, shrouded portrait of the woman who has fascinated Delmarva residents and researchers in the 181 years since her death in 1829.

In the early 1800s, Patty Cannon and her gang operated an inn west of Seaford in the border town of Johnson's Crossroads. Its location precisely on the Mason-Dixon Line was a major reason why her criminal career lasted so long. Basically, Patty made her living, and fortune, killing travelers that stopped by her home to spend the night. She disposed of the evidence by burying bodies in her fields and garden, and keeping the victims' belongings for her time and effort. It's said she had "the Room" in the cellar, where she stacked many of the unburied corpses and kept them until, eventually, there was nothing left but irregular groupings of scattered bones.

Patty also operated a "reverse" Underground Railway. In the early 1800s, she and her gang stole free blacks from the northern counties and nearby states, tied them up, and sold them to eager slave traders who took the unfortunate captives back down South, delivering them a second time into slavery. A federal law passed in 1808 that restricted the importation of slaves into America made the human product scarce. As the value of plantation workers skyrocketed, Patty took advantage of the Southern businessmen's needs, fulfilling the principle of supply and demand. By kidnapping free blacks, she made a very good living. Patty kept the captives chained to the walls in her attic, above her bedroom, until the buyers arrived. She manacled others to trees on nearby islands in the Nanticoke River, which were convenient sites for loading the cargo onto boats bound for the slave states.

Eventually, area residents noticed that a fair number of people were going into Patty's inn, but few of these folks were coming out. Authorities could not catch the murderess in the act, however, because of the Mason-Dixon Line. Patty's home stood at the Maryland edge of the state border. Her barn, across the road, was located in Delaware. When Maryland authorities on horseback approached her residence/inn to investigate a reported crime, Patty would walk across the road to her barn in Delaware and wave at the arriving constables. When Delaware officials would approach her property from the east, the gang leader would step across the line and be safe on her front porch in the adjacent state of Maryland. For years, she avoided the law by hopscotching the Mason-Dixon Line. Parents used Patty's reputation to make unruly children behave. They told ornery youngsters that Patty Cannon was coming over to get them. This quieted them down quickly, since Patty was known to despise children, especially when they caused the slightest fuss.

In one book it's said she beat small children to death by crushing their skulls with blows from heavy tree limbs. A slave woman's child would not be quiet, so Patty stopped the child's screams by shoving the baby's face into the hot coals of the inn's fireplace until the child stopped breathing. These victims joined others in the Room or were buried in shallow graves under the tavern's porch.

Patty was not arrested or captured red-handed at the scene of a crime. Instead, she brazenly left her inn, site of countless crimes and murders, to entertain rich ladies on the Eastern Shore with tales and stories. Members of her audiences thought she had a wonderful imagination to think up such legends of suspense and horror. Little did they know that this teller of tales was the real-life source of Patty's local folktale repertoire.

Before leaving Reliance, the mistress of death rented her land to a local farmer. While plowing a field behind the inn, his horse fell into a hole and he discovered a trunk, containing what he thought was pirate's treasure. Unfortunately for him, but more so for Patty, the chest offered up the dead body of a Georgia slave trader. He had been stabbed in the chest and the corpse was wrapped in one of Patty's tablecloths, obviously another victim of Patty's unique brand of Southern Delmarva hospitality. The Georgian had come up to Reliance with $15,000 in gold to purchase slaves. Patty sat him down at her table and, while he was dining on her homemade vittles, shot him in the back and had her gang members dispose of the corpse in a nearby field.

While she was living in Maryland, one of Patty's old gang members was captured. To help save himself, he agreed to testify against her. With the traitor's help, an indictment against Patty and several other members of her gang was issued in April 1829. She was charged with four murders, but it was believed she was involved in up to ten times as many. Somehow, Patty was enticed to cross the Mason-Dixon Line and enter into Delaware, where a task force made up of law officers from both states snatched her up. When charges against her were filed in May 1829, news of the arrest spread quickly in towns and villages throughout the Eastern Shore. Delmarva's most famous murderess was under lock and key in the Georgetown, Delaware, jail. Her trial was set for October.

Sometime in May, Patty disappointed those who were eagerly awaiting the gory tales she would certainly tell in the Sussex County courtroom. She killed herself in her jail cell by taking poison that she kept in the hem of her skirt. (It's rumored she previously had disposed of two husbands with the poison and always kept it close at hand.) Others suggest local politicians and landowners, to keep her from divulging their roles in her crimes, murdered Patty before her trial.

But Patty Cannon's story did not end with her death. According to official records, she was buried in a pauper's grave in an unmarked plot behind the Georgetown jail, where her body rested until the early 1900s. At that time, Patty's corpse was among scores of others moved to make way for an addition that was being built to the original building. According to a document written by the late Alfred W. Joseph, dated May 2, 1963, and now on file in the Dover, Delaware, Public Library, in the early 1900s, James Marsh, a Sussex County deputy sheriff, was involved in the exhumation of Patty's casket for reburial in another potter's field.

"Somehow, while moving these bodies, Patty's skull came into the possession of James Marsh," the document states. When Mr. Marsh moved to Colorado for health reasons in 1907, he gave the skull to a relative, Charles I. Joseph, for keeping. It was kept on a nail in the family barn until the late 1930s, ". . . by which time it had become quite a curiosity. To save it from damage or possible theft, he put it in a box and stored it in the attic of his home," according to Alfred Joseph's statement. After his father's death in 1946, Mr. Alfred Joseph took possession of the skull and, in 1961, put it on loan to the Dover Library, where it sits to this day, in a round, red hatbox in the workroom on the first floor, or in a safe elsewhere in the building.

According to a 1994 interview with Bob Wetherall, then Dover Public Library director, people occasionally called and asked to see Patty, and he agreeably responded to their requests. Several national periodicals, including *Reader's Digest*, have called and inquired. Some have sent photographers to capture Patty's jawless, toothless remains. Many who have seen the skull question whether it really is that of Patty Cannon. Some claim it's too small, since Patty was said to be a very large woman. But the real answer will never be known. "It's an interesting curiosity," Wetherall admitted. "There's no way of authenticating it. We usually bring her out at Halloween and tell ghost stories. And we've not had any sightings."

Delmarva author Hal Roth wrote what many consider the definitive book about Patty Cannon. In *The Monster's Handsome Face*, the Vienna, Maryland, author and oral historian included a children's song about the murderess. One can imagine it being sung by small children in the border state area as they jumped rope or held hands skipping in circles:

> Old Patty Cannon
> Is dead and gone.
> Can't you hear the devil
> Draggin' her along?

The murderess's reputation has lingered into the present and has been introduced to a new generation of readers, web users, and television viewers. In an entry filed under the name "Patty Cannon" and posted on the Internet site MySpace, the host seems to have assumed Patty Cannon's identity and tavernkeeper occupation. This new claimant of the murderess's identity argues against the bad publicity her namesake has received over the centuries, and has posted the eerie regional children's rhyme printed above.

Historians from the Public Broadcasting System's program *History Detectives* investigated the Patty Cannon home in Reliance, Maryland, which hosts a state historical marker on its front lawn designating the building as the serial killer's residence. Patty's criminal exploits were referenced in the award-winning television series *Homicide: Life on the Streets* in the episode entitled "Sins of the Father." In one scene a nursery rhyme/poem, taught to a Baltimore detective by his grandmother about a slave-stealing character named "Patty Ride-nour" (a rough French translation meaning to ride at night) seems based on Delmarva's infamous female kidnapper/killer. That rhyme goes:

Hush your mouth
Go to sleep
Old Patty Ridenour
Take you back deep
Got a gang of seven
Taking slave and free
Riding day and night
On her coal-black steed

If it's true that for every good there exists evil, and that each heart of gold is balanced by a horrifying creature capable of inflicting suffering, pain, and death, then Patty Cannon certainly was the dark balance in the simple, good-bad equation of life along Maryland's Eastern Shore side of the Mason-Dixon Line.

Author's Note: An ornate metal historical marker, designating "Patty Cannon's House," stands at Johnson's Crossroads, at the Maryland–Delaware border at Reliance. The structure, now privately owned, is believed at one time to have been Patty Cannon's residence. Other research, however, indicates that the existing building simply stands at the site of the inn and slavenapper's house, which was torn down in the 1940s and actually was located several yards away. Perhaps a Sussex County, Delaware, builder has provided the most unusual anecdote related to the centuries-old Patty Cannon legend. Along River Road—a few miles south of Reliance, near the Woodland Ferry that carries vehicles across the Nanticoke River—is a suburban housing development. At its entrance is a large green-and-white sign proclaiming "Patty Cannon Estates." As one local remarked, "It's like living in Charles Manson Manor. I wonder how many of the current residents realize their neighborhood is named after a serial killer?"

Night Visitor

Along Maryland's northeastern boundary there are numerous legends and tall tales associated with centuries-old buildings. But the incidents in this story did not take place in a historic farmhouse or barn. They occurred in a modern gas station/convenience store. It's a major chain, built at a busy intersection so travelers can do some quick bread-and-milk-and-sandwich shopping while they fill up the tank on the way home from work.

Originally, two workers who we'll call Jane and Stella declared they wanted to "tell it all," and they were excited to get their picture taken for a newspaper story about their unusual experiences. They were sure their eerie incidents would make the front page of the local paper, and they were strong believers in the supernatural and delighted they had a close paranormal encounter.

Unfortunately, as usually happens, deep-thinking, corporate "higher-ups" didn't want them talking on the record and calling attention to the respected retail chain's "haunted store." So the dejected women agreed to let me share their tale, as long as the site and their real names weren't identified. The around-the-clock business where they work is located at a relatively busy intersection, and it sits atop a long-ago-demolished historic site. Some suggest it's also where a battle occurred and several troops died. One longtime area resident insists the store is near a forgotten or unmarked graveyard. Others claim it once was a stagecoach stop, or the crossroads where a centuries-old inn or tavern catered to weary travelers. There were lots of taverns in the old days. Whatever it was, it is no more. But something, or a spirited someone, seems to have stayed behind.

Jane is the manager. She usually gets to the store very early, before the going-to-work rush hits full force. She said one morning, before sunrise, she noticed something out of the corner of her eye. When she turned quickly, she was sure she saw a "misty figure in a top hat and dark coat, standing in the corner, near the freezer that holds the bags of ice." As she tried to focus on the indistinct image, it disappeared. Within the next few minutes, Jane said her mind convinced her that what she thought she witnessed was so unusual, that she was not really sure of what she saw. As the day passed, she began to think she might have been sleepy or out of sorts, and hadn't seen anything at all. Either way, Jane decided to keep the sighting to herself. "No sense having everybody think I was crazy," she said.

A few days later, Stella, the assistant manager, said she heard something that "sounded like whispers," and then she felt a sense of "sudden coldness." When she turned to look, she was sure she saw something out of the edge of her eye. "But it wasn't anything I could identify," Stella recalled. "It was like a moving, dark blur." Like her boss, she decided to keep the experience quiet. "I didn't want anybody laughing at me or teasing me. Once that gets started it's never going to stop," Stella said. "I know that for sure."

As the days and weeks passed, both women would hear a voice call out their names and see a shadow disappear in the corners of the building. The activity occurred in the storage room, behind the counter and deli, and also near the ice freezer. One day they were sitting together during a slow time in the store, in early afternoon just after the lunch rush. Somehow, they began talking about a ghost show that was on television the night before.

"One thing led to another," Jane said, "and we started mentioning the crazy stuff happening in our store." Relieved, they began sharing their unexplained experiences, and both women said they felt better knowing each of them wasn't imagining things. As weeks passed, spooky events were rare. But one day Jane had to work well into the early-morning hours. The next morning Stella, who had arrived before sunrise, noticed that items were knocked off the shelves, and she heard a few unexplained sounds. When she mentioned this to Jane, who had been up most of the night and finally arrived about noon, the manager admitted she had probably stirred things up. She said had brought a Ouija Board into the building the previous night, and she had been trying to make contact with the spirit when she took a break in the middle of the night.

After the resumption of strange incidents, Jane left her spirit-attracting board at home. The women noticed that the sightings and sounds still increased, but at irregular and indefinite intervals. A few friends who lived in the area suggested some bizarre reasons for the mysterious visitor's appearances, but no one had come up with a sensible suggestion.

Stella, however, smiled and offered a rather unusual theory that no one else had voiced. "I think," she said, "that he wants to be Jane's boyfriend. After all, he shows up more frequently when she is here alone. And I think she likes it, and that's why she sneaked in here that night along with the Ouija Board. It might sound crazy, but why not?"

Cold House

The original neighborhoods in this small Maryland border town are accented by older houses, which are well-spaced on their roomy lots. Most were built during the mid-1800s, and while many have been restored there are a few that are showing the scars of old age and neglect. Weathered shingles, peeling paint, sagging porches, ripped screens, and overgrown landscaping give the worst of the bunch a "haunted house" appearance. Under a full moon on a fall night, this Addams Family impression might make even the toughest construction worker decide to walk along the opposite side of the street.

The residence where our story takes place stands on a corner, only a short bicycle ride from the Pennsylvania border. It has a wraparound porch and a third-floor turret room, is surrounded by overgrown shrubs and trees, and sits on a rise that gives the impression the aging structure is larger than it really is. And some say it's haunted.

Ted worked as an engineer. To him, everything in life had to occur logically. Even the most unusual incident could always be rationally explained. But on a winter night during one Christmas season, he witnessed a series of incidents that even his lifetime of logical reasoning could not, and still cannot, explain. And, he admitted, that still bothers him immensely.

Ted said his daughter, Tracey, was visiting a high school classmate who lived with his mother and sister at this particular home. On previous occasions the young girl stayed at her friend's place until about 10 P.M. and would call her father for a ride back home. One night, Ted answered his phone shortly after 9 P.M. and heard his daughter say, "Dad, please come over right away. There's stuff happening here." After making sure his daughter wasn't talking about an intruder or something that might cause her to be in immediate danger, he drove directly to the old house in the middle of town.

As he stopped his car, he noticed that all of the lights were on, both inside and outside the home. The boy's mother, Sally, greeted him at the front door and he walked into the entry hall. The owner apologized and led him toward the living room. "That's where things really got weird," Ted recalled. "The whole family was sleeping in the living room. They each had their bedclothes and pillows scattered on the couches and across the floor. They said they had been sleeping together down there for over a week."

Before Ted could ask what was going on, the mother and her two children—a son, Billy, and daughter, Janice—began offering explanations involving a series of unusual scary incidents. "It was the typical stuff you see in horror movies," Ted recalled, such as noises coming from the upper floors, furniture being tossed over, clothes being thrown around, stomping sounds on the stairs, and the impression that someone or something was sitting on the edge of the bed. Electrical items in the home also would turn on without anyone touching them and without being plugged into an outlet. Clocks would not work properly, even after being reset several times during the same day. They would be fine for a week or two and then malfunction again.

Billy, who was Tracey's friend from school, went upstairs to his room and invited Ted to follow. The boy showed his visitor an oversized black handprint on the wall. It was more than six feet off the ground, and despite efforts to clean the impression or cover it over with paint, the handprint kept reappearing in the same spot. Ted said the size of the hand outline was very large, much bigger than his own hand, and he was more than six feet tall. There was also another mark that looked like a hand in the corner of the room, but this one was at the base of the wall near the floor. Ted said it looked like whatever it was had gripped the small corner of the wall and pulled itself across the floor.

Ted followed Billy into the hall bathroom, where the boy pointed to scattered red dots in the sink and bathtub. The boy said these tiny marks appeared for no apparent reason and the family referred to them as "blood spots." Whenever anyone noticed them, there seemed to be an increase in unexplained activity throughout the house for the next few days.

When Ted returned with Billy to the first floor, Sally introduced him to her friend, Renee, who had arrived while he was upstairs. The owner said Renee was a friend of the family and a self-proclaimed psychic. Renee told everyone she had discovered her gift to "discern signals from the other side" following a vehicle accident in which she almost died. "I believe the Lord gave me a second chance at life, and I'm using his gift to help others, like Sally and her family," Renee announced quite casually, as if she had recited the explanation frequently.

Pausing to wonder what he had gotten himself into, Ted forced his scientific personality to remain tolerant of what he thought was a bunch of mumbo jumbo and a gathering of whackos. He kept silent while Renee walked the house with a Bible clutched in both hands, and eventually she announced with conviction that there were two unsettled entities residing in the home. One was a very scared young girl. The other was an evil, older man, who had no desire to move on and who enjoyed controlling the younger spirit and aggravating the families that have lived in the house. Renee the psychic told Ted, his daughter, and the family to remain downstairs as she ascended to the second floor. After about ten minutes of roaming through the rooms, Renee's screaming voice reached the downstairs living room.

"Then she shouted that she was okay," Ted recalled. "She announced she had cornered him, the evil one, in the closet of the boy's room, where the black handmark appeared. Renee proclaimed loudly, 'He showed me the face of Satan, but I'm okay.' Then," Ted added, "like in the movies, this gray cat appears at the top of the stairs. It's hissing like it's on fire and it seems like it's looking directly at me. Suddenly, it flies off the second-floor landing and heads for the first floor. All of us are standing together, like statues, in the hall near the front door. The cat runs between our legs and disappears behind us. But the thing is, the family didn't own a cat, and the front door was locked. So where did it go?"

With his mind running on overdrive, Ted admitted he couldn't come up with a logical explanation for the disappearing cat. But he didn't have time to dwell on that incident. Renee had appeared at the top of the stairs and began walking down toward the small group. She announced she had been able to send the young girl to "the light on the other side." She added that the group should have seen her, since the girl's spirit was heading toward them down the stairs. No one mentioned the mysterious gray cat, but all of them thought that might have been the manifestation of the newly released spirit of the girl. But Renee immediately presented the bad news.

"I wasn't able to harmonize the other entity," she said, her voice weaker than when she had entered the second floor. "He's not as powerful anymore, but he's still here. I seriously suggest you and your family move. You have got to leave this house as quickly as possible. Tonight. I have never encountered anything this dangerous or powerful. I've got to go, immediately. Sorry. There's nothing more I can do here."

Ted recalled the woman was very agitated, nothing like the calm and self-assured psychic he had talked to only minutes before. Her hands were shaking, her eyes glancing away from the group and looking toward the door, as if she wanted to make sure the path was clear for her to get out in a hurry. Without saying good-bye, she walked swiftly toward the street and unlocked her car.

Sally and her family and Ted closed the door and were about to speak when they heard several blasts of a car horn coming from the street. When the group ran outside to check on the source of the sounds, they saw Renee, trapped in her car, trying to get out. But the car doors wouldn't open, and the door locks were going up and down, making clicking sounds. It looked to Ted like the car locks were operating on their own. Then the strange activity stopped suddenly, and Renee started up the car, depressed the accelerator, screeched her tires, and drove away like she was fired from a cannon.

Sally and Ted led the children toward the front steps of the building and paused for a moment. "We weren't thrilled about going back inside the house," he said, noting they all were shocked by the words and actions of the experienced, terrified, and long-gone psychic. "We thought if she dealt with this stuff all the time, and she was freaked out, whatever was in the house had to be something serious."

But Ted still was trying to figure out some logical reasons for all of the strange stories, the troubling reactions of the paranormal expert, and the car lock malfunction. As he sat in the parlor-turned-family bedroom, trying to calm his daughter and the full-time residents of the home, the downstairs room became extremely cold.

"It was like an icy blast from a freezer filled the area where we were sitting. It was so sudden and so cold, the family grabbed blankets and wrapped themselves in them, and I zipped up my jacket. When I could see clouds of frost escaping from their mouths, I walked to the baseboard heat source, and it was blasting out. But when I pulled my hand two inches from the heater, it was like I was in the North Pole. That's when I gave up trying to attribute logic to anything happening in that house."

Sally, with her head peeking out from a quilt, shouted, "It's here!" As the children started crying and shouting "We have to get out of here!" the phone rang. It was Renee, checking to see if Sally and her family had left. Sally told her the room was like an icebox, and confirmed they were leaving right away. Without taking anything but her purse, and the children not bothering to grab a change of clothes, everyone followed Ted down the porch steps to the curb.

"We stood there for a few minutes," he recalled. "I gave Sally about fifty dollars, which I thought would help her get a motel for the night. My daughter's hands were clutching onto me. It was obvious she was scared to death."

Ted said he waited at the curb until the frightened family drove off. Then he and his daughter headed for home. During that short, nervous ride, Tracey recalled an incident that had occurred a few months earlier, when she was leaving the house. She said she had turned back to look up at Billy's room. The lights were on, and a shadow looked down on her and waved. Thinking it was her friend, she waved back. Suddenly, Billy came running down the driveway to return a homework assignment. Perplexed about who she had just seen, she looked back at the window, but the dark figure was gone. There was no one there. She said she never told anyone about it, because she didn't want to cause her friend any concern.

Within a month, Sally's family moved from the house. During the weeks it took them to find another residence, they stayed with relatives and friends. No one stayed in that house. When Sally and her children needed to enter to pick up any possessions, they went inside during the day and never alone.

"I heard no one after them rented the home for very long," Ted said. "There seemed to be a steady turnover of tenants, many of whom seemed to leave abruptly." Pausing, Ted said a strange thing related to the same house happened to him four years later.

After separating from his wife, Ted found himself looking for a place to live. For a short time he stayed with some friends, but he regularly read the classifieds in the paper, seeking a cheap but clean place of his own. He had not thought of the strange events that happened that night in Sally's home for years, particularly since he was not a fan of paranormal tales. He also said he probably was annoyed that he was never able to figure out any logical reasons for the things that occurred. As a result of his frustration, he probably shoved the memories out of his mind.

But while riding around checking out a short list he had compiled of possible rentals, he found himself driving on the street where he had rescued his daughter from the unknown entity several years before. He stopped his car in front of the house and double-checked the address, which had been given to him by a rental agent. Amazed at the coincidence, he found himself looking up at the very same house where the bizarre events had happened.

"I said aloud, 'No way!'" Ted recalled. "I mean, what were the chances that would occur? It was vacant. There were no cars in the driveway. Of course, I didn't leave my car, or go on the porch, or look in the window. Here I am, Mister Logical, and I was careful not to step foot on the property. I drove by a few times later, at night, to see if any lights were on. There was no one in there—no one living, anyway. It was dark inside, but in a threatening sort of way. At the time, I thought whatever was there years ago hadn't left. It's still there."

Ted admitted that he had been bothered for some time by events he witnessed that winter evening. "I found it ironic that the same logical, tested methods I had used to shoot down unexplained events actually resulted in making me think, to a degree, that there might be something of substance to paranormal occurrences. The icy cold in the room, despite the heat blasting from the baseboard, was what really perplexed me. And it has to this day, as well as the door locks going crazy in the psychic's car. The other things, like the sounds and shadows. They all could be written off as overreactions by the recipient or emanating from natural causes or explainable sources."

Renee the psychic had mentioned that the house's evil entity probably was someone trapped and unable to enter the calmness of the other side, the afterlife. "From an early age," Ted said, "we're taught about a religious afterlife, that there is something comforting after death. We learn about faith and hope and that after we die we will find peace and be reunited with our loved ones. For some, it's hard to actually accept that faith, to make the long leap from this world we know to belief in the next life—one that we can't see and have to imagine and believe in, based on no clear evidence, only faith.

"But that night, I got the sense that whatever evil entity was in that house, it knew it would never be able to find comfort on the other side. I don't know what it did in this life. But whatever horrible thing it was, that frustrated spirit didn't ever want to leave. It didn't want to be judged. However miserable it was trapped here, in our dimension, was better than what was waiting in the afterlife. That's just my guess. I don't know for sure. But the one thing I know for certain is that I would never, ever go into that house again. Not for all the money in the world."

Old Blackie

At the Atlantic Ocean, the Trans-Peninsular Line separates Ocean City, Maryland, and Fenwick Island, Delaware. Stone makers along the border indicate the line's straight path. Each stone bears a coat of arms of Lord Baltimore and the Calvert family of Maryland on the south side and the coat of arms of the Penn family on its north face. These historic stones can be found near Fenwick, Gumboro, Delmar, and Selbyville.

In this last-mentioned community stands the home of Old Blackie. The ghost's presence was discovered by accident, since its name isn't on the mailbox or on a folk-art plaque above the front door. But several residents had encounters with this roaming spirit. And they were so unsettling that the families moved out hurriedly and took their belongings and ghost tales with them.

Al and Diane had been married for five years when they rented an old, weathered, frame farmhouse in a small, rural town along the

Maryland-Delaware border. Al was a truck driver and worked an irregular schedule. He slept during the day or night, depending upon his assignments, which often came in with short notice and erratically. The couple needed to live in a house and area where it was quiet, away from traffic and noisy neighbors. They found what they wanted near Hudson Crossroads. The house was a two-story rental with two bedrooms and a small storage area on the second floor. The only bathroom was downstairs.

They moved in during the winter, in January, and decided to make one of the downstairs rooms their bedroom. That would give Diane time to paint and decorate the upstairs room they had selected as their eventual master bedroom. Besides, there were no heat vents on the second floor, so their temporary, first-floor bedroom would be warmer during the cold-weather season.

Soon after they moved in, Diane was home with the couple's two children. Al was out on the road. She kept a dimmer light on throughout the evening so that she could get up and take care of the children whenever they needed a drink of water or had to go to the bathroom. "I woke up for some reason," she said, "and I saw a black figure move across the downstairs. It went from one room to the next, sort of like it was floating. I remember it was shaped like a monk with a hood and hunched over, like it was wearing a black shroud." she said. "It may sound silly, but I remember thinking if he sees me looking at him, maybe he'll bother me. So I'll just peek, and then he'll go away. The next morning I tried to tell myself it was all a dream, or just my imagination."

Diane didn't tell Al about the black monk when he returned home from a long haul, but she did mention the racket that seemed to be coming from the second floor. "I would hear noises, like something was moving big pieces of furniture up there during the night," Diane recalled. "It seemed to be coming from the attic area that was off to the side of the narrow stairs. It was coming from an older area that was built above the kitchen. I told Al to go and put some rat killer up there, but he told me he had done that before we moved in."

When spring arrived a few months later, the couple moved their bedroom upstairs and Diane said she started hearing laughter. It sounded like a woman's voice, and it occurred both during the day and night. It too seemed to be coming from the storage area next to their just-finished bedroom. "I'm not the kind of person to be afraid," she said, referring to her work as a medic with several volunteer fire company emergency care units. "I specifically didn't tell my husband, because I thought he'd think I was going crazy."

As their first fall in the home approached, Al and Diane were reading in their bedroom, which was entered by the old stairs that led up directly from the kitchen. They had secured the wooden stairway door on the first floor with a hook and eye. They wanted to keep it open so the downstairs heat would travel freely up the staircase.

Just as Al shut off the light and his head hit the pillow, he heard an unusual sound and immediately jabbed Diane with his elbow. She nodded that she also had heard something, and they both listened to the distinct sound of footsteps that they were sure were coming up the wooden stairs. Realizing the intruder would soon be standing at the open bedroom doorway, Al pushed Diane off the side of the bed and pulled his pistol from beneath the mattress. As the concerned husband and terrified wife both crouched down behind the far side of their bed, Al pointed the barrel of his weapon toward the open doorway. The steady steps became louder. The sounds were very close. As the footsteps advanced, he pulled back the hammer, ready to unload all six rounds into whoever had broken into their home.

Then everything in the house was silent. No sounds on the stairs at all. It was as if whatever it was had evaporated into thin air. Al and Diane held their breath, and then after several minutes the footsteps returned. But they were softer and fading away. It was as if the unseen stranger was descending the stairs and leaving. When Al finally got up and walked down the steps, gun pointed and ready for use, there was nothing in the house. They searched every room and found no sign that anyone had broken in. Only one thing was out of place: the door at the foot of the stairway that had been secured open was now unlatched and swinging back and forth. Whatever had been there had left a calling card, as if to tell the couple that they had not imagined the strange, unexplained incident.

"It took about ten days for us to move out," Diane said. "We told the landlord we had to have a larger place, because the children were growing and we needed more room for their things. He was a nice man, and we didn't want to tell him his house was too spooky for us to live in."

Diane and her family relocated only about a half-mile down the road. Over the next eight years that they lived in the area they noticed that the next several renters of the old haunted farmhouse never stayed there too long. Every group of new renters would be long gone after only a few months. "That house sat empty more than it was rented," Diane said. "Word in the area was that the landlord's mother had lived there all alone for a long time and she died in the house."

Once in the safety of their new residence, Al admitted that he, too, had seen the dark, monk-like figure roving the downstairs of the old house soon after they moved in. He added that he didn't want to mention the incidents for fear of scaring his wife.

One day about ten years after they had left the haunted house, Diane said she was working part-time at a convenience store in Ocean City. It was a hot, thick, humid August afternoon. She thanked the Lord for having the good fortune to work in an air-conditioned building. A young woman came into the store, bought a soda, and asked if she could hang out and soak up the free air conditioning.

"I said, 'Sure,'" said Diane, before pausing to explain the rest of the strange, chance encounter. "But now, this next part of what happened really scared me to death. It made my hair stand up on end."

The woman, who Diane had never seen before, said, "I didn't get much sleep last night. My son kept me awake."

"Is he teething or sick?" Diane asked.

"No," the woman said, giggling. "Our spook was moving furniture around all night."

"What in the world are you talking about?" Diane asked her.

Rolling her eyes, the embarrassed woman said, "The place we live in has got spooks. And the bad part of it is, when I went downstairs to get my son a drink of water, there was Old Blackie floating through the living room."

A chill went through Diane's entire body, and although she tried to remain calm she said she practically shouted out her question: "Where do you live?"

"In an old frame house out near Hudson Crossroads."

Diane was shocked, and asked, "How do you live there? We used to live there years ago, but had to get out. We couldn't take it."

The girl smiled, finished her soda and headed toward the door. "As long as they leave my son alone, I can handle it. But they better not bother him. Then I'll have to go after them or leave the place."

"When I got home," Diane said, "I rushed into the house and told my husband what happened at work, about the girl. He stared at me. Was real still for a minute, then he said, 'I think I'm going to be sick.' Diane continued, "I remember that girl looking at me. I must have turned white. I never saw her again. I think her name was Kristen, but I can't be sure about that. But I tell you, it still sends chills up my back. But in a way I'm glad it happened, because it confirms what we saw, and it proves that we weren't crazy."

Red Rose Inn

The historic brick building is closed now, the front door locked and the drapes pulled, keeping out the sunlight. A large "For Sale or Lease" sign stands on the front lawn. Across the road a large, modern shopping center with specialty shops, fast-food restaurants, and a huge supermarket cater to shoppers too busy to notice the empty, weary-looking building. But from its establishment in 1740, until only a few years ago, the Red Rose Inn, now overlooked and deserted, was the center of attention at the busy Jennersville intersection of U. S. Route 1 and Pennsylvania Route 796.

The centrally located stagecoach stop on the Old Baltimore Pike, which connected Philadelphia and Maryland's largest city, catered to the great and famous—members of the Penn family, Helen Keller, the Grand Duchess of Luxembourg, and noted politicians. They all stopped there as they traveled north and south along the Mid-Atlantic coast. As the inn's brochure stated: "It became a meeting place where the drover and farmer could transact business, where the Indian could trade coonskin for gunpowder, and where the food and drink could provide hearty fare before a warming fire."

But less significant stories of local history were passed down for centuries about incidents involving the welcoming inn. During a 1999 interview, the owners of the business referenced a tale of an Indian who murdered a young girl. He later was hanged for the crime and was believed buried in the inn's cellar. Some claim to have seen the Indian's face staring out from an upper-floor window, and the little girl's spirit was seen floating in the area of the ladies' room. Other women, dressed in old-fashioned clothing, appeared and disappeared suddenly in the Carriage Lounge bar. Dolls were found tossed onto the floor in the gift shop, as if a little girl had been playing with them and left them behind. There also were stories that the building had been a stop on the Underground Railroad. Experts pointed out marks in the rock formation of the inn's foundation that were used as signals to slaves traveling north from the nearby Maryland border.

The Red Rose Inn took its name from the 1731 agreement between the Penn family and the King of England. According to the deed, the Penn heirs, who had received five thousand acres of land, were to "forever pass one Red Rose on the 24th day of June, if same be demanded," to the Crown. The painting of three red roses, which was displayed above the fireplace in the inn's parlor dining room, symbolized the original land payment agreement. Some residents of the Jennersville-Kelton area recalled a time when there was an annual rose-payment ceremony held at the inn each year on June 24.

But that event, like banquets with hundreds of guests, and private dinners for romantic couples, is long gone. Only the ghosts and their stories survive. If no one responds to the real estate sign's plea for the inn's survival, within a short time a gas station/convenience store no doubt will conquer the old historic site—and the building that hosted Indians, slaves, mule drivers, soldiers, aristocrats, business leaders, and ordinary saloon patrons will become another victim of progress.

Sudden Death

The small hamlet of Conowingo hugs the rocky banks of the mighty Susquehanna River near the Pennsylvania border. Travelers passing through the area along old Route 1 can sense the age of the area from the appearance of the rolling farms and historic homes built of attractive gray stone. The topography of the land in that northernmost sector of Maryland, with its deep valleys and rocky landscape, is dramatically different from the flatness of the lower Eastern Shore.

For slaves secretly heading toward freedom before the Civil War, the change in the scenery and presence of hills was an indication that they were close to the Mason-Dixon Line, the symbolic border that separated the slave-holding Old Line State from the abolition-minded Keystone State.

In the 1970s, a contractor bought a farmhouse located along one of the area's winding country roads. One of his first projects was to build a three-room apartment in the basement. Soon after the man moved into the site, a large barn located on his newly acquired property collapsed to the ground. As the contractor and his crew began to sift through the rubble, the owner decided that the weathered barn paneling, with its attractive silver patina, would be ideal for the walls of the farmhouse's recently renovated basement bedrooms. But soon after the siding was installed, unusual events began to occur.

The family's French poodle, which initially had been content in the new homestead, refused to descend the farmhouse stairs leading to the recently finished basement. Unexplained sounds were heard throughout the house, especially after dark. While raking leaves in the yard one afternoon, the contractor turned and noticed an old Amish man standing nearby. The bearded stranger in dark clothes and a straw hat seemed to be helping with the fall chore. As the new owner took a few steps in the man's direction, and began to call out a greeting, the unexpected helper disappeared. The family became more concerned when a metal cross, placed on the newly paneled wall in the basement, flew off the wood, traveled across the open area, and landed on the floor at the opposite end of the room.

Desperate and concerned, the owners contacted a medium, who agreed to hold a séance in the farmhouse. When she arrived for a preliminary visit, the psychic took a cross, which she wore around her neck, and hung the gold chain on a nail protruding from the paneling. Immediately, the nail bent downward and the cross and chain fell to the floor.

When the evening of the gathering arrived, the psychic and several of her students sat in the haunted farmhouse basement and began to meditate under a dim light. A black woman who was a member of the medium's group announced that she had made contact with two disturbed spirits. Several others present at the session said they saw the hazy impressions of what seemed to be a pair of young black men appear in the room. In the midst of the séance the two unearthly visitors focused on the black woman at the table, to whom they cried out, pleadingly, "Help me!"

The clues to the solution of the mystery came in segments. Psychic messages were relayed silently to several in the medium's group, who later shared them with the others. When the isolated statements and incidents were interpreted, the following explanation was developed: Because of its proximity to Pennsylvania, in the late 1850s the large Maryland farm had been one of the final stations on the Underground Railway. Originally, an Amish man had owned the property. He and his family helped the slaves reach freedom by offering them shelter and then guiding them across the nearby Mason-Dixon Line.

When the Amish farmer died, the property was sold to a man who did exactly the opposite. He held the slaves for his own use and also took many down south and sold them back into slavery for large amounts of money. After holding two slaves, who were brothers, for some time, he took them outside, had them stand against the side of his barn, and shot them without warning. As they fell to the ground, their blood splattered on the wooden walls behind them. Apparently, the shooting happened so fast that the two lost souls didn't realize they were supposed to be dead. The spirits and blood of the restless slaves mingled with the barn paneling near the spot where they were shot. Then the confused ghosts moved into the farmhouse when the wooden planks were salvaged from the ruined barn and erected in the home's basement.

The medium claimed she was able to communicate with the spirits of the two dead men. She convinced them to rest in peace by leading them through the open psychic door, which she said she closed behind them as they passed. As she walked up from the basement, the psychic and the relieved family members noticed the immediate change in attitude of the small French poodle. It cheerfully ran down the stairs toward the new rooms for the first time in months.

Headless Horseman

The Headless Horseman still rides. But it is not the ghost of the decapitated Hessian soldier of Sleepy Hollow who's the subject of this tale. It's the roaming nogginless rider who has been reported along the narrow winding path of Welsh Tract Road. Like Washington Irving's fictional creation, the Maryland–Delaware version of the headless ghost traces its origin to the Revolutionary War. But this mid-Atlantic character is more heroic than its Hudson Valley counterpart. His exploits were passed down through word of mouth, rather than in print, and without this creature's heroic intervention the American Revolution would have been lost—at least, according to the legend.

The story begins in 1777, more than a year after the signing of the Declaration of Independence in Philadelphia. By late summer, the British force's objective was Penn's City of Brotherly Love. Both land and naval forces were heading to the American hotbed of revolution. More than fifteen thousand British troops, including four thousand Hessian mercenaries, arrived in three hundred wooden ships at the top of the Chesapeake Bay. They disembarked in Cecil County, Maryland, after a month-long sea trip from New York. The invaders were hungry, miserable, and ready for battle.

Men, horses, and supplies landed on the west bank of the Elk River and headed east. They were only about fifty miles from Philadelphia and the warning was sounded throughout the region: "The Redcoats are coming!" Like the minutemen of New England, Maryland and Delaware volunteers assembled to stall the enemy's advance. But the defending force's number was minute in comparison to what would be called the "largest land invasion of North America." General Washington, along with the young French general Marquis de Lafayette, came south from New Jersey and assembled American troops in defensive positions in nearby Wilmington, Delaware. The colonial army planned to intercept the British before they reached Pennsylvania. Washington himself conducted the reconnaissance from a high point along the Delaware–Maryland border. When a severe thunderstorm erupted, the American military leader hid in a nearby barn and was nearly captured by advancing enemy troops.

Several weeks earlier, an area grain merchant named Charles Miller and his teenage son, Charlie, were delivering supplies to Washington's headquarters. When the American general apologized for being unable to pay the local miller, Charles senior replied, "I'm doing this for my country, general. But my generosity is also for the sake of my son. I want this war to be over before it takes young Charlie from me."

Embarrassed by his father's comment, the younger Miller said to Washington, "I'm not afraid of the British, sir. I'll kill as many Redcoats as I can. In fact, sir, I am ready to stay and join your army right now, and I will fight as hard as any grown man."

Washington put his hand on the enthusiastic young patriot's shoulder and said, "You do your part in your own way, Charlie. Right now, bringing much-needed food for our men is your way of fighting this war. If the day ever comes when you are needed, I know you will be there, right beside me and my men. And you will demonstrate your conviction and courage."

In August of 1777, Charlie's time had arrived. At the age of sixteen, the boy mounted his family's white horse, took his father's sword, and headed toward Newark, Delaware, where American volunteers were gathering to halt or stall the steadily advancing British invasion.

On September 3, at Cooch's Bridge, a small creek crossing south of Newark, the Stars and Stripes flag, designed earlier that year by Betsy Ross, was flown in a land battle for the first time. But it eventually would be carried in defeat, rather than in victory, as waves of invaders attacked the American defenses. The Battle of Cooch's Bridge was fought at several scattered locations. One strong outpost was within the walls surrounding the cemetery of Welsh Tract Church.

There were only about three dozen volunteer defenders in the graveyard, and most had nothing more than the supplies they carried to the fray. Charlie Miller was one of the few Americans with a horse. When a cannonball hit the ground, men scattered in all directions and Charlie's horse strained to get away from the area. To calm the animal, Charlie mounted the steed and began racing across the west side of the church, intending to secure the horse behind the building. But as he passed across the center of the brick structure, a British cannonball struck his head, decapitating the young man. Without slowing, the black iron sphere carried Charlie's head along with it as the ball smashed into the center of the west wall of the church. The beheaded American's friends screamed and ran off in retreat. In the bedlam, Charlie Miller's white horse carried its headless rider into the woods and was never seen again. At least that's what everyone thought.

On September 8, the British left Newark and marched toward Chadd's Ford, Pennsylvania. On September 11, the opposing armies would meet in the famous Battle of the Brandywine, the largest land battle of the Revolutionary War. On the evening before the fight, Washington was walking from his headquarters toward a group of tents where a few of his men were talking around a fire. While Washington was speaking to the soldiers, two British snipers in the nearby woods aimed their muskets at the American general. By killing the colonial army's leader, they knew they could win the war for England more quickly. The patient riflemen cocked the hammers of their muskets, aimed, and held their breath. The general stood still and was close. It was a sure shot. There was no way they could miss.

Suddenly, their impressive target turned and looked toward his left, for no apparent reason that anyone could see. Washington's men jumped up, straining to see or hear what had attracted their commander's attention. Then it appeared. Riding directly toward the general, as if intending to run him down, was a large white horse that had materialized out the darkness. But the animal seemed to pass through the group of soldiers now surrounding their leader.

Washington and his men stared at the animal's headless rider. The eerie figure sat erect in the saddle, holding a sword in his outstretched arm as it continued charging swiftly toward the dark line of trees only a few hundred feet away. The shocked British marksman instinctively shifted their aim. They fired at the chest of the approaching, threatening figure. Although both shots hit their mark, the blue-coated ghost and its galloping white horse did not stop. Then a deep voice came from an unseen source, its volume filling the surrounding darkness. "I WANT MY HEEEAAAD!"

The shout became a growl, turning the blood of those who heard it to ice. "I WANT MY HEEEAAAD!" it repeated, as the phantom rider increased his already breakneck speed.

Despite their determined efforts to reach their horses at the other end of the field, the two Redcoats were doomed. With one flashing sweep of his razor-sharp sword, the ghost of Charlie Miller claimed each British sniper's head. Washington and his mesmerized troops were silent spectators, watching the amazing scene unfold. Just as suddenly as it appeared, the specter vanished into the darkness and mist that shrouded the banks of the nearby Brandywine Creek.

The next day, during the famous battle, soldiers from both sides reported seeing a blue-coated, headless rider atop a white horse. But the specter was riding along the British lines—chopping off heads of the enemy troops manning the Redcoats' cannons.

After losing this important battle, Washington and his army retreated to Valley Forge. The victorious British wintered in comfort in Philadelphia. Apparently, Charlie's ghost was not through with his enemies. Although no battle was fought at Washington's winter encampment, the headless rider apparently guarded the perimeter of the camp, making sure the general was safe from any British snipers. When the spring thaw melted the heavy snows, more than three dozen headless British soldiers were discovered in the woods of Valley Forge, proof that Charlie Miller continued to take his revenge on those responsible for his death.

It's recommended that those who visit the graveyard at Welsh Tract Church near Cooch's Bridge, the historic Brandywine Battlefield, and the fields and valleys of Valley Forge National Park wear colonial blue, rather than British red—just in case the ghost of Charlie Miller is still about, planning to demonstrate his distaste for his enemies in a very permanent way.

Author's note: Welsh Tract Church is just north of Interstate 95 at the Maryland–Delaware border. Take Route 896 north; turn left (west) at Welsh Tract Road. The historic church and graveyard are on the left. On the Maryland (west) side of the church, between the two first-floor windows, is a small section of patched brickwork. This marks the site where the cannonball that decapitated the young American volunteer during the Battle of Cooch's Bridge smashed the soldier's head into the wall of the historic church.

The Walker

Thousands of acres of farmland surround the southern portion of the Maryland–Delaware border. A blindfolded person dropped off near these flat stretches would think he was in the middle of Kansas. Every few miles, large farmhouses with even bigger barns dot the landscape, indicating generations-old family operations. Surrounding the main homes are older buildings inhabited by renters and tenant workers. Many of these places are cheap, because they're off the beaten track, need a fair amount of repair, and aren't much to look at. But they offer basic conveniences, like a tight roof, running water, electric service, and, nowadays, cable connections or a satellite dish. Then there are the hard-to-rent ones that also come with a story, a very bad story. Like the weatherworn house where Darryl and his family lived with "The Walker."

It was the 1980s when the young couple with three small children agreed to rent a run-down, rustic farmhouse. The moved in the very day they did the walk-through. The owners were an elderly couple that looked like the farmers in the famous painting *American Gothic*, but more chubby and short rather than tall and thin. They informed the lookers the very reasonable amount of the monthly rent, and then they said the dirt-cheap figure also included utilities.

"Where do I sign?" Darryl asked excitedly. He said he laughed at the great deal, shook the owners' hands, and immediately started unloading his pickup. His wife, Laura, said she didn't mind the cleaning she would have to do to get the long-neglected place back into shape. She was a stay-at-home mom to two toddler boys and a ten-year-old daughter, so the minor repairs, decorating, and painting would be fun and keep her busy at home all day.

Since the couple's queen-size bed wouldn't fit up the stairs, they turned the first-floor dining room into their bedroom. "That meant we would have to take the stairs up to the one and only bathroom on the second floor. But I figured I could use the exercise," said Darryl, as he patted the small bulge above his wide leather belt.

Their stay was uneventful—for about two weeks. "Then strange things began to happen," Darryl said. Running off the eerie memories like he was reciting a shopping list, he mentioned such common incidents as doors slamming, lights flickering, shadows moving and disappearing, personal items going missing and returning an hour later, and his boys looking up at the ceiling and waving at some unseen object.

Although each parent and the older daughter had experienced something unusual, initially no one told anyone else. "We were afraid we would sound like we were nuts!" Darryl said, referring to the commonly offered excuse many people use for keeping strange experiences private for as long as they can bear. "We sort of didn't want to admit anything was happening, and by sharing it we thought it might make it come true. And if it was nothing, we didn't want to be laughed at," Darryl said. "But looking back on the situation, I wish I would have said something sooner. But that's always the case, isn't it?"

He decided he couldn't remain silent after the "corn flakes incident." "That shook me up, big time," he said, thinking back twenty years. "I can see it in my mind, clear as the picture on my big-screen TV," he added, chuckling. "I can laugh now, but it wasn't funny when it happened."

Darryl was home alone. His daughter was in school, and Laura had taken the youngsters with her shopping. As Darryl was finishing a bowl of corn flakes at the kitchen table, he heard a scraping sound coming from the cabinet near the sink. Instinctively, Darryl turned his head to look in the direction of the noise, and he stopped breathing when he saw the narrow silverware drawer sliding open. It moved about eight inches away from the front of the cabinet and stopped. It was open, with the handle just hanging out there, away from where it should have been closed. "I just stared. I didn't know what to do," Darryl recalled. "Part of me wanted to say something, another part of me wanted to run out the door. There was nobody home to show it to, and who would believe me if they came in from another room? They'd just say it was my imagination, and that I had left the thing open. So I took a few deep breaths, closed up the corn flakes, and put the milk back in the fridge. Then I went outside, worked around in the yard, and stood out near the back shed for about an hour. Then I went back in—and as I passed by the cabinet I shoved it back into place and kept walking."

Darryl said that while he was outside, he didn't know whether to hope the drawer was still open or had closed. Either way, he was afraid to look. And either way, he wouldn't be able to explain what had happened. If it was still open, the ghost did it. If it was closed, the ghost shut it. "I couldn't win either way," he said. "But that was the thing that made me decide to tell Laura what had been going on. And it was a good thing, 'cause she had stuff to share with me that she'd been keeping quiet about, too."

It was the sound of heavy footsteps that bothered Laura the most. She heard them on the old wooden floor in the second-floor hall when she was home alone with the two toddlers. For fun, she would raise her eyes and say to her children, "There goes the Walker again." And the dining room chandelier, which hung above the couple's queen-size bed, would sway in the middle of the day when no one else was around to push it. She said it was like some unseen force was shoving it extremely hard.

After their conversation, the couple began to talk a lot about the unexplained. Laura took out a batch of books on the topic from the library. Darryl began asking people at work and longtime area residents if anything strange had ever happened in the old tenant house where they lived.

"The books gave us more information than the folks did," Darryl admitted. "In back roads areas, locals don't like to talk too openly to outsiders and newcomers, like we were. So they just listened politely to my questions, nodded a bit, and then said they 'didn't know nothin' worth repeating.' I found out that was sort of a code way of saying there was something they were aware of, but they weren't about to tell me. That way they weren't actually lying. 'Cause that woulda been a sin, since most of the folks down that way being Sunday, go-to-church, religious types and all."

But other people mentioned the uncomfortable feelings they experienced while visiting the old house. A few of Darryl's work friends came over on weekends, and they would sit near the work-bench in the cellar and drink beer. Individually, they told him the hair on the backs of their necks would stand up when they got too close to a certain corner in the basement.

One of Laura's friends said she had seen a shadow moving in the upper-floor hallway, right after she had left the bathroom. Out-of-town relatives would only visit the home one time. Afterwards, they insisted on meeting the couple and their children at the motel where they were staying. One told Laura the old house "looked like it belonged in a horror movie." Another said the place "gave her the chills."

Since the price was right, and the kids weren't complaining—and Darryl and Laura decided nothing horrifying, threatening, or truly dangerous had occurred in their rented homestead—they stayed there for more than six years. But two incidents made them decide it was time to go. The first happened to Darryl; the other involved their older daughter, Mindy, who had just turned sixteen.

Since the only bathroom was upstairs, Darryl said it was necessary to make a second-floor climb to use the facilities. In the middle of one night, about three o'clock in the morning, he said he walked slowly up the narrow stairway. All the lights were off, but he knew his way so that wasn't a problem. When he reached the top and turned to his right to head down the hall, Darryl said he felt a sudden, intense pressure all around him, like he was begin pushed or pressed in from all sides. Shaken from his sleepy state and now fully awake, he thought if he could get into the bathroom and shut the door he would be safe.

Forcing his body to move against the unseen pressure, which was also getting warmer and causing him to sweat, he stumbled against the bathroom door, got inside, and slammed it shut. After he hit the light switch, he moved quickly to the sink, turned on the cold water, and began splashing it in his face.

"I felt a hundred percent better," he said, wiping a bead of sweat from his brow, as if the memory of the incident that had occurred years earlier was affecting his body temperature. "It was cool and bright and safe in there. I didn't want to go back out in the hall. But I had to pass through that horrible hallway to get back to my bed. I mean, I was just worried about me. I didn't even think about the kids, whose rooms were up there. They slept there every night. I wondered what was going on that I didn't know about. But that thought came to my mind a day or two later. At that moment in the bathroom, I just wanted to make it back downstairs where I would be safe."

After a lengthy portion of time, Darryl opened the door but left the bathroom light on and slowly placed a foot into the hallway. Nothing happened. He got about four steps away from the bathroom doorway, still a half-dozen steps from the top of the stairwell, and the threatening force returned.

"It swooped down from all sides, all at once," he said. "Like it was waiting for me, like an ambush. I was terrified, probably 'cause I knew what it felt like from before, and I didn't want to go through it again. I didn't know what to do. I got to the top of the stairs and I knew whatever evil it was, it was going to toss me down the stairs. I knew I was going to die, with a crushed spine or a broken neck. I just closed my eyes, grabbed onto both sides of the wall at the top of the stairway, raised my head, and shouted as loud as I could: "Sweet, Jesus. Please help me! Deliver me from this demon!"

Immediately, Darryl said, the hot pressure evaporated, like a tornado had sucked the life out of whatever was threatening him. He opened his eyes, raced down the stairs, jumped into bed and recited prayers of thanks to the Lord until he fell asleep. The next morning he was telling his wife the story when Mindy came into the kitchen. She had been listening in the hall. After taking a seat at the table, their daughter offered her own report on a series of unexplained and frightening experiences. The most troubling was the apparition of a high school-age girl with bulging eyes, who floated in the air above her bed. She seemed to be pressed up against the ceiling and was dressed in a long white gown. Mindy said the ghostly visitor had been in her room several times, the most recent on the previous morning about three o'clock.

"That's when I decided we were moving out, and doing it that afternoon," said Darryl. "Bad enough it was coming for me, but I didn't want whatever it was getting my kids."

They made some quick calls, arranging to stay a few nights with friends. That weekend they returned and loaded up their furniture and clothes in three or four pickups and headed to a modern apartment in a nearby town. They were done with old houses. Darryl decided the longer they were there, the greater the chance that a remnant of some tragic incident or troubling history would latch onto them or follow them when they left.

Darryl and Laura were waiting on the side porch of the farmhouse when the landlords arrived to say good-bye and return their deposit.

They thanked the renters for their prompt payments and for the repairs they had made on the property over the years.

"You stayed the longest of any of them," the old farmer said.

"Your six years is the record, way beyond the next longest," the old man's wife added with a smile and nod.

"How long was that?" Laura asked.

The elderly couple exchanged glances, and the woman said, "Eight months. Most left after about three weeks. It was a hard place to keep rented."

No one talked for a few minutes. Then the farmer stared at the younger couple and asked, "Did ya see her?"

Darryl waited a minute, breathed deeply and said, "My daughter did. Me and my wife, we only saw the shadows every now and then and we heard the footsteps. Upstairs in the hall. But my daughter said she saw a girl. Teenager in a white gown."

"That'd be her," the old farmer said. Turning to his wife, he asked, "Ain't that right, mother?"

The woman nodded grimly, and then wondered aloud, "Which room?"

"Next to the bathroom, in the back. Overlooking the cornfield. That was our daughter's room. Said a girl in a white gown was floating around the room. Happened a few times."

Nodding again, the farmer said, "That was where it all happened. Long time ago."

Darryl and Laura waited. They knew they didn't have to ask. The rest of the story would come in a minute, when the old man was ready. "She came back from a school dance. First one she ever went to. Mother here made the dress, but I guess some of the other girls made fun of her, 'cause it wasn't store bought. Children can be cruel. Our little girl, Missy we called her, she got a rope outta the barn and hung herself in the attic, just above her bedroom. The same one your girl slept in. Mindy's her name, right?"

Darryl and Laura nodded.

"To tell the truth," the farmer added, "she musta liked you folks, 'cause she didn't come out much. With the others, she was mean. She run them off real fast."

As the landlords handed over the envelope to Darryl, they explained there was a few extra hundred dollars inside to thank them for being good tenants. They said they were going to tear the house down and try to get rid of the bad memories, if that was possible. Hopefully, that would put their daughter's soul to rest and help her spirit move on.

"I rode by the place a few times after we moved out," Darryl said. "The last time, about six months had passed since we left, and it was gone. But I think there was more to that house than that girl's suicide. I don't think that's what started it all. There was stuff going on there before she killed herself."

He explained that some time after they moved away, his two boys began talking about the spiders that would crawl on the ceilings, move down the walls and get into their cribs and playpens. They also mentioned seeing an old man with a red face and horns like a goat that would sit in the corner of their playroom.

"Some people would say that's just kids' imaginations," Darryl admitted. "But after living there, and going through some of that crazy stuff, I'd bet there was more than what the landlords said. That girl wasn't the cause of the problems in there, she was just another victim. I mean, there could be an old burial ground under that place, or maybe some slaves were killed or an Indian tribe massacred somebody nearby. We'll just never know what happened before they built over that ground. Best thing is to plant soybeans or corn there. That's what I think, anyway."

George M. Reynolds Sr.

Knocking at the Door

Except for the time he served on submarines and the submarine tender USS *Beaver* in the U.S. Navy during World War II, George Reynolds has lived in Elk Mills for more than eighty years. The sleepy rural village is both a ten-minute walk and a full century removed from the heavy traffic flow traversing nearby Interstate 95.

Reynolds—a licensed Methodist minister, past president of the Archaeological Society of Maryland, Mutual UFO Network field investigator and regional director, and local historian—can relate a litany of fascinating stories of the old mill town along the Big Elk Creek. Some are historical, some hearsay, and some are from personal experience.

One story comes from the summer of 1777, during the Revolutionary War, when the British invaded Cecil County on their overland march to capture Philadelphia. That's when a local miller mixed glass into sacks of his flour, which he knew the hungry Redcoats would confiscate. And that's exactly what they did, hauling off the miller's precious food supplies without paying as much as one thin farthing. But a few days later several vengeful British soldiers returned to Elk Mills, pulled the miller from his home and hung him from a tree along the nearby creek. The invaders figured out the guilty patriot's sabotage after several Hessian mercenaries, who had eaten freshly made bread, started expelling streams of clotted blood containing slivers of made-in-America crushed glass.

Then there was the time local youngsters came upon a man's body on a gray winter afternoon. The fully clothed stranger was discovered face-up in the shallow creek, staring skyward from beneath a thick layer of ice. Finding that dead body trapped beneath the frozen surface put a damper on afterschool skating parties for a while, Reynolds said. Soon after the stiff corpse was extracted from its frozen location, the ghost of the unknown murder victim was said to haunt the rocky streambed for several decades until the story eventually died out. But one of Reynolds's most fascinating stories involved his experiences in a house—more specifically, a haunted house—where he lived and in which, he said, there were several ghosts.

For the most part, Reynolds said, his ghosts were benevolent, rather friendly, in fact; not the chain-rattling, blood-dripping sort. Still, a few times he felt the hair of the back of his neck stand up and icy chills travel up his spine. As a retired electronics technician from the Ballistic Research Laboratories of the U.S. Army's Aberdeen Proving Ground, Reynolds has a strong background in science and logic. But he has always kept an open mind regarding the possibility of unseen forces that might cause incidents that most people refer to as "the unexplained." And there were quite a few unusual, unexplained occurrences that happened while he lived in the old Simpers farmhouse on Elk Mills Road.

The building is a typical, two-story frame structure with a front porch and small attic, built sometime before 1856. There's nothing fancy, ornate, or unusual about the architecture. A small side porch leads off into the yard. Today, the building hugs the two-lane blacktop road, located near an entrance to a busy quarry. Years ago, the house must have been farther removed from traffic, when the passing roadway leading down to the creek, mills, and center of the village was narrow and made of dirt.

Reynolds moved into the vacant home in 1985. It was in late October, during the Halloween season. The previous owner, named Hanna, died at the age of eighty-six after lying on a couch for three years in a small room located off the kitchen. A bachelor at the time, Reynolds set up a sofa bed in a small room where he was only about twelve feet from the back door. A short time after Reynolds settled into his new home, something began waking him up four or five nights a week around 3 A.M. "It sounded like someone scuffling along the floor with bedroom slippers on, in the kitchen," Reynolds said. "After a while, it got annoying, something waking you up in the middle of the night. And I started creeping to the kitchen with a flashlight, turning it on, looking all around, but no one was there. I couldn't find anything."

After the disturbances continued for a lengthy period of time, Reynolds became frustrated. One night, he said he was so bothered that he went into the kitchen and began talking to what he thought had to be an annoying ghost. "I said, 'Hanna! What's wrong with you? I've known you since I was a little child. And I'm a Christian like you are. And I bought your house and I'm going to try to rebuild it. And here you are, keeping me up every night. Now, for God's sake, leave me alone!' And there I was in the dark, talking to Hanna," Reynolds recalled, laughing. "And after that, the noise, it got less and less. And after three or four months the footsteps finally disappeared."

Apparently, Reynolds wasn't the only person to experience strange incidents at the old Simpers farmhouse. About twelve years before he bought the empty house, a couple had purchased a property adjacent to the Simpers spread. Because it was going to take some time to build their new home, the couple and their children made arrangements to rent the Simpers farmhouse and live there until their dream home was finished. They would be close to the construction, be able to keep an eye on their building materials, and send their children to the same school they would attend when their new home was completed. They stayed in the old house two nights.

During the first night, everyone in the family felt something just wasn't right about the place. In a story in the *Rising Sun Herald*, the father said, "There was a presence in the house someplace. I mean, it wasn't right."

"On the second night, the parents were in the upstairs bedroom," said Reynolds, "and they said they could feel a strong presence, bending down over them. They were holding onto each other when their three children came running into the room, yelling 'Mommy! Mommy! There's somebody in the room with us.' And it all happened to all of them at about the same time."

That family moved out and lived elsewhere until their home was built. When they moved into the new house, the wife said Hanna would walk over and pay her visits. Frequently, the older woman would talk about the pounding on her door and sudden loud sounds waking her up at three in the morning. "Old Hanna was scared herself," the husband told the *Rising Sun Herald*. "She called me a million nights. This is going on, and that's going on—and there would be nothing going on."

Reynolds said several neighbors knew about the ghostly happenings, but no one bothered to tell him about the terrified family's encounter and other stories until after he had moved in. He later learned that Hanna had told a fair number of her friends about hearing strange sounds, specifically loud knockings on the door at 3 A.M. One of Hanna's nephews, who lived nearby, said he knew about his aunt's noisy disturbances. She told him about the pounding on the door, and when she went to investigate there was no one to be found. Neighbors and family members who responded to Hanna's pleas for help never found anyone either. They all assumed it was the work of local youths who had decided to annoy the elderly woman—or her imagination.

But the same pounding incidents happened to Reynolds. "Whatever it was would be beating on the door, three and four times a week," he said. "When I got up and got dressed and opened the door, no one was ever there. I was getting to the point of losing my religion." The last time Reynolds heard the knocking was on the night before Easter in 1987. It was cold and snowing, and he had just arrived back home from a church service. "But this night," he remembered, "the monster was ignorant. And it just wouldn't stop. It was a constant rapping, loud. I got to the door, pulled it open, and then I went outside with my flashlight and checked for footprints in the snow. Nothing. There was no physical evidence that anything was there. Then I sassed the thing, preaching a sort of spontaneous, anti-demonic sermon, and that was the last I heard of it."

At least that's what he thought at the time. A few months later, Reynolds returned home from a shopping trip with a friend. He placed his groceries on the kitchen table. His friend was standing within two feet of the door when the loud, obnoxious knocking occurred. The friend quickly opened the door and found no one there. Reynolds jumped up and exclaimed, "Oh, my God, the thing's back. It's back again. My Lord, what's the matter with that monster? I got rid of it once."

When the two men closed the door and returned to the kitchen, the annoying and unexplained pounding resumed. Losing his patience, Reynolds went outside and confronted the unseen nuisance. "I preached it another demonic service," he said. "I called it ugly names, and told it to get away and leave me alone." Apparently, the fire-and-brimstone lecture accomplished its purpose, but that wasn't the end of Reynolds's supernatural encounters.

Reynolds experienced a different type of incident in the front hallway of the house, just inside the door at the foot of the stairs. He was doing some work, moving a mattress and singing an Easter hymn, "Christ Has Risen," to make the furniture lifting seem easier. "When I leaned over," he said, "all of the sudden I felt all the hair on my body stand up. I felt a presence was glaring right at me. I felt cold all over. I could tell right where it was coming from—at the top of the steps on the landing. I felt like there were these two big red eyes peering down on me. It was a demonic experience, probably caused by the religious song I had been singing. But when I looked up, there wasn't anything there. And that was the only time I ever was scared."

Later Reynolds carried the mattress to his couch in the old parlor and worked on other projects. He recalled that Hanna's brother, Curley, had died in the house, so he went back into the entry hallway, looked up the stairs and shouted, "Curley, I'm going to bed. I'm shutting the door. Leave me alone." Reynolds said the threatening feeling never occurred again. "That was the end of it, and the only time I felt that uneasy in that house."

On Christmas night in 1987, Reynolds arrived home from a party. As soon as he went into his first-floor bedroom and placed his head on a pillow, he heard music. It was about midnight, and he initially thought it might be from a passing car. But it was loud and constant. When he stepped into the hallway, he discovered the sounds were coming from the second floor. "Blaring wide open, at the top of its volume," said Reynolds, "was an old clock radio, that I had never had set or used for anything up there but a clock." Reynolds couldn't figure out why the radio had been turned on or who could have played with the alarm. With no explanation for the sudden activation of the appliance, Reynolds pulled the plug from the wall and shouted to Curley to leave the radio alone, because Reynolds had experienced a long Christmas Day and was going to bed. The next day, Reynolds ran into one of Hanna's relatives and he told the story of the clock radio. The man told Reynolds that the perpetrator of the mysterious Christmas night disturbance wasn't Curley, but more probably Winfield.

Recalling the conversation, Reynolds said, "I asked, 'Who is Winfield?' And the man replied, 'Uncle Winfield was a brother, and he died up there, too. And the reason the radio was on is because Christmas was Uncle Winfield's birthday. So that's why he came back.'"

Some time later, Reynolds found the previous owner's family tree in the old house. It indicated Winfield had been born on December 25, 1901, and had died on November 19, 1961.

One of Reynolds's overnight guests had an unusual experience while staying in the old Elk Mills farmhouse. Mike, Reynolds's friend, had stopped by to pick up Reynolds for their drive to an amateur radio convention in Atlanta. The two men had planned to get on the road early the following morning. After spending a restless night in the second-floor bedroom where the radio incidents had occurred, Mike mentioned at breakfast that his bed had been torn up during the night, with blankets and pillows tossed all over the floor. He told his host that "something was in that room" with him, and that he swore he heard voices during the night. "He said," Reynolds recalled, "that he would never sleep in that house again."

Reynolds said his daughter heard a similar comment from the man whose family had experienced frightening events in the old house a few years earlier. "My daughter," Reynolds said, "tried to get him to tell her of his ghost experience. She said the man replied, 'All I will say is, I wouldn't stay in that house one night, even if you gave it to me.'"

Ghostly incidents fell off dramatically after that, said Reynolds. There were no more sightings, no noises or disturbances. Things died down to a minimum. "The guy quit knocking. Hanna quit stomping. I didn't feel any more threatening presences, and Winfield didn't turn on the radio," Reynolds said.

After doing research for a lecture he was scheduled to give at the local library, Reynolds came across a theory that states visits by some spirits are related to seasonal events. As a result of that discovery, he said his senses were a bit keener during certain times of the year, particularly around Winfield's birthday. But nothing dramatic ever occurred.

In 1990, Reynolds subdivided the property, and he built a new house on a plot directly behind the old Simpers farmhouse. Making sure to cover all contingencies, when Reynolds put the farmhouse on the market he figured everyone in the area knew about—or the new buyer would eventually find out about—the home's eerie reputation. Therefore, Reynolds inserted a unique clause in the sales contract, informing potential buyers they were buying the house "as is, with all contents," an apparent reference to Hannah, Curley, and Winfield.

The home eventually sold and Reynolds hasn't heard of any reports by subsequent owners about strange sightings, knocking doors, or bumps in the night. But, unlike Reynolds, folks tend to downplay unexplained events and keep such strange stories to themselves.

While reflecting on his years living in what some consider a haunted house, Reynolds said people would often ask him if he believes in ghosts. Without hesitation, he said, "I told them that I've tried to keep an open mind on the subject. I really believe there's something to this. But I can't put a label on it. I guess I'd have to say, if there's such a thing as ghosts, while I lived in that house, I met a few."

Selected Bibliography

Books, Documents, and Film

Anderson, Elizabeth B. *Annapolis: A Walk Through History*. Centreville, MD: Tidewater Publishers, 1984.

Botkin, B. A. *A Civil War Treasury of Tales, Legends, and Folklore*. New York: Promontory Press, 1993.

Brown, Stephen D. *Haunted Houses of Harpers Ferry*. n.p., Little Brown House, 1976.

Brugger, Robert J. *Maryland: A Middle Temperament, 1634–1980*. Baltimore: Johns Hopkins University Press, 1988.

Byron, Gilbert. *St. Michaels: The Town That Fooled The British*. St. Michaels, MD: St. Mary's Square Museum, 1985.

Cannon, Timothy L., and Nancy F. Whitmore. *Ghosts and Legends of Frederick County*. Frederick County, MD: s.p., 1979.

Carey, George C. *Maryland Folklore*. Centreville, MD: Tidewater Publishers, 1989.

Cockey, Genevieve, and John Stanley. *Selected Ghost Stories, Legends and Folklore of the Elkton, Maryland, Area*. Elkton, MD: Cecil County Historical Society, 1999.

Dahlgren, Madeleine Vinton. *South Mountain Magic: Tales of Old Maryland*. Maple Shade, NJ: Lethe Press, 2002.

Flowers, Thomas A. *Shore Folklore: Growing Up with Ghosts 'n Legends, 'n Tales, 'n Home Remedies*. Easton, MD: Economy Printing, 1989.

Force, Peter. *A Documentary History of the English Colonies in North America, from The King's Message to Parliament, of March 7, 1774 to The Declaration of Independence by The United States*. Washington: M. St. Clair Clark and Peter Force, 1839.

Hammond, John Martin. *Colonial Mansions of Maryland and Delaware*. Philadelphia: J. B. Lippincott, 1914.

Hauck, Dennis William. *The National Directory of Haunted Places*. New York: Penguin Books, 1996.

Haunted History: Haunted Baltimore. New York: A&E Television Networks, 2000.

Jackson, Elmer M., Jr. *Annapolis: Three Centuries of Glamour*. Annapolis, MD: Capital-Gazette Press, 1936.

Johnston, George. *History of Cecil County, Maryland*. Baltimore: Genealogical Publishing, 1989.

Lake, Matt. *Weird Maryland*. New York: Sterling Publishing, 2006.

Legends of St. Mary's: A Collection of Haunts, Witches and Other Strange Occurrences. Leonardtown, MD: St. Mary's County Historical Society, n.d.

McAllister, Elizabeth, and Anne Turkos. *Ghost Tour*. College Park, MD: University of Maryland, October 13, 2006.

McAllister, Elizabeth, and Jennie Levine. *Mysterious Maryland: The Strange and Supernatural on Campus and Beyond*. Exhibit in the Maryland Room Gallery, Hornbake Library, University of Maryland, College Park, MD: September–December 2007.

Merriam, Anne Van Ness. *The Ghosts of Hampton*. Towson, MD: Orangerie and Gift Shop Committee of Historic Hampton, 1985.

Moose, Katie. *Annapolis: The Guide Book*. Annapolis, MD: Conduit Press, 2001.

Mumma, Walter McKendree. *Ghosts of Antietam*, Sharpsburg, MD: s.p.,1977.

Norman, Michael, and Beth Scott. *Haunted Heritage*. New York: Forge Books, 2002.

Okonowicz, Ed. *Annapolis Ghosts: History, Mystery, Legends and Lore*. Elkton, MD: Myst and Lace Publishers, 2007.

———. *Baltimore Ghosts: History, Mystery, Legends and Lore*. Elkton, MD: Myst and Lace Publishers, 2004.

———. *Crying in the Kitchen*. Elkton, MD: Myst and Lace Publishers, 1998.

———. *Haunted Maryland*. Mechanicsburg, PA: Stackpole Books, 2003.

———. *Horror in the Hallway*. Elkton, MD: Myst and Lace Publishers, 1999.

———. *In the Vestibule*. Elkton, MD: Myst and Lace Publishers, 1996.

———. *Opening the Door*. Elkton, MD: Myst and Lace Publishers, 1995.

———. *Phantom in the Bedchamber*. Elkton, MD: Myst and Lace Publishers, 2000.

———. *Possessed Possessions 2: More Haunted Antiques, Furniture and Collectibles*. Elkton, MD: Myst and Lace Publishers, 1998.

———. *Presence in the Parlor*. Elkton, MD: Myst and Lace Publishers, 1997.

———. *Pulling Back the Curtain*. Elkton, MD: Myst and Lace Publishers, 1994.

———. *Terrifying Tales 2 of the Beaches and Bays*. Elkton, MD: Myst and Lace Publishers, 2001.

———. *Up the Back Stairway*. Elkton, MD: Myst and Lace Publishers, 1999.

Papenfuse, Edward C., Gregory A. Stiverson, Susan A. Collins, and Lois Green Carr, eds. *Maryland: A New Guide to the Old Line State*. Baltimore: Johns Hopkins University Press, 1976.

Riley, Elihu S. *The Ancient City, a History of Annapolis, in Maryland, 1649–1887.* Annapolis, MD: Record Printing Office, 1887.

Scarborough, Katherine. *Homes of the Cavaliers.* Centreville, MD: Cornell Maritime Press/Tidewater Publishers, 1969.

Scott, Harold L., Sr. *Legends of Allegany County.* Cumberland, MD: H. L. Scott Sr., 1994.

Strain, Paula. *Tales of Mountain Maryland.* New York: iUniverse, 2005.

Stump, Brice. *A Visit With the Past: Legend and Lore of Dorchester County.* s.p., 1968.

Taylor, Troy. *The Haunting of America: Ghosts and Legends from America's Past.* Alton, IL: Whitechapel Productions, 2001.

Trapani, Bob, Jr. *Lighthouses of Maryland and Virginia: History, Mystery, Legends and Lore.* Elkton, MD: Myst and Lace Publishers, 2006.

Weinberg, Alyce T. *Spirits of Frederick.* Braddock Heights, MD: s.p., 1992.

Weller, Bob. *Prince George's Bounty.* Upper Marlboro, MD: Queen Anne School, 1984.

Wiley, Flora H. *Harford Ghosts.* s.p., 1985.

Wright, C. Milton. *Our Harford Heritage: A History of Harford County, Maryland.* s.p., 1967.

Selected Interviews

Andrew, Louis C., Caroline County Detention Center

Browning, Ron, La Cle D'or Guesthouse

Currier, Jane, Currier House

Dixon, Michael, Historical Society of Cecil County

Evans, Jennings, Smith Island Museum

Hammett, Donnie, Point Lookout State Park

Hook, Kevin, Point Lookout State Park

Jerome, Jeff, Edgar Allan Poe House and Museum

Lively, Carter C., Hammond-Harwood House

McAllister, Elizabeth, Hornbake Library, University of Maryland

Nemeth, Carol, Spencer-Silver Mansion

O'Brien, Lynn, Brice House

Pearl, Susan, Historical Society of Prince George's County

Reid, Beau, Druid Ridge Cemetery

Reynolds, George, Cecil County historian

Schatz, Mark, Ann Arrundell Historical Society Inc.

Schaumburg, Wayne, Green Mount Cemetery

Sheads, Scott, Fort McHenry National Monument and Historic Shrine

Tucker, John, Atlantic Book Warehouse

Vaise, Vincent, Fort McHenry National Monument and Historic Shrine

Verge, Laurie, Surratt House Museum

Williams, Leslie Harper, Kent Manor Inn

Wilson, Vince, Baltimore Society for Paranormal Research

Newspaper and Magazine Articles

Alexander, Sandy. "Eerie Tales—Based On Facts," *Baltimore Sun*, October 30, 2003.

Alvarez, Rafael. "Oh, Say, Can You See Ghosts At Fort?" *Baltimore Sun*, October 31, 1996.

Anne Arundel Times, "Ghosts (Civil War Nurses?) Haunt St. J. Dormitory," n.d.

Arcieri, Katie. "Parole Development Rising from the Dirt: Construction on Area's First Target Begins." *The Capital*, February 11, 2007.

Associated Press, "Maryland Courthouse Employees Hunt Ghost in Kent County," August 7, 2004.

Bache, Ellyn. "Baby-Sitting Ghosts." *The Sun Magazine*, October 31, 1982.

Baker, Kimball. "From Maryland's Past: Ten Paces to Death." *Maryland*, Winter 1982.

Baltimore American, "Ghostly 'Blue Dog' Still Wags Legend," September 9, 1962.

Baltimore News-American, "Favorite Haunts In Frederick County," November 2, 1975.

Baltimore Sun, "Maryland Superstitions: Sign of a Crowing Hen—Bad Luck to Move Parsley," May 1898.

Birchfield, Jim. "Ghost of Dent's Place." *Sunday Star Magazine*, February 21, 1960.

Blake, Allison. "Ghosts Give 'Living History' New Meaning." *The Capital*, November 1998.

Bragdon, Julie. "The Unseen Presence: Ghosts In Annapolis." *Annapolis Magazine*, October 1984.

Briscoe, Betty. "Know Your County." *Calvert Independent*, March 23, 1979.

———. "Know Your County: Ghost Story Near Prince Frederick." *Calvert Independent*, December 3, 1975.

———. "Know Your County: As It May." *Calvert Independent*, November 12, 1975.

Browning, Ron. "Be Safe Around the Ghosts, Goblins." *The Record*, October 29, 2004.

Burdett, Hal. "Brice House Ghost Stories." *Evening Capital*, n.d.

Burnes, Brian. "Spirits That Go Flat In the Night." *Prince George's Post*, October 28, 1976.

Carman, James. "GHOST Stories." *National Parks*, September/October 1986.

Challmes, Joseph J., and Tom Horton. "Marylanders Compile Rich Legacy of Ghostly Tales and Legendary Lore." *Baltimore Sun*, October 31, 1972.

Chappell, Helen. "Ghosts of the Eastern Shore."

Chronicles of St. Mary's (Monthly Bulletin of the St. Mary's County Historical Society). "How the Cavalier George Beckwith Returned to His Home from Over the Sea," July 1966.

Colimore, Edward. "Ghostly Visits Enliven North Point House." *Baltimore News-American*, August 11, 1976.
———. "Teacher's Home A Ghost's Castle?" *Baltimore News-American*, June 8, 1976.
Colley, David. "Nightfall Livens Two Homes." *Evening Sun*, October 31, 1968.
Collins, Nancy Bromley. "Share Spooky Stories." *Maryland Independent*, October 27, 1995.
Conboy, Don, and Marian Conboy. "Baltimore's Spookiest Ghost Stories." *Baltimore Magazine*, October 1979.
Cushwa, Patricia. "Spooky Myths." *Hagerstown Cracker Barrel*, October 1976.
DeSocio, Charles. "Talking To the Spirits." *Rising Sun Herald*, October 21, 1992.
Dowd, Maureen. "The Ghosts of Montgomery." *Washington Star*, October 31, 1977.
Duke, Jacqueline. "Historic Haunting Ground." *The Capital*, October 30, 1982.
DuPont, Dale. "In Prince George's, a Haunted Hideout." *The Sentinel*, October 20, 1975.
Emanuel, David. "Glenn Dale Hospital Rich In History, Ripe With Legend." *Bowie Blade News*, October 26, 2000.
The Enterprise, "Ghosts from St. Mary's Past: Tom White & The Devil's Ball Yard," October 31, 1979.
Erlandson, Robert A. "'Ghost Writer' Collects History That Chills Bones." *The Sun*, February 20, 1992.
Ernst, Ora Ann. "'Poltergeist' Nothing New for Washington County." *Daily Mail*, June 16, 1982.
Evening Capital, "Celebrated Brice House Ghosts Now Believed Gone: New Owners Haven't Seen Single One," October 31, 1957.
Farley, G. M. "The Weird Legend of Williamsport's Veiled Lady." *Hagerstown Cracker Barrel*, January 1972.
Frank, Pat. "'Are You Ready Gentlemen?' Code Ruled In Fighting Of Duels." *Washington Herald*, January 22, 1934.
———. "'Are You Ready Gentlemen?' Congressmen Meet On Field Of Honor Over a Trifle." *Washington Herald*, January 29, 1934.
Gallagher, Lynda. "House and Garden Tour Features Local Haunts." *Calvert Independent*, April 18, 1990.
Gardner, Bonnie. "Seeing Isn't Always Believing: Homeowner Recalls Ghostly Visit." *Calvert Independent*, July 13, 1983.
Gay, Lance. "Is Oxon Hill Grave His? New Battle on John Hanson." *Washington Star*, April 20, 1971.
"Ghost Story." Vertical File, College of Southern Maryland..
Ginn, Molly, Jon Ginn, Kristi Ginn, Kerri Ginn, and Porter Ginn. "Gross Coate Plantation 1658," s.p.
Glass, Jesse Jr. "The Silver Mine," *Carroll County Times*, October 31, 1984.
Gostomski, Christina. "Old 'Spooks Hill' Rumors Not Much More than Talk," *Weekly Record*, June 29, 1993.

Gottlieb, Robin. "Do Ghosts Haunt All Saints Parish? Some Parishioners Believe They Do," *The Calvert Recorder*, November 2, 2001.

Historical Society of Harford County. "The House That Booth Built, A Revisit: Harford County's Tudor Hall," *Harford Historical Bulletin*, Winter 1997.

Heavey, Bill. "The Ghosts of Antietam: Past and Present Collide On One of the Civil War's Bloodiest Battlefields," *Washington Post*, February 11, 1998.

Hubbard, Louise. "The Poker Game Lasted 40 Years." *Washington Post*, January 24, 1959.

Humphrey, Theresa. "Legends of Suicide Bridge Lend Mystery to Area in Dorchester," *Baltimore Evening Sun*, January 21, 1985.

Hunt, J. William. "Across The Desk," *Cumberland Sunday Times*, March 17, 1957.

———. "Across The Desk," *Cumberland Sunday Times*, December 26, 1965.

———. "Across The Desk," *Cumberland Sunday Times*, February 11, 1968.

Julius, Erin. "Reporter Haunts Pry House," *The Herald-Mail*, October 28, 2007.

Kaltenbach, Chris. "Shades of History," *The Sun*, October 28, 1999.

Kobler, John. "Was John Hanson Our First President?" *Saturday Evening Post*, June 1957.

Koehler, Charles, and Margaret Koehler. "Politic and Pistols At Bladensburg," *The Star Magazine*, July 31, 1990.

Kumpa, Peter. "John Hanson: The Forgotten 'First President' From Maryland," *Baltimore Evening Sun*, April 6, 1983.

Manger, Dyan. "Ghosts Haunt Annapolis," *Annapolitan*, October 1973.

Martin, Bill. "In Montgomery County, a Poltergeist With Style and a Night Visitor," *The Sentinel*, October 29, 1975.

Martin, Katie. "Tour Stakes Out Spots with Spooky Legends," *The Sun*, October 30, 2005.

Mellin, John. "Who Says Parole Was Prison Camp?" *The Capital*, February 8, 1990.

Meyer, Eugene L. "House That Booth Built Has Friendly Ghost," *Washington Post*, January 10, 1980.

Mezensky, Catherine. "Monumentally Speaking, Black Aggie Baltimore's Most Mysterious Statue," *The Urbanite Magazine*, February 2001.

Michael, J. L. "Rose Hill and Blue Dog Ghost to Change Hands," *The Star*, February 8, 1955.

Minnich, Dean. "Carroll County Farmhouse is 'Spirited,'" *Baltimore News-American*, August 29, 1976.

Mohsberg, Margot. "An Inn With Spirit," *The Capital*, June 3, 2001.

Montgomery, David. "On the Hunt For Haunts," *Washington Post*, October 28, 1993.

New York Times, "A Historic Old Town: Bladensburg Near Washington, Famous As a Battle Ground," July 30, 1893.

Norris, Joseph. "The Hills of Halloween," *The Enterprise*, October 28, 1976.
———. "The Hills of Halloween," *The Enterprise*, October 18, 1981.
———. "More Ghost Stories from St. Mary's County," *The Enterprise*, October 26, 1977.
———. "Weird Occurrences At Point Lookout," *The Enterprise*, October 29, 1980.
Oakey, Jane, and Terry King. "Do Spooks Feel The Cold In Annapolis? Ghost House Undergoes Renovation," *Anne Arundel Times*, February 15, 1979.
Okonowicz, Ed. "Md. Man Is Successful Ghostbuster," *Wilmington News-Journal*, October 1990.
Oman, Anne H. "Where Eighteenth Century Is Like Yesterday," *Washington Post*, August 18, 1978.
Osborne, Audrey. "Get To Know the Legends & Tales of Calvert County," *Calvert Independent*, October 25, 1995.
"Parole, Former Civil War Troop Encampment Site and Racetrack."
Peniston, Bradley. "Local Haunts, Guided Ghost Tours Unearth Annapolis' Haunted History," *Sunday Capital*, October 23, 1994.
Perry, Jodi. "County's Haunted Hallways," *The Gazette*, October 30, 1991.
———. "Historical Hauntings in Montgomery County," *The Gazette*, October 20, 1995.
Pugh, Dorothy. "Ghost Stories of Montgomery County," *Montgomery County Historical Society Bulletin*, November 1988.
Pugh, Dorothy, and Karen Yaffe Lottes. "Be Aware of the Tommyknocker—and Beware!" *The Gazette*, n.d.
The Publick Enterprise, "Get Spooked!—Halloween Is a Great Time to Meet the Ghosts of Annapolis," October 1994.
Py, Ray. "Hillish Haunts," *The Sentinel*, October 26, 1989.
Rasmussen, Frederick N. "Emmitsburg's Musical Ghost," *Baltimore Sun*, October 27, 2001.
Reppert, Ralph. "Parole, Maryland."
The Sentinel, "County's Mansions Attract Well-Sheeted, Non-Chain Ghosts," July 26, 1956.
The Sentinel, "A Haunted Bridge," March 17, 1896.
Simmons, Melody. "Alleged Ghost Spooks Workers at Courthouse," *Evening Sun*, October 31, 1980.
Sutton, David. "Looking for Ghosts at Montanverde," *The Gazette*, October 30, 1991.
Sword, Gerry. "Is It Haunted? Committee Hears Ghosts," *The Enterprise*, September 17, 1980.
Sykes, Shelley. "Things That Go Bump in Carroll County," *Carroll Magazine*, October–November 2005.
"The Curtis Creek Furnace and Iron Works," Ann Arrundell County Historical Society document.
Warr, Bonnie. "Myth and Mystery Of Old Homes," *Towson Times*, October 30, 1969.

Waters, Sarah. "The Otherworldly Side of St. John's," student paper by 1988 graduate provided by St. John's College Communications Office.

Webb, Vanessa. "Close Encounters With the Unknown," *Daily Grind*, October 31, 1997.

Weeks, Linton. "Be True to Your Ghoul," *Washington Post*, October 30, 2002.

White, Michael. "Haunted Neighborhood?" *Cecil Whig*, May 22, 2002.

White, Tom. "Spotlight: Only a Ghost Of a Chance," *Baltimore News-Post*, February 6, 1959.

Wilfong, James C. "Historically Speaking: Salubria," *Prince George's Post*, April 24, 1969.

———. "Of Historic Interest: These Family Cemeteries," *The News Leader*, October 16, 1965.

Wilson, Becky. "The Whistler—and the Wayward Elevator," *Diversions: The Wide World of Other*, November 1982.

Woods, Amber. "Haunted: A Tour of HDG," *The Record*, October 13, 2006.

Wooten, Orlando V. "Bloody Tales of Murder and Piracy Cloak Mystery of Old Cellar House," *Salisbury Daily Times*, October 13, 1966.

Selected Online Sources

http://www.angelfire.com/scary/marylandhauntings/
http://www.associatedcontent.com/article/421469/the_local_folklore_and _legends_of_6.html?cat=37
http://bsprnet.com/
http://funkmasterj.tripod.com/mdf.htm
http://www.greater-maryland-paranormal-society.com/
http://www.msa.md.gov/msa/homepage/html/homepage.html
http://www.prairieghosts.com/hauntmd.html
http://theshadowlands.net/places/maryland.htm

Adams Rib's Restaurant
http://www.paranormalinvestigators.com/Adams/Adams_report_additional.htm

Antietam National Battlefield
http://www.nps.gov/anti/index.htm
http://www.nationalparktraveler.com/2007/10/haunted-house-antietam-national-battlefield
http://www.herald-mail.com/?cmd=displaystory &story_id=177840 &format=print

Barbara Fritchie
http://query.nytimes.com/mem/archive-free/pdf?_r=2&res=9406EEDF1539E43BBC4E51DFB266838E669FDE

Black Aggie
http://www.baltimoremd.com/content/blackaggie.html
http://www.prairieghosts.com/druidridge.html

Bladensburg Dueling Grounds
http://www.hmdb.org/marker.asp?marker=8177
http://www.prairieghosts.com/bladensburg.html
http://query.nytimes.com/gst/abstract.html?res=9807E0D9143EEF33A2575
3C3A9619C94629ED7CF

Blue Dog Ghost
http://en.wikipedia.org/wiki/Port_Tobacco_Village,_Maryland

Braddock Treasure
http://www.hmdb.org/results.asp?SearchFor=Braddock
http://www.post-gazette.com/pg/05167/522060.stm

Brice House
http://www.annapolis.org/
http://www.bsos.umd.edu/anth/aia/james_brice_house.htm

Carroll County
http://www.carrollcountytourism.org/PDFs/Ghost-Walk-Brochure-2009.pdf

Cellar House
http://www.cellarhouse.com/
http://www.cellarhouse.com/articles.htm

Club Charles
http://lostcitydiner.com/ghosts.htm

Cyprus Swamp Monster/Wampus Cat/Snarly Yow
http://www.bigfootforums.com/index.php?showtopic=10801
http://www.dnr.state.md.us/naturalresource/spring2005/parkticulars.asp
http://www.essortment.com/all/wampuscat_rvmr.htm
http://wesclark.com/jw/s_yow.html

Deer Creek/Rocks State Park
http://books.google.com/books?id=8JhHAAAAIAAJ&dq=Rocks+of+Deer+Creek+wysong&printsec=frontcover&source=bl&ots=hAhfrVZqly&sig=VTg5JarTcxeQk_rhphIpgz6jVpk&hl=en&sa=X&oi=book_result&resnum=1&ct=result#v=onepage&q=&f=false

Ellicott City Ghosts
http://www.ellicottcity.net/tourism/attractions/patapsco_female_institute/

Emmitsburg Fiddler
http://www.emmitsburg.net/archive_list/articles/history/stories/chris-mas_legends.htm

Fells Point
http://www.baltimorestories.com/main.cfm?nid=2&tid=59
http://www.fellspointghost.com/
http://www.gadling.com/2009/12/21/at-fells-point-maryland-ghosts-reside-year-round/

Fort McHenry National Monument and Historic Shrine
http://www.nps.gov/FOMC/index.htm
http://www.examiner.com/x-29424-Baltimore-Hauntings—Paranormal-Examiner~y2009m11d10-The-ghost-of-Levi-Clagett-at-Fort-McHenry

Fort Washington State Park
http://www.stateparks.com/fort_washington.html

Frederick Ghosts
http://www.suite101.com/article.cfm/civil_war_ghosts/85654

Furnace Creek Slave
http://www.heritage.uMDedu/CHRSWeb/AssociatedProjects/chidesterre-port/Chapter%20VI.htm

Glenn Dale Hospital
http://www.opacity.us/gallery57_vines.htm
http://www.waymarking.com/waymarks/WM54D

Governor's Bridge
http://www.realhaunts.com/united-states/governors-bridge/
http://www.snopes.com/horrors/madmen/hook.asp
http://en.wikipedia.org/wiki/Goatman_(cryptozoology)

Green Mount Cemetery
http://www.greenmountcemetery.com/index.html

Hammond-Harwood House
http://www.hammondharwoodhouse.org/

Hampton National Historic Site
http://www.nps.gov/hamp/index.htm

Havre de Grace Inns
http://www.spencersilvermansion.com/
http://www.lacledorguesthouse.com/
http://www.currier-bb.com/

Hell House
http://hellhouse.ellicottcity.net/press_cuttings/#Firedamageshistoricsem-
    inaryinIlchester

Jericho Bridge
http://www.dnr.state.MDus/publiclands/jerusalemhistory.html
http://jerusalemmill.org/bridge.html

Kunte Kinte Monument
http://www.annapolis.gov/info.asp?page=1717
http://www.kuntakinte.com/memorialelements.html#wall
http://www.mdslavery.net/

Lovers Leap
http://www.qufriary.org/Hoebing/lleap.html

Maidstone
http://www.calvert-county.com/maidston.htm

Mount Airy Plantation
http://www.prairieghosts.com/mtairy.html

Mount Savage
http://www.rootsweb.ancestry.com/~mdallegh/MtSavage.htm

Oaklands
http://www.prairieghosts.com/oaklands.html

Parole
http://www.bayweekly.com/year04/issuexii18/leadxii18.html
http://www.cem.va.gov/pdf/Annap.pdf
http://www.civilwararchive.com/Unreghst/unnyinf5.htm#53re
http://www.pa-roots.com/~pacw/campparole.html

Patty Cannon
http://books.google.com/books?id=d8wOAAAAIAAJ&pg=PA524&lpg=PA524
    &dq=Patty+Cannon&source=bl&ots=IdH-U4wao6&sig=wOXGV-
    VQXUsBaZSSxqcwUbv2dsA&hl=en&ei=6LKrSpegN83jlAfx3-
    W7Bg&sa=X&oi=book_result&ct=result&resnum=5#v=onepage&q=Patty
    %20Cannon&f=false
http://www.globalclassroom.org/jane.html
http://www.ket.org/tvschedules/episode.php?&cd=1&nola=HIDE++000104
    #details
http://www.prairieghosts.com/patty.html
http://www.unsolvedmysteries.com/usm397105.html

Phantom Black Dogs
http://www.mysteriousbritain.co.uk/folklore/black_dogs.html

Poe House and Museum
http://www.ci.baltimore.md.us/government/historic/poehouse.php

Point Lookout Lighthouse
http://www.bayweekly.com/year00/issue8_42/lead8_42.html
http://www.ptlookoutlighthouse.com/
http://somdthisisliving.somd.com/vol6num3/point_lookout.html

Rosaryville State Park
http://www.dnr.state.md.us/publiclands/southern/rosaryville.html

St. John's College
http://www.examiner.com/x-2363-UFO-Examiner~y2010m3d24-Blue-
translucent-discs-captured-on-camera-over-Annapolis-MD
http://www.stjohnscollege.edu/asp/home.aspx

Sampson Hat
http://www.carfaxabbey.net/spheres/features/1800.sampsonhat/
http://www.prairieghosts.com/furnace.html

Spook Hill
http://www.dnr.state.MDus/publiclands/spookyparks.html
http://www.roadsideamerica.com/tips/getAttraction.php3?tip_Attrac-
tionNo==600,

Suicide Bridge
http://www.suicidebridge.com/legend.html

Surratt House Museum
http://www.surratt.org/

Todd's Inheritance
http://www.myedgemere.com/todd's_history.htm

Tudor Hall
http://www.harfordhistory.net/Booths.htm
http://www.harfordhistory.net/th.htm
http://www.surratt.org/su_tudor.html

University of Maryland/Mysterious Maryland
http://www.newsdesk.umd.edu/undergradexp/release.cfm?ArticleID=1513
http://wikimapia.org/35565/University-of-Maryland-College-Park

Westminster Hall/Burying Ground
http://thecabinet.com/darkdestinations/location.php?sub_id=dark_desti-
    nations&letter=o&location_id=old_westminster_burial_ground
http://www.westminsterhall.org/

Wise's Well
http://www.cmhl.org/fox.html
http://www.cmhl.org/wise.html

Zodiac Restaurant
http://baltimoresnacker.blogspot.com/2006/10/zodiac.html

Acknowledgments

I'd like to thank Kyle Weaver for inviting me to write this book. This is my third project with him and his company. The experience has been very satisfying. I also appreciate the excellent work of production editor Brett Keener, whose review and suggestions added significantly to the content and final outcome of this project. This book involved significant document research and a fair number of personal interviews. For their assistance in offering research, materials, personal sessions, or other information, I appreciate the help of: Patricia Anderson, Montgomery County Historical Society; Louis C. Andrew, Caroline County Detention Center; Penny Chandler, Nottingham, MD; Mike Dixon, Historical Society of Cecil County; Molly Ginn, Gross' Coate; John Lewis Graham, Cellar House; Donnie Hammett and Kevin Hook, Point Lookout State Park; Mike Hillman, Emmitsburg Area Historical Society; Jeff Jerome, Edgar Allan Poe House and Museum; Carter C. Lively, Hammond-Harwood House; Michael Kyne, Washington County Historical Society; Jennings Evans, Smith Island historian; Billie Keller, Perryman historian; Susan Pearl, Historical Society of Prince George's County; Cassandra Pitts, Allegany County Historical Society; George Reynolds, Cecil County archaeologist; Elizabeth McAllister, Hornbake Library, University of Maryland; Lynn O'Brien, Brice House; Nadine Rosendale, Finksburg Branch, Carroll County Library; Hal Roth, Nanticoke Books; Mark N. Schatz, Ann Arrundell County Historical Society; Wayne Schaumburg, Green Mount Cemetery; Karen Sykes, Calvert County Historical Society; Troy Taylor, Whitechapel Press; Bob Trapani, American Lighthouse

415

Foundation; John Tucker, Milford, DE; Vince Vaise and Scott Sheads, Fort McHenry National Monument and Historic Shrine; Laurie Verge, Surratt House Museum; Ed Wells, Elkton, MD; Bonnie White, College of Southern Maryland; Vince Wilson, Baltimore Society for Paranormal Research and The Haunted Cottage; and staff at the Maryland Room at Baltimore's Enoch Pratt Library. My wife, Kathleen, was invaluable for her helpful comments and endless patience during this and all of my writing projects. While working on this book, I enjoyed learning more about the wide range of history and legends associated with the state of Maryland. Finally, if I have neglected to mention anyone with whom I had contact during this project, I truly apologize.

About the Author

*E*d Okonowicz is a storyteller and a regional author of more than twenty-four books on Mid-Atlantic culture, oral history, folklore, true crime, and ghost stories. His books include short story collections, sports biographies, oral history collections, and novels. He also teaches folklore as an adjunct professor at the University of Delaware. In 2005 he was voted Best Local Author in *Delaware Today* magazine's Readers' Poll. His popular two-book series titled *Possessed Possessions: Haunted Antiques, Furniture and Collectibles* led him to appear in October 2005, with psychic James Van Praagh and other paranormal investigators, on The Learning Channel's two-hour special, *Possessed Possessions*, filmed onboard the *Queen Mary*. His book *Civil War Ghosts at Fort Delaware* is based on ghost/history tours he has conducted at the island prison since 1997. His two most recent books, *Haunted Maryland* and *True Crime: Maryland*, were published by Stackpole Books. His Web site, www.mystandlace.com, provides information on his books, public presentations, and programs.